SONIC LITURGY

STUDIES IN COMPARATIVE RELIGION

Frederick M. Denny, Series Editor

SONIC *liturgy*

Ritual and Music in Hindu Tradition

GUY L. BECK

The University of South Carolina Press

Published by the University of South Carolina Press
Columbia, South Carolina 29208

www.sc.edu/uscpress

Manufactured in the United States of America

21 20 19 18 17 16 15 14 13 12 10 9 8 7 6 5 4 3 2 1

Library of Congress Cataloging-in-Publication Data

Beck, Guy L., 1948–
Sonic liturgy : ritual and music in Hindu tradition / Guy L. Beck.
p. cm. — (Studies in comparative religion)
Includes bibliographical references and index.
ISBN 978-1-61117-037-5 (cloth : alk. paper)
1. Music—Religious aspects—Hinduism. 2. Sound–Religious aspects—Hinduism. 3. Hinduism—Rituals. 4. Hinduism—Liturgy. 5. Liturgics. I. Title. II. Title: Ritual and music in Hindu tradition.
BL1215.M87B43 2012
294.5'38—dc23

2011031529

This book was printed on a recycled paper with 30 percent postconsumer waste content.

CONTENTS

SERIES EDITOR'S PREFACE

This new book is an important sequel to Professor Beck's pioneering earlier book in this series—*Sonic Theology: Hinduism and Sacred Sound,* published in 1993. The earlier book focused on theoretical understandings of sacred sound in Hindu traditions from the earliest times, whereas this sequel takes us into the actual, lived world of Hindu ritual and liturgy, which the author refers to as "sacred sound in practice as opposed to sacred sound in theory." "Sonic liturgy" is a new category for understanding religious music in comparative perspective, thus enriching the traditional fields of ritual and religious studies. Although this book focuses principally on Hindu ritual and its musical dimensions, it provides a universal methodology for the study of sacred sound in whatever religious traditions are being studied.

Frederick M. Denny

PREFACE

This book is dedicated to all the musicians and ritual specialists of Hindu India who have diligently maintained their traditions with unswerving devotion over the centuries. *Sonic Liturgy: Ritual and Music in Hindu Tradition* may be viewed as a sequel to the previous *Sonic Theology: Hinduism and Sacred Sound* (1993), also published by the University of South Carolina Press. While the former deals with theories of sacred sound in Hinduism, the present work covers some of the practical aspects of sound and music. Financial support for the research conducted in 1992 and 1993 was provided by the Council for the International Exchange of Scholars (CIES) in the form of a Fulbright Research Grant and by the American Institute of Indian Studies (AIIS) in the form of a Senior Research Fellowship. During the periods covered by these grants, I greatly appreciate the assistance provided by the Vrindaban Research Institute for fieldwork in the Braj area and the ITC Sangeet Research Academy in Calcutta for instruction on Indian music theory and history.

For the present work, thanks go to Professor Ed Johnson, chair of the Philosophy Department at the University of New Orleans, for providing me with a wonderful office while I taught courses at UNO from fall 2008 through fall 2009. During this time most of the actual writing took place in the peaceful solitude of the third floor of the Liberal Arts Building. In addition, the fact that the Tulane University School of Continuing Studies kept me on board during the difficult post-Katrina years will never be forgotten. Without the employment support of these two institutions, the completion of this book would not have been possible.

I sincerely extend a vote of thanks to Professor Fred Denny for graciously accommodating this text in his USC Press series, Studies in Comparative Religion. I also thank James Denton and the editors of the University of South Carolina Press for taking an interest in a work on Hindu ritual and music and for their help through the acquisitions and editorial processes.

Last, Kajal Beck, my wife, deserves much credit for her patient assistance and encouragement through all phases of the project, including in Vrindaban and Rajasthan in northern India when I was the recipient of the Fulbright and AIIS grants.

NOTE ON TRANSLITERATION

For the many terms in this book that are derived from Sanskrit, Hindi, Bengali, Telugu, and Tamil languages, the diacritical marks have been omitted in the main text but appear in the appropriate entries in the glossary and in the titles listed in the notes and bibliography. Several of the Hindu proper nouns are given in standardized form as Vishnu, Krishna, Siva, Sarasvati, Durga, and so on, while terms used repeatedly in the text are given in uppercase as Yajna, Puja, Seva, Sama-Gana, Gandharva Sangita, Kirtan, Bhakti Sangit, Pada-Kirtan, Dhrupad, Dhamar, Haveli Sangit, Samaj Gayan, Apurva, Adrishta, Raga, Tala, and so forth. For consistency omission of diacriticals and the uppercasing of foreign terms has also been applied when quoting sources within the text.

Introduction

THE ONLINE DESCRIPTION OF THE GRADUATE program in liturgical studies at the Graduate Theological Union in Berkeley, California, contained the following statement in August 2010: "The goal of this program is to promote the study and understanding of Christian worship as it is lived and expressed through the churches' various traditions and cultures. It assumes that worship is at the heart of the theological enterprise, since it is both the primary context of the churches' encounter with the mystery of the Triune God and a primary actualization of the ecclesial body. Study in this area requires an interdisciplinary approach to liturgical studies that integrates the historical, theological, and social-scientific study of Christian ritual practice" (www.gtu.edu/academics/areas/liturgical-studies).

At first glance this statement suggests that "liturgical studies" is essentially a Christian concern. In fact this notion is found throughout the curricula of many theological schools and seminaries. But despite this seemingly closed perspective, there are multiple indications of the widening of the liturgical lens within Christianity, as is evident in the number of non-Christian entries found in *The New Westminster Dictionary of Liturgy and Worship* (2002), edited by Paul Bradshaw. There are entries regarding Jewish worship, Islamic worship, Hindu worship, Buddhist worship, Sikh worship, and Shinto worship. In each case the presence of music and chant is briefly woven into the description of the ritual and liturgical dimensions of each tradition. Outside the Christian fold scholars in the phenomenology of religion and music have also been struggling to break the ironclad hold of sectarianism on otherwise neutral terms and categories such as *liturgy, ritual,* and *sacred music.* These expressions, and others, are now increasingly employed by Christian as well as religious studies scholars as comparative categories, understood not to be the "possession" of certain religious groups. Hence despite some programmatic setbacks, the field of liturgical studies, along with ritual studies, has the potential of developing into a rewarding comparative discipline and one that also provides new elements of method and theory with regard to Hindu tradition.

Recent scholarship in musicology has broadened the scope of music and religious worship by explaining the various ways in which music and song play central roles in all known religions: "In some religions sound itself is a cosmological starting point. As such, it represents the essence of the universe and to be in harmony with the universe means to hear accurately its sound. . . . Further, sound may be the medium of revelation by which the gods have chosen to make themselves known. Further still, sound may be the believer's means of communication to the gods and/or preparing oneself for such communication. The content of this preparation and communication is combined with the music to become songs, that is, music with an articulated goal. Music has been used cosmologically, liturgically, and devotionally in all the world's religions."[1]

One of the tasks in the study of religion and music is to recognize and document common denominators among varying forms of religious music. For example, a parallel feature shared by religious practitioners is the conservative attitude with which they approach their music as it relates to ritual and liturgy. In most religions throughout the world, there are strict rules regarding the performance of music and chant in ritual contexts. Traditional psalms, chants, hymns, and liturgical songs are generally predetermined and contain little scope for alteration beyond fixed parameters: Latin Gregorian chants, Calvinist psalmody, Lutheran chorales, gospel hymns, church litanies, and prayers in the Christian tradition; Qur'an recitation and Majlis in Islam; Chinese ceremonial songs and chants in Confucian or Taoist contexts; Buddhist chants throughout Asia; musical forms of ancient Egypt as described by Plato; Vedic invocations and hymns, Gandharva music, Sanskrit mantras and Stotras, scriptural recitations, Kirtana and Kriti in South India, Bhajans, Bhakti Sangit, Haveli Sangit, Samaj Gayan, and Padavali Kirtan in North India, and Shabad Kirtan in Sikhism. A widely held assumption is that these traditional musical forms are performed in connection with one God, specific deities, sacred ancestors, or spirits. They are handed down from the hoary past and effectively produce expected results only if performed precisely according to canonical standards.

Among the various forms of "conservative" music used in religious worship around the world, this book focuses on the exploration of ritual and music in the Hindu tradition. For this purpose the author has advanced the category of *sonic liturgy* as a flexible template with which to examine the co-appearance of ritual and music as they have evolved within the Hindu tradition. While sound and music are certainly present in most if not all religious rituals, the Hindu tradition provides perhaps the most consistent and enduring exemplification of the notion of sonic liturgy—the ritual order or pattern of specific events that include sound and music on a variety of levels. Moving beyond the mere description of ritual or musical practices, this book seeks formally to engage the issue of why music is so profoundly significant in Hindu ritual. This quest for the deeper meaning of ritual and music in Hindu tradition touches upon the Western field of liturgical studies in several ways. Liturgist Edward Foley had already raised the central question—why is music so widely used in ritual?—that has partly led to the formulation of this study. Additional aspects of method and terminology are adopted from liturgical studies and ritual studies that articulate the subtleties and nuances of the Hindu ritual and musical experience.

In terms of format this book follows a chronological scheme that reveals the historical roots of the consistently close connection between ritual and music in Hindu tradition, from the ancient Vedic religion to modern times. Selected traditions of Hindu sonic liturgy throughout India's long legacy of ritual sacrifice, temple music, and devotional traditions are presented in sequence, with references from the appropriate Sanskrit and vernacular sources. After discussing the Vedic religion associated with Yajnas (fire sacrifices) and Sama-Gana, this book outlines the emergence of Gandharva Sangita as the principal music designed for Puja, a new form of worship that abandoned the use of fire in favor of offerings placed on an altar. Following this, it covers the medieval tradition of Hindu temple worship that became standardized in the Agama literatures and began to include vernacular poetical expressions of devotion set to regional music in the shape of Bhakti Sangit, variously known as Kirtan and Bhajan. As these traditions flourished, sonic liturgies became associated with sectarian branches of Hindu traditions, primarily those of Siva and Vishnu and, especially, Krishna. The book consequently examines selected cases of Vaishnava temple worship that have adopted the classical music styles of Dhrupad and Dhamar in the form of Haveli Sangit and Samaj Gayan. The purpose is to elaborate upon these genres of Hindu music and to reinforce the growing comparative nature of the field of liturgical studies by applying some of its approaches to the Hindu religious realm.

RELIGIOUS STUDIES

Despite their obvious significance, sound and music as categories of special inquiry have been neglected in the academic field of religious studies since the pioneer work of Rudolf Otto (1920s) and Gerardus Van der Leeuw (1950s). Systematic studies of texts, communities, social issues, artifacts, tools, architecture, verbal testimony, clothing, utensils and other objects associated with a religion are routinely carried out, often at a distance from the actual practice of living religions, which is rarely silent and almost always sound-full, musical, and frequently noisy. The visual dimension of religion has received plentiful attention from art historians, iconographers, mythographers, and anthropologists. However, complementary studies in the audible or sonic realm of religion have not been forthcoming, leaving a lacuna. For instance, two recent examples of important authoritative works in the field do not contain references to music: Mark C. Taylor, ed., *Critical Terms for Religious Studies* (Chicago: University of Chicago

Press, 1998), and Willi Braun and Russell T. McCutcheon, eds. *Guide to the Study of Religion* (London: Cassell, 2000). Moreover, many standard textbooks and dictionaries on religion are mute with regard to sound and music, as discussed in the introduction to my 2006 volume *Sacred Sound: Experiencing Music in World Religions* (Waterloo, Ont.: Wilfrid Laurier University Press). This book issued a clarion call for more serious attention to the roles of music and chant in comparative religious thought and practice and for increased emphasis on the actual experiences of believers in the embodied context of worship, experiences that invariably involve sonic or musical activity.

In the twentieth century two of the principal founders of the academic field of religious studies, Rudolf Otto and Gerardus Van der Leeuw, highlighted sacred music and sacred sound in their writings. While both were Protestant theologians, they were among the first to inaugurate a nonsectarian approach to the presence of music in religious experience across religious borders. Otto (1869–1937), a Lutheran theologian, in *The Idea of the Holy* (published in German in 1917 and in English in 1923), set the parameters for the phenomenological study of religion and music with a few well-chosen remarks on the feelings associated with music, which in his view were very similar to feelings associated with the holy itself, the numinous, the "wholly other": "Music, in short, arouses in us an experience and vibrations of mood that are quite specific in kind. . . . The resultant complex mood is, as it were, a fabric, in which the general human feelings and emotional states constitute the warp, and the non-rational music-feelings the woof. . . . The real content of music is not drawn from the ordinary human emotions at all, and . . . is in no way merely a second language, alongside the usual one, by which these emotions find expression. Musical feeling is rather (like numinous feeling) something 'wholly other.'"[2] Accordingly, the human response to music is composed of feelings and experiences similar to those evoked by the numinous, such as *mysterium tremendum* (mystery and awe) and *fascinans* (attraction).

Building upon the work of Otto, Van der Leeuw (1890–1950), in his now classic *Religion in Essence and Manifestation* (1938), broadened the scope by stating that "musical expression of the holy occupies an extensive domain in worship. There is hardly any worship without music."[3] In a subsequent work, *Sacred and Profane Beauty: The Holy in Art* (1963), an entire section entitled "Music and Religion" includes the subsections "Holy Sound," and "Theological Aesthetics of Music." In sum, he affirmed that "almost all worship uses music; . . . religion can no more do without singing than it can without the word. . . . Music represents the great struggle of reaching the wholly other, which it can never express."[4]

However, the fruits of the work of Otto and Van der Leeuw in this respect seem to have disappeared from mainstream trends in religious studies and the history of religions. Serious concern about this lack was voiced as early as 1970 by

S. G. F. Brandon in his *A Dictionary of Comparative Religion:* "The connection between music and religion is so generally recognized that it is surprising to find how little work has been done, particularly from the side of comparative religion, in relating the phenomenology of the two." Equally disconcerting was the work of anthropologists and musicologists: "musicologists, ethnomusicologists and anthropologists have assembled details of instruments, scales, rhythm, harmony (if any) and performance from many ethnic and religious areas. But, although so much is known about the practical function of music in various contexts, little attention has been paid to its significance as an aspect of religious action."[5]

Reasons for the gradual disappearance of sacred music and sacred sound as recurrent academic categories post-Otto lie partly in a misguided understanding in the West of religion as merely a set of beliefs and doctrines incorporated in scripture or sacred texts. Ritual studies scholar Catherine Bell, in her article "Performance," traces the neglect of the oral and performative aspects of religion much earlier, to the Enlightenment period: "Most theories of religion since the Enlightenment have tended to emphasize the more cognitive aspects of religion no matter how rooted these were thought to be in emotional, doctrinal, or communal experience."[6]

The emphasis on "silent textual study" and cognitive aspects in modern religious studies may also expose certain Protestant notions of scripture as primarily a written document to be read quietly in private. After the invention of the printing press, the radical shift from hearing scripture chanted or sung aloud by priests in churches to the reading of the printed word in churches and homes led the way to the modern academic attachment to written language as the primary carrier of religious meaning. The arena of a "silent religion" also does not faithfully represent other religious worldviews, least of all the traditions of Hindu devotional poetry that are the subject of this book. In fact, sacred texts in virtually all religious traditions are chanted or sung in a living context. For example, oral recitation of ritual texts is upheld as statutory in Judaism. The Qur'an in Islam is not considered authentic when it is studied in translation or read silently. Buddhist Sutras are almost always chanted, as are Sikh prayers and songs. For thousands of years Hindu dharma (law) forbade the writing down of scriptures, and the chanting and hearing of sacred verses and mantras, even without full comprehension, still constitutes the most common form of access to the sacred for the pious multitude of Hindus. Since music and chant are located at the core of religious life for most cultures, including ritual and liturgical action, it is just as improbable to understand a religious liturgy without the oral dimension as it is to penetrate a religious tradition without examining its musical dimension.

Historians of pagan and pre-Christian cultures have affirmed the important role of music in ancient religious ritual and ceremony. Johannes Quasten, in

Music & Worship in Pagan & Christian Antiquity (1983), writes: "The legends and myths of nearly all pagan peoples have sought to explain the elaborate use of music in their worship by indicating that the art of music was a gift of the gods to men."[7] He cites Censorius who explained how music was pleasing to the gods in the ancient world, and Horace, who stated that sacred music was a means of appeasement which, like the fragrance of incense and the blood of animals, disposed the gods to act favorably toward men. As such, music held an extremely importance place in all sacrificial ceremonies, such that flutes, cymbals, lyre, and tambourine were required in Greek sacrifices. Instruments and songs were also required in the mystery cults of Cybele and Isis. At a more profound level music as cultic action was understood to exercise a magical influence over the gods, so that it became a means by which men controlled the deities. For example, the worshippers of Isis made a din with their bells during the liturgy so as to keep the wicked Set away from the sacred action.[8] This kind of action has strong parallels with ancient Indian music and its control over the Devas.

Quasten summarizes the role of music in the ancient world by applying the classical terms *epiclesis* and *apotropaia*: "Inasmuch as all of antiquity was convinced that music had the power of epiclesis [calling down the gods], the step to its use as sacrifice was a short one, for both apotropaism [removing unwanted spirits] and epiclesis played a major role in sacrifice."[9] The term *epiclesis* was subsequently borrowed by the Christian tradition to refer to the drawing down of the Holy Spirit during the Eucharist, and is a useful category for understanding the general role of music as invitation to the deities as found, for example, in the Hindu tradition.

Celtic historian Karen Ralls-MacLeod, in her book *Music and the Celtic Otherworld: From Ireland to Iona* (2000), has affirmed the central role of music in all ancient Celtic traditions: "From the beautiful, enchanting music of the fairy harp to the sacred singing of the choirs of angels, Celtic literature has many references to a spiritual or supernatural dimension of music. This sacred dimension is called the Celtic Otherworld, in which music is often prominently featured."[10] Examples included fairy harpers, songs of mermaids, the power of the saint's bell, the singing of angels in heaven, musical trees, and so on. In Celtic literature "music is portrayed as one of the most potent forces of the Celtic imagination." In earlier times music was an integral part of culture that provided access to unseen realms: "The mysterious, sacred dimension of a people's culture and experience is most often described in terms of their religious beliefs and rituals, but various art forms can also be used to show this, including music. It seems as though many of these experiences are of a non-verbal nature, and that music can serve as an important communicative or expressive medium. . . . By a careful examination of the sources, it appears that the early Celts believed that music can give access to reality in both every day, mundane and otherworldly contexts."[11] Music for the Celts was the definitive link from this world to the next: "Music is seen as a universal 'connector' to the Otherworld, and as an especially effective link between this world and the Otherworld."[12]

Musicologists and ethnomusicologists agree that music is a universal aspect of culture that is also central to religion in various ways. From the side of ethnomusicology, Bruno Nettl has strongly affirmed the ubiquitous connection between religion and music in his textbook *Excursions in World Music* (2001): "In all societies, music is found in religious ritual—it is almost everywhere a mainstay of sacred ceremonies—leading some scholars to suggest that perhaps music was actually invented for humans to have a special way of communicating with the supernatural."[13]

The complex interlacing of music and religion is articulated further by musicologist Robin Sylvan in *Traces of the Spirit: The Religious Dimensions of Popular Music* (2002): "Music is capable of functioning simultaneously at many different levels (physiological, psychological, socio-cultural, semiological, virtual, ritual, and spiritual) and integrating them into a coherent whole. So for a complex multidimensional phenomenon like religion, which also functions simultaneously at multiple levels, the fact that music is capable of conveying all these levels of complexity in a compelling and integrated package makes it a vehicle par excellence to carry the religious impulse."[14]

RITUAL STUDIES

The quest to understand the seemingly intrinsic connection between religious ritual and music takes us to the discipline of ritual studies, where the arguments for the special significance of ritual are the most pronounced and a basis is provided for a broad definition of ritual that fills our expectations with regard to the presence of music. Ritual studies serves to underscore the central importance of ritual for religion and, in many cases, for all human existence. Anthropologist Mary Douglas has stated it succinctly: "As a social animal, man is a ritual animal. If ritual is suppressed in one form it crops up in others, more strongly and more intense the social interaction."[15] Anthropologist Victor Turner explains that ritual "holds the generating source of culture and structure."[16] Taking this notion further by tying ritual directly to religion, Nathan D. Mitchell, in his book *Liturgy and the Social Sciences* (1999), holds that "what is at stake in ritual behavior—as it develops in individuals and is ritually enacted by groups—is nothing less than the survival of the social order; . . . culture cannot be defined apart from cult."[17] In some areas of ritual studies the lens has become so wide that today in this field a scholar may use just about any term he or she likes for any concept.

Scholars in ritual studies have tended to hold an etic, or outsider, perspective on ritual. There are inherent values to this approach, as emphasized by ritual studies pioneer Ronald L. Grimes: "The value of etic theories lies in the uncovering of hidden meanings associated with otherwise obscure phenomena. . . . [For example] performance theories [of ritual] can be especially incisive when applied to events in religious settings, since religious leaders sometimes deny or even cover up performance aspects of their rites. Rites are enactments rendered special by virtue of their condensation, elevation, or stylization. They are not necessarily religious, but since religious rites often determine how practitioners and theorists alike conceptualize other kinds of ritual, it is crucial to study them."[18] Grimes then cautions against the uncritical application of terminologies with regard to ritual: "Any label—'ritual,' 'liturgy,' 'art,' 'dance,' 'music,' 'religion,' or 'drama,'—used without qualification to describe a traditional activity would likely be misleading, since the term would segregate a phenomenon that many intend to be deliberately integrative. So if we are to talk about religious activities as rites or performances, our definitions must be broad and provisional rather than restricted to what we in the West usually label 'religion' or 'theater.'"[19]

Accordingly, some of the most widely circulated theories are integrative in their approach. Anthropologist Roy A. Rappaport, in his monumental study *Ritual and Religion in the Making of Humanity* (1999), argues that ritual is fundamental and indispensable to the human species.[20] And besides being the fundamental social act—in Mitchell's words, "the social act basic to humanity"—ritual is also transcendental or connected to transhuman dimensions, what Rappaport calls "Ultimate Sacred Postulates." For Rappaport, as Mitchell puts it, rituals' "deepest and most stable messages are canonical (consisting of messages concerned with ultimate realities not visibly present but conveyed through symbols). Canonical messages are never invented or encoded by participants; they are 'found' or 'discovered' as already given in and by the rite."[21] As stated elsewhere by Rappaport: "Ritual is not simply an alternative way to express certain things; . . . certain things can be expressed only by ritual."[22]

Adding weight to the etic perspective, Adam B. Seligman, Robert P. Weller, Michael J. Pruett, and Bennett Simon, in *Ritual and Its Consequences: An Essay on the Limits of Sincerity* (2008), discuss how rituals—like play—function to create "as if" worlds, rooted in the imaginative capacity of the human mind to create a subjunctive universe. Ritual, the authors claim, defines the boundaries of imagined worlds, including those of empathy and other realms of human creativity, such as music, architecture, and literature. Dismissing ritual as mere convention, the authors show how the conventions of ritual function to allow us to live together in a broken world. Ritual is work, endless work, but nonetheless highly important work. The Hindu sonic liturgy, seen from this etic perspective, is a purely human construct of the imagination that functions as a remedy for the abject world of brokenness and pain. While there is some truth to this claim, the long history and persistence of the coexistence of ritual and music in India reveals more about the transhuman basis of creativity and adjustment than this scenario is willing to afford.

William Sax, Johannes Quack, and Jan Weinhold, in *The Problem of Ritual Efficacy* (2009), bring together nine scholars who address the issue of how rituals work, ranging across the fields of history, anthropology, medicine, and biblical studies. These essays place ritual in various contexts and address a set of debates between positivists, natural scientists, and religious skeptics on the one side and interpretive social scientists, phenomenologists, and religious believers on the other.

Tom F. Driver's *Liberating Rites: Understanding the Transformative Power of Ritual* (2006), offers valuable insights derived from his functional study of ritual in Haiti. This book illustrates ritual by presenting it as something raw, basic, and central to all living beings. Driver examines the many ways people use ritual to give order to their lives, to deepen feelings of communal belonging, and to transform the status quo. There are interesting points here, especially as he discusses creative performance as essential to religion and addresses the human longing for rituals that "work," combining meaning with power.

Fresh topics covered in ritual studies scholarship lend more credence to the present project, as ritual becomes increasingly identified with almost all religious behavior, even that which is normatively "anti-ritual." In Steven Heine and Dale S. Wright's edited volume, *Zen Ritual: Studies in Zen Buddhist Theory in Practice* (2007), ritual in Zen is presented very convincingly, shattering older conceptions of the anti-ritual nature of this branch of Buddhism. Although Beat poets had written about the demythologized, anti-ritualized spirit of Zen, this collection of essays discuss various Zen rituals, including those of zazen. As a more useful etic approach it uncovers aspects that are not affirmed within the tradition, setting aside what religion says about itself and focusing on what religion is actually about as discovered in historical records and sociological observation. Zen is revealed as inextricably associated with many varieties of ritual behavior.

Regarding the role of women in religious ritual, Stephanie W. Jamison, in *Sacrificed Wife / Sacrificer's Wife: Women, Ritual, and Hospitality in Ancient India* (1995), discusses the conceptual position of women in early India, specifically in the Vedic and early epic periods. By focusing on a single female role—the activities of the "Sacrificer's Wife" in solemn ritual, the book makes some valuable suggestions on how gender and social class may be important factors in the experiences of sonic liturgy.

While the field of ritual studies includes broad and integrative approaches, attempts to incorporate music in ritual theory have remained sporadic and undeveloped within the discipline. The early work of Ronald L. Grimes, such as *Beginnings in Ritual Studies* (1982), while helpful in theoretical and reflective aspects of ritual in a generic sense, is not directly concerned with either liturgy or music. His more recent work, *Rite Out of Place: Ritual, Media, and the Arts* (2006), confesses to cover areas not within traditional religious parameters, such as film, theater, public discourse, and so on. Studies of related emic (insider) categories in other religious cultures serve to underscore the prevalence of the deliberate demarcation of ritual from other areas of normal life, especially those dealing with religious rites and ceremonies. What are needed are studies of religious rituals in context whereby the role of music and sound is brought out and examined.

In order to construct a working definition of ritual that best engages the phenomena of Hindu ritual and music, I draw on a recent volume of essays edited by Jens Kreinath, Jan Snoek, and Michael Stausberg entitled *Theorizing Rituals: Issues, Topics, Approaches, Concepts* (2008). Coeditor Jan Snoek, in his article "Defining Rituals," while not proclaiming a strict definition, offers a series of helpful parameters that help to focus attention on the special place of ritual in human society. After describing the problem of arriving at a satisfactory definition of ritual, he outlines, using superlative adjectives, a series of characteristics of ritual: "Ritual behavior is a particular mode of behavior, distinguished from common behavior. Its performers are (at least part of) its own audience. In general, all human actions can be part of ritual behavior, including speech acts. However, in each particular case the large majority of these will be traditionally sanctioned as proper ritual actions. Most ritual behavior takes place at specific places and/or specific times. Most ritual behavior is more formally stylized, structured, and standardized than most common behavior. Most ritual behavior is based on a script [written or oral]. Most ritual behavior is to some extent purposeful and symbolically meaningful for its participants. At least those playing an active part consider themselves to be participating in non-common behavior."[23] He indicates that there are polythetic or fuzzy areas and that much behavior in society may be ritual-like without being in effect ritual. Some additional clarification of terms is given in this article: *rite* should refer to the smallest unit of a larger complex of ritual behavior. It has also meant a regionally accepted version of a ritual, as in Roman Rite, Coptic Rite, and so forth. *Ceremony* is the smallest configuration of rites into a meaningful whole, that is, a short sequence of rites. *Ceremonial* is the total configuration of ceremonies for any ritual occasion. The term *ritual* may also be understood as the actual script or playbook, oral or written, outlining each step of any ritual procedure.

The emic perspective lends primary credence to the insider definitions and perspectives on ritual. While the etic, or outsider, perspective has many critical advantages, it does not suffice by itself and must be balanced with the insider views, especially in topics of religious practice and belief. The discipline of phenomenology of religion has always taken seriously the positions advanced by practitioners and believers. In the lengthy account of emic perspectives in the field of ritual studies edited by Michael Stausberg, "Ritual: A Lexicographic Survey of Some Related Terms from an Emic Perspective" (2008), categories of religious ritual are described by scholars from different cultures. They are unanimous in accepting the notion of sacred ritual as a separate endeavor or realm apart from other ordinary activities. Thus the etic concept of "anything can be considered ritual" is strongly called into question.

At odds with etic assumptions, the entry by Alex Michaels titled "Sanskrit" (2008) in Stausberg's survey clarifies the contours of Vedic and Hindu rituals and how they are construed as separated from other activities. He explains: "In Sanskrit, there is no one single word or term that could be considered equivalent to 'ritual' (whatever it might mean), but a number of terms that come close to it."[24] The terms *karma* or *kriya* (from *kr*— "to do") refer to religious rites or ceremonies in Vedic texts but in the Upanishads are expanded to include all actions within the world (*samsara*) leading to rebirth in the cycle of reincarnation. The term *samskara* ("to put something correctly together, to make something perfect") includes the life-cycle rites, including birth, tonsure, *upanayana*, marriage, cremation, and any purificatory rite. The word *Yajna* is understood to mean a Vedic sacrificial rite, a fire sacrifice, including domestic (*grihya*) and public (*srauta*). *Utsava* (*mela*, "fair") in Hindu parlance means a communal festival related to mythic events, harvest cycle, ancestors, or pilgrimages. Rituals or rites are subdivided into *nitya* (compulsory), *naimittika* (occasional), and *kamya* (optional). *Puja* (either from Skt. *puj-* , "to honor," or from Tamil *pucu*, "to anoint" somebody with something), means worship, adoration, respect, or homage. As elaborated by Michaels: "Puja basically denotes the worship of deities according to a ritual script that traditionally includes sixteen elements of service (*upacara*) that can be reduced to five essential parts (*pancopacara*): anointment of the deity (*gandha*, *anulepana*), flowers (*puspa*), incense (*dhupa*), lights or lamps (*dipa*), feeding of the deity (*naivedya*)."[25]

What is significant throughout the Hindu literature and testimony is that religious ritual is always separated from ordinary action by virtue of the results that are believed to occur for the practitioner. This insider perspective is crucial in understanding the nuances attached to the various terminologies. Michaels recalls the philosophical position as argued by the Mimamsakas and stressed in the *Bhagavad-Gita:* "The Mimamsaka classification of acts makes it clear that Indian scholars of ritual generally distinctively separated sacrificial acts from normal or worldly acts. Each ritual act begins with a declaration of what the ritual is intended to do. . . . Rituals are seen as constructions of a world with which man ritually identifies himself. . . . Only by ritual, but not by 'normal' (karmic) action, can he be liberated. Thus, ritual action has to be separated from non-ritual action, as the Bhagavad-Gita (3.9) clearly says: 'this world is bound by the bonds of action (karma) except where that action is done sacrificially.'"[26]

In light of the Indian materials Michaels issues a word of caution to modern ritual theory that may be tempted to see all action as ritual: "Within the Vedic-Brahmanic worldview it is always clear and demarcated . . . when ritual (sacrificial) action begins and where it ends. Whatever is not construed by ritual (sacrificial) action is not seen as ritual. This could be regarded as a kind of warning for modern ritual theory when [in India] 'ritual' is seen as a construction of acts that are regarded as separated from 'normal' or 'natural' action."[27]

As examples of both approaches, one etic and one emic, two studies of Jain rituals and Jain music in India are of timely interest and relevance here. Caroline Humphrey and James Laidlaw, in *The Archetypal Actions of Ritual: A Theory of Ritual Illustrated by the Jain Rite of Worship* (1994), present a detailed ethnography of the ritual of daily worship before a temple idol (Puja) by Svetambara Jains in western India. In typical etic fashion they argue that ritual is not a logically separate type of activity but rather a quality that can be attributed to a wide range of everyday activities. They argue that Jain worship, while ostensibly similar to Hindu Puja, may be distinguished from it by examining the intent of the worshippers and the overall perspective on life of each community. Mary Whitney Kelting, in *Singing to the Jinas: Jain Laywomen, Mandal Singing, and the Negotiations of Jain Devotion* (2001), offers a thorough emic account of the practice of Stavan singing by laywomen and how Jain vernacular hymns are performed in ritual context. Jain women both accept and rewrite the idealized roles received from religious texts, practices, and social expectation, according to which female religiosity is a symbol of Jain perfection. This study is close in theme and spirit to the present book and stimulates comparative discussion with regard to both gender and the nature of music in Hindu and Jain experiences.

Attempts by contemporary musicians have strengthened the case for the serious study of sound and music by insiders. Canadian composer R. Murray Schafer coined the term *soundscape* in the 1970s to indicate "the sonic environment, the sum total of all sounds within any definitive area which surround us as a result of certain historical, technological, and demographic processes." Schafer's soundscape, comprising keynote sounds, sound signals, and soundmarks, has been used effectively to describe the "auditory environment" of religious communities, as in "The Auditory Environment of Emerging Christian Worship," chapter two of Edward Foley's *Ritual Music: Studies in Liturgical Musicology* (1995), and in Charles Hirschkind's *The Ethical Soundscape: Cassette Sermons and Islamic*

Counterpublics (2006), which describes the Islamic "pious soundscape." Steven Feld, in *Senses of Place* (1996), advanced the notion of "acoustemology" (acoustic epistemology), whereby the bodily experience of sound is a special way of knowing. As an examination of how subjects know the world in and through sound, acoustemology also has wide implications for the study of religion.

Instead of the domains of religious studies and ritual studies, however, the field placing the most attention on the oral or sonic dimensions of ritual, including music, is, not surprisingly, the place where an interest in Rudolf Otto's work has been consistently on the rise. The most visible and credible attempts to take up the themes and issues originally outlined by Otto and Van der Leeuw more than a half-century ago, including the gradual reconciliation of religion and music, have come from Christian theologians and historians working in the field of liturgical studies. Though emerging in renewed form out of conservative reactions to the delimiting of the sacred liturgy after Vatican II, this field, when expanded beyond the Christian base, is the most developed and useful discipline of discourse for the study of ritual and music in non-Western cultures such as the Hindu tradition.

LITURGICAL STUDIES

Liturgical studies is a field that, while initially grounded in Catholic and Protestant Christian tradition as well as in Judaism, has been rapidly expanding to included non-Western traditions. When seen in cross-cultural perspective, the role of music often parallels the role of worship in religion. And when music is understood as sacred or "religious," then it generally functions within the ritual or liturgy in some kind of relationship to what is of absolute value to believers, such as the sacred or a transcendent reality. Thus almost all liturgical action in religion involves music and chant.

The term *liturgy* (from *laos*, "people," and *ergos*, "work" or "action") is understood within the field of liturgical studies to be a series of rites that combine word, music, action, symbol, and/or object that is performed on behalf of a group. This term most often refers to the public ritual or worship of a religious community that is performed by priests or other functionaries. The term *paraliturgical* denotes private or individual rituals that are nonetheless tied symbolically to larger public liturgies, such as rites of passage and other domestic ceremonies.

Liturgical studies, while normally a realm of specialized research, has been expanding its corpus of material beyond dealing with music and chant in Jewish and Christian liturgies. But while still theoretically rooted in Western religion, the methods and structures of analysis of liturgical studies apply equally well to Hindu traditions of worship. The obvious presence of "liturgy" in many other religious traditions expands the theoretical possibilities for the presence of "liturgical music" worldwide, as current opinions in liturgical studies are moving toward endorsement of music as a central element in all religious action. Liturgical scholar Joseph Gelineau has affirmed the embedded nature of singing and music in all liturgies: "The liturgy is the shared activity of a people gathered together. No other sign brings out this communal dimension so well as singing."[28] In fact, his ecumenical perspective indicates profound restructuring of the categories of sound, music, and sacrifice, as he states his premise with examples from the Bible as well as Hinduism:

> Sound—voice or music—constitutes a sacred link with the transcendent being. The religious significance of the sacrifice of sound is global, at once evocation and adoration, invocation and praise, from the syllable "OM" which contains within it all the acoustic powers, to the vocal expression of a kyrie or an alleluia. The sacrifice of sound is at the root of all cults containing song and music. In the biblical revelation, it constitutes a force which carries us from blood sacrifices to the pure sacrifice of the lips, already present in the prophet Hosea (Hos 14:2) and taken up again by the Epistle to the Hebrews (Heb 13:15). It will culminate in the sacrifice of thanksgiving (*sacrificium laudis*) from Psalm 50, vv. 14 and 23, to the Christian Eucharist where it becomes the sacrament of spiritual sacrifice.[29]

The documents of the Second Vatican Council (1963–1965) on sacred music reveal the close and necessary connection between the divine word and musical expression as directives for all types of liturgical activity within Roman Catholicism, including the sacraments: "Liturgical worship is given a more noble form when it is celebrated in song. . . . The unity of hearts is more commonly achieved by the union of voices. . . . One cannot find anything more religious and more joyful in sacred celebrations than a whole congregation expressing its faith and devotion in song."[30] The effects of this pronouncement, while expressing traditional intentions of piety and surrender to Roman Catholic beliefs, was soon believed to have compromised the liturgy through the withdrawal of Latin as compulsory and the allowance of too much flexibility in the musical dimensions of the service.

As a conservative response to what appeared as the "deterioration of the Liturgy," theologian Aidan Kavanagh affirmed that the real meaning of the liturgy was "symbolic, enduring, invariable, and ultimately independent of human agents. It is neither produced by participants, nor defeated by their emotions, nor exhausted by repetition." By this he meant that the liturgy, once fixed, must not be tampered with, as it served to guarantee continuous religious meaning for the community. Kavanagh then warned that we should "adapt culture to the liturgy rather than liturgy to culture."[31] To make his case stronger he appealed to other religious traditions to make a universal proposition about liturgical activity in religion: "The liturgy is an art constrained by rule. . . . Every liturgical system in existence, Christian or not, is based on this principle simply because so highly complex a social art as liturgy must maintain a defined order of regular expectations lest it fail to be a participated event."[32] In order to understand Kavanagh's concerns and methods fully, it is useful to note that already at the time of Vatican II some Roman Catholic theologians had begun to address the issue of ritual or liturgy in religion. They understood that in order to build a more solid case for authentic liturgical activity, the Church needed to situate its own liturgical tradition within the broader inherent sacrality of the universe. And to work this cause to its real fruition, the phenomenology of religion became an effective tool, as culled from the writings of Otto, Van der Leeuw, and its more recent exponent, Mircea Eliade (1907–1986).

Theologian Louis Bouyer, in his erudite study *Rite and Man: Natural Sacredness and Christian Liturgy* (1963), acknowledged the role of Mircea Eliade in effectively articulating the natural religious impulse of humanity: "More effectively than anyone else, Eliade has helped us to understand that the religious attitude is not merely a primitive attitude of man in the face of reality. It is a permanent attitude. For it is the relation of man to his whole experience. Through that relation man discovers the world as a totality which is also a unity, and a unity perceived as being at once both immanent and transcendent. . . . The history of comparative religions has had to recognize the fact that religion is a permanent, irreducible, and generally dominating element in all human experience."[33]

Bouyer then explained the primacy of ritual within the universal history of religion: "A rite is not simply one type of action among many others. It is the typical human action, inasmuch as it is connected with the word as the expression and realization of man in the world, and to the degree that this expression and realization are immediately and fundamentally religious. . . . A rite is a human action in which man apprehends himself as a religious being, . . . what a man does in the rite is a divine action, an action which God performs through and in man, as much as man himself performs it in and through God."[34] He then opined that rites are rites because of their natural sacredness, as bestowed by divine favor: "This is why at all times and in all places rites are considered to be the work of the gods. The men who celebrate these rites would not celebrate them as they do if they thought that they were themselves their authors. . . . Rites exist precisely as rites because it is believed that if they can be instituted at all, it is the gods who have instituted them and are the real agents of the rites, working through and beyond the action of the priests."[35] These ideas were soon to circulate among many theologians.

In the subsequent anthology *The Study of Liturgy* (1978), theologian J. D. Crichton discussed Otto's paradigm in relation to worship in his essay "A Theology of Worship": "Worship is seen to have a value and significance of its own that cannot be explained or explained away as superstition or magic or the expression of fear. Worship is a religious phenomenon, a reaching out through the fear that always accompanies the sacred to the mysterium conceived as tremendum but also fascinans, because behind it and in it there is an intuition of the Transcendent. But if in this sense worship is profoundly religious it is also profoundly human."[36]

Theologian Richard Viladesau then broadened the scope of the issue to include all religions and the arts in *Theology and the Arts: Encountering God through Music, Art, and Rhetoric* (2000), in which he presented a case for the theological foundations of culture, including music, in all its forms of expression. Building upon the categories presented earlier by Otto, he stated:

> My proposal is based on the conviction that that there is an underlying implicit or transcendental dimension of religious experience. Its object—the mysterium tremendum et fascinans, the numinous—would then be ontologically identical with the ultimate object of aesthetic or moral or intellectual experience; it would never be experienced simply in itself as a categorical object but would always be "co-experienced" as the dimension of mystery implicit in all human knowing and loving; and it would ground the analogies that are in fact found in the human reaction to the beautiful, the good, the true, and the holy. In this perspective, the ultimate reason for music's ability to mediate the spiritual is not merely that it echoes emotions that are felt in religious experience, but also and more profoundly that its object is the beautiful, which itself is godly and thus leads toward God.[37]

Viladesau broke new ground by qualifying the distinction between the specific "Christian revelation" and a "universal revelation" that encompassed all experiences of sacred music: "There is a universal revelation of beauty, of which all music partakes. This is separate from the uniqueness of the Christian revelatory Word in Christ. This is why mere instrumental music may be a potent factor in the experience of the sacred."[38] He therefore opened the distinct probability of non-Western cultures participating in authentic experiences of the sacred through music. Taking this further in terms of natural theology, Anthony Monti, in *A Natural Theology of the Arts: Imprint of the Spirit* (2003), fully affirmed that the arts are theological by their very nature and not simply when they are explicitly religious and argued that art conveys the real presence of God, even when not labeled as such.

Liturgical studies scholars have routinely stressed the correlative association of myth (narrative words) and ritual. Kavanagh maintained this point by explaining that myth is the "conceiving" aspect, and ritual the "enacting" aspect: "Both myth and ritual thus appear to me as strictly correlative and inseparable junctions: their reciprocal union is what I mean by cult. The outcome of cult, so understood, is what I understand as culture."[39] Frederick M. Denny and Rodney L. Taylor, in their introduction to the edited volume *The Holy Book in Comparative Perspective* (1985), distinguished the two closely related dimensions of scripture, the informative (myth) and performative (ritual).

Indeed, in order for religion to be natural and authentic, rites cannot stand alone but must always be tied with sacred words in a kind of balance. Bouyer emphasized the balance between myth and ritual such that an imbalance would jeopardize the status of religion itself: "Sacred words and sacred actions are as a matter of fact always found joined together. . . . If words and rites are distinct and are to a certain extent reciprocally opposed, their constant connection must mean a natural relationship. This is so true that a decisive dominance of one over the other effects a change in the dominant element itself which seems to foretell the downfall of religion and perhaps quite simply of the religious man himself."[40] Bouyer cited both extremes of imbalance as situations to be avoided, that is, meaningless rituals versus abstract meaning without ritual practice. For example, the Sabian priests in Roman cults had many rituals but forgot the meaning of the words, and modern Protestant services stress the spoken word without ritual and sacraments.

According to Bouyer, the true authenticity of language is in its natural connection to ritual. Words alone do not suffice, nor does a ritual without words. For there to be authentic or natural religion, both must inhere in each other in a kind of mystical bond. And while Bouyer recognized the imbalance within religion, we have underscored the similar problem in the study of religion. Thus while words have become devitalized in religious life, words have become stale and lifeless in the academy because of their divorce from living rituals.

We argue in this book that sound and music provide that necessary bond between myth (words) and ritual (action) in religion. And for ritual worship to sustain that necessary element of mystery within religious life, music must be acknowledged as the most important and vital balancing factor between word and action in religious rituals, public and private, preventing their decline into the extremes of either verbal pedagogy or mindless ritualistic actions.

LITURGICAL MUSICOLOGY

A scholar of liturgy who has outlined some useful parameters for developing further insights into ritual and music and a liturgical professor, Edward Foley, has addressed many of the salient issues regarding the role of music in ritual behavior in *Ritual Music: Studies in Liturgical Musicology* (1995). At the beginning of chapter five entitled "Toward a Sound Theology," Foley raises the basic question of why sound/music is integral to religious worship, noting that, "even if one accepts the premise that music is integral to worship, few have attempted to explore why this is so. As a result, most commentators on the subject—be they musicians or liturgists—find themselves addressing questions of how music is integral to worship rather than questions of whether or why music is integral to worship."[41] In this work Foley presents some resolution with careful insights into the meaning of sound and music in religious ritual and experience.

During the course of his analysis Foley defines ritual in line with Eliade's notion of *homo religiosus:* "Ritual is patterned, shared, public behavior, expressing a meaning and purpose that cannot be put into words alone, in the face of some reality larger than ourselves."[42] He then quickly brings music into the discussion with reference to the realm of symbols that inhabit a space beyond rational discourse: "Rituals achieve the inexpressible by means of symbols; and although all art is symbolic, opening up levels of reality which can be broached in no other way, the most highly developed type of such purely connotational semantic is music."[43]

Employing a phenomenological method he calls "liturgical musicology," or simply the ritual-music approach, Foley begins by stating that "sound, as such, does not really exist in the world around us. What does exist is vibration. . . . In other words, there is no sound until we hear it; . . . it is not only a physical phenomenon, but also the response to that phenomenon and to a lesser degree the intentionality behind the phenomenon that enables us to distinguish between noise and communication."[44]

Foley then argues that sound events "are not only active events in and of themselves, but dynamic to the extent that they engage the other and captivate the listener; . . . sound events like human song are fundamentally unitive: uniting singer with the song, listener with the song, singer with the listener, the listener with other listeners, and even in a new way the listener with her or himself."[45] He reflects on the uniqueness characteristic of religion in its encounter with a personal "other" rather than an abstract One or essence. Speaking of religious music as "sound events," he presents sound as an "experience of the personal," and sound-events are not simply "experiences of something other, but of another." Reminiscent of Martin Buber's "I and Thou" approach, Foley states that "sound encounters are keyed to personal encounters. They occur in the realm of acoustic space which is translated by the human imagination as an arena of personal presence. Thus the sound event by its very nature supports the revelation of God who is perceived as a person. Music, in particular, is an infallible indicator of human presence since music, properly speaking, is a human creation that does not otherwise occur in nature. Consequently music serves as a special sound metaphor for the unnamable God who chooses to reveal Self in personal terms."[46] The concept of a personal deity is directly relevant to the Hindu materials discussed herein, as Hindu sonic liturgy entails a participatory experience of the listeners and the musicians in relationship with God or the numinous.

Foley then explains that since music is the most refined of all sound events, it reflects the characteristics of all sound phenomena to the highest degree. Music is thus the most suitable feature for ritual worship because "music's temporality, human genesis, dynamism and apparent insubstantial nature enable it to serve as a unique symbol of God [the sacred], suggesting presence without confinement, eliciting wonder without distance, and enabling union which is both personal and corporate. More critical than any other characteristic for liturgy is music's capacity to wed itself to word and share in its power, for music like word is both event and utterance. Music can, therefore, be understood as necessary or integral to liturgy because it has the capacity to reveal images of God and the community as well as to realize the implications of those images in a unique and irreplaceable way."[47]

In line with Otto, Foley affirms that music comes closest to expressing the meanings associated with the numinous or higher truths: "Music has symbolized the mysterious and wholly other since the dawn of creation. . . . This elusiveness in form and content is part of the reason why music is so often used for communicating with the spirit world. In the Judeo-Christian tradition music is an effective means for communicating with a God who is both present and hidden."[48] He continues: "Music creates that acoustic space which—as much as any other environment—enables ritual precisely to express meaning and purpose that cannot be put into words alone, in the face of some reality larger than ourselves. . . . Traditional societies have known that beautiful sounds convey feelings and thoughts more powerfully, more completely, and more exactly than does any word, and consequently is universally tied to their rituals. Thus, music's most important and frequent use is in religious rituals."[49] Foley even suggests a kind of "natural alliance between text and tune . . . [whereby] music has a special capacity to heighten and serve the word which occupies a central place in worship."[50]

The irreplaceable nature of music's contribution to religious worship is a function of its special acoustical properties, which enable music to engage the assembly, reveal the divine, and enable the communion between the assembly and God or the sacred in ways unique to this art form. Accordingly Foley enumerated four acoustic properties which allow music to accomplish these things: music is time-bound, music is the indicator of personal presence, music is dynamic, and music is intangible.

Music is time-bound. Music requires performance in historical time in order for it to exist: "Sound as one of the basic ingredients of music is considered more real or existential than any other sense object and situates us in the midst of actuality and simultaneity (cf. Walter J. Ong 1967: 111, 128). Because of this existential quality, music is able to image a God who . . . intervened in time and reveals Self in human history. Furthermore, this time-bound art has the ability to engage the community in the present reality of worship."[51]

Music is an indicator of personal presence. Music is one of the universal symbols of human civilization and a symbol of human presence: "Since it is a human creation, music is itself a symbol of human presence. . . . God . . . is not only believed to be an abstract power intervening in history but a personal God who intervenes on behalf of a beloved. . . . This intervention . . . took an auditory form. . . . In view of this auditory bias in God's self revelation . . . music as the most sophisticated form of sound has the capacity to symbolize the personal nature of God's self will especially as it unites to the Word."[52]

Music is dynamic. Sound and music have the ability to announce presence and also engage another in dialogue: "Because of sound's ability to resonate inside two individuals at the same time it has the capacity to strike a common chord and elicit sympathetic vibrations from those who hear it. It, therefore, is dynamic in its ability to enter the world of the other and elicit a response."[53]

Music is intangible. In line with Otto, Foley states that "the paradox of all sound phenomena including music is that sound/music is perceivable but elusive, recognizable but uncontainable. The apparently insubstantial nature of music is one of the reasons why it has symbolized the mysterious and wholly other since the dawn of creation. Music as a non-discursive symbol is not only perceived as insubstantial but itself seems to have an ambivalence of content. . . . Furthermore, music offers itself as a powerful symbol for the Divine Self who is recognizable while remaining the unnamable. Music thus enables us to encounter and know God without presuming to capture or contain the divine Self."[54]

Instead of simply prioritizing songs according to the religious importance of texts, as previous scholarship had done, Foley's ritual-music approach affirms that there are four types of ritual music:[55]

Music Alone: Music without text or ritual action. Examples: drums before a Buddhist ritual, organ prelude before the Eucharist, *shehnai* music before Hindu ceremony, taps during a funeral, drums and hand cymbals between Puja activities.

Music and Ritual Action: Music without text but tied to ritual activity. Examples: organ mass during preparation of the Eucharist, dirge or slow march at a funeral, "Hail to the Chief" during arrival of the president, "Pomp and Circumstance" at graduation, "Wedding March" at a wedding.

Music and Text: Music tied to text without ritual action. Examples: Gregorian chant (for example, Vespers), Qur'an recitation, Torah cantillation, Christian hymns, Theravada Buddhist chanting, Vedic Stotras preceding the Yajna, national anthem at sports events.

Music and Text and Ritual Action: Music united with words and tied to ritual activity. Examples: Haveli Sangit and Samaj Gayan in Hindu worship, Latin chants performed during the Mass, Tibetan Buddhist chanting during rituals, Jazz funeral hymn "Just a Closer Walk with Thee" in procession.

A fifth category would be Text and Ritual Action without Music. This would still be a sound event including speaking or reading something during a ritual activity. Examples: Pledge of Allegiance, swearing of oaths on the Bible.

When these rubrics are expanded and amplified with examples from other religions, they provide useful frameworks for the more neutral work of "sonic liturgy." Although Foley outlined the four acoustical properties and the four types of ritual music described above in order to analyze sound and music as part of Christian ritual and liturgy, he indicated the need for more cross-cultural work to be undertaken in this field: "There is so little comparable work on the theology of music or liturgical music."[56] In answer to this call the present book seeks to contribute to the concerns raised by Foley by attempting to present a lucid understanding of why music plays a central role in Hindu worship.

Mary E. McGann, an American liturgical scholar and faculty member at the Graduate Theological Union, has endorsed Foley's call for more comparative studies in music and religion by orienting her academic approach to the need for wider understanding of the central role of music in a variety of world religious cultures. According to her, music and the arts "are a compendium of religious, social, and cultural realizations of relatedness. From the perspective of liturgical theory, they are not embellishments but constitutive of what takes place in liturgy, affecting how all other elements are experienced and participating in the creation of meaning that takes place."[57] Music and song are thus not used as mere decoration or background ambience but express key cultural factors within the worship communities themselves. She stresses that the holistic approach is more effective in understanding the role of music as it is inseparable from ritual: "Music making and ritualization must be interpreted as an integrated whole. Music unfolds not only in ritual but as ritual, as a mode of ritual performance. An assembly's musical performance inevitably influences the whole ritual process."[58]

In making a strong case for the importance of ritual for sacred music, Stephen A. Marini, in *Sacred Song in America: Religion, Music, and Public Culture* (2003), argues that merely the mythic content of a song, that is, the lyrics and their narrative dimension, is not sufficient to make it sacred or "religious"; it must contain the ritual element. He states: "For a song to be sacred, it must possess not only belief content but also ritual intention and form. Ritual is the defining performance condition for sacred song, as mythic content is its defining cognitive condition. . . . In order for song to be religious expression it must be presented with sacred intentionality as part of effective ritual action. . . . Sacred song is an extraordinary vehicle for conducting believers into the ritual dimension. It may indeed be the single most powerful medium of the ritual process."[59]

For both McGann and Marini music and song are the key modes of ritual expressiveness. Music structures time in various ways, song inhabits the acoustical space, and the singing of songs permits specific words to take on the cultural resonances and style of a community. McGann is optimistic about the trends in liturgical studies toward increasing attention to performance traditions rather than the mere study of texts. Yet she is apprehensive about the current state of research into musical aspects of liturgies in different contexts. Despite advances in specialized fields, "little has been done to develop methods for studying music within a community's worship performance, and for assessing how a community's musical performance affects the entire continuum of liturgical action, shaping and expressing an embodied theology."[60]

Specific research methods for developing the field of comparative liturgy and music are revealed in *Exploring Music as Worship and Theology: Research in Liturgical Practice* (2002), in which McGann describes an interdisciplinary approach: "The method is necessarily interdisciplinary. Each of the three fields of Liturgical Studies, Ethnomusicology, and Ritual Studies offers us a different yet complementary view of what takes place when a liturgical assembly makes music. Taken together, the perspectives, theories, and methods of these three disciplines provide a basis for studying and interpreting music as an integral part of liturgical performance."[61] She offers a persuasive call for more interdisciplinary work in music and liturgy in various religious cultures: "It is my hope that other scholars will take up the work of studying worship music, using all or parts of this method, or developing comparable methods of their own. The approach I take can be used in a variety of cultural and denominational settings, and can be adapted to a range of musical idioms."[62]

Terry Muck, in his innovative essay "Psalm, Bhajan, and Kirtan: Songs of the Soul in Comparative Perspective" (2001), provides a good example of the type of comparative and interdisciplinary research into religion and music that both Foley and McGann are recommending. Muck discusses three varieties of sacred song—one Western and two Indian—and finds that they each reflect the "ineffable" or "sublime" realm in a unique way: "The difficulty in identifying defining characteristics of religious song is that these characteristics are precisely those that go beyond definition. Religious song refers one to the sublime dimensions of life, the ineffable, the beyond, the indefinable. Perhaps the best definition is one that acknowledges it is really no definition at all because it admits that its subject is indefinable. . . . Religious songs, then, are those that have the capacity to present the unpresentable, the sublime. . . . Clearly Psalms, Bhajan, and Kirtan have as their subject matter, their evocative basis, and their performance this area called the sublime."[63] Psalms, Bhajans, and Kirtans each have their own religious context within a specific community of worship, whether in Judaism, Christianity, Hinduism, or Sikhism, and exemplify the notion of what Otto described as a personal encounter with God or the ineffable:

> Psalm, Bhajan, and Kirtan speak truth and open one to God. Their singing represents one aspect of the quintessence of the religious act. But these religious, devotional songs are more than theology, worship, and liturgy. They are all of these together—and more. . . . Religious, devotional songs are directed from human beings toward the object of devotion. . . . Humans direct their religious songs to the transcendent object with awe and reverence in the face of sacred power; they are sung with confidence and trust that the transcendent is real; and they are sung with a single-minded concentration that befits the sincerity required of such an endeavor.[64]

Utilizing his own particular expertise, Muck establishes the basis for serious comparative discourse about music in religious worship: "Clearly the consensus in all three traditions is that religious, devotional songs may be used individually or in groups for purposes of worship, and/or petition with a wide variety of musical styles, as long as they are faithful to the religious traditions' understanding of the transcendent and effective in generating ways of connecting singers to that transcendent."[65]

Muck cites the present author's earlier work *Sonic Theology: Hinduism and Sacred Sound* (1993) in order to underscore his comparative viewpoint about the devotional object of sacred music: "The art of intoning sacred sound has been seen (in Hinduism) to both inaugurate and sustain the soteriological quest toward whichever Hindu god, goddess, or heaven is targeted."[66]

Those who engage in the study of other cultures, religion, and music, must be able to move beyond their own categories of interpretation, to see things from another point of view and to reach an empathetic awareness of how a community makes meaning musically and ritually. While this approach should contain some of the etic perspective, including the element of functionalism of the social sciences, the ideal case combines it with a deeper empathy and subtle awareness of the absolute value that ritual and music have for the believers and practitioners.

TERMINOLOGY FOR SONIC LITURGY

In preparation for the study of ritual and music in Hindu tradition, it is useful to list some precise terms drawn from various disciplines that are helpful in examining sound or music events as they occur in various liturgies.

Anamnesis: Remembrance of a past historical or mythical event, as in music during Passover or Christ's Passion or in the remembrance of Rama's victory over Ravana in the Hindu epic Ramayana.

Apotropaia: Removal of unwanted spirits or demons, through the chanting of specific texts or the playing of loud and brash instruments. This effect is obtained in Hindu, Buddhist, Shinto, and tribal religions.

Catharsis: Purification from sin or defilement. This is found in mantra chanting in Hinduism and in Buddhist recitation of the Pali Canon.

Cosmogony: Reenactment of the creation myth. Examples of music in this function would include the music of New Year ceremonies in many religions as well as ritual combat. Several of the Vedic sacrifices reenact the cosmogony and involve complex styles of chant and the singing of hymns.

Didactic: Teaching doctrine, as found in Jewish lessons, Hindu Puranic recitation, and the chanting of the Buddhist Pali Canon.

Doxology: Praise or glorification of God or a deity. In response to receiving the gift of life from their creator, humans offer praise. As such, ethically speaking, humans are under a kind of obligation to make music for the glory of God and not for their own amusement. This function is termed doxological (doxa, "glory") because music is used to glorify or praise the divine. Music as "doxology" is also fully present in other theistic musical traditions: Kirtan and Bhajan in Hinduism, Qawwali in Islam, and Shabad in Sikhism, but not in Buddhism, which does not recognize a creator.

Epiclesis: Invitation of a god or divine being to a sacrifice or worship occasion. Borrowed from classical pagan vocabulary, this term is used to depict the priestly action of inviting the Holy Spirit into the sacramental bread and wine in Roman Catholicism. In a broader sense it may refer to the mantras in a Vedic Yajna, Hindu devotional music, and other forms of religious practice in the world. Music here serves a distinct purpose apart from mere praise or expiation.

Eschatology: Expressing the end times. Music that is eschatological represents or expresses a future state of being, such as those described in the biblical books of Isaiah (6:3) and Revelation (5:8–10). This type may also be found in Jewish messianic songs, Christian hymns, Hindu Bhajans, Buddhist prayers, or Sikh Shabads. The Hindu ritual music studied herein fits with this mode, as the units of ritual/musical time accumulate to provide rewards in the heavenly afterlife.

Eucharistic: Giving thanks, as also found in Sikhism, temple Hinduism, and Judaism.

Expiation: Asking forgiveness of sin or transgression from a deity or divine being.

Exstasis: Ecstasy, as in Sufism, Hasidism, Hindu Bhakti, and some Buddhist sects. Music is employed to achieve particular states of ecstasy and bliss, termed exstasis in the texts of ancient mystery religions.

Katanyxis: Contrition or remorse. Besides Christianity, this is found in some forms of Hindu Kirtan and Sikh Shabads.

Koinonia: Communion between the human and divine world. The notion of musical unity among human beings, martyrs, and saints is found in the Christianity and also in archaic and Asian religions where music celebrates a communal meal among humans and the gods, as practiced in ancient Vedic India or in temple Hinduism.

Litaneia: Petitionary prayer, as in the Roman Catholic Kyrie Eleison ("Lord Have Mercy"), in Judaism, temple Hinduism, or in many of the Sikh Shabads.

Propitiation: Seeking the favor or blessing from a deity or divine being.

RITUAL AND MUSIC IN HINDU TRADITION

Many of the theoretical aspects of sacred sound in Hindu traditions have been discussed in the present author's earlier book, *Sonic Theology: Hinduism and Sacred Sound.* These may be summarized as follows. As a basis for approaching the study of sacred sound in Hinduism, the Vedas and Upanishads (4000–1000 B.C.E.) offer information about chant and vocal utterances in relation to cultic sacrifices to the gods. These ancient Indo-Aryan texts are said to be eternal, authorless, and the embodiment of the primeval sound that generated the universe. This sacred sound is variously known as the syllable *Om* and as Sabda-Brahman and is described as the Supreme Absolute in the Upanishads. The compact elemental sound of Om becomes manifest through the power of oral chant and music and is first discussed in terms of Nada-Brahman in the Agamas, Pancaratras, and Tantras. In the later theistic traditions, whether Vaishnavism (Vishnu or Krishna worship), Saivism (Siva worship), or Saktism (goddess worship), the term and concept of Nada-Brahman ("sacred sound") gained ascendancy while simultaneously being articulated in musicological texts as well those of the Tantra and Yoga traditions. Nada-Brahman encompassed, in addition to linguistic sounds and utterances, all musical and other nonlinguistic sounds. The term *Nada-Brahman* referred to the cosmic sound that may be either unmanifest (*anahata,* "unstruck") or manifest (*ahata,* "struck"). Since the Upanishadic Brahman pervaded the exterior cosmos as well as the interior human soul at its core, the notion of sacred sound as Nada-Brahman provided a veritable thread binding the human realm to the divine. Musical treatises discussed Nada-Brahman as the foundation of musical sound, and Yoga texts used the term *Nada-Brahman* to refer to the musical sounds heard during deep meditation. Nada-Brahman was thus essential to Indian views of the salvational dimension of music, for music, as a direct manifestation of Nada, was seen as a means of access to the highest spiritual realities. Music was viewed as both bhukti (entertainment) and as a vehicle toward Moksham (liberation). Combining the metaphysical notions of Nada-Brahman, the aesthetics of Rasa theory, and the structures of Raga (melody types) and Tala (rhythms), the various schools of Indian classical music have carried forth the formal traditions of music to the present day.

The present work, *Sonic Liturgy: Ritual and Music in Hindu Tradition*, builds upon these premises and is in many ways a sequel to the earlier work. Yet it is more than that, since it pursues a practical application and exploration of some of the important commonalities associated with sacred sound on the ground, so to speak, in ritual and liturgy, especially through the new category of sonic liturgy. This work may also be seen as describing sacred sound in practice as opposed to sacred sound in theory. The "practice" that is focused upon is primarily the musical dimension in the context of ritual worship, beginning with the Vedic Yajna, then the Hindu Puja, and lastly, the Vaishnava Seva.

If one were to ask casually about the role of music in Hindu worship, the question would undoubtedly elicit some common-sense responses: "Well, of course Hindu worship includes music" or "all the Hindus I know sing songs in the temple." But if one were to inquire seriously about why music is so prominent in ritual life, a moment of silence would probably follow. Moreover, if the question was raised about scholarly publications in this field, there would be some hesitation, even among academics. There are in fact many books and articles about Indian classical music and its history, yet most of these trace the history of Indian music as if it were a secular art divorced from ritual or liturgical life. Indeed, there are many competent studies of scale systems, the classification and evolution of musical instruments, musicological texts, and biographies of great musicians. There is even an abundance of literature on selected religious practices, but there are few works documenting the precise role of music and chant within the daily or seasonal worship routines of specific traditions and liturgical systems. What is needed at this juncture is a comprehensive survey of the role of music in Hindu ritual over the centuries, revealing the rationale for its importance across several traditions of worship. This book is an attempt to provide that overview.

The academic categories of ritual and liturgy are only beginning to be applied to Hindu traditions. For example, in the field of Vedic ritual the work of Frits Staal is foundational, including his *Ritual and Mantras: Rules without Meaning* (1989, 1993) and *Agni: The Vedic Ritual of the Fire Altar* (1983). Uma Marina Vesci, in *Heat and Sacrifice in the Vedas* (1985), has examined the details of Vedic ritual in terms of heat and fire symbolism. Musashi Tachikawa, Shrikant Bahulkar, and Madhavi Kolhatkar have documented in detail the rituals of Agnihotra and domestic sacrifices in *Indian Fire Rituals* (2001). Brian K. Smith, in *Reflections on Resemblance, Ritual, and Religion* (1989), has provided the most provocative and refreshing examination of the meaning of Vedic ritual in our time. G. U. Thite's *Music in the Vedas: Its Magico-Religious Significance* (1997) is the most important work on Vedic music.

Gudrun Buhnemann's groundbreaking study of Puja rituals, *Puja: A Study in Smarta Ritual* (1988), has opened the field for further research. Regarding Puja in the ancient drama productions, Natalia Lidova, in *Drama and Ritual of Early Hinduism* (1994), makes a significant contribution. The field of Siva Puja and the Agamas is remarkably enhanced by the recent book of Richard H. Davis, *Worshipping Siva in Medieval India: Ritual in an Oscillating Universe* (2000).

There are also some excellent specialized studies of Puja. Hillary Peter Rodrigues, in *Ritual Worship of the Great Goddess: The Liturgy of the Durga Puja with Interpretations* (2003), has laid down the entire sequence and format of the liturgy associated with the worship of the goddess Durga. He also acknowledged that music played an important role: "It is traditionally prescribed that particular musical pieces, known as Ragas, be performed during the Great Bath on Saptami, Astami, and Navami. These may be sung or preferably played on the shehnai or the harmonium, although other instruments are not inappropriate. These performances may be accompanied by dancers and other musical accompaniment."[67] In addition, the complete Puja of the deity of Jagannatha in Puri has been documented by Gaya Charan Tripathi in his mammoth work *Communication with God: The Daily Puja Ceremony in the Jagannatha Temple* (2004). These Vaishnava rituals are rife with mostly Sanskrit mantras and incantations.

Focusing attention on music in ritual or liturgical context, it is incumbent on us first to acknowledge where modern scholarship has affirmed the importance of music and performance as vital to understanding the Hindu religion. Countering the traditional emphasis on textual analysis in Indian studies, Hinduism scholar Vasudha Narayanan broadly stated: "The performers of music and dance, the transmitters of the religious traditions, speak for Hinduism. We should listen to them."[68] Susan L. Schwartz has more recently stated that "so central has the religious context been to understanding and achieving the goals of performance that it is possible to study the religions of India through her performing arts. The forms performance takes and the ways it is studied, learned, and experienced reveal ways in which religion may be understood in India."[69] These views have found adept practical application in the works of Selina Thielemann, such as *Divine Service and the Performing Arts in India* (2002) and *Sounds of the Sacred: Religious Music in India* (1998). In terms of liturgical music, Meilu Ho (2006) has produced a full-length study of the Vallabha tradition.

Sonic Liturgy: Ritual and Music in Hindu Tradition seeks to draw upon the insights and information from the studies mentioned above in order to build a case for the overall significance of music within Hindu ritual and worship. This goal is achieved by tying together several diverse traditions into a near-seamless continuity over time and geographic area. The principal focus is on the portable category of sonic liturgy and how it serves as a flexible template with which to understand the constantly changing and developing process of human interaction with the divine in the context of ritual and music.

From the singing of the ancient Vedic hymns, known as Sama-Gana, to the earliest classical music called Gandharva Sangita, to the medieval forms of devotional temple music or Bhakti Sangit, Indian music is rooted both in the theological principles of sacred sound inscribed in Hindu scriptures and in the performance of ritualistic activity in relation to the divine. Many sages in ancient India were chanters of the Vedic texts, while founders of religious lineages were patrons of music or musically adept. Most teachers, in fact, of Indian musical styles were directly associated with religious lineages.

Considered divine in origin, music was closely identified with the Hindu gods and goddesses and formed an integral part of Indian mythology. The goddess Sarasvati, depicted with the Vina instrument in hand, is believed to be the divine patron of music and receives the veneration of all students and performers of Indian music. Brahma, the creator of the universe, fashioned Indian music out of the ingredients of the *Sama-Veda* and also plays the hand cymbals. Vishnu the Preserver sounds the conch shell and plays the flute as the avatara known as Krishna. Siva as Nataraja plays the Damaru drum during the dance of cosmic dissolution. Each of these instruments symbolizes Nada-Brahman, sacred cosmic sound. Divine manifestations of these deities on earth have stimulated the cultivation of music throughout India as an integral part of both religious and secular realms.

The Hindu rites of worship studied here are Yajna ("sacrifice"), Puja ("worship"), and Seva ("divine service"). Yajna involves offerings placed into a fire and is the mainstay of the Indo-Aryan or Vedic cult. Puja and Seva involve the worship of images and require offerings of flowers, food, incense, lamps, and the sounding of conches and bells. While the systems of Puja (and Seva) most probably originated outside of the Vedic or Indo-Aryan tradition, they were quickly adopted into it as part of ancient sacred dramas and temple traditions that worshipped a deity according to a strict liturgical calendar. The liturgical calendars of the Hindus as developed over the years are a combination of solar and lunar observation. Beside the solar calendar based on the sun, the lunar calendars are of two types, depending on the way in which the months are calculated. A lunar calendar that is marked by months beginning on the full moon is called Purnimanta, and one that begins each month with the new moon is called Amanta. The Purnimanta is followed in most of northern India, while Amanta calendars are found in South India and Bengal. Both also apply the solar calendar, depending on the observance.

Indian music that fills a liturgical function requires close attention to the text and to clear pronunciation, at the same time maintaining established patterns of performance throughout the year over many generations. Although melody and rhythm are important, improvisation and musical virtuosity for its own sake are normally discouraged in Hindu temples or religious gatherings, in contrast with the developing classical traditions that laud improvisation and technical mastery. Most Hindu religious gatherings today include chant and music that frequently form part of congregational rites in which there is a sharing of Bhakti experiences. Modern scholarship has noted and confirmed that, despite differences in theology or philosophy in the Bhakti movements and sects, a common factor in most is devotional music, since religious leaders consider music essential for propagation of their faiths in order to make those faiths more attractive. While there may be differences in the content of their Padas (stanzas), there is little difference in principle in their style of singing or performance. Thus an understanding of music and its relation to liturgical activities is vital to a full comprehension of Hinduism.

To reiterate our premise with regard to Hindu tradition, the worship of God through or with music has remained at the center of most Puja and Seva activities, whether in the North or in the South: "Evoking the presence of God through song, dance, enactments and narrations represents the core task of the ritual service."[70] From this position we can demonstrate that from Vedic chant to Sama-Gana to Gandharva Sangita to Bhakti Sangit and from Yajna to Puja to Seva, there is a continuity of ritual and music within various forms of sonic liturgy in Hindu tradition.

The ancient ritual practices of the Indo-Aryans are discussed here in the context of Indo-Iranian mythology, the Avesta, Zoroastrianism, and Yajna (Yasna in Persian), the fire sacrifices that included the chanting and reciting of portions of the Veda. The ancient Vedic fire sacrifice always included chant and meditation on sound. The chanting of Sanskrit hymns from the Vedas was performed by priests during public and private fire sacrifices. Ritual chanting was viewed as a powerful means to interact with the cosmos and to obtain unseen spiritual merit toward a heavenly afterlife. Sound and speech also had a feminine connotation as the goddess Vac, said to inhere in the pronunciation and metrical structure of the mantras. Verses from the Rig-Veda were chanted in roughly three distinct musical tones or accents. These three were expanded to seven notes in the Sama-Gana, the singing of hymns from the *Sama-Veda* that were set to preexistent melodies for use during elaborate Soma sacrifices involving the offering of Soma juice. This juice, mixed with milk and honey, was particularly enjoyed by the god Indra and was imbibed by the priests as a sacrament after the ritual. The *Sama-Veda* was also connected with the worship of ancestors, whose abode was the moon, Soma.

The chanted Samans were believed to possess supernatural powers capable of petitioning and supporting the deities that controlled the forces of the universe. The Vedic gods even seem to have had a sense of music appreciation. The singing of Sama-Gana with sustained musical notes was essential to the sacrifice and indicates that music was mysteriously linked to the divine at this early stage of Hindu ritual practice. The Sama-Gana, referring to the more musical rendering of *Sama-Veda* hymns by specialized priests during Soma sacrifices, is explained as one of the forerunners of Indian classical music. The earliest form of sonic liturgy emerges here in the scenario of the Yajna and the rendering of Sama-Gana. The Vedic sacrificial process of Apurva is described with reference to ritual sequence, whereby unseen "soteriological" merit is accrued in increments to the participants. This scheme recurs within the dynamics of language comprehension as well as in the rhythmic dimensions of Hindu devotional music.

The tradition of Sama-Gana was paralleled by the creation and development of Indian classical music, known first as Gandharva Sangita, which was heavily tied to drama, and then simply as Sangita. The three divisions of Sangita, vocal, instrumental, and dance, have always been intertwined, whether in religious observances or as courtly entertainment. Gandharva Sangita ("celestial music") was the counterpart to the sacrificial Sama-Gana and was considered to be a replica of the music performed and enjoyed in Lord Indra's court in heaven. This ancient religious music was primarily vocal but included instruments such as the Vina, flutes, drums, and cymbals. As part of the changeover from Yajna to Puja as the principal Hindu ritual, Gandharva Sangita played a significant role in the evolving devotional worship of the great gods Siva and Vishnu. Gandharva Sangita, as represented in the ancient texts of the *Natya-Sastra* and the *Dattilam*, is discussed with reference to Puja, the new form of non-Aryan worship that replaced fire with flowers and other offerings on an altar. There is a description here of the various elements of Puja with the insertion of chant and music as necessary components.

Indian mythology contains frequent narrations of the gods and their heavenly music. Images of the gods as musicians serve as prototypes or paradigms for the human musicians, who in many ways are oriented toward the divine realm in their performances. The roles of Brahma, Sarasvati, and Narada Rishi, the giver of music to the world, are discussed with regard to the genesis of music in human society. The oldest surviving texts of Gandharva Sangita are the *Natya-Sastra* by Bharata Muni and the *Dattilam* by Dattila (ca. 400–200 B.C.E.). These, as well as the *Naradiya-Siksa* (first century C.E.), provide glimpses of Gandharva Sangita and its evolution. Gandharva music was the music performed in sacred dramas, festivals, courtly ceremonies, and temple rituals in honor of the emerging great gods and goddesses, including Siva, Vishnu, Brahma, Ganesha, and Devi. Special songs used to propitiate the gods, called Dhruva, were rendered, not in Sanskrit but in Prakrit, a derivative language with less rigid grammatical construction. The Dhruva was the prototype of the medieval Prabandha which was the basis of the later classical and devotional forms of Bhakti Sangit sung in vernacular, called Dhrupad (Dhruvapada), Haveli Sangit, Samaj Gayan, or Kirtan in the North and Kriti in the South.

Rhythm, or Tala, is fundamental to all Indian music. Mimamsa philosophy is useful in understanding why this is so. As explained by Mimamsa philosophers, Vedic chants and Sama-Gana were punctuated by metrical divisions that, through the principle of Apurva, generated distinct units of unseen merit called Adrishta that accrued to the priest or sacrificer leading to afterlife in heaven. In Gandharva music similar metrical units were marked by the playing of hand cymbals and drums. Since Vedic chant was metrical, religious music must have a distinct rhythm or division of musical time sequence for it to provide the benefits noted above to the listener or performer. The ancient theory of music held that the musicians and audience earned liberation through accumulation of unseen merit as exemplified in the marking of ritual (musical) time. However, the emerging sense of release (Moksha) within the Bhakti traditions was also dependent on the emotion or feelings of the practitioners with regard to the developing personal relationship with their deity, including the proper Rasa and Bhava states. The strong emphasis on cymbal playing in most forms of Bhakti Sangit, including Haveli Sangit and Samaj Gayan, supports the contention that the Mimamsa theory of merit accumulation has continued into the present time, though often unrecognized.

By the sixth century C.E. in the Tamil region of South India, Bhakti movements emerged as powerful forces favoring a devotion-centered Hinduism with song-texts composed primarily in regional vernacular languages, called Deshi Bhashas. Within the rising Bhakti movements, there were a number of new styles of Deshi Sangit, or regional devotional music. Bhakti Sangit was often formalized as music accompanying liturgies in the temple Hinduism of medieval times and followed a simple aesthetic that reflected the perspective of music as a means toward communion with a chosen deity. In theistic Vedanta, Brahman was conceived of as the supreme personal deity, whether in the form of Vishnu, Siva, or Sakti.

As the Vedic fire sacrifices and Sama-Gana were eclipsed by Gandharva Sangita and Puja rituals, classes of orthodox Brahmins called Smarta attempted to estrange Gandharva Sangita from mainstream Hindu tradition. Yet in response a new fusion developed between Gandharva Sangita, which was widened to include vernacular poetry and regional melodies, and sectarian orthodoxies derived from the thrust of the Bhakti movements. Temple Hinduism emerged in honor of the great gods Siva and Vishnu, with icons (Murti) of these gods installed with regular Puja services according to new scriptures called Agamas. In line with Bhakti devotion the new Hindu sonic liturgies were obliged to contain chant and music and also to incorporate musical instruments. As such, various new forms of liturgical music, referred to as Bhakti Sangit, evolved that were both endorsed by Bhakti scriptures and chronicled in musicological texts. These new musical forms, also called Kirtan and Bhajan, appeared to diverge from earlier models but nonetheless carried forth the soteriological dimensions of unseen merit accumulation (Adrishta) as outlined in Mimamsa texts, which are here referenced to practical musical time in temple worship, providing a hitherto unrecognized continuity between India's religious past and the present Hindu practice of rendering devotional music.

The radical switch from Sanskrit to vernacular languages as found in the flood of medieval Bhakti poetry and temple music traditions was believed to have had scriptural sanction in the canonical text known as the *Bhagavata-Purana*, which speaks of "ancient," that is, Sanskrit, hymns, as well as of verses composed in local languages. Consequently the Bhakti movement has produced a tremendous amount of vernacular devotional poetry that is sung in temples all over India. The earliest examples of vernacular hymns being placed on an equal level with the Veda are the *Tevaram* hymns of the Saiva saints known as the Nayanars, and the *Divya Prabandham* hymns of the Vaishnava saints called Alvars. Both of these were compiled from the fifth to ninth centuries C.E. These traditions overlapped with the classical music of the South known as Carnatic. Sometime after the thirteenth century the classical music traditions separated into northern Hindustani and southern Carnatic. Hindustani music stemmed from the classical Dhrupad and Dhamar that had become a mainstay in the courts of Rajasthan, Maharashtra, Gujarat, Bengal, and Uttar Pradesh. Parallel to this were the classically influenced forms of Bhakti Sangit, sometimes referred to as Pada-Kirtan, that were composed in vernacular languages. The presence of Persian and Sufi culture also influenced the development of Hindustani classical music.

Music has always been closely associated with Vaishnavism, the rising theistic tradition that placed Vishnu, and most often, Krishna, at the center of religious practice. During the Late Middle Ages (1200–1600 C.E.), the deity of the youthful Krishna emerged as the principal object of Bhakti Sangit and inspired the creation of several new "Krishna sampradayas" in the region of Braj in North India. The Vallabha, Radhavallabha, Nimbarka, and Haridasi sampradayas are the most prominent Vaishnava traditions of northern India that have incorporated classical forms of Bhakti Sangit into their Seva or temple liturgies. Based on classical forms of Bhakti Sangit or Pada-Kirtan, this music comes under the name of Haveli Sangit, and Samaj Gayan.

In the North, Dhrupad and Dhamar were the principal classical vehicles for the vernacular Bhakti lyrics and provided a formal structure for several related genres of devotional music including Haveli Sangit and Samaj Gayan. These various types of Dhrupad-influenced music became instrumental components of the Seva of several new Vaishnava traditions of Bhakti established in Braj by the sixteenth century. The Vallabha Sampradaya or Pushti Marg tradition, founded by Sri Vallabhacharya, was instrumental in developing and refining the notion of divine service or Seva. The deity of Krishna that was worshipped in this early sect was Sri Nathji, discovered in Braj. A group of eight poets called Ashtachap began to compose songs for the Seva at different times of the day. These poets included Sur Das and also Chaturbhuj Das, Chitaswami, and Govind Prabhu. This tradition is examined with reference to Seva, Kirtan, and Haveli Sangit, the later name of the temple music tradition associated with this group.

Haveli Sangit is believed to be one of the forerunners of Hindustani music and is composed of songs in Braj Bhasha that describe the pastimes of Krishna, including especially the festival associated with Holi in the spring season and the Rasa Dance in autumn. Haveli Sangit is now practiced in the Vallabha headquarters in Nathadvara in Rajasthan, as well as at temples and centers in Rajasthan, Gujarat, and Mumbai.

Besides the tradition of Haveli Sangit associated with the Vallabha Sampradaya, Samaj Gayan is the most significant form of classically based devotional music in northern India, figuring centrally in the worship of three new Krishna sampradayas: Radhavallabha, Nimbarka, and Haridasi. Samaj Gayan, though based on Dhrupad and Dhamar, reveals innovative methods of "interactive" choral music that require years of study and training to perform. Rendered in styles related to Hindustani classical music, Samaj Gayan is sung according to Ragas (scale formulas reflective of distinct emotional moods set within daily or seasonal formats) and Talas (rhythmic cycles). The compositions of Samaj Gayan are usually sung in call-and-response form with musical accompaniment of harmonium, Tanpura (lute), Pakhavaj (barrel drum), and Jhanjh (hand cymbals). The various festivals and observances throughout a liturgical year make up the solar-lunar calendar of these groups, which provides a framework for the inclusion of a vast assortment of songs and hymns. Although a compelling genre of Bhakti Sangit, Samaj Gayan is, unlike Haveli Sangit, largely unknown outside of the Braj area.

In the mid-sixteenth century Sri Hita Harivamsa founded the Radhavallabha Sampradaya in Vrindaban and was the first promulgator of the interactive vocal style known as Samaj Gayan. Samaj Gayan, as an integral part of Radhavallabha temple Seva, is believed to have been continuously practiced since the founding of this tradition. Samaj Gayan was adopted by the Nimbarka Sampradaya, founded by Sri Nimbarka (ca. twelfth century C.E.), shortly after the Radhavallabha Sampradaya. The Haridasi Sampradaya, founded by Swami Haridas (ca. 1500–1595 C.E.), also adopted Samaj Gayan but not until the eighteenth century.

As this book may serve as a companion to the author's earlier work *Sonic Theology: Hinduism and Sacred Sound,* which outlined the philosophical and theoretical dimensions of sacred sound in Hinduism, it also advances the premise that theory is not enough to understand fully the role of music or sound in religion. Such understanding requires the study of its practical application in ritual and liturgy.

Research in the Braj region of Uttar Pradesh in North India in 1992–93 has allowed the author to study the temple music as well as the liturgical use of devotional song-texts in four living traditions of Vaishnavism established in Braj between 1200 and 1600 C.E.: the Vallabha, Radhavallabha, Nimbarka, and Haridasi traditions.

A close study of the four types of Vaishnava Seva, or sonic liturgy, reveals a vast multileveled "auditory environment" illumined with poems describing divine pastimes sung to melodic formulas (Ragas), penetrated with rhythms (Talas) played on drums and cymbals, punctuated with conches and bells, and suffused with emotional moods associated with the times of the day and the colorful seasons of the year. The music employed in worship can be properly comprehended only when it is viewed as a contributive part of an interlocking network of liturgical meaning. As such, this study hopes to broaden knowledge and understanding of Hindu worship, where meaning surpasses mere musical or literary effect, and heighten awareness of sonic liturgy as a comparative category.

I

Ancient India

Yajna and Sama-Gana

INDIAN MUSIC AND ITS EMPLOYMENT IN WORSHIP as a sonic liturgy is traceable to the earliest roots of Indian civilization. Comprising the Yajna or Vedic fire sacrifices, the Soma sacrifices, and the singing of Sama-Gana in Sanskrit, the concept of sonic liturgy in Vedic religion first developed as a uniquely Indo-Aryan tradition. With the parallel rise of early classical music and its association with drama and Puja rites, sonic liturgy became enlarged with non-Aryan elements. And as the ancient Vedic culture gradually blended more and more with indigenous features and vernacular expression, new forms of Hindu liturgical tradition emerged, leading ultimately to the concept of Seva, a fully comprehensive worship experience that nonetheless retained ties to the Vedic tradition as well as to the earliest classical music, Gandharva Sangita. The earliest Hindu musical expression was the singing of *Sama-Veda* hymns (Sama-Gana), rendered during Soma sacrifices, and Gandharva Sangita, performed during Puja (services to the Hindu gods) associated with early religious dramas. As these traditions developed further in conversation with the devotional input of the Bhakti movements, they were codified into new forms of sonic liturgy by schools of orthodoxy. Consisting of what has been called temple Hinduism in the medieval period, and devoted primarily to the gods Siva and Vishnu, these traditions combined Vedic chant in Sanskrit with regional musical forms and vernacular poetry. Several new forms of Seva that were established from the fifteenth to sixteenth centuries were focused on the Vaishnava deity of Krishna and became fully integrated and interactive systems of sonic liturgy that often involved all of the creative arts. In order to understand the roots of Hindu sonic liturgy, we first turn to the religion and culture of the ancient Indo-Aryans.

INDO-ARYANS

The terms *Hindu* and *Hinduism* were unknown in ancient India, as was the idea of a unified religious system. Instead there were wider networks of language, culture, and ritual that may be defined as Arya-Dharma, the dharma or religious culture of the ancient Indo-Aryans, the South Asian branch of the broader Aryan cultural and linguistic milieu. What we understand today as Hinduism is actually a complex blend of Indo-Aryan traditions and many indigenous elements, including those associated with the Indus Valley Civilization. The term *Aryan* was originally identified with peoples across the entire region from India to ancient Persia (Iran) from about 3000 B.C.E. The Aryan languages, Sanskrit and ancient Persian or Avestan, belong to the larger family known as Indo-European, comprising Greek, Latin, Celtic, Germanic, Slavic, and other languages that share many features.

The ancient Persians (Iranians or Avestans) and Indians (Vedic) were the only groups who applied the term *Aryan* to themselves. It was not a racial or geographic classification but a cultural one. And despite the use of the Aryan appellation by various interest groups in recent times, modern scholarship tends to confirm the conservative ascription: "The Rig-Vedic and Avestan people are called Aryan because that is how they described themselves in their texts. The term should be reserved for them alone, and not used as an umbrella term for Indo-Europeans."[1] It has also become apparent that the Persian and Indian cultures shared a similar origin and remained closely bound together for many years: "The institutions, customs and ways of thought of the Vedic and Avestan people are so similar that there can be no doubt the two peoples are very closely related. Both call themselves Arya. . . . Any statement that is made about the history of the Vedic people should not only be consistent with the Vedic texts but also with the Avesta."[2]

The similarity of the two cultures has been confirmed on linguistic grounds by Harvard philologist Michael Witzel: "Vedic Sanskrit is indeed so closely related to Old Iranian that both often look more like two dialects than two separate languages. . . . [In fact] the comparison of the many common features found in Vedic Indo-Aryan and Old Iranian has led to the reconstruction of a common parent, IIr, spoken (at least) c. 2000 B.C.E., by a group of people that shared a common spiritual and material culture."[3]

The early religions of both "Aryans" were closely bound up with sun worship, fire rituals, the Soma cult, and solar phenomena. Since they both utilized the mysterious Soma (Haoma in Avestan) plant in rituals, the native habitat for this plant weighs in heavily as the most probable geographic place of Aryan origins. This author accepts the view of both Karl Geldner and Rajesh Kochhar, namely, that the Soma plant was not a hallucinogenic mushroom as has been suggested by R. Gordon Wasson, but a species of Ephedra common to the mountainous regions of Iran, Afghanistan, and Pakistan. The importance of the Soma plant and its cult nonetheless cannot be overestimated in connection with Aryan religion, as Soma was the central focal point of both Vedic and Avestan ritual life: "Soma is the mascot of the Aryans. Whatever the Avestan and the Rig-Vedic people needed or wished for at the individual and collective level, they asked Soma/Haoma to provide. Soma/Haoma is thus perceived as a giver of immortality, health and longevity, offspring, happiness, courage, strength, victory over enemies, wisdom, understanding and creativity."[4]

Not only the name and function, but many other facets of the Soma cult are shared as well by the Iranians and the Indians, as pointed out by C. Kunhan Raja: "The Soma worship is common between the two [*Rig-Veda* and Avesta religion], the Soma-Yaga of the Veda and the Haoma Yasna of the Avesta. In the matter of the way in which the Soma is pressed and offered at the worship, there is some agreement. The stories preserved in the Vedas about the original abode of the Soma in the Heaven, the transfer of the Soma to the earth, the place of its growth, namely, on a mountain, the properties and the powers of the Soma, are common with the same features of the Avestan Haoma."[5]

At a still uncertain period (ca. 2500–2000 B.C.E.), there was a bifurcation between the Irano-Aryans (Persians) and the Indo-Aryans (Indians), who gradually settled in present-day India and Pakistan. According to Vedic scholar Kunhan Raja, "the generally accepted view is that the group of Aryans who may be called the Indo-Iranians lived together in a common land for some time and developed a common culture, till they themselves were separated into two groups, one group having migrated to the West and the other to the East; their former common home may have been to the North."[6]

This separation resulted in groups of Indo-Aryans migrating into the Indian subcontinent, as described by Vedic scholar Frits Staal: "More than three thousand years ago, small groups of semi-nomadic peoples crossed the mountain regions that separate Central Asia from Iran and the subcontinent of India. They spoke an Indo-European language, which developed into Vedic, and imported the rudiments of a social and ritual system. Like other speakers of Indo-European languages, they celebrated fire, called Agni, and like their Iranian relatives, they adopted the cult of Soma—a plant . . . which grew in the high mountains." Vedic civilization developed on the Indian subcontinent when the migrating Indo-Aryans gradually blended with local inhabitants, including those of the urbanized and sophisticated Indus Valley Civilization: "The interaction between these Central-Asian adventurers and earlier inhabitants of the Indian subcontinent gave birth to Vedic civilization."[7]

In the wake of archaeological discoveries in the Indus Valley beginning in the 1920s, there have been heated debates surrounding the original homeland of the Aryans, whether it was India or outside of India and, if outside, whether the Aryans "invaded" India or simply migrated there. Despite current studies and academic conferences that have examined the issue of the original homeland of the

Aryans in great detail (see Edwin Bryant, 2001, 2005, and Thomas R. Trautman, 2005), the situation has not been resolved, and so we are content to leave things as summarized by Kunhan Raja:

> It is the people who developed the civilizations in Iran and in India that survived in these two regions, whom we call by the common name of the Indo-Iranian Branch of the Aryans, that use the term Aryan very prominently. It is supposed that they came from another region; but the exact region from which they came, the region that may be called the original home of the Aryans, has not yet been fixed. Scholars differ very widely on this problem. The only point on which they all agreed is that the Indo-Iranians belonged neither to India nor to Iran, but to another region from which they migrated. Nor is the time of the separation of the Aryans into different groups and their migrations into the various regions definitely fixed.[8]

According to Thomas R. Trautman (2005), the consensus among scholars is the scenario of a long series of migrations from somewhere in central Asia, echoing the original position of F. Max Muller (1888). This is still the most plausible explanation, as it still has not been proven conclusively that either Iran or India was their original homeland. The issue of an Aryan military invasion and defeat of native Dravidians has been closed, however, since "the Vedas do not show any sort of conflict with religious practices and beliefs that could be accepted as Dravidian."[9] The alternative position is that the Indo-Aryans, and indeed all Aryans, originated within India and spread outward, a position that does not stand up to scholarly scrutiny.

VEDIC RELIGION

Current academic attempts to define Hinduism place the acceptance of the authority of the Veda as the core concept. In the words of Brian K. Smith, "Hinduism is the religion of those humans who create, perpetuate, and transform traditions with legitimizing reference to the authority of the Veda."[10] But while many Hindus refer to the Veda as a kind of symbolic icon, Smith's observation relies on the dynamic relationship that Hindus maintain with the Veda by means of worship and ritual, in a kind of perennial ritual process: "The Veda, then, symbolizes nothing short of transcendence itself and maintains its authority by being intentionally divorced from human reality. . . . Hinduism, I would argue, is to be defined as a process, not an essence. It is not the essential nature of the Veda (or what it 'symbolizes') that is of defining import as much as it is the particular relationships Hindus establish and maintain with it."[11]

The primary sources for an understanding of Vedic religion are the Vedic literatures themselves, as there is virtually no archaeological evidence that is reliable, including artifacts or inscriptions. Vedic religion may be discovered only by extensive study of the four Vedas: *Rig-Veda, Yajur-Veda, Sama-Veda, and Atharva-Veda.* The first of the Vedas is the *Rig-Veda,* which is a collection of Sanskrit poems, mantras, hymns, and invocations reflecting myths, rites, battles, and metaphysical insights of many kinds. The *Rig-Veda* is the oldest of the Vedic texts and consists of hundreds of verses or Riks (*Rig*). The term *Rik* (also *Ric*) is derived from the root *arc,* to worship. Later derivative Sanskrit terms include *arcana* (worship) and *arcaka* (worshiper). The verses of the *Rig-Veda* are metrical, mostly in the form of prayers or hymns addressed to a large number of deities. Some of the deities have the appearance of being personifications of the phenomena of nature such as the sun, dawn, storm, and rivers. The precise nature of many others is indefinite. The *Rig-Veda* has 10, 450 verses grouped into 1,017 poems designated as hymns (Suktas). Suktas are grouped into ten Mandalas (books or circles). Book one comprises various ancient poets not in books two through seven, the so-called Family Books. Books two through seven present the compositions of Rishis (sages) and members of their families. They are named after the appropriate Rishis: Gritsamada, Visvamitra, Vamadeva, Atri, Bharadvaja, Vasishtha. Book eight is by Rishi Kanva, book nine is made up almost entirely of Soma hymns for Soma-Yagas (Soma sacrifices), and book ten includes later philosophical prayers. The fact that several of the Rishis, as well as their families, were antagonistic to each other (for example, Vasishtha vs. Visvamitra) suggests that the compilation of all of the *Rig-Veda* hymns into one volume is a late event in the history of its transmission.

All fire sacrifices or Yajna required mantra chant. Special priests known as Hotri chanted verses from the *Rig-Veda* in a type of monotone, reflecting an ancient Aryan, and indeed pan-Asian, belief in the magical power of tonal recitation. The *Rig-Veda* verses were generally recited in a kind of tonal speech, often understood to mean a monotone with a small degree of variation that included at most two other notes. This practice could be called metrical cantillation in Western terminology, while biblical cantillation was generally nonmetrical. The "recited" or read portions of the *Rig-Veda* were called Sastra. The second Veda is the *Yajur-Veda* which consists of metrical verse and prose: both verse and prose sections were recited during Vedic rituals, with the prose sections involving description and interpretation of the ritual acts themselves. The *Sama-Veda* consists essentially of verses of the *Rig-Veda* that were set to preexisting melodies. The resulting musical hymns are called Samans, and the genre of performance is called Sama-Gana. The rendering of Samans is best understood as a type of chant that includes more notes and their prolongation beyond the simple monotone (or three tones) of the *Rig-Veda* with the addition of meaningless syllables called Stobhas to fill out the text in order to fit the melodies. Groups of individual Samans are known as Stotra. The fourth Veda, the *Atharva-Veda,* consists of later verses composed by different authors from those who wrote the first three Vedas;

it was utilized less for public liturgies and sacrifices (Srauta) and more for private or domestic (Grihya) use.

The Vedic authors depict their religion as a sonic liturgy, a system or order of ritual events that included sound and music and was directed toward divine personifications of the forces of nature. Vedic religion was only secondarily a mythology or speculative system. Rather than simple outpourings of literary or poetic expression, the hymns and verses of the Vedas were essentially composed for, and linked to, sacrificial and liturgical activity: "The four Vedas are directly connected with the ritual they depict because portions of three of them are recited and chanted as part of these ritual performances."[12] Though remaining in oral form for thousands of years, the Vedas are still the oldest Indo-Aryan documents and our primary sources for understanding Vedic religion.

The Vedas are not the composition of one person but a library or collection of poetic writings of several Rishis, gifted persons with a special spiritual faculty to receive divine wisdom. According to Kunhan Raja, "Veda is first class poetry; truth is revealed in the transcendental poetic vision of some persons of superhuman faculties. It is not a revelation to an individual; it is a revelation to a class of poets."[13] The Rishis were not renunciates or ordained priests in any official sense but were householders and ordinary citizens of the time:

> The Rishis in the Vedas are not people who are supposed to have renounced the world, who wear special robes and who live in special habitations and for whom there are special rules of conduct. This is a later phase in the development of Indian culture. But the Rishis in the Rig-Veda were normal citizens in their private life, who lived in the usual homes with their family; the only factor that distinguished the Rishis from the general citizens was their special poetic gift, their ability to see things beyond what the general people were able to see. As such the word Rishi in Vedic tradition came to mean "one who can see."[14]

They were thus not priests in the formal sense of a class or caste. And since the Vedic literatures were not the production of one person, the oral texts were a kind of corporate possession that were nonetheless placed in the care of a group of learned priestly intellectuals who memorized the texts and administered their performance as part of sacrificial activity. These persons organized the texts in terms of specified rituals, along with their hymns or chants that were obligatory accompaniments to the rituals.

The importance of Vedic religion is reinforced by the antiquity and enormous sophistication of the Vedic rituals, serious attention to which has been largely neglected by scholars in ritual studies and anthropology. While it is tempting to think of Vedic ritual as primitive or primordial with regard to the evolution of religion, the facts do not support this assumption. It is perhaps best to regard it as both a peak moment in the history of ritualistic behavior and as a measuring tool with which to compare the parameters of rituals of other traditions. According to Frits Staal, "Vedic ritual is not only the oldest surviving ritual of mankind; it also provides the best source material for a theory of ritual. This is not because it is close to any alleged 'original' ritual. Vedic ritual is not primitive and not an Ur-ritual. It is sophisticated and already the product of a long development. But it is the largest, most elaborate and (on account of the Sanskrit manuals) best documented among the rituals of man."[15]

Although the Vedas were not necessarily composed by a priestly class, Vedic knowledge was preserved and expanded by evolving groups of priestly specialists called Brahmins who orally taught and passed on the Vedic texts and instructions to succeeding generations for nearly three thousand years. Accordingly, "though Vedic ritual contained popular as well as more exotic or extravagant elements, it was confined to an elite of professionals who spent much of their life learning and preserving its oral tradition. These experts became the Brahmins of India. Performances must have been relatively common for at least five centuries, from about 1000 to 500 B.C.E. Then Vedic ritual began to decline and new cultures and traditions rose to prominence."[16] These new traditions included Jainism, Buddhism, and the developing theistic traditions of Hindu worship that began complementing or replacing the outdoor Vedic sacrifices or Yajnas as the central religious practice, with Pujas inside of temples and enclosed spaces, such as drama stages, to deities in visual and material form.

The wider impact of Vedic ritualism has been duly acknowledged. Although Buddhism initially rejected the Vedic ritual system and the supremacy of the Brahmins, "in due course it evolved its own hierarchies and ceremonies, incorporating again Vedic rites. Vedic fire ceremonies became part of the Buddhist tradition and were exported all over Asia. The 'piling' (cayana) of the Vedic fire altar was transformed into the Buddhist Caitya (from the same root ci) or Stupa (Tibetan: choten). Originally a funeral pile, it became the primary cult-symbol of Buddhism throughout Asia."[17] Current scholarship has brought attention to the largely unrecognized importance of Vedic fire rituals (viz., the Homa rite) in the history of religion: "The fire ceremony, basic to Vedic ritual, was also eventually incorporated into Tantric Buddhism, and the Homa rite thus absorbed by Indian Mahayana Buddhism was disseminated throughout Nepal, Tibet, China and Japan. For an understanding of the structure of Buddhist Homa too, knowledge of the structure of Homa as it was performed in ancient India is indispensable."[18] As a case in point the Japanese Buddhist fire ritual known as the Goma was modeled upon Vedic prototypes.

Although the larger dimensions of Vedic sacrificial culture have suffered a decline in India, Vedic ritual is by no means absent from current Hindu life.

Smaller fire sacrifices and ceremonies are still associated with key Hindu rites of passage (*samskaras*) such as initiation (*upanayana*), marriage (*vivaha*) and cremation (*antyesti*). As confirmed by Staal, "fragments and features of Vedic rites survive to the present day in India in the Grihya or domestic ceremonies of high caste Hindus, for example, in marriage ceremonies."[19] And the theoretical or ideational importance of the Vedas has remained strong on a broad scale: "Hinduism continued to look upon the Vedas as its source, formally transmitted by the Brahmin members of its highest caste, regarded as an eternal revelation, of non-human origin, and no longer understood."[20] Even within the realm of metaphysics, such as Vedanta ("End of the Vedas"), whereby philosophical speculation subordinated practical rituals, many ritual elements were retained and Indian philosophy continues to bask in the ancient glory of the Vedas.

YAJNA

Vedic religion was defined by ritual activity, at the center of which was the fire sacrifice or Yajna, alternatively referred to as either Yaga or Homa. Vedic chant, employing passages of the Vedas, was intertwined with rituals at every level, creating some of the world's oldest examples of sonic liturgy. The fire sacrifices were conducted by a priestly cult that ensured stability and sustenance to the universe. The ancient Vedic systems of ritual chanting were direct predecessors of the later Hindu temple traditions of singing and musical worship.

The Vedic Yajnas were divided into two groups: 1) Srauta, that is, the sacrifices described in the Sruti ("revelation") found in the Samhita and the Brahmana portions of the four Vedas. The practical dimensions of Vedic rituals are elaborated in Sutra form in the *Srauta-Sutras*, a part of the *Kalpa-Sutras*; and 2) Grihya (domestic rites), otherwise called Smarta based on Smriti (remembrance), laid down in the *Grihya-Sutras*, another part of the *Kalpa-Sutras*. The *Kalpa-Sutras*, composed between eighth and fourth centuries B.C.E., are excellent primary sources for the study of Vedic ritual. The Srauta rituals are generally older and more complex, sometimes considered public or solemn. The Grihya rituals refer primarily to household ceremonies associated with rites of passage (domestic or life-cycle rites) such as birth, initiation, marriage, and death. The Srauta rituals were dedicated mostly to Agni and Soma and included offerings of clarified butter (ghee), vegetable and animal substances, and juice extracted from the stalks of the Soma plant, which were given as oblations into sacrificial fires installed on altars. There was a also kind of hierarchy of Srauta rites: "The Vedic Srauta rituals consist of a hierarchy: four basic rituals that involve oblations of milk, rice or barley (the most important of these are the Full- and New-Moon ceremonies); one ritual that involves animal sacrifice; seven varieties of Soma rituals; and finally the Agnicayana which incorporates one or more occurrences of most of these others."[21] Vedic rituals ranged from the simplest Agnihotra, consisting of an oblation of milk offered every morning and evening by a householder, to opulent and lengthy performances involving up to seventeen priests, such as the Agnicayana. The rites were performed by the priests on behalf of and for the benefit of a Yajamana (ritual patron).

In Sanskrit terminology the Yajnas, as a general class of sacrifices, consist of a variety of species. The Yaga referred to the public "Greater Rites," usually including an animal sacrifice, lasting several days or more. The best example is the Soma-Yaga. The Agnistoma was the basic or simplest form of the Soma sacrifice that lasted about three days. Other Yagas included the Vajapeya (offering of alcohol), Rajasuya (consecration of a king), and Asvamedha (horse sacrifice). The private "Lesser Rites" were known as Ishti that normally lasted one day only, including the New Moon (Darsa) and Full Moon (Paurnamasi) sacrifices. These were much less complex than the Yagas. Some other Ishtis were the Agrayana (harvest), Vaisvadeva (spring sacrifice to all the gods), Varuna Praghasa (rainy season offering to Varuna), and Sakamedhas (autumn). Another class of rites was the Sattra, lasting many days, weeks, or years. Additional terminology related to the Yajnas included Ghrita (offering of clarified butter or ghee), Purodasa (offering of sacrificial rice cakes), Ida (offering of sacrificial food), Barhis (sacred grass), and Samadheni (hymns recited to kindle the fire).

Several theories regarding the meaning of Vedic rituals have been advanced. Perhaps the most controversial have been those of Staal. In several of his works he argues for the inherent "meaninglessness" of Vedic rituals. Theories of the meaninglessness of rituals maintain the idea that rituals are formal actions and that the actual forms and symbols of ritual actions are independent of cultural context and thus meaningless: rituals are thus pure and primary activity, without function, aim or goal. All language, and thus meaning, was created by religion. Staal states: "The chief provider of meaning being religion, ritual became involved with religion and through this association, meaningful."[22] Thus ritual plus meaning equals religion. For Staal rituals have meaning only because human beings have given them meaning, when in fact rituals reflect archaic modes of structural behavior that are found even in the animal kingdom. While rejecting the functionalism of Emile Durkheim and the symbolic analysis of anthropologists Victor Turner and Clifford Geertz, Staal turns to Claude Lévi-Strauss and the application of linguistic analysis to ritual syntax and semantics. In the words of ritual studies scholar Alex Michaels, "Staal understands ritual . . . as anti-religion. It is not a subdimension of religion or society but an autonomous practice with its own rules. Thus ritual should not be studied as religion but as syntax without semantics or semiotics. Consequently, and following Levi-Strauss, Staal proposes to study ritual 'in itself and for itself' and as 'syntax' without reference to semantics."[23] Since semantics is viewed here as a later addition to the structure of syntax, Staal claims that rituals are meaningless because they exhibit structural syntax before they become semantic, or have cultural meaning by virtue of language.

Recently Michaels has refuted Staal's views in the essay "Ritual and Meaning" (2008). He notes that scholars M. Houseman and C. Severi (1998) "have rightly criticized Staal's biological reductionism, speculations about the animal origins of language, and atomized view of ceremonial behavior, in which the sum and arrangements of supposedly meaningless ritual elements do not count at all." Moreover, religionist Hans H. Penner (1985) has also pointed out that "Staal is mistaken in his understanding of language and, consequently, ritual. . . . If rituals have a syntax, they must have semantics, or meaning, for they cannot be separated. Syntax means the combination of signs, and signs always refer to something (which is their meaning). In other words, there cannot be a syntax without signs, and there cannot be signs without meaning. Thus syntax is always combined with meaning. . . . Staal's position is simply wrong."[24]

Michaels began his dismissal of the "meaninglessness theory" with some general observations: "Given the many more-or-less explicit reasons for the performance of rituals, given the magnitude of exegetical literature on rituals, theories that claim that rituals are meaningless are indeed difficult to accept—for both practitioners and scholars of rituals." Furthermore, for many outsiders the meanings of rituals are sometimes impossible to perceive because they are undisclosed or even occult: "The meaning of rituals is more often regarded to be hidden (unconscious) or esoteric than self-evident—even for insiders."[25]

One aspect of rituals that is often overlooked by scholars outside of religious studies is the significance of the origin of the ritual for practitioners. Historians of religion refer to this point of origin as *illo tempore*, or the time before history, a foundational basis of myth. Michaels explains further with reference to the invariability of rituals over time: "The first time . . . became an extremely important focal point for rituals that are often treated as unchangeable. In myths, rituals often refer to these archetypal, idealized, or sacralized origins when nothing had to be changed because everything was in a perfect state or golden age. It seems to me that rituals, especially religious rituals, are intrinsically bound up with this notion of changelessness. Rituals are regarded as rigid, stereotypical, and unchangeable because they are *per definitionem* difficult to change. This does not mean that rituals are unchangeable. On the contrary, they are altered without giving up the claim of being invariable." Thus, for Michaels, Vedic rituals have inherent meaning because of their apprehension as unchangeable and invariable vessels of the eternal realm: "If people identify themselves in rituals with invariability and timelessness (in Vedic rituals, for instance, with the timeless Veda and the sacrifice), they resist the uncertainty of past and future, life and death. In rituals they become eternal, related to something that has always been there, never changed and detached from everyday life and profanity. Thus rituals are staged productions of timelessness, the effort to oppose change, which implies finality (and, ultimately, death)."[26]

Apart from their invariability, rituals have polysemy, the quality of holding a multitude of meanings and functions, as can be demonstrated through any history of ritual. The tradition of commentaries on specific Vedic rituals also demonstrates the history of the meaning that was attached to them. Michaels concludes his argument: "The persistence of rituals requires that they serve some (adaptive) functions. If they were entirely without function, it would be unnecessary to transmit them. My point is that the significance of rituals lies in the fact that they often create an auratic sphere or arena of timelessness and immortality—at least in religious or semi-religious contexts. Seen from this perspective, rituals can indeed do without any specific meaning, but this in itself is not meaningless, that is, without significance."[27]

MYTHIC ORIGINS

The antiquity of Vedic Yajnas or fire sacrifices is vouchsafed by the Indian mythological accounts of the origin of humankind. By way of comparison, in the biblical tradition Adam and Eve are described as the first human beings, but they do not offer sacrifice to God in Eden. Their sons, Cain and Abel, first present sacrificial offerings to God, consisting of both meat and nonmeat items. However, the precise rules and regulations for pleasing God through sacrifice do not appear until the revelations given to Moses on Mount Sinai, as recorded in the Books of Numbers and Leviticus. In the Indian context the first humans were the brothers Yama and Manu. As in the West, these figures are not supported by history. Yama and Manu are believed to have been sons of the sun god Vivasvat. Yama was the first to offer sacrifice and attain immortality in the netherworld, while his brother Manu laid down the rules of sacrifice for succeeding generations. According to Kunhan Raja, the accounts of Yama and Manu in the Vedic texts establish that the Vedic religion had human founders, one who first led the path and another who set down the laws for posterity:

> There is a person who is the founder of the Vedic religion. . . . It has been said in the available texts of the Vedas that Yama first saw the Path, that he went over to that region beyond and that others followed him and continue to do so. Yama rules over that region. . . . Manu is the first man who gave form to the religious rites that were continued by the people later. . . . Being sons of Vivasvat, [Yama and Manu] were the fathers of humanity and also established the rituals and the

> codes of life for humanity. Thus the religion is conceived of as having started along with the appearance of humanity in the world. There is no period in the history of humanity when there was neither a religion nor a set of codes for moral life.[28]

Although Yama and Manu are given divine lineage as descendents of the sun god Vivasvat, there is no prescribed worship of Yama or Manu in the Vedic religion. Divine worship is reserved only for the deities praised and described in the *Rig-Veda.* Yet Yama and Manu are highly regarded as pathfinders for humanity. According to the texts, Yama, being the first human to reach the netherworld, made it possible for others who followed the path of sacrifice to obtain immortality with the gods. As such, according to the earlier Vedic view that predated the concept of reincarnation as delineated in the Upanishads, deceased persons go to heaven and retain the same body. According to Kunhan Raja, they have the same names as when they had life on earth, and enjoy music and good food and drink and other human pleasures: "They have the same enjoyment; . . . they all enjoy life there and those who go there later also have the same life of immense joy. They have drink and food and music."[29] As will be shown, the Vedic (and later Hindu) association of music and chant with ritual life on earth as a sonic liturgy is linked with enjoyment and fulfillment in the hereafter.

VEDIC CHANT

In India sacrifice and chant have been bound together from the very beginning, and the style and manner of the chanting of Vedic verses and hymns represent both the beginning of Indian music as well as the earliest form of sonic liturgy that can be documented in history. In fact, the chants and hymns associated with Vedic rituals comprise the oldest surviving tonal system in the world. According to *Sama-Veda* scholar Wayne Howard, "the chanted Veda, the Sama-Veda, contains probably the world's oldest notated melodies. Like the Rig-Vedic recitation, the Sama-Vedic songs have been passed on orally to the present day though they are also preserved in manuscript form."[30] In recent scholarship in musicology Vedic chant is regarded as an ancient form of collective singing: "One of the oldest known forms of singing together was the recitation of the Vedas. . . . Chanting the hymns of the Vedas or reciting the mantric formulae was an essential accompaniment to the Vedic sacrifice."[31] Indian or Hindu music did not develop from this stage in an evolutionary manner, however. It coalesced over many centuries by drawing upon many different strands and channels, both Indo-Aryan and indigenous, that contributed in a layered fashion to its present state.

Vedic chant comprised the rendering of metrical verses whose syllables were measured according to a system of precise time duration. The powers of sound and speech found in the Vedas are said to inhere in the pronunciation and metrical structure of the mantras, or ritual chants, themselves. In fact each poetical meter was associated with a particular demigod or divine power, and accurate chanting by the priest meant a degree of control over a specific power or being. The accumulated powers of the mantras and meters were gradually condensed into the syllable Om, symbolizing and representing the metaphysical Sabda-Brahman, or Sound-Absolute. The power of Om was also represented as Vac, goddess of speech and "Mother of the Vedas," or the goddess Sarasvati, patroness of music and learning, and later transformed into Nada-Sakti or female sound-energy.

The syllable *Om*, A-U-M, was construed as the condensed powers of the Vedic mantras and became associated in Hindu metaphysics with Sabda-Brahman or Nada-Brahman (the Sound-Absolute). In theistic speculation Brahman, the Absolute Truth of the Upanishads, was represented as the combination of the male Isvara ("Lord") with his female energy (Nada-Sakti). Henceforth each male deity in the evolving Hindu pantheon contained this element of sacred sound as represented by the female consort or Sakti. Nada-Sakti (female sound-energy) thus remained ever present within the evolving Vaishnava, Saiva, and Sakta theistic and devotional (Bhakti) traditions of worship, and the notion of sacred sound as manifest through chant and music provided an abiding link between the human and divine realms.

Aesthetics is also rooted in Vedic literature. The major Upanishads describe Brahman as full of Rasa, the essence of taste and bliss (*Taittiriya Upanishad* 2.7: See Robert E. Hume, trans. 1921, 287). Hence the performing arts, such as theater and music, were closely aligned with religion since their goal was to produce Rasa which led to liberation or Moksha. Brahman as Isvara (personal deity, whether Vishnu, Siva, or Sakti) was the prime source of the emotional pleasure produced by musicians (and actors).

The four Vedas, the corresponding priests, and the various meters that governed Vedic chanting formed a unitary religious world that was instigated by divine sanction. Citing the *Markandeya-Purana* (45.31), Vedic scholar G. U. Thite explained how the god Brahma first created the four Vedas, the Samans, and other chants: "Facing towards the East, he created the Gayatri meter, Rig-Veda, Trivrt-stoma and Rathantara-Saman; facing towards the South, he created the Yajur-Veda, Tristubh Meter, Pancadasa Stoma and Brihat Saman; facing towards the West, he created the Sama-Veda, Jagati Meter, Saptadasa Stoma, and Vairupa Saman; finally facing towards the North he created the Atharva-Veda, Ekavimsa Stoma, Anustubh Meter and Vairaja Saman."[32]

The precise manner in which the *Rig-Veda* was rendered, whether recited in a speech pattern with three accents or chanted in a monotone with two additional tones, has been debated for some time. Early notations in manuscripts suggest at least three accents that most probably referred to three separate tones: Anudatta (grave, "not raised"), Svarita (circumflex, "sounded"), and Udatta (acute, "raised"). One compelling reason for this, and still a cause for some debate, is that the same word in Sanskrit was used for both accent and tone or note, namely, *Svara*. According to *Sama-Veda* scholar G. H. Tarlekar, "the Rig-Veda has three accents. This accent is called a Svara. The word is derived from the root 'svr' meaning 'to sound.' The three accents are Udatta, Anudatta and Svarita. The Udatta is unmarked; Anudatta is shown by a horizontal line below the syllable while Svarita is indicated by a vertical line over the syllable."[33] Tarlekar then confirms that "the word Svara is used both for the accent and the musical note. The Svara of Vedic recitation was of three types namely Udatta (high), Anudatta (low) and Svarita (circumflex)."[34]

According to Chitrabhanu Sen in *A Dictionary of Vedic Rituals: Based on the Srauta and Grhya Sutras*, the term *Svara* is best defined as tone when applied to mantras in ritual context: "Svara—m. tone or accent pitch of the Vedic texts, especially of the Samhitas: udatta or acute (raised), anudatta (not raised) or grave and the third, svarita (provided with tone?) or circumflex. The mantras in the ritual are to be pronounced in tones as given in the Samhitas or in the Brahmanas. But actually all mantras are to be pronounced in monotone (Tana = Ekasruti)."[35] What is most likely is that, according to the context, certain portions of the *Rig-Veda*, called Sastra, were read in a kind of tonal speech with accented syllables and other parts in ritual context, Stotra, were strictly chanted in up to three notes. This may represent a sort of compromise when, in fact, various scholars have wavered between two positions, namely, that either the oldest form was speech recitation that developed into musical tones, or vice versa.

One of the earliest Western assessments of this phenomenon argued for the primacy of tone, as found in one of the classic works on Indian music, *The Music of Hindostan* (1914) by A. H. Fox-Strangeways:

> The Rig-Veda is recited now, as it has always been, to three tones; for the accent was originally a mark of musical pitch, and became a mark of stress only after the beginning of our era. The "raised" (Udatta) and "not raised" (Anudatta) sounds represent the two main pitches of the speaking voice; this is the prose accent of the Brahmanas; and there is nothing to show whether these two prose accents had any musical relationship. In addition to these two there was, for the reciting voice, the "sounded" tone (Svarita), which is shown on philological grounds to have been originally between the two others in pitch, but which is in the Rig-Veda above the Udatta.

For Fox-Strangeways there is a question about the meaning of the term *sounded*, since no explanation is given. Suggesting it may mean something like graced, he then states: "The Svarita is in effect a falling accent of a dependent nature, marking the transition from an accented to a tuneless syllable."[36] This is the original theory of recitation, but it has been modified in practice—the Svarita marked with a perpendicular line over the syllable, the Anudatta with a horizontal beneath; and Udatta and Pracaya are unmarked.

In accord with this, musicologist Thakur Jaideva Singh has more recently affirmed that the three accents were tones: "The Vedas were musically recited. Udatta (raised, Greek oxyu, sharp or acute), Anudatta (not raised, grave, Greek baryu), and Svarita (Greek oxyubaria, acute grave or circumflex) were the three pitches used in Vedic recitative. . . . There three were not merely accents or stress on words; they were musical pitches used for simple recitative."[37] Musicologist Shahab Sarmadee also accepts the musical interpretation of the three accents: "The Yajnas were conducted with Veda-patha and Gana, employing three musical notes (Svaras) known as Udatta, Anudatta and Svarita." Yet the Vedic recitation (Patha) was always done in a monotone: "Veda-Patha, other than that of the Sama-Veda, was done as a monotone (referred to by Panini as Ekasruti, 1, 2. 33–34 [see below])."[38]

Musicologist Solveig McIntosh explains in a recent work that the three accents represent a kind of evolutionary development from an original monotone into three tones and finally into a seven-tone system. She affirms that

> the system of sound organization for different traditions of Vedic recitation (but not including Sama-Veda recitation), which has been handed down through the oral tradition to the present day, involved the use of up to three accents. At first the Rig Vedic hymns, it is said, were sung on one note, in a monotone and without melodic life. This hymnal period has been called Archika. Another early period of Vedic recitation pivoted around two notes, referred to as Udatta and Anudatta. . . . They are also referred to as Brahmana Svaras and described as belonging to the Gatha or Gathika period. In the course of time a third intermediary tone known as Svarita, was established. This period of Vedic music is known as Samika.[39]

With the gradual addition of notes, the full seven-tone scale is developed by the time of the *Natya-Sastra* (ca. 200 B.C.E.).

There is an ancient reference in the Srauta-Sutra literature regarding the chanting of the *Rig-Veda* in monotone. The *Katyayana Srauta-Sutra* (Rules for the Vedic Sacrifices) introduces the term *Ekasruti* (I.8.18–19), often translated as a single tone (monotone): "One should rather recite the mantras in a single tone (i.e. *ekasruti*), since it is constant by usage. . . . A single tone is to be used either while addressing someone from a distance or during the performance of sacrifice excepting while pronouncing a Subrahmanya chant, Saman, Japa (muttering), Nyunkha and the mantras to be uttered by the sacrificer."[40] Sen defines *Ekasruti* as "f. monotone, i.e. the neutral tone in which the mantras are pronounced in ritual, except in cases like subrahmanya, japa, nyunkka, and Saman recitation to be done by the sacrificer."[41] The other term given above is *Tana* (fixed tone): "Tana—m. tone which, on account of its 'fixed' (nitya) character, is to be followed in pronouncing the mantras."[42]

Tarlekar has explained the earliest notational symbols for the three Svaras of the *Rig-Veda*: "Svarita is indicated by vertical over the syllable and Anudatta by horizontal line under the syllable. Udatta is left unmarked." The chanters of the verses would then enunciate the texts accordingly. This method is contrasted with the early methods of musical notation of the Saman chants, whereby numbers were applied directly above the syllables ranging from one to seven: "the musical notes are indicated by the numerals 1 to 7. The first note indicated by the numeral 1 in the series of the numerals 1 to 7 would be the highest note."[43] The grammarian Panini (fifth century B.C.E.), in describing these accents or tones, is believed to have witnessed the living tradition.

Scholars interpret this notation, in Western terms, to mean that Udatta was the tonic (middle C) and the principal note upon which the chants were generally intoned. The Anudatta was a whole step below (B-flat) while the Svarita was a half step above (D-flat). According to Tarlekar, "from the musical point-of-view, the Udatta, Anudatta and Svarita are heard in the present practice of Vedic recitation as the notes Sa, Ni and Re respectively."[44] This would mean that both Re and Ni are komal or flattened. Other scholars place the Svarita in the middle position C with the Udatta as the raised note (D-flat) and Anudatta as the "not-raised" note Bb.

In renditions of *Rig-Veda* (RV) verses it is apparent that chanters most often utilize the three-tone system of Bb, C, Db, with the tonic on C. Renditions of Rig-Vedic chants in Sanskrit such as the *Purusha-Sukta* continue to follow this three-tone system as they are still incorporated within selected rites of Hindu Puja. The most famous complete "hymn" from the *Rig-Veda* is in fact the *Purusha-Sukta* (RV 10.90), in which a sacrifice of the Cosmic Man (Purusha) is described with reference to the creation of the universe. The Purusha is beyond time and space, yet manifests partially (that is, one fourth) within the created universe. The pantheistic language is symbolic and figurative. As such, terms such as *thousand-headed* and the like refer to the multiplicity of living beings. *Viraj* refers to the splendor of the deity in its feminine dimension. This is also the hymn in which the Varna (social divisions or caste) system is first articulated as a revelation from the gods. Portions of this hymn continue to be chanted during Hindu worship rituals known as Puja in addition to being employed in strict Vedic rites.

For purposes of ritual application many stanzas, such as the *Purusha-Sukta* from the *Rig-Veda*, were selected and rearranged in the *Yajur-Veda* according to specific sacrificial formats. This process included additional prose formulas inserted for utterance by Adhvaryu priests as they performed the material functions of the sacrifice, such as making oblations into the fire. Hindu music as manifested in worship over the centuries owes a significant part of its origin to the *Sama-Veda.*

SAMA-GANA

Musicologist S. S. Janaki has placed Sama-Gana, the singing of the Saman hymns, in the forefront of the historical scenario of Indian music: "For purpose of treatment of the subject [Indian music] the entire history may be said to have approximately six phases—the Saman music, the Gandharva system, the synthesized common old Indian music, the Hindustani-Carnatic division, and the modern development of both the systems on somewhat different lines of style. . . . The earliest music of India is in the chants of the *Sama-Veda,* a work of more than 4000 years ago. . . . The fact that Saman chanting is the basis for Indian music has been mentioned by all musicologists dealing with the history of Indian music."[45]

Renowned Indologist V. Raghavan has described Sama-Gana as the "parent-source" of Indian music and a useful model for study in terms of the singing techniques: "In fact, the Saman, which is just the *Rig-Veda* hymns set to music, is mentioned in all treatises and remembered in the entire tradition of Indian music as the ultimate parent-source of the art. Music is deemed a second Veda—the Gandharva Upaveda, attached to the main Sama-Veda. Apart from the tradition, a study of the technique of Saman-singing convinces one of the close relations that exist between Saman-singing and several practices of later classical music."[46]

The *Sama-Veda* text itself comprises many verses from the *Rig-Veda,* but these verses were set to music and sung by another group of priests known as Udgatri. The Samans, hymns of the *Sama-Veda,* were especially rendered during elaborate public Soma sacrifices involving the offering of the juice of the Soma plant, a still unidentified plant believed by some scholars to have hallucinogenic properties. The Soma juice, sometimes mixed with milk and honey as an oblation, was particularly enjoyed by the god Indra. After the ritual the priests imbibed any remaining juice as a sacrament. The *Sama-Veda* was also connected with the worship of ancestors, whose abode was the moon. Great importance was given to the *Sama-Veda* in the Upanishads, particularly in the *Chandogya-Upanishad.* Saman singing, as part of sacrificial ritual, is in fact frequently mentioned in the Sruti texts of the Brahmanas, Aranyakas, and Upanishads—*Taittiriya-Brahmana* III. 12. 9. 1; *Satapatha-Brahmana* XI. 5. 83; XII 3. 4. 9; *Aitareya-Brahmana* V. 32. 1; *Aitareya-Aranyaka* III. 2. 3; *Chandogya-Upanishad* I. 3. 7; III. 3. 1. 2.

Sen has described the relationship between the text of the *Rig-Veda* and the collection known as the *Sama-Veda:* "The Sama-Veda Samhita is also a liturgical collection. But by no means it is an original one. It is almost entirely a verbatim copy of the Rig-Veda Samhita. Of the total 1810 verses or 1549 verses (261 verses are repetitions) contained in the arcika and the uttarcika all but 75 are found in the 8th and 9th Mandalas of the Rig-Veda Samhita." The *Sama-Veda* Samhita has been assigned to the Udgatri priests who chant sets of verses called Stotras in melodies called Saman chiefly in the Soma sacrifice: "The Udgatri priests have hardly any role in the sacrifice apart from chanting the stotras. While the Adhvaryu priests have discarded the accent of the Yajur-Veda Samhita, the Udgatri priests adopt a peculiar fashion in chanting the Stotras. The verse is broken up in various parts . . . , and then by repetition of the Padas [Stoma] . . . and interpolations of syllables [Stobha] . . . , the chant assumes a bizarre form. It is so intricate that it is almost impossible to determine its exact nature."[47]

One of Europe's premier Indologists, Hermann Oldenberg, had described Soma sacrificial chant by distinguishing it from Rig-Vedic recitation in his work of 1894, *Religion of the Veda:*

> They [Soma singers], numbering three, did not participate in the minor sacrifices, but had to recite during the Soma sacrifices, individually or together, different verses of the sacrificial songs interspersed with interjections, exultations and magic words. These songs can be divided into two major groups. On the one hand a song or a complex of song-recitations to the Soma (Soma pavamana) strained and refined through the sieve of goat-hair, was part of every Soma-pressing ritual that took place on the sacrificial day at morn, at noon and in the afternoon. These songs are of a quite different type from those of the Rig-Veda with the invitations to the gods. It may be said that the note of good cheer of the priests at the emergence of the intoxicating, divinely animated drink meant to scare away demons has been developed into songs which are directed to Soma in hundredfold repetitions throughout the whole of the Rig-Veda: stream forth purified; mingle with the milk of cows; strengthen Indra and the gods; drive away every wicked enemy; bring us light and salvation. But the singers recited the second large group of sacrificial hymns to the usual sacrificial gods, on the whole such that the more prominent deities, who were given the offerings after the regulation governing the three pressings of the Soma and to whom the litanies were sung by the Hotar, also received their praise in songs.[48]

The rendering of Sama-Gana in the Soma sacrifices followed a liturgical structure, and forms a principal example of sonic liturgy in ancient India. Three priests, collectively called Udgatri, were each named Udgatri, Prastotri, and Pratihartri. The Samans were chanted or sung by these three Udgatri priests in five sequential parts, as follows:

1. Prastava: This prelude begins with "Hum" sound, sung by all the priests together.

2. Udgitha: This portion of the song is commenced with "AUM" (Om) and sung by the Udgatri priest. This is the main part of the song.
3. Pratihara: The singer of this portion is known as Pratihartri. Pratihara is divided into two sections—Upadrava and Nidhana.
4. Upadrava: This is only a section of Pratihara which is repeated by the Udgatri.
5. Nidhana: This is the remaining section of Pratihara which is sung together by all the three priests, viz. Prastotri, Udgatri, and Pratihartri. The syllable Om is added to this portion of the song. This is the concluding portion.[49]

Unlike the *Rig-Veda* chant, which followed a strict metrical execution limited to about three tones but in actuality tending toward monotone in recitation, the Samans of the *Sama-Veda* were more "musical" in that they were rendered according to preexistent melodies that included up to seven notes. The lexical definition lends additional insight. According to Sen, "Saman: (etymology doubtful) n. a melody set to a verse (ric), and it is considered as a mantra. . . . It is a melody mostly set to verses of Rig-Veda, hence the word sometimes designates the chanted verse (Giti), but actually Saman is simply a melody independent of the verses. A Saman is primarily associated with certain verses, which are, therefore, called svakiya. But a Saman can be set to verses other than its own. Thus by Rathantara (a Saman) its own verses are meant. But the same melody can be set to different verses." The most unique feature of Sama-Gana was the insertion of a number of "meaningless" words or syllables (Stobha) for musical and lyrical effect, such as *o, hau, hoyi, and va.* The Stobhas were inserted according to the metrical format of the stanza yet were extended vocally with longer duration on specific notes by the singers: "A chant is executed by resorting to certain changes in the verse itself such as, distortion of vowels, repetition of syllables, and addition of musical interjections (Stobha)."[50] The *Sama-Veda* priests and singers thus enhanced the function of epiclesis, summoning the gods to the sacrifice, through extended vocal droning on these notes all of which were believed to hold magical properties. The chanting and hearing of sustained musical notes was thus mysteriously linked to the divine at this early stage of Hindu ritual practice.

Adjusting and enlarging upon the *Rig-Veda* tone system, the singing of Sama-Gana required an expansion of the original three tones of the *Rig-Veda* chant to a maximum of seven distinct musical notes, forming a new "Sama-Veda scale." These seven notes correspond roughly to the notes of the Western diatonic scale yet were understood to be in a descending order beginning with F above middle C to G below by way of the movement A-B-G. They were called (from F above to G below middle C), prathama (F), dvitiya (E), tritiya (D), caturtha (C), mandra, (A), atisvarya (B), and krusta (G). These notes are in descending order as the melodies of the Samans were usually descending in contour. Yet most Saman singing continued to utilize three to four to five notes primarily, with occasional use of the other two. Jaidev Singh, in observing the broad span of Vedic religion and culture, has outlined the process of development of Sama-Gana from one tone to seven tones, each with useful nomenclature: "This classification shows that there were three stages in the development of Sama-Vedic music. At the first stage, it employed only three notes. In the next stage, it employed four to five notes. In the final stage, it employed six to seven notes."[51]

1. Arcika—one note. This was nothing but a musical chant of a mantra of one syllable.
2. Gathika—two notes. This was sung usually in praise of some king or feudal lord or one who paid for a particular sacrifice (Yajna).
3. Samika—three notes. Many hymns of the *Sama-Veda* were originally sung in three notes. This accounts for a song of three notes being called Samika.
4. Svarantara—four notes.
5. Odava—five notes.
6. Sadava—six notes.
7. Sampurna—seven notes.

The Sama-Gana in this early stage of development was not a mere supplement to the sacrifice, utilized on the margins for entertainment purposes. On the contrary, singing of the Saman played a central role, was highly respected and even used with caution. Thite underscored the central importance of the Saman in Vedic ritual life: "Music [Saman singing] is immensely used in the Vedic sacrifice; It is an important, essential and constitutory part of the sacrifice. Many forms of Vedic sacrifice are products of merely particular ways of singing employed in them. Music helps the sacrifice by making it continuous, well-established, well-supported, entire, well-protected and defectless. Music is double-natured. It can be useful or harmful. Therefore it must be used carefully."[52]

The chanted *Sama-Veda* hymns or Samans were themselves believed to possess supernatural qualities capable of petitioning and summoning the deities in charge of the forces of nature. Thite has described the powerful nature of Sama-Gana vis-à-vis the Vedic gods: "The poet-singers call, invoke, and invite the gods with the help of musical elements. In so doing they seem to be aware of the magnetic power of music and therefore they seem to be using that power in calling the gods."[53] The Vedic gods even seemed to have had a sense of music appreciation: "Gods are fond of music. They like music and enjoy it. The poet-singers sing and praise the gods with the intention that the gods may be pleased thereby and having become pleased they may grant gifts."[54] Sama-Gana was so essential to the sacrifice that "without it no sacrifice can go to the gods."[55]

The power of music was sought after by humans and divines alike: "The Samans are supposed to possess power, valor, etc. and also helpful for the sake of obtainment of power, etc. Even the gods become strengthened by means of the power of Samans. Thus Indra killed Vritra."[56] Music, considered as a kind of autonomous power substance, could function independently of gods or humans: "In the Veda, music is considered to be a power substance. By means of it one can control natural phenomena and perform miraculous deeds; the power of music is sometimes considered to be superior and sometimes inferior to gods; it can work sometimes independently and even upon gods; but sometimes it requires the help of gods for its effectiveness. Thus the power of music is magico-religious."[57]

Thite has summarized the overall magico-religious role of Sama-Gana in Vedic India as follows:

1. Gods and music are closely connected with each other in the Veda.
2. Music has an attractive power. So it attracts the gods. Music also goes to the gods. One may please the gods with music and ask them to come. Gods are fond of music. They enjoy it.
3. One barters with gods by means of music and gets the desired results granted by them.
4. Music helps gods in many ways. Particularly it is often said that it strengthens them. Gods use music and get their desired results. They come under the influence of music and are sometimes inferior to music.
5. Sometimes, however, they themselves help the music in various ways and are superior to it.
6. Thus music has got a magico-religious role in connection with the gods.[58]

As a means to achieve immortality and liberation from the material world, the singing of the Samans was considered essential in the *Yajnavalkya-Smriti:* "Singing of Samans as well as music in general is helpful for reaching to the highest principle viz. Brahman and obtaining salvation. Thus, according to the *Yajnavalkya-Smriti* III.112 ff, if one chants verses from the *Sama-Veda,* according to the rules and attentively, one would reach, by this practice, the high Brahman."[59]

Precise methods of singing the Samans were established and preserved in three different schools, the Kauthuma, Ranayaniya, and the Jaiminiya, the oldest. Each school has maintained a distinct style with regard to vowel prolongation, interpolation and repetition of Stobhas, meter, phonetics, and the number of notes in a scale. Accordingly there has been a fervent regard for maintaining continuity in *Sama-Veda* singing to avoid misuse or alteration over the years. Since written texts were not in use, in fact prohibited, the priests memorized the chants with the aid of accents, melodies, and hand gestures called Mudras, enabling them to pass down this tradition orally from one generation to the next for more than three thousand years.

THE PURPOSES OF VEDIC RELIGION

Vedic religion incorporated a different worldview from that found in most other religions. Vedic fire rituals and sonic liturgies were not primarily employed to glorify, thank, or honor a deity (doxology) but actually assisted in the higher purpose of sustaining and integrating the cosmic order by inviting divinities (epiclesis) to the sacrifice and bringing the cosmos to completion or perfection through their nourishment and satisfaction. This view has strong implications with regard to the importance of sound events and their integration within ritual. Sonic liturgies in Vedic times were thus perpetually linked to the ongoing process of healing, rebuilding, and reinforcing the cosmos. Since the universe as created contained inherent flaws, it was incumbent upon humans to engage in ritual activity in order to correct the imperfections. Contrary to the theories of Staal and J. C. Heesterman (1978), who viewed Vedic ritual elements as either meaningless or divorced from reality, Brian K. Smith has argued that Vedic ritual acted as a kind of "functioning workshop" that strove to guarantee the continued healing and stability of the cosmos: "Reality, according to the Vedic savants, is not given but made. . . . Sacrifice, for them, was not primarily an honorific gift-giving representation of an already concretized reality. The Brahmin ritualists themselves certainly did not understand the sacrifice to be meaningless activity done for its own sake or as a ritualized realm of anti-reality. Rather, the ritual was the workshop in which all reality was forged."[60] Thus the binding of sound within liturgical structure was not simply an act of praise or a meaningless repetition of past models but functioned on several levels to bring order and continuity to the universe.

Contrary to biblical perspectives on the inherent goodness and completeness of God's creation, the natural world in the Vedic view required the continuous performance of ritual by humans in order to fuse it together as a complete unit incapable of dissolution. Explaining that creation did not produce a perfect cosmos, Smith states that "the natural is the chaotic, the disorganized, the unformed. In cosmological terms, what is merely procreated by the creator god is not a cosmos or a universal whole made up of ordered parts. The origins of true cosmos are not found in this primary generative act but rather in a secondary operation—a ritual act that lends structure and order to a chaotic creation."[61] The bringing forth of a true cosmos as well as a truly authentic human being was a result of correct and proper ritual procedures.

The academic field of religious studies has often viewed ritual as expressing or symbolizing some inherent human need or merely reenacting a myth. Opposed to this perspective, Vedic ritual, building upon the original acts of the gods, was believed to perform real tasks in real time, as it were, to insure the completion and perfection of the universe: "For the Vedic priests and metaphysicians, ritual activity does not 'symbolize' or 'dramatize' reality; it constructs, integrates, and constitutes the real. Ritual forms the naturally formless, it connects the inherently disconnected, and it heals the ontological disease of unreconstructed nature, the state toward which all created things and beings perpetually tend."[62] In a very real sense then, in this view true cosmos is fabricated and continually reconstructed by ritual and liturgical activity.

The Vedic texts delineate creation as a complex series of stages from undifferentiated unity (Sarva) to totality of assembled parts (Visva) to a perfected unity (Samana): "The creation myths. . . may also be understood as the tracing of the transition from Sarva to Visva, a transformation from a perfect unity without parts to a defective totality. Another step in the metamorphosis is required for true cosmos: the reintegration of the totality (Visva) into a constructed whole, a composed unity of parts the texts call Samana." The end product is not the same as the beginning but the result of ritual work of both the gods and humans: "The move toward cosmogony and ontology in the Vedic conception is one not of return to primordial unity but rather of rebuilding a complete structure without eliminating diversity."[63] Therefore the ritual acts bring completion and perfection to the already produced cosmos: "This constructive activity combating natural imperfection is usually said to be ritual activity. The sacrifice is the cosmogonic instrument, for the ritual process completes all the stages necessary for making an ontologically viable universe—Sarva, Visva, Samana."[64]

From a linguistic perspective we may underscore the inclusion of language and music in this ritual process as vital elements. Smith explains this in terms of a shift in prefixes attached to verbal roots in Sanskrit: "The procreative dispersal, marked by words prefixed with *vi-* , is later counteracted by action of cosmic healing, repair, and construction described with verbs beginning with *sam-* , conveying, conjunction, concentration, and assembly (samkri- , samtan- , samklp- , sampad- , samyuj- , etc.)."[65] The choice of the words *Samskrita* (that is, Sanskrit, "well-formed") for the classical language and *Samgita* ("well-sung") for music imply that these verbs (speaking, chanting, and singing) are drawn into the cosmic healing process by which both the universe and the individual soul (Atman) are refined and perfected. The musical counterpart to the series of *sam*-prefixed words is the name of music itself, *Sangita,* or *Sam-gita.* Music, as Sam-gita, symbolically combines the disparate elements of tone, language, and rhythm. The applications noted above bear some similarity, as cognate elements in the Indo-European language family, to the use of the Latin prefixes *com-* and *con-* , appearing in English words such as *combine, communicate, confluence, consolidate, consonance,* and so on.

Even the term for rhythmic "convergence" in Indian music is indicative. The *Sam* is the initial beat or Matra of the time cycles known as Tala in Hindustani classical music. This was prefigured in the concept of Samya outlined in the texts of Gandharva Sangita. At the instant of the Sam, all three aspects of Svara (note), Tala (rhythm), and Pada (word) come together in unison or harmony. According to Rajagopala Aiyar, the word *Sangita* further connotes "the simultaneous and perfect blend and play of the components of music. . . . What are the components of Sangita? They are 1) Bhava, 2) Raga, 3), Tala, 4) Sruti and 5) Laya. The happy, simultaneous exercise and blend of all the above five essential adjuncts is denoted by the prefix 'Sam' in the term Sangita."[66] The development of Sangita or classical music is elaborated later.

Vedic ritual and Sama-Gana as a unified sonic liturgy thus functioned on several levels to rectify or perfect what was raw and natural in the beginning: the human being on the micro level and the cosmic creation on the macro level. Both enterprises were the object of ritual activity, such that, Vedic ontology—the creation of the human being—was a process of ritual labor and construction that replicated at the anthropological level the ritual construction of the universe at the cosmological level. Just as the cosmos was rebuilt and reactivated each time a ritual was performed, the human soul or Atman was also reconstituted and perfected a result of ritual activity. The analogy is best understood in terms of Prajapati, the Cosmic Man, as described in the Brahmanas:

> The body of Prajapati, the Cosmic Man, was joined together, reintegrated, and healed by the ritual acts of the gods. So also is the Atman of the human made whole and perfected in his sacrificial activity. Each sacrifice expresses and regenerates the sacrificer's Atman, and the ritual life of the individual becomes like a canvas on which is painted the picture of his self. The portrait is complete in itself at any particular sacrificial performance and is filled out over time. It is at once an index and a projection, a gauge of the relative realization of the self in this world and in the other world beyond death. Sacrifice constitutes being, on both the cosmic and human planes, through a process that is equally one of construction and of discovery, of making and of finding.[67]

In short, "human life is a process of ritually constructing and refining a self, Atman, out of the raw materials of aboriginal creation, just as the Atman of Prajapati is reconstituted (literally 'remembered') by the post-creation rituals of the gods."[68]

The sonic ritual act on the microlevel actually builds or constructs an eternal spiritual self for the human being called the Daiva Atman: "The divine self [Daiva Atman] is born out of the sacrifice; that is, it is a ritual construct."[69] Citing the *Aitareya-Brahmana* (AB 6.27), Brian K. Smith describes the Soma sacrifice with reference to the ritual construction of a spiritual self by means of the sound and rhythm of the mantras: as a "ritual of self-perfection (Atma-samskriti) . . . the sacrificer 'fashions (samskurute) his own self in a rhythmical way' [by the meters] through the ritual chants that are likened to seeds being poured into the womb." Citing the *Kausitaki-Brahmana* (KB 3.8), he states that "in the ritual the priests construct and perfect (samskurvanti) a 'heavenly self' (daiva atman) for the sacrificer."[70]

Another Sanskrit word applies here with regard to the life-cycle rituals: *samskara.* Often translated "rites of passage," Samskaras are "really rituals of ontological healing, construction, and perfection."[71] The building of the true and authentic human being or "Aryan" is made possible by the sonic rites of Samskara, especially the initiation ceremony known as the Upanayana: "The Upanayana delivers a reborn Aryan, who was supposedly more really human because more fully realized, activated through the activity of ritual."[72]

The Samskaras as life-cycle rituals are obligatory for Hindus since they carry the process forward of refining and reconstituting the spiritual self in preparation for the afterlife, or journey to heaven: "Humans are responsible for creating an ontologically viable self for themselves and the world (loka) for that self to inhabit. And both self and world are ritual constructs." As Smith notes, quoting the *Satapatha-Brahmana* 1.3.2.1: "Man is the sacrifice"[73] and "each sacrifice has a different sustaining power for the divine self in the next world."[74] Like the law of karma, Vedic ritualism, including the reciting of mantras, was premised on the assumption that acts have consequences for those who act, both in this life and in the future.

YAJNA AND THE AFTERLIFE

Participants in religious rituals the world over claim to be changed by them; they are consecrated, made sacred, by virtue of the power of ritual activity. In India a large part of that change is the transformation of the self after the death of the body. In Vedic ritualism the divine self and the place in the netherworld are sonic ritual constructs, and the transformation is portrayed as a journey: "The ritual creation of the Daiva Atman and Svarga-loka was part of a transformative process that the texts liken to a journey, with the sacrifice itself the vehicle."[75] The ritual process is one in which a place in the afterworld is reserved by means of sacrifice and chant: "The sacrificial journey places the sacrificer in the other world only temporarily, just long enough to mark out and reserve a space for the next life."[76] As Smith further explains, "man's divinity, his Daiva Atman, is also forged by the ontological (and transcendental) power of ritual work, and so, too, is his heavenly world—both the heaven reached in every sacrificial performance and the heaven to which the sacrificer ascends and in which he dwells after death. . . . Both the self and the world that one builds for oneself here and those that one constructs for the afterlife are products of the rituals one performs."[77] Music and chant are the eminently proactive elements in the ongoing ritual process of unifying, rebuilding, and solidifying the cosmos as well as the individual self in this world and the next. In short, ritual is necessary to fix the defective universe: "Life in the historical present, no less than in the mythic time or origins, is regarded as intrinsically faulty without the formative structure only ritual can provide."[78]

Regarding the eschatological dimension of Vedic chant, a poignant technical aspect is found in the notion of measured time and its application in Yajna. While Vedic ritual is divided into units of "ritual time," Vedic chant or mantra, as metrical chant, is subdivided into syllables that have a distinct time unit. The English word *meter* is cognate with the Sanskrit word *matra,* which derives from the Sanskrit root *ma,* to measure across, to mete out, to mark off, as in a unit of time, a measure, a foot. In Sanskrit poetics a Matra is equivalent to the time it takes to pronounce a short vowel, with two Matras equivalent to a long vowel (*Monier-Williams Sanskrit Dictionary,* 804). One of the original usages of the concept of measure is found in relation to the god Vishnu in Vedic mythology. In the first book of the *Rig-Veda* there is the story of Vishnu, as Trivikrama, taking three strides to "measure the expanse from the earth to the stars." In *Rig-Veda* 1.154, where this aspect of Vishnu is described, the term *vimame,* past perfect of *ma,* to measure, is used in reference to his three strides (*tri-vikrama*). These three strides have sacrificial associations beyond the merely mythological, however, as they in fact lay down the foundation for the concept of a "measured distance" between earth and heaven. This distance is expressed in ritual acts, meters, and rhythmic Matras. The story of Vishnu as Trivikrama presents a kind of Vedic archetype for the journey from earth to heaven. As a type of measured soteriological space, the distance to the heavenly abode may be traversed by the worshipper through the medium of sacrifice that is necessarily modulated with measured sound in the form of mantra and Sama-Gana. This idea resonates very well with the later practices of theistic Hinduism, especially within Vaishnava traditions, in which rhythm in Bhakti Sangit to this day is measured according to Matras or beats. The attainment of an eternal afterlife through the performance of chant and music in measured time units is thus a concept that spans from ancient Vedic sacrificial chant to modern practices of devotional music.

APURVA AND ADRISHTA

The Vedic system of sacrifice, as explained in the philosophical school of Mimamsa, endorsed a primary theoretical dimension to ritual events in its approach to the afterlife. In the sacrifices correct pronunciation and performance of rites guaranteed entrance into Svarga or heaven through a principle of Apurva, whereby the result of the sacrifice was delayed or stored away. The unseen merit or Adrishta that accumulated within the soul of the practitioner over a lifetime of ritual activity on earth could then be reclaimed in the future. The ritual stages in the Yajna as well as the chanting of mantras were believed to contribute merit toward this end. While the rite would finish, the result derived from its execution remained invisible to the performer only to be reclaimed after death in the form of a heavenly reward or immortality. This notion was paralleled in the Mimamsa linguistic theory of Varnavada, whereby in mantra recitation there was a quantified accumulation of merit via chanted syllables. What is most significant in our study is that the ritual notion of Apurva or Adrishta has a counterpart in the marking of rhythmic units in music.

The concepts of Apurva and Adrishta in relation to Mimamsa philosophy have been described in *Sonic Theology: Hinduism and Sacred Sound* (Beck 1993, 55–62). The Veda is said to be the purest form of Sabda, as it is the most reliable source for knowledge both of the visible world (Drishta) and the invisible world (Adrishta). As language or Sabda encompasses both dimensions of reality, Drishta and Adrishta, language in the form of chant or song is directly related to both these dimensions and is of crucial importance in understanding reality. The central place for the mediation between these two dimensions is the Vedic sacrifice or, more specifically, the Vedic injunctions and the action they engender within the sonic ritual context. Language is the only link since it prescribes particular actions for the sacrificer, whose own efficient force causes unseen merit to accrue known as Adrishta. This merit is the direct result of actions commanded by Vedic injunctions in the form of verbs and gains the aspirant entrance into svarga or heaven. Verbs or verbal phrases, not nouns or names, are more directly connected to the unseen dimension of reality through the principle of Apurva that allows for the delay and storage of the results of ritual activity. Thus an act in the visible realm, according to Vedic injunction, inevitably—namely, only after death—leads to an unseen result—namely, heaven—in the invisible realm. And heaven is not experienced by sense perception, but is only realized and made possible by being involved in ritual acts.

Mimamsa, or Purva-Mimamsa, is one of the six schools or Darsanas that developed as interpretive tools for Vedic ritual and metaphysics. The ancient *Mimamsa-Sutra* of Jaimini (ca. 300 B.C.E.) is the earliest Mimamsa text. Jaimini mentions the term *Apurva* about twenty times, but only as indicative of dharma action-related injunctions. Sabara, the orthodox commentator on Jaimini, articulated the notion of Apurva to explain how the invisible result of sacrifice is redeemed at a later time. Sabara was followed by two interpretive schools, both about 700 C.E.: Kumarila Bhatta and Prabhakara Misra. The close continuity of text and commentary in Mimamsa requires that the tradition be viewed as a whole: "The text in its tradition is ultimately what must interest us most, and through our understanding we become in a sense members of that tradition—commentators of sorts, as we engage in criticism of older commentators. To understand the Mimamsa we must also try to make sense of the tradition from the worldview of Jaimini to that of his commentators; we must enter their world too. . . . Prabhakara school most faithfully adheres to the system of the Sutras, while Kumarila's system is the logical expansion and completion of Sabara's interpretation of Jaimini."[79]

In order to explain the phenomena of the unseen result of the sacrifice being sustained after the burning of the ashes, the notion of Apurva was developed by Sabara in his commentary on the *Mimamsa-Sutra* and furthered principally by Kumarila Bhatta in his work *Sloka-Varttika*. Francis X. Clooney, S.J., in *Thinking Ritually: Rediscovering the Purva Mimamsa of Jaimini* (1990), discusses Apurva with the indication that it was Kumarila Bhatta who is responsible for the complete notion of Apurva, embodying the idea of an invisible residue or spiritual potency (Sakti) from the burnt sacrifice that inheres in the soul of the practitioner and is available as a reward in the afterlife. In reference to Kumarila Bhatta and Apurva, Clooney explains that "Kumarila's main contribution is to suggest that Apurva is a potency (Sakti) having its basis (asraya) in the soul (Atman) of the performer. . . . which did not exist prior to the performance of the action, and which is duly based upon the authority of Scripture."[80] In fact,

> the notion of Apurva (as the unseen link between the sacrifice and its results) is so central to the intelligibility and coherence of Sabara-Kumarila Mimamsa that to speak of it is to speak about their systems as a whole. . . . The growing importance of Apurva in Sabara-Kumarila Mimamsa testifies to a devaluation of the action of the sacrifice and a new grounding of the significance of sacrifice on a more permanent basis, a transcendent reality surviving the sacrificial ashes. This reality, the Apurva which survives the sacrifice and is ultimately determined by Kumarila to precede it as well, is in turn implanted in the eternal Atman of the performer of the sacrifice.[81]

The logic leading to Sabara's and Kumarila's conclusion regarding the existence of Apurva may be explained further. "Desirous of heaven, one should sacrifice" is taken as a Vedic theological injunction. For this statement of Vedic scripture to be true, there must be something that connects the sacrifice to a result. The reasoning of how the injunction to sacrifice presumes the existence of Apurva is presented by Clooney with reference to Sabara's commentary: "Otherwise, if there were no such thing as Apurva, such an injunction would be meaningless. For the act of sacrifice itself is perishable, so that if the sacrifice were to perish without bringing into existence something else, then the cause having ceased to exist, the result (in the shape of heaven) could never come about. From this it follows that the sacrifice does bring into existence something, . . . some force or potency which continues to exist and operate till such time as the result is actually brought about."[82] Sabara's (and Kumarila's) view is that if there is no such thing as Apurva, the Vedic injunctions would be meaningless: "The Veda states that the sacrifice yields certain results, but we observe that the sacrifice ends, the offerings reduced to ashes, without any evident attainment of heaven by the performer. This means that the Vedic promisc of heaven must be untrue, unless there is something more, an intervening Apurva. . . . [Thus] words expressive of activity [in the Veda] are expressive of the Apurva."[83]

The notion of Apurva, according to the commentators, also applies to ancillary rites that support the principal rituals and even applies to other activities such as secular duties. Apurva is described as evolving over time, maturing like a sprouted plant. In the developing classical music of India, this same principle has been indicated in the ancient musicological texts and commentaries, whereby it is the performative act of singing or playing instruments in real time (that is, ritual time), not simply the melodies or beats by themselves, that produces the positive merit (Apurva or Adrishta) that earns a person heavenly rewards such as Moksha. The notion of Apurva will continue to manifest itself through the measurement of musical time and even guide the performance of Bhakti Sangit within Hindu temple traditions.

The tradition of Sama-Gana and its manifestation within ancient Vedic sonic liturgy set the stage for the creation and development of Indian classical music, known first as Gandharva Sangita, or simply Gandharva, and then as Bhakti Sangit, Carnatic music, and Hindustani music. Hinduism is one of the few traditions of religious music in which the transition from religious cantillation or chant, normally comprising a minimum of notes, to music, utilizing the full gamut of notes, has occurred directly within the same textual tradition. Gandharva Sangita, however, was not merely music for entertainment but was integrated within the early Puja ceremonies that accompanied rituals and drama associated with scenic presentations of Vedic and epic narratives. Thus new forms of sonic liturgy emerged that incorporated both Vedic and non-Vedic or indigenous elements. And as Hindu sonic liturgy evolved and changed through time, music continued to grow and expand as a core element of Hindu ritual practice.

2

Classical India

Puja and Gandharva Sangita

AS WE HAVE SEEN, VEDIC INDIA WAS dominated by a culture that promoted fire sacrifices and the melodic chanting of the *Sama-Veda*. Vedic literatures provided information about the means to propitiate the gods in order to gain desirable goals, as well as about how the universe functioned. The mode of access to the Vedic gods was through the combination of the chanted text and fire and not through images or other iconic manifestations. Yet the Vedic gods were frequently depicted in language as spiritual beings with names, form, and activity. Indeed, rather than depicted in terms of impersonal principles as in the Upanishads, the gods portrayed in Vedic descriptions were generally anthropomorphic and personal. The historical details regarding the transition from literary description to concrete images or icons have been widely debated. New research suggests that this transition took place by means of ceremonies known as Puja which were originally tied to sacred drama and indigenous rites that surfaced visibly in the classical period from 400 B.C.E. to 300 C.E.

The narratives of the Vedic gods and their heroic exploits became the substance of Indian mythology and ritual reenactment in the post-Vedic period. Chief among the early means by which these narratives were reenacted was through sacred drama. The sacred dramas or Natyas began with special ceremonies of veneration and worship called Puja in the earliest texts. Early Indian music called Gandharva Sangita was also closely associated with these Pujas and sacred dramatic performances, as evidenced in Bharata's *Natya-Sastra* and Dattila's *Dattilam*, the two earliest texts on drama and music believed to have been composed between the fourth and second centuries B.C.E. The tradition of Puja did not directly derive from Vedic models, however, but was linked to indigenous practices involving the ritual offering of selected items such as flowers, water, and food, not as oblations into a fire but as objects placed at the foot or base of an icon or symbol of the divine being. These practices, along with rites for temple construction and icon worship, were later described and codified in medieval texts called Agamas which, though postdating the Vedas, likely reflect pre-Vedic and non-Vedic dimensions of ancient India. The proliferation of Agamic traditions also facilitated the ascendancy of the gods Siva and Vishnu as the most prominent deities in the Hindu pantheon.

Gandharva Sangita, or simply Gandharva, was the sacred music associated with the early Pujas and sacred dramas during the classical period. It was the principal style of music performed in Hindu festivals, courtly ceremonies, and rituals in honor of the emerging great gods and goddesses such as Siva, Vishnu, Brahma, Ganesha, and Devi. In the ancient epics of the *Mahabharata* and *Ramayana*, as well as in the mythical histories called Puranas, there are descriptions of temple musicians and dancers who performed Gandharva Sangita for the pleasure of these deities.

PUJA

While the Yajna was central during Vedic times, the ceremonial rites of Puja became widespread in the post-Vedic or classical period, coming to the foreground as the quintessential Hindu ritual. Gandharva Sangita, in combination with early Puja, indeed helped to create a new form of sonic liturgy that offered striking distinctions from Yajna and the culture of Sama-Gana and fire sacrifice. To appreciate more fully the differences between the Vedic realm of fire sacrifice and the emergent Puja ritualism involving images, it is essential to compare these two forms of liturgical worship, beginning with some basic definitions and descriptions of Puja.

Appearing initially in the scenic rites of sacred dramas and more fully developed within the textual tradition of the Agamas, Puja or Deva Puja was a form of religious ritual that Hindus began to perform on a variety of occasions to petition or show respect to their chosen gods or goddesses. Puja may be defined as any act of showing reverence to a god, a spirit, or another aspect of the divine through invocations, prayers, offerings, songs, and rituals. An essential part of Puja for the Hindu devotee is making a personal connection with the divine. Most often the contact is facilitated through an object: an element of nature, a sculpture, a vessel, or a painting. During Puja an image or other symbol of the god serves as a means of gaining access to the divine. The icon is not the deity itself; rather it is believed to be filled with the deity's cosmic energy or spirit. It is a focal point for honoring and communicating with the god. For the devout Hindu the icon's artistic merit is important but is secondary to its spiritual content. The objects are created as receptacles for spiritual energy that allow the devotee to experience direct communication with his or her chosen deities.

Many devout Hindus in the modern world still perform Puja once or twice a day. As such, Puja should be done after a shower or bath, and it is recommended that Puja rites be performed before food intake to ensure purity (*sattva*) and full concentration (*dhyana*). Puja is performed on special occasions in addition to the daily ritual. Examples of these occcasions include Durga Puja, Siva Ratri, Kali Puja, Pongal and Lakshmi Puja.

Puja normally includes activities or observances like meditation (*dhyana*), the practice of austerity (*tapas*), chanting (mantra), scripture reading (*svadhyaya*), offering food (*naivedya*) and prostrations (*ashtanga pranama, dandavat*). The individual may apply a *tilaka* mark on the forehead with sandalwood paste and then a vermillion (*kumkum*) dot in its centre. This signifies submission to the divine presence. Puja is usually concluded with an Arati ceremony to the deity, including a series of offerings.

Puja may be performed by an individual or as part of a group. The ritual may be observed in silence or accompanied by prayers and songs. Sometimes a Puja is done for the benefit of certain people for whom priests or relatives ask blessings. A Hindu priest (called a Purohit or a Pujari) chants prayers in Sanskrit or some other language while performing Puja. Large Pujas require the presence of fellow believers and involve a full day's ritual, with people present for the actual Puja ceremony and the partaking of *prasad* (food sacrament), followed by Bhajans (religious prayer songs) and a meal. Most sects, families, and even individuals have their own way of conducting Puja.

As part of the overall Puja ritual sequence, an Arati ceremony is usually conducted in which the flame from burning wicks soaked in ghee (clarified butter) or camphor is offered to one or more Devas or Devis. Arati is generally performed two to six times daily in temples and usually at the end of a Puja or Bhajan session. In relation to food offerings, it takes place just after the food is placed on the altar and "consumed" by the deity. Generally Arati is performed during most all Hindu ceremonies and occasions. The activity involves the clockwise movement of the offered article, whether incense, flower, lamp wick, plate, or other, before the image or symbol and is generally accompanied by the singing of songs in praise of a deva or holy person. In the process the article itself is supposed to acquire sacred power. The priest may then circulate the article, especially the plate with burning lamp wick, among all those present, who cup their downturned hands over the flame and then raise their palms to their forehead. The purificatory blessing, passed from the divine to the flame, has now been passed to the devotee. The Arati plate is generally made of metal, usually silver, bronze, or copper. On it may rest a lamp made of kneaded flour, mud, or metal, filled with oil or ghee. A cotton wick is put into the oil and then lighted or camphor is burnt instead. The plate may also hold flowers and incense.

One of the purposes of performing Arati is to ward off evil effects and the malefic influence of the "evil eye." This procedure is generally called apotropaia (removing malevolent forces), which may also be a goal of certain types of music. To ward off evil effects Arati is performed on people of high social or economic status; small children during various ceremonies; people who are going on or coming back from a long journey; a bride and bridegroom when they enter their house for the first time; at harvest; on any other occasion of importance. It is also performed on newly acquired property or before an important task. It is believed that the image of a deity too is susceptible to the evil eye, and thus needs regular Arati, with the singing of special Arati songs. These songs laud the glory of the deva and describe the benefits that one might gain by praying to that particular figure. Sometimes they also include information on the life of the gods. While there may be similarity in musical structure and tune across sectarian divides, the lyrics of Arati songs are usually specific to each deva.

The *Vishnudharmasutra* (chapter 65) provides one of the earliest (ca. 300 B.C.E.) detailed descriptions of Deva Puja of Vishnu. This Puja ceremony has integrated the Vedic chanting of the Gayatri Mantra and the *Purusha-Sukta*. The Pujaprakasa section presents the details of this Deva Puja in sixteen stages or Upacaras that have become more or less standardized in temple ritual sequences: *avahana* (invite), *asana* (offer seat), *padya* (wash feet), *arghya* (wash hands), *acamaniya* (offer water to drink), *snana* (bathe), *vastra* (clothe), *yajnopavita* (offer sacred thread), *anulepana* (offer sandalwood paste), *gandha* (offer fragrances), *puspa* (offer flowers), *dhupa* (offer incense), *dipa* (offer lamp wick), *naivedya* (offer food), *namaskara* (offer prostrations), *pradakshina* (circumambulate) and *visarjana* (conclude). In these texts and in many of the succeeding delineations of the Puja ceremony, it is recommended that the priest repeat one of the verses of the *Purusha-Sukta* (RV X. 90) before offering each of the sixteen Upacaras. Otherwise one may utter the mantra *Om sivaya namah* or *Om vishnave namah*, "I salute Siva," "I salute Vishnu."[1]

There are comparisons with the Vedic Yajna that can further delineate the singular status of Puja in Hindu tradition. According to the Vedic texts, at the beginning of the classical period the Yajna system was divided into three types:

1. Soma Yajna. Libations of Soma, performed only by elite class of Brahmins and the most complex rites based on the ritual patterns of the Agnistoma;
2. Havir Yajna. Libations and oblations of milk, ghee, and grain, performed by lesser Brahmins, which were less complex and included daily Agnihotra rites;
3. Paka Yajna. Home worship, also called Grihya rites, performed by householders, which were the simplest.

In each case the dualism of fire and offering had an all-embracing significance in Vedic theology. Identified with the god Agni, fire had an exceptional ritual function as the intermediary between the heavenly and mortal worlds. In Vedic worship gods were ideal presences at the altar, so that only the unseen offering consumed by Agni could reach them. In the Paka Yajna and Havir Yajna, milk and melted butter were poured onto the fire and grain thrown in it. Soma Yajna added the offering of sacrificial animals which were dismembered and cooked on one of the altars. However, it was the Soma libation that embodied the universal offering. Gathering the Soma stalks, squeezing and diluting the juice, and pouring the juice on the fire were the most sacred events in the Soma or Agnistoma type of worship.[2]

Richard H. Davis, a scholar of medieval Hinduism, notes several differences between Puja and Yajna: "Vedic deities when invoked remain invisible. In Puja deities are summoned to inhabit material embodiments and so make their presence evident even to humans of limited vision. . . . Sacrificial offerings cannot be presented directly to the divinities; another deity, the fire god Agni, is required to act as intermediary, conveying the offerings to the other gods. Offerings of Puja, by contrast, may be made directly to the highest god in the central image and to other subsidiary deities also present in their own individual embodiments." The Yajnas were portable rituals that were not performed at permanent sites, while the Puja sites housed the deity or icon: "While Vedic public sacrifices are performed in temporary ritual settings constructed for the occasion, public Puja . . . takes place in a durable structure, built to last out of stone or brick and elegantly decorated by sculptors and painters. Such a temple serves as an enduring home for the divine image and for the god himself who dwells within it."[3]

The differences between Yajna and Puja were sometimes mitigated by some common ground. As Davis notes,

> both center on acts whereby humans offer food to the gods. Both require that the human participants attain a personal state of purity of godliness consonant with the solemnity of the ritual action, and both provide means through which divinities are summoned to be present at the ritual terrain. Once invoked, the divinities are treated with all the respect due them and presented with a repast of the finest order. In most cases the remainders of the meal are subsequently distributed among the community of human worshippers in a prescribed hierarchical order. Both, accordingly, involve an enactment of proper relations between humans and deities, as these are understood by each, and may articulate as well status relationships within the human community.[4]

Regarding the offering of food, in the Yajna whenever animal sacrifices occurred, meat was cooked first before being offered to the deity, unlike in ancient Israel. In Puja offerings, by contrast, the cooked food that is offered is predominantly vegetarian.

What mattered most in the area of Puja ritual was the simultaneous transcendence and immanence of the deity. In the Vedic sphere a deity was viewed as beyond the material domain, accessible only through the media of fire and mantra. For the process of image worship the deity had to be accessible through material form, which was also consecrated by mantra nonetheless. According to Davis, "transcendent as they are believed to be, these gods are also fully immanent, pervasive throughout the cosmos, and capable of manifesting themselves visibly in the world through incarnation (*avatara*), emanation (*vyuha*), or embodiment (*murti*) in order to enter into direct relations with other divinities and lesser beings such as humans. Schools might differ from one another as to which divinity is supreme, but they share the theological premise that, to be supreme, God must be both transcendent and immanent."[5]

Image worship in ancient India, though consisting of material objects, operated on a higher level than mere adoration of matter or material form. According to Vedic scholar P. V. Kane, image worship was always associated with a higher spirituality: "Image worship was not absolutely necessary for everybody and the ancient writers never thought that when they worshipped an image they were simply paying homage to a material object. They believed that they contemplated the One Supreme Spirit in the form of the image or symbol before them, which helped ordinary people to concentrate their mind on the Godhead to the exclusion of other external and engrossing objects and pursuits."[6]

While image worship has remained a staple of Hindu religious life for centuries, it was not part of the original Vedic revelation nor did it exist among the ancient Indo-Aryans: "One can say without much fear of contradiction that the religious practices among the higher strata of the Vedic Aryans did not include the worship of images in the house or in the temples."[7] As such, the process of the gradual shift from Vedic fire sacrifices directed toward invisible deities to the devotional service of anthropomorphic deities embodied in material form has sparked continuing debate.

One side of the argument states that image worship naturally arose within Vedic sacrificial worship. Although the Vedas and Brahmanas are mute regarding image worship itself, the process of Deva Puja (image worship) appears in several of the canonical authors of the Hindu tradition, suggesting a kind of natural or spontaneous arising. One principal example is found in the *Manu-Samhita* (II.176), which directs the brahmacarin (celibate student) to worship images (see also VIII. 87, III. 117, IX. 285). Kane cites the practice in Panini (ca. fifth century B.C.E.), where Puja is nearly equated with Yajna: "The word 'Deva Puja' occurs in the Vartika on *Panini* I.3.25."[8] Panini is also cited as the first reference to image worship in India, one which indicates that Puja was already widespread: "The earliest testimony to the existence of an iconic cult goes back to the mid-first millennium B.C.E. Thus, Panini's grammar, the *Astadhyayi*, dated fifth to fourth century B.C.E., mentions of images of gods (arca). . . . The *Astadhyayi* gives enough information to conclude that by the mid-first millennium B.C.E., Puja worship was widespread in India alongside the Vedic Yajna. We come across repeated references to Puja in Panini's grammar (*Panini* 3.3.105, 8.1.67)."[9] Most of the canonical references try to demonstrate that, just as a Yajna consists in giving up materials accompanied by a mantra with reference to a deity, so a Puja is a type of Yajna, wherein there is also a giving up (or dedication) of materials to a deity.

In the debate about the origins of Puja, the citations above have lent support to the argument that Puja "evolved" out of Yajna. Based partly on these as well as a modern nationalist tendency to "discover everything Indian in the Vedas," this fairly prevalent view argues for a natural evolution from the poetic descriptions of deities in the Vedas to their gradual iconic worship. Considering the anthropomorphic personification of deities as described by the Vedic poets, Kane entertains this possibility: "It is extremely doubtful whether images were generally worshipped in the ancient Vedic times. In the Rig-Veda and the other Vedas, there is worship of Agni, the Sun, Varuna, and various other deities; but they were worshipped in the abstract, as powers and manifestations of the One Divine Person or as a separate deities or functions behind natural phenomena or cosmic processes. There are no doubt passages where the deities of the Rig-Veda are spoken of as possessed of bodily attributes."[10] Kane then affirms a similar perspective in the Brahmana literatures: "If we look at the Vedic cult described in the Brahmanas where sacrifices of butter, cakes and boiled rice or other grain are offered to several deities in the fire, or animal and Soma sacrifices are described in great length, it is clear that the ancient sages hardly ever thought of the worship of idols, but of deities in the abstract to whom they ascribed different functions and poetically represented them as being endowed like human beings with hands and feet and other limbs. It cannot be denied that here and there occur passages that suggest images as objects of worship."[11]

Regarding the shift toward image worship, one argument on the opposing side has been to view the switch as caused by abrupt foreign influence, such as the influx of Greek statues and images after the rise of Buddhism (sixth century B.C.E.). But again this view is not supported by the consensus of scholarship that gives an earlier date to Panini, who mentions image worship. As concluded by Shahab Sarmadee: "It could be more plausible to suppose, therefore, that Panini lived and wrote before the time of the Greek invasion—sometime between the sixth and fifth centuries of the pre-Christian era."[12]

More recent scholarship on the rise of image worship in Hinduism presents a rather different view from the prevailing arguments and counterarguments. According to this approach, the essentials of Puja were adopted by the Indo-Aryan culture from the indigenous non-Aryan populations and subsequently integrated within Hindu culture. Russian Indologist Natalia Lidova has championed this view, stating unequivocally that "the sum total of the available ritual, historical and linguistic information testifies to the non-Aryan origin of the Puja."[13] While the Yajna and the Puja may have existed simultaneously in ancient India, Lidova concludes that "the Puja as a practical form of cult rather denies than follows the Yajna."[14] This is a declaration based upon the completely different ritual structure and theology of the Vedic Yajna and the Puja as outlined in the *Natya-Sastra:*

> We can thus state that not one of the essential aspects of religious practice, which determined the arrangement of the ritual space, the way of offering sacrifices and the ritual goals of the worship, offered a coincidence between the Vedic system and the *Natya-Sastra* rites. . . . In fact, the Vedic and the *Natya-Sastra* rites served different gods, and actualized different sacral ideas. As we see it, Yajna could not evolve into Puja through any transformation, without shattering the pivots of Vedic ritualism. We could suppose equal coexistence of Yajna and Puja within Vedic culture, if not for the conspicuous absence of Puja in all ritual sources of the Vedic era. In other words, this type of adoration was absent in the Vedic ritual system.[15]

The word *Puja* is argued to be completely foreign to the Vedas: "The Rig-Veda never uses the verb '*puj*,' semantically connected with the rite and meaning 'revere' or 'glorify.'"[16] In fact *puj* is not an Indo-Aryan root or term. Deriving the term *Puja* from the Dravidian root *pu* (flower), Lidova offers the suggestion of Dravidian influence with regard to both icons and Puja: "Ritual statues of gods, unknown in the Vedic era, were by no means part and parcel of the Yajna cult. By this alone, the Puja could not inherit them from the Vedic ritual system. Possibly they could be borrowed from Dravidian tribes together with the Puja."[17] Hinduism scholar Wendy Doniger has concurred with this etymology in her definition of Puja: "Puja (from the Dravidian *pu*) consisting of making an offering to an image of a god (flowers, fruits, sometimes rice), and/or moving a lamp through the air in a circular pattern, walking around the god, and reciting prayers, such as a litany of the names of the god."[18] Puja in its origin was thus a kind of "flower sacrifice" that, when integrated within Indo-Aryan culture, eventually did away with the need for animal or blood sacrifices: "Vedism had bloody offerings on special altars, as against Hindu bloodless sacrifices of incense, flowers and water before the images of divinity."[19]

The Vedic cult of Yajna did not employ any form of flower sacrifice, the cornerstone of Puja. In fact the Pujas described in the *Natya-Sastra* and the Agamas did not involve fire but required offerings made directly to the deities as embodied in material form: "Both Agamas and the *Natya-Sastra* demanded flowers spread on the site throughout the ceremony. This was an essential component of Puja sacrifice."[20] As explained further, "the *Natya-Sastra* rites imply offerings of an entirely different kind. Fire is neither the only nor even the basic way of sacrifice.

The ritual offerings of flowers, incense, unguents, food and water don't need it [fire] as an intermediary, with sacrifices piled at the foot of a ritual symbol [or object, such as a statue]."[21] The author or compiler of the *Natya-Sastra* must have been well aware of the Yajna-Puja difference, so that "his comparison merely emphasized the elevated status of Puja sacrifice, with sacral results no lesser than Yajna."[22] And as evolving Hindu traditions turned away from the Vedic prescriptions of fire sacrifice as central and assimilated the exterior religious form of Puja, the fire sacrifice became marginalized as part of the life-cycle rituals known as samskaras.

Regarding the origins of the flower sacrifice and other practices, there was most likely a selective adoption of these rites by the early Indo-Aryans from indigenous practices (that is, from Dravidian-speaking groups and others), rather than the wholesale importation of a native cult: "There is no reason to think that Aryans borrowed a whole religious system from Dravidians—a cult whose constituent features included templar construction and liturgical imagery. Such a cult, most probably, never existed at all." Thus it is more likely that certain aspects, such as the offering of flowers, were adopted from outside the Indo-Aryan sphere. As the offering of flowers was the definitive aspect of Puja, in contrast to the Vedic cult, Lidova argues that "it would be more correct to assume that only an idea or, at most, the basic pattern of flower sacrifice was borrowed. With its developed symbolical semantics, this pattern gradually gave rise to sophisticated ceremonial rites which we know from the *Natya-Sastra* and the Agamas."[23] Yet these outside influences were not simply cosmetic or transitory but brought about an immense and permanent overhaul of Hindu ritual life: "If we acknowledge that a non-Aryan rite became the basis of the Hindu ritual-mythological system, largely at the Yajna's expense, we have to recognize that these influences were not external but structural and involving the heart of hearts of the ancient Indian ritual culture."[24]

The necessity to reform Brahmanic ritualism combined with certain innovative trends in the classical period of Indian history led to the sweeping primacy of Puja as the central domain of Hindu practice: "The Puja had a magnetism as a worship form new to the Aryan community—first, as a rite sanctified by its very age and, second, offering an alternative to the Yajna, which no longer corresponded to the new spiritual values. . . . The ritual and mythological system which, presumably, arose in the mid–1st millennium B.C.E. round the non-Aryan Puja was immediate historical predecessor of Hinduism which, in the first century C.E., ousted all other religious trends from India to become its leading religion for a long time."[25] The Puja system also provided a veritable bond between the religion of the Vedic period and later Hinduism.

The beliefs and practices associated with Puja and image worship, first visible in drama texts like the *Natya-Sastra,* were later laid down systematically in a completely different corpus of texts called the Agamas. The continuity between the *Natya-Sastra* and the Agamas is remarkable in terms of the prescriptions for Puja and image worship. Agamic texts name Puja as the basic ceremonial rite, and present its content and details exactly like the *Natya-Sastra* worship: "The Agamic rituals were also performed with flowers, fruit, incense, water and foods in honor of gods and basic ritual symbols."[26] The essentials of Puja were even similar across sectarian divisions: "All Agamas, Hindu ritual texts, irrespective of confession (Saivite, Vishnuite, and Krishnaite) describe one type of sacrifice, with variants within the single Puja ritual pattern."[27] In fact one may consider with a degree of certainty that the Trimurti idea of Brahma, Vishnu, and Siva reached its first concrete expression within the scenic rites of the *Natya-Sastra* and later in the Agamas.

Since the Agamas postdate the *Natya-Sastra* by several centuries, they represent a more mature stage in the development of image worship: "The Agamas know the tradition of templar worship of gods' images in a well-developed and finally established form. Doubtless, the Agamas make us think of a widespread and flourishing religious culture, whereas the *Natya-Sastra* . . . reflects a much earlier period of its existence. . . . The essential features of ritual specifics of the Agamic Puja have direct analogies in the *Natya-Sastra.*"[28] Consequently, "the *Natya-Sastra* turns out to be much older than all the Agamic literature available today. It fixes many features of the emergence of the iconic cult and, at the same time, is the earliest source on the Puja ritualism."[29] All of these rituals, evident in the *Natya-Sastra* and the Agamas, contrasted with the Vedic system: "There was a world of difference between the Vedic liturgical practice and Hindu worship."[30]

The Agamas continued the ritual sophistication of the *Natya-Sastra* with its emphasis on the Mandala as a kind of magic center: "Scenic ritualism demanded the magic circle made during the rites. Agamic texts also refer to permanent Mandalas in places of worship, which structurally repeated the scenic Mandala. The Agamic Mandala was the most sacred point in the center, where flowers were spread during the rituals, and kumbhas placed—essential ritual symbols of Hindu deities."[31] While the Mandala as a magic circle was never known in Vedic ritualism, the sacred Mandala in both scenic rites and Agama worship represented the center of the universe or *axis mundi* in accordance with the explanations of Mircea Eliade and the school of religious studies known as history of religions. In "both in Agamic and scenic rites, the centre of the Mandala represents the centre of the Universe, its circle the world border-line, and the banner the cosmic axis and arbor mundi. This makes the arranged ritual space a miniature replica of the whole and organized Universe."[32] As this and further comparisons reveal, "the basic, archetypal aspects of the *Agamic puja* coincided with rites described in the *Natya-Sastra.* The closeness of symbols and worship structure hints at direct genetic links—not mere typological likeness—between the *Natya-Sastra* and Agamic rites. This is borne out by numerous particular analogies, as connected with liturgical practices."[33] Other examples include the replication of hand gestures and postures such as Nyasa and Mudra that correspond with the worship of an anthropomorphous god.

In the Saiva Agamas, Agamic texts devoted to Siva, ritual objects were placed in the center of a Mandala denoting Siva: "Special among the jars of various shapes and sizes was the Siva-Kumbha [pitcher], ritual embodiment of Siva, always placed in the center of the principal Mandala. Thus, Agamic rites were analogous to the *Natya-Sastra* as the center of the sacral space protected by the supreme god—Siva, in this particular confessional tradition."[34] In fact, according to Lidova, the Saiva Puja traditionally comprised sixteen obligatory stages comparable to the basic parts of the *Natya-Sastra* sacrifice.[35] Even the deities guarding the borders of the Mandala were replicated in the Agamas: "The circle of the Agamic Mandala—visible border of the particular sacrificial space and at the same time of cosmos—was guarded by the Lokapalas, as in the *Natya-Sastra* rites, who took their places to the four cardinal points."[36]

Another point of contrast between the Vedic Yajna and the Agamic Puja exposes the emergence of the important role of the community or congregation in Hindu rites. The fruits of Vedic sacrifice were generally reserved for the individual sacrificer (Yajamana) or his family. Thus the donor who arranged the sacrifice would reap the rewards in this world and the next: "The Vedic rite was always ordered by a particular donor, who often took part in it, on his own or with his wife, as the case might be. The rite served his well-being, and all the fruit of an auspicious sacrifice belonged to him alone—the person who paid for the ceremony and distributed the *dakshina* [gratuities] among the priests."[37] There was little sense of communal experience or collective elation in anticipation of liberation. In opposition to this, "the *Natya-Sastra* rites had no such personal address. . . . Instead, as the treatise says on several occasions, the rites served the prosperity of the country and nation, i.e., had a pronounced communal message." As explained further,

> as we study the ritual goals of the *Agamic* worship, we must point out that, like the *Natya-Sastra,* it had a communal message and was meant not for a particular donor but for the affluence of the whole community. The communal idea was intrinsic in Hindu ritualism. The entire congregation directly participated in the liturgy, the priest made sacrifices on its behalf, and success of the rite guaranteed protection and well-being for each of its members. As the Puja made him closer

> to the divine world, every believer could address his prayer to god with his personal entreaty, whereas the Vedic religion gave this right only to the person who ordered the offering, and sometimes his family.[38]

The communal or congregational idea was also crucial to the development of liturgical music in the temple Hinduism of the medieval period.

NATYA-SASTRA OF BHARATA

Despite the scattered and often elusive references to image worship or Deva Puja among early Indian canonical sources, the most informative source for the wholesale adoption of Puja into Hindu culture is the *Natya-Sastra* by Bharata, the earliest text on ancient dramaturgy and music (ca. 400 B.C.E. in its original form). The *Natya-Sastra* is now available only in parts, but is believed by experts to be based upon a still older text called the *Natya-Veda*, which was one of the four Upavedas that extended over 36,000 *slokas* composed by a figure named Bharata Muni. Among the commentators the names of Udbhata, Lollata, Sankuka, Bhattanayaka, and Abhinavagupta have come down to us, yet the only commentary available today is the *Abhinava-Bharati* of Abhinavagupta (950–1020 C.E.). All these commentators are known to have hailed from Kashmir and flourished from the eighth century to the eleventh century.

Although some scholars cite a later date for the *Natya-Sastra*, the rituals and scenic prescriptions are most certainly older, according to Vedic scholar G. H. Tarlekar: "The well-settled practice of the earliest available classical dramas presupposes the existence of Sanskrit drama at least a few centuries earlier. The *Natya-Sastra* (400 B.C.E. to 200 C.E.) gives such minute details of the dramatic art that it must have had a long tradition of centuries to possess such perfection. Hence, it is reasonable to conclude that in the times of Panini, the Sanskrit drama was definitely in vogue."[39]

The arrival of Puja as a central feature of Indian drama tradition is first outlined in this text and revolves around a series of scenic rites and ceremonies invoking the presence of many Hindu deities as both preliminary to and part of the drama event. Deva Puja, including the music of Gandharva Sangita, developed around the needs for dramatization of Vedic and epic narratives that involved the gods and heroes of ancient India.

A summation of the signal importance of the *Natya-Sastra* for Hindu religion and culture has been provided by Susan Schwartz: "In short, the *Natya-Sastra* is an exhaustive encyclopedic dissertation on the arts, with an emphasis on performing arts as its central feature. It is also full of invocations to deities, acknowledging the divine origins of the arts and the central role performance plays in achieving divine goals. It is clear that in Bharata's text, and in the tradition that uses it as a primary source, Rasa and those arts that attempt to achieve it hold transcendence of the microcosmic reality as their ultimate purpose. The story of the text's origins leaves no question as to its divine source, Brahma, and it is often called the Fifth Veda."[40]

Several of the salient points are corroborated by Tarlekar, who stresses the intimate bond between religion and the origin of drama: "The effort to call the *Natya-Sastra* the fifth Veda, the Puja in connection with the stage, the relation with gods, Brahma, Vishnu, and Mahesa [Siva], the occasions of the performances which were the festivals in honor of the deities, the preliminaries to satisfy the deities, all point to the religious connection of the drama."[41] Consistent with the label of "Fifth Veda," the *Natya-Sastra* (NS 36.26) equates the arts of music and dance with Vedic chant: "Music, both instrumental and vocal, dance and songs are equal to the recitation of Vedic mantras."[42]

The theory of Rasa, aesthetic experience or taste, was first delineated by Bharata in his text. He outlines eight separate Rasas (NS 6.14) and identifies them with specific deities (NS 6.44):[43]

1. Shringara Rasa—love in union and separation: Vishnu;
2. Hasya Rasa—humor: Pramatha;
3. Karuna Rasa—pathos, sorrow: Yama;
4. Raudra Rasa—anger, wrath: Rudra (later Siva);
5. Vira Rasa—heroism: Mahendra (Indra);
6. Bhayanaka Rasa—fear/panic: Kala;
7. Bibhatsa Rasa—distaste, disgust: Mahakala;
8. Adbhuta Rasa—wonder/surprise: Brahma.

By the eighth century C.E. a ninth Rasa, Santa Rasa, was added, which means peace and tranquility. These Rasas have been subsequently aligned with some of the Ragas or scale formulas of Indian classical music.

In *Studies in the Natyasastra: With Special Reference to the Sanskrit Drama in Performance*, Tarlekar explains how Natya (the drama) incorporated a blending together of speech, music, and dance: "The actor [Nata] takes the role of the character and adopting the gestures, the speech and the mental states as well, of that character, creates before the spectators, the life that character lives, making them one with that life. Music helps this representation by intensifying the particular mood. The grace of physical movements is supplied by dance. Thus, the Natya becomes the art of representation in which speech, music and appropriate graceful gestures are all harmoniously blended."[44]

Tarlekar also mentions six views on the origin of Natya. The first is the traditional account given in the *Natya-Sastra*, chapter one. Here it is stated that Brahma created the *Natya-Veda* (a lost ancient text on drama) for the benefit of all the castes, since Sudras could not be instructed in the Veda. Brahma then gave the *Natya-Veda* to Bharata, who compiled the *Natya-Sastra* from it. In another account Siva had given the *Natya-Veda* to Brahma through his student Nandikesvara. It is in the *Natya-Sastra* tradition that the Trimurti (Brahma, Vishnu, Siva) emerge triumphantly as distinct divine beings responsible for the establishment of the arts: "The origin of the dramatic art goes to Brahma according to one tradition and to Siva according to the other."[45]

In *Natya-Sastra*, chapter 36.33–76, the full account of how drama came to earth is presented. Bharata's one hundred sons performed the drama in heaven but, under the effects of intoxication, offended the sages by caricature and mockery. Angry, the sages cursed the sons to become Sudras. In response the gods headed by Indra were worried that drama would hence disappear as an art form. The sons, out of sadness and desperation, threatened to kill themselves, but Bharata comforted them and told them to perform acts of purification (*prayascitta*). Meanwhile King Nahusa, who had gained heavenly status, observed the dramatic performance and subsequently desired to have these spectacles performed in his own palace on earth. Though the gods refused to lift the curse of the sages, Bharata arranged to send his sons to earth to perform the music and drama and thus lifted the curse. Bharata's sons, Kohala, Vatsya, Sandilya, Dattila, and the others were ordered to stay on earth as mortals to carry on the tradition by writing treatises and teaching.[46]

The second theory of origin claims that drama emerged out of selected dialogue passages in the Vedas. The Indologist Max Muller even suggested that a Vedic dialogue between Indra and the Maruts (storm gods) was repeated aloud or acted out with two parties in conjunction with sacrifices.[47] The dialogue hymns are regarded as precursors of the later classical drama by P. V. Kane, who had also argued for the Vedic origin of Puja. But Tarlekar had reservations about this theory: "In connection with the dialogues and monologues in the Rig-Veda, it can be reasonably said that the recitation would have been accompanied by necessary physical gesticulation. But their dramatic representation cannot be understood definitely in the absence of positive evidence."[48] A. B. Keith also held that the Vedic ritual contained the germs of drama, yet these were only that, germs.

The third theory was based on possible evidence from the epics. Though the *Ramayana* and *Mahabharata* do not reveal knowledge of Sanskrit drama, the epic and Puranic gods are nonetheless prominent in dramatic performances: "The influence of Krishna cult on the Sanskrit drama is evident. The normal prose language of the drama is Sauraseni Prakrit. It was so because it was the ordinary speech of the people among whom the drama first developed into a definite shape. Siva occupied an important place as the inventor of dance. The part of Rama is equally significant in connection with drama."[49]

The theory of its secular origin in mime, puppet-play, and shadow play, has been dismissed, despite the support of such scholars as Alfred Hillebrandt and Sten Konow. The theory of Greek influence is also untenable according to Tarlekar: "About the Greek influence in the creation of Sanskrit drama we can see that there are marked differences between the Greek drama and the Sanskrit drama. Scholars like Dr. V. Raghavan, Dr. Keith and Mr. G. Banerjee have shown that the Sanskrit drama is indigenous. The Indian drama is distinguished from the Greek drama, on account of its rich variety of dramatic form and the absence of anything like Greek tragedy and the chorus. . . . The highest influence of Hellenism in India was in the first century B.C.E. But we know that the Sanskrit drama was already well-established by that time."[50]

Regarding the last theory, the origin from dance, "the *Mahabharata* tells us that the Gandharvas and the Apsaras delighted the priests in the intervals of sacrificial rites by the arts of dance and music." Citing an account of pre-Aryan tribes in India, Tarlekar mentions the primitive drama of the Santals, in which "the role of the Goddess of the village, the god of the village and the mountain god are played by men in their flower festival." This reference to a flower festival has interesting implications for its possible tie to the role of flower sacrifices in the earliest Pujas of the *Natya-Sastra*. In Tarlekar's words, another scholar, Shri I. Shekhar, "favors the non-Aryan origin of the Sanskrit drama. According to him, Bharata was a scion of the non-Aryan family of artists who did his best to secure recognition for the members of his troupe. When Bharata felt helpless and depressed a result of the curse on the Natas, he found a non-Aryan patron in the person of Nahusa. The Nataraja Siva is the non-Aryan god. . . . In ancient India there was a fusion of Aryan and non-Aryan cultures."[51] Yet the Bharatas were an Indo-Aryan tribe mentioned in the *Rig-Veda*.

The *Natya-Sastra*, though often cited as a principal authority on ancient Indian drama and music, is seldom included in general histories of Indian religion. Little is known about the author, which may help to explain the hesitancy of many scholars to take up the serious study of the *Natya-Sastra*'s religious themes and their context within the history of Hinduism. Nonetheless, Lidova has attempted to redress this imbalance. In this text music is not described as a peripheral art but is essential to the presentation of sacred dramas and the felicitation of deities before and during the performances. The rites of Puja, including music, that are prescribed in the text are the earliest descriptions of this form of worship and are thus of great significance in understanding the development of ritual and music in Hindu tradition. The *Natya-Sastra* should also be considered as a prescriptive text for Puja, drama, and music, and not a mere description of Indian society of the times as some scholars have claimed. The term *Sastra* attached to any text indicates this difference.

By the era described in the *Natya-Sastra* (ca. mid–sixth to fifth century B.C.E.), Puja, as well as the adoration of images, was well integrated into the system of drama and scenic rites outlined by Bharata. Lidova, quite rightly, attributes the rise of icon or image worship not so much to wholesale borrowing from indigenous traditions but to developments responding to the needs of the sacred drama and the incorporation of innovative features of worship within scenic rites. Yet the primordial events outlined in the *Natya-Sastra* occur in *illo tempore*, mythical time before creation, a scenario in which sacred drama is inaugurated with the application of Puja by the gods themselves: "The mythological time of the *Natya-Sastra* combines three crucial events: the birth of the Natya, the construction of the first theater, and a Puja in it."[52] As such, the entire enterprise is rooted in religious consciousness: "With different ritual goals, all *Natya-Sastra* ceremonies demonstrated one and the same type of religious mentality, sharing ritual semantics, liturgical structure, arrangement of the sacrificial site, ritual symbolism and the manner of offering—in short, all components of which consists the conceptual basis of religious mentality."[53]

The *Natya-Sastra* describes rituals in chapters two, three, and five, which characterize three basic rites connected with the ancient Indian scenic practice: the foundation of and consecration of a theater and the Purvaranga. While the theater construction and consecration usually occurred only once, the Purvaranga was performed before every performance of a sacred drama, directed toward the gods. Music, including ritual songs known as Dhruva, was central to these rites and was regulated according to the ritual action of the Puja. The preliminary stages of the dramas were accompanied by ritual songs called Dhruvas, with rhythm, meter, and tempo clearly specified in chapter five of the *Natya-Sastra*. According to Lidova, "these detailed instructions as to the singing and instrumental accompaniment did not appear by chance. The entire Purvaranga is subjected to music, the kernel of the scenic action, the unseen director and conductor of the entire rite. At first slow, the tempo gradually quickened and became louder as the Purvaranga went on to reach its peak at the principal instant of the offering. The ritual events gained a suspense, proceeded to a climax, and then denouement in correspondence to it."[54]

The specific name for music as described in the *Natya-Sastra* and performed during the Puja and drama activities is Gandharva, or Gandharva Sangita. As explained by Lidova: "A unique, celestial music accompanying the Purvaranga belonged to the Gandharva system (NS 28.9). According to ancient Indian musicological treatises and the music sections of the *Natya-Sastra*, this music could be played only with ritual ceremonies to give the congregation a proper mood and make it part of the performance, and thus played an essential sacral role."[55] More details of Gandharva Sangita are given later.

Although the *Natya-Sastra* does not directly allude to the Purvaranga as the official rite consecrating a play, it repeatedly stresses its status as a special liturgy in Puja form that was independent of the drama. The Purvaranga was to be a Puja to gods "conducive of Dharma, fame and longevity" (NS 5.57–58). As Lidova observes, "the drama proper was separated from the Purvaranga—more than that, non-obligatory, as far as the inner ritual logic was concerned. In other words, it did not matter so much whether a play followed it or not. The ritual events were important for themselves."[56]

The author Bharata appears to be a staunch devotee of Siva, as there are several places in the text where prayers and ovations to Siva are presented. For example, NS 31.114 states: "I have come to take refuge with Hara (Siva) the terrible one, the benefactor of the three worlds, who is worshipped as the Lord God by the gods, and to whose feet Daityas and Yaksas bow down."[57] Verses 115 and 116 contain longer prayers to Siva.

As a preliminary to each drama, the Purvaranga was composed of two parts: part one was performed on stage with the main curtain closed, and part two was performed before the audience with the curtain open. Part one ends with the *Gitavidhi* hymn in honor of the gods (NS 5.17–21). The sections of each part indicate how music and dance were integrated within the structure of the ceremony as a sonic liturgy.

Part I

Pratyahara—the opening, offered to Nagas and Raksasas
Avatarana—offering to Apsaras
Arambha—vocal exercises for Gandharvas
Asravana—tuning of instruments, offering to Danavas
Vaktrapani—rehearsal of manners, offered to Danavas
Parighattana—tightening strings to the desired sound, for Raksasas
Samghotana—manual gestures to indicate rhythm, for Guhyakas
Margasarita—sound of strings merged with the drums, for Yaksas
Gitavidhi—hymn in honor of all the gods

Part II

Ten Obligatory Episodes
Madraka or Vardhamanaka type of song for Rudra, with dance
Utthapana; raising of the Jarjara, Indra's banner and weapon, which protected the Natya from demons
Parivartana; in honor of the Lokapalas, protectors of the world and the four directions
Nandi; hymn to the gods, Brahmins and the king, was said in honor of Soma
Suskapakrsta; in honor of the Pitrs, ancestors

Rangadvara; praise in honor of Vishnu
Cari; expressed Shringara Rasa in honor of Uma
Mahacari; Raudra Rasa in service to Siva
Trigata; conversation between Sutradhara and assistants
Prarocana; praised the drama, hinted at the plot

The initial part of the Purvaranga ceremony was meant to elevate the scenic action above the everyday reality of the profane world and give it a universal sacral meaning. As explained by Lidova, "the sacral message of the Puja signified the acquisition of supreme cosmic harmony, directly linked to the harmonization of the integrated scenic space, brought into order beforehand—to all appearances, through the special solemnity of ritual postures, music, measured movement and the beauty of white lotuses spread on the floor. During the Puja, the performers were supposed to be the closest to the supra-personal world. The ritual replica of the Universe on the stage was considered merged with its cosmic prototype." As such, the Purvaranga started with the worship of Brahma by establishing the Brahma Mandala, which was equivalent to the center of the universe. Subsequently "the *Natya-Sastra* connected the following ascent of scenic sacrality with the worship of the three supreme gods, Siva, Brahma and Vishnu, in neuter, male and female hypostases."[58]

The Sutradhara was the architect, masterbuilder, leader of the plays, and chief priest of Purvaranga. Since the stage as yet had no special ritual symbol to be identified with a deity worshipped in the Puja, the ritual officer Sutradhara "assumed this part, as flowers were heaped at his feet. By communicating with the supra-personal world throughout the Purvaranga, he increased his own sacrality by posing as a visual embodiment of a god in the Puja."[59] The high point of recognition and veneration of each of the gods was the flower sacrifice, for flower sacrifices concerned all deities of the Hindu pantheon. Aside from the Sutradhara and the gods, the Puja honored the Jarjara, Indra's banner staff, as well as the musical instruments. The *Natya-Sastra* gave a mythological substantiation to Jarjara worship, since the Jarjara was the first ritual symbol visually present on stage. The veneration of the art of music through its instruments places music in a central ritual position: "The worship of musical instruments—other Puja objects—in the flower sacrifice, clearly shows that the performers were aware of the key ritual function of music."[60]

Music was indeed crucial both to replicating the structure of the cosmos on earth and to sustaining human society against the always possible decline into chaos. In Lidova's words, "the exceptional importance attached by the *Natya-Sastra* to the music played throughout the Purvaranga makes us suggest that the tunes and songs had not so much an outer decorative as concrete ritual goal: they brought concord into the spatial and temporal characteristics of the cosmic model on stage. . . . Most probably, the musical harmony gave an earthly manifestation to the cosmic order and protected the organized world from chaos."[61]

From a comparative perspective in liturgical studies, the Indian role of music in drama reenactment may be successfully juxtaposed with Western models: "The Purvaranga, as appealing to a wealth of Hindu myths, was universal and autonomous enough—a cyclic liturgy which demanded regular re-enactment and, in the ritual typological aspect, resembled nothing closer than Christian liturgies. As a regular rite, it not so much precluded or consecrated a drama as worshipped gods in a specific form, the Puja, accompanied with the Natya. In this sense, the Purvaranga-Natya correlation is typologically comparable to the relation between the liturgy and the liturgical drama, which existed in the Christian ecclesiastical practice."[62]

The full description given in the *Natya-Sastra* of the Puja surrounding the construction and consecration of a new theater provides even more insight with regard to the primordial bond between Puja, sacred drama, and ritual music associated with Hindu deities. The close connection with sacred architecture is also recalled: "The playhouse originally had a templar status and manifold sacral functions centered round the Puja and ritual drama. . . . The *Natya-Sastra* allows us to assume that the templar Puja practice with the accompanying Natya emerged in the earliest days of sacral architecture."[63] In fact the *Natya-Sastra* never treats the theater as a mere secular building intended for entertainment of the laity: "a theater is Brahma's creation, an abode of gods and the site for Puja—in other words, a purely sacral building analogous to a temple."[64] Moreover, the god Visvakarman, the divine architect of the universe, was believed to have built the first playhouse.

The specific Puja for theater consecration in the *Natya-Sastra* had three parts.

1. Mystical protection: Through special prayers and Puja, the Sutradhara created a unique sacral space analogous to the universe as substantiated and given by Brahma.
2. Consecration of the stage: The visible Mandala representing the universe, the abode of all the gods, was drawn on the stage by the Sutradhara. This was the longest Puja in the *Natya-Sastra,* with extensive offerings to the Trimurti, followed by a special liturgy to sanctify the stage.
3. Puja to all gods, musical instruments, and the Jarjara: Flower sacrifice to the Jarjara consecrated this divine weapon by tying it with multicolored fabrics to mark the abodes of Brahma, Siva, Vishnu, Skanda, and the Nagas to the sounds of a mantra invoking them to their appointed places: "Consecration made the Jarjara not so much Indra's weapon as an analogue of the arbor

mundi [Cosmic Tree Pillar], with the top in the highest spheres and roots reaching the underworld—the status it had in the Purvaranga."[65]

Natya-Sastra, chapter 3, describes the Puja to all the gods after the theater has been constructed. The seating arrangement in the Brahma Mandala for the Puja is given in NS 3.23–30.[66] Once the various deities were placed on stage, they were offered incense, garlands, and unguents. All received ointments and flower garlands. The concrete references to material forms of the deities point to the inauguration of Murti-Puja taking place within the scenic rites of the *Natya-Sastra* traditions: "The characteristics of supreme deities . . . presuppose actual sculptures, in particular, 'Brahma seated on a lotus' in a posture which clearly points to the widespread Indian iconography of the god who, according to tradition, was born of a lotus flower. To all appearances, all the other gods mentioned in the treatise were also represented by ritual statuary."[67]

The *Natya-Sastra* required that the priest arrange the statues of Siva, Vishnu Narayana, Indra, Skanda, Sarasvati, Lakshmi, Agni, Yama, Mitra, and other gods around Brahma in eight sectors oriented on and between the four cardinal points. In correct order "the image of the god to whom the temple was consecrated was the first to take its place, in the center of the edifice. Next, sculptures of other gods were placed to its four sides, oriented on the cardinal points. The ceremony ended with equal intervals measured out to arrange other holy images midway between the cardinal points." This requirement allows us to assume with a high degree of certainty that scenic ritualism incorporated divine images as objects of worship. Consequently "the *Natya-Sastra*, as the Agamic treatises, records a syncretic cult which demanded not only the worship of an unseen god materialized only in worshippers' imagination but ritual adoration of his physical form open to visual perception."[68]

The breakaway from the Vedic sacrifice to the realm of Puja entailed much more complexity than may be assumed from the rather clear-cut distinctions outlined above. In fact the multitude of overlap between Vedic tradition and indigenous culture appeared almost seamless in many instances. For example, there was a close affinity between the Jarjara staff and the Yupa, the Vedic sacrificial pillar erected in the ceremonial rites: "They looked exactly alike—long wooden poles made in a special way—and had analogous ritual functions: The Yupa and Jarjara as one and the same ritual symbol common to the *Natya-Sastra* and Vedic rites. . . . They shared not only the cult mission but the ritual semantics."[69] In addition many of the priestly preparations and activities were similar for Vedic and *Natya-Sastra* rites: fasting, ablutions, wearing new robes, sprinkling water to purify areas, chanting of mantras in Sanskrit, cooking of sanctified food, observances of astrological signs in determining rituals according to season and time.

The Homa fire sacrifice, performed in the royal rite of the *Natya-Sastra*, was also inherited by the Agamic tradition from Vedic culture without essential change and continued to be prominent in Hindu rites: "The Agamas provide numerous descriptions of Homa varieties with flaming braziers brought to the sacrificial site. Like in the Vedic era, *ghee*, melted butter, and milk were poured into the consecrated flame, and grain and other food thrown—all this to mantra recitals. . . . All features of Vedic ritualism revealed in the *Natya-Sastra* rites are present in Hindu ones. In fact, this is one more proof of the close link between Agamic and scenic Puja."[70]

Another major change of direction in the classical period involved the issue of the Vedic Soma sacrifices and rituals. By the time the Vedic culture had blended together with Puja rites, scenic rituals, and accompanying Gandharva music, the Soma cult, the core of Aryan liturgical rites, had virtually disappeared: "The system of the Puja adopted the rites that were only in the background of the hierarchy of the Brahmana texts and secondary in the religious system of the Yajna, whereas the Soma offering—the heart of Vedic ritualism—went into oblivion." The Puja with its concomitant flower sacrifices had all but replaced the need for Soma plant preparation and offerings: "The main goal of the Puja was to oust Soma libations, whose practice died away in the post-Vedic era."[71] The flexibility of the concept of sonic liturgy is portrayed here with the abandonment of certain features and the adoption of others.

The transition from the textual descriptions of deities in the Vedas to their actualization in the form of statues or icons is most visible in the process of dramatization in the *Natya-Sastra*. Lidova makes the argument that it was the actors in full costume and their roles as gods that spawned the process of image making and deity veneration. She states that "paintings and sculptures of gods, most probably, received their attire, make-up and postures from actors who played gods. . . . Sculptures of Hindu gods on temple facades have poses described in the *Natya-Sastra*. . . . Instead of imitating iconographies from static images which appeared out of the blue no one knows when, the stage, with its sophisticated tradition of enacting Hindu myths, produced sets of divine features later fixed in paintings and statuary. . . . It was easy to go over from scenic images, with their fixed costumes, hairdos and coloring, to more lasting likenesses—statues."[72] In fact, the dramatic portrayals in Natya provided the raw impetus for the standardized representations in material form: "Make-up, costumes and other expressive means known in the stage world sufficed to create highly individualized and at the same time conventional image of any deity."[73]

With these facts in place, we can establish with some degree of certitude the evolution of Hindu temple worship and the veneration of images as derived, at least partly, from the tendency to dramatize the myths of the gods through theatrical representation. As Lidova concludes, "in the final analysis, this evolution conditioned the appearance of anthropomorphous images of gods as repeating the symbolism of actors' costumes, movement and make-up. The coherent performance of the flower sacrifice and the scenic myth alone can explain why the playhouse known from the *Natya-Sastra* was at the same time referred to as the first temple for Puja offerings in the legend." The religious dimension of the drama served to establish archetypal images and modes of being that were later codified in the Puja rites and in the Agamic texts: "At first, gods acted in the flesh only in the ritual drama, which had particular techniques to represent them. Step by step, these techniques grew to be treated as a way to communicate with the suprapersonal world. So they found their way to the rites connected with dramatic performances, and later into the Agamic forms of the Puja."[74]

Once established in the Agamas, the protocols associated with worship were solidified over many centuries until the present time, as Hindus still acknowledge the multiple ways in which the divine may be manifested: "Characteristically, self-identification with a divine being through conventional poses and gestures not merely became an Agamic sacred practice but survived to this day in the many forms of Hindu ritualism." To this end Hindus attest to all three forms of earthly manifestation of the divine power: "Three kinds of divine incarnation—through the actor in the drama, through the priest performing the Puja, and through the sculptor as he worked with stone, wood or metal—share a symbolism and appeal to one system of ritual ideas."[75]

While the singing of Sama-Gana was a prevalent part of the Vedic sonic liturgy, the transition into scenic ritualism and Puja provided the more suitable venue for the incorporation of classical music, initially termed Gandharva Sangita, into new forms of sonic liturgy. Although the Puja received influences from Vedic ritualism, other elements arose, in Lidova's words, from "independent efforts of pious creativity—especially the singing, music, dancing, its specific movements, conventional poses and precise iconic gestures which were the symbolical bases of the sacred rite rather than decorations of the Puja. Unknown in the Vedic ritualism, all these innovations have a pronounced scenic nature. As we see it, nothing but a long parallel evolution of the rite and the ritual drama could make the sacral techniques of the Puja so close to scenic expressive means."[76] The role of Gandharva music became central to the mutual development of sacred drama and Puja, such that Pujas and temple Hinduism in general required music as did theater productions: "Another trait that brought together the Agamic and scenic worship was obligatory musical accompaniment with instruments, ritual singing and dancing."[77] The ancient dramatic texts such as the *Natya-Sastra* as well as the *Dattilam* contain our earliest descriptions of Gandharva music, which was well interlinked with scenic rites and Puja.

GANDHARVA SANGITA

Gandharva Sangita ("celestial music"), or simply Gandharva, was the courtly or royal counterpart to the Vedic Sama-Gana that came to full form during the classical period of Sanskrit drama, as recounted in the *Natya-Sastra* and the *Dattilam.* In ancient times all classical music was indicated by the word *Gandharva.* This held true up until the time of Sarngadeva (thirteenth century), at which time music was referred to simply as Sangita or Gita and had become detached from the drama tradition.

As a gift from the gods, Gandharva Sangita was considered similar in kind to the music performed and enjoyed in Lord Indra's court in Svarga, or heaven. Viewed as a replica of heavenly archetypes, this ancient religious music was primarily vocal but included instruments such as the Vina (harp or zither), flutes, drums and cymbals. While the Gandharvas, as a group or as individual musicians, are not mentioned in the *Rig-Veda,* they appear in an abundance of references in the epics and Puranas. Therein, the celestial performers of Gandharva (ancient music) were known as the Gandharvas, a class of male singers and gods led by Narada Rishi, the mythical son of Brahma who resided in heaven but was capable of journeying throughout the universe. The Gandharvas were accompanied by their wives, the dancing Apsaras, and by the Kinnaras, players of musical instruments. All of the arts, including vocal music, dance, and instrumental music, were considered divine, being performed by divine beings. Besides authoring seven hymns in the *Rig-Veda* (and the *Sama-Veda*), Narada Rishi was believed to be the inventor of the Vina and the sage who instructed human beings in Gandharva Sangita, having learned it from the goddess Sarasvati who had received it from Brahma himself. Yet in some accounts Siva is the original instructor of sacred music to Brahma.

Complex rules and regulations governing scales, rhythms, and instrumental styles of Gandharva music were said to have been set down in very early texts known collectively as the *Gandharva-Veda,* an auxiliary work attached to the *Sama-Veda.* Because these ancient works are lost, including the original *Natya-Veda,* the oldest surviving Sanskrit texts of Indian music are the *Natya-Sastra* by Bharata and the *Dattilam* by Dattila (both ca. 400–100 B.C.E.). These works, as well as the *Naradiya-Siksa* (first century B.C.E. in its final form), provide information on Gandharva Sangita and provide literary evidence of the sophisticated musical thought in ancient India. Gandharva Sangita was intimately connected with drama, as confirmed by Sarmadee: "Natya, Pathya and Gana all went together those days, and music of the time happened to be dance-drama-dominated."[78]

Alain Danielou, the Western savant of Indian music, praised the rise of Indian music theory as a groundbreaking event. In *Introduction to the Study of Musical Scales* (1943), he stated: "Since the remotest antiquity there has existed in India, besides a general theory of sounds, a theory of musical modes which seems to have been the source from which all systems of modal music originated. The Hindu theory is not, like other systems, limited to experimental data; it does not consider arbitrarily as natural certain modes or certain chords, but it takes as its starting point the general laws common to all the aspects of the world's creation." The ancient Indians were true theorists in that they experimented with various scales and tunings, just like the Greeks. But music for the Hindus, as we have seen, begins with strong theological or metaphysical premises: "Starting from metaphysical principles, the Hindus have re-created the theory of sounds. They have analyzed and classified all the possible ratios and relations between sounds. The result is, obviously, an astronomical number of theoretical chords, modes and combinations, of which few only are utilized in practice; the others, however, remain accessible for the day when new conditions, or the inspiration of musicians, may require new modes or new musical forms."[79]

While ancient Indian classical music is initially known as Gandharva, it is later referred to as simply Sangita ("well-formed song"): "In ancient times music is indicated by the word Gandharva. By later authors, however, it is called Gita or Samgita."[80] Sangita, however, is defined as having three divisions: vocal music, instrumental music, and dance. All three have usually been intertwined, whether in religious observances, in sacred dramas, or in courtly entertainment, though in modern times music has fully emerged in its own right. As a word with the *sam-* prefix, *Sangita* (Sam-Gita) conforms to the Vedic ritualistic notion of rebuilding or reassembling the cosmos that initially began in an imperfect state. Sangita thus serves this end by combining the musical and performative arts into a viable unit that is an instrument for cosmic and spiritual reunification within the context of sonic liturgy.

Gandharva Sangita was not simply one of India's ancient musical forms; it was the form-supreme. It was said to be born of the Saman singing of the *Sama-Veda* (*Dattilam* 222): "In this way the vocal music, which originated from the Sama-Veda, was sung by the wise (Rishi, plural)."[81] Seven other kinds of songs developed from this music, referred to here as Gita (see NS 1.17: "He [Brahma] took the vocal music from the songs of the Sama-Veda").

Gandharva Sangita was as sacrosanct as Sama-Gana and emerged as the primal body of music of India to which can be related our own present-day musical forms. Gandharva has even been called the progenitor of all subsequent musical forms by Indian musicologist Mukund Lath: "The process of unfoldment and creative change which was initiated with Gandharva in our musical culture has continued over the centuries and is still alive in current music. . . . Much that is distinctive of all post-Gandharva music is, in essence, existent in Gandharva."[82] Remarkably, in the text of the *Dattilam* the musical terminology associated with Gandharva-Sangita is almost precisely the same as used today in classical music instruction: *svara*—note; *pada*—words; *tala*—time measurement; *sruti*—micro-intervals; *grama*—tone-system; *murchana*—scale; *tana*—series of notes; *sthana*—register; *vritti*—style; *suska*—instrumental music; *sadharana*—overlapping; *jati*—mode; *varna*—ornamentation; *alankara*—grace; *mandra*—lower register; *madhya*—middle register; *tara*—higher register; *dhvani*—musical sound.[83]

While the Sama-Gana singers were connected with sacrifice, the Gandharvas were professional singers or musicians who were nonetheless bound with religion. Svara (notes and melody), Pada (words and lyric), and Tala (beats and rhythm) were the three principal constituents of Gandharva music, as defined by both the *Natya-Sastra* and the *Dattilam*, a near-contemporary work of immense significance in studying ancient music. Lath explains the spiritual significance of Gandharva music as a body of music that was pervaded by a transcendental significance not only in spirit but in every detail of its melodic (Jati, later "Raga") and rhythmic (Tala) content as well: "Every movement in Gandharva, whether of melody or of Tala, was sacrosanct and had to be rendered as prescribed by specific injunctions which spelled out each particular detail. Recording these prescriptions was the function of authoritative manuals like the *Dattilam*. Gandharva was thus akin to religiously prescribed and liturgically regulated musical forms such as were known in ancient Egypt and other ancient cultures. It reflected the same tendency which has been preserved to a great extent in the Gregorian chant of Europe. It was a body of music the like of which we no longer know in India."[84]

The practice of Gandharva Sangita was devoutly and diligently maintained as a distinct form of music for many centuries and occupies a unique position in the history of Indian culture as a link between Sama-Gana and current classical music. According to Lath, it merits close and detailed study by scholars of religion and music: "Gandharva, historically speaking, occupied a crucial position. It arose from Sama and in turn gave rise to those later forms which have come down to the present through transformations and transitions. To know Gandharva will thus help us to understand later musical forms in a historical perspective and will also provide a key to their links with tradition as well as a cue to the nature of change. Gandharva thus stands as a doorway between the now extinct Saman and subsequent musical forms. To know and distinguish Gandharva can provide many handy clues to a historian of music."[85]

Gandharva Sangita was believed to be more efficacious than other forms of religious observance, including recitation of the names of God on beads (Japa). The *Natya-Sastra* had stated (NS 36.27): "I have heard from the god of gods

(Indra) and afterwards from Sankara (Siva) that music vocal as well as instrumental, is in fact a thousand times superior to bath [in holy waters] and to Japa."[86]

In line with the principle of apotropaia (see the introduction, above), playing Gandharva Sangita also had the power to remove evil forces and sin: "Just as injury by weapons is warded off by armor, or sin wiped away by sacrifice, so sins in the form of obstacles are to be removed by worshipping gods, by praising gods, by benediction, by describing peace of mind, by the resounding playing of musical instruments, by the sound of singing."[87] In fact, Gandharva warded off all demons and inauspiciousness: "In so much space as is filled with sound of musical instruments there will be there no Raksasas [demons] or leaders of Vighnas [NS 36.24]. . . . In places in which there occur instrumental music and dramatic performance, or song and instrumental music, there will surely be there never any kind of inauspicious happening [NS 36.28]."[88]

The musical scale employed in Gandharva Sangita utilized a different pattern from that of Sama-Gana. The original descending *Sama-Veda* scale was gradually recast into a new ascending and descending seven-note structure in Gandharva Sangita. Still employed today, the seven notes of the standard Indian scale are labeled (in Sanskrit) *sa ri ga ma pa dha ni* (cf. C D E F G A B of the Western diatonic scale). These appear in both the *Natya-Sastra* and the *Dattilam* (11–15). In *Dattilam* 15 the term used for the seven notes (*svara-saptak*) is Svara-Mandala—circle of notes.[89] This usage resonates well with the term *Mandala* in the *Natya-Sastra* as a circle of the gods in the preliminary Puja rituals.

Establishing Vedic continuity with these seven notes was not far behind. In the *Naradiya-Siksa* (first century B.C.E. but perhaps older than *Natya-Sastra* in its original form), Narada (an historical person, not the Vedic Rishi), explained how these seven notes were directly determined from the original three Vedic accents: Udatta into *ni* and *ga*, Anudatta into *ri* and *dha*, and Svarita into *sa*, *ma* and *pa*. The seven notes are also named here, metaphorically, after the sounds of different birds and animals: *sa*/peacock, *ri*/bull, *ga*/ram, *ma*/crane, *pa*/cuckoo, *dha*/horse, *ni*/elephant.[90] The F *(ma)* may be raised, and the notes D E A B (*ri ga dha ni*) may be lowered (like the Western sharp and flat notes, respectively) to create multiple variations of scale formulas, while the tonic C *(sa)* and the dominant G *(pa)* generally remain fixed. The term *Raga*, as a special set of notes with a unique character or mood containing aesthetic elements associated with Rasa, was derived from the Jati scale-formulas of *Natya-Sastra* and *Dattilam*.

In the *Natya-Sastra*, about nine chapters have been dedicated to Gandharva music, both vocal and instrumental. The author describes each Svara (a musical note) and its use in expressing a particular aesthetic sense, that is, Rasa. Gandharva music is said to be derived from the *Sama-Veda*, since seven notes were already established in Sama-Gana. The chapters of *Natya-Sastra* on Gandharva

Sangita are of equal stature with the Puja sections and must also be considered ritual or liturgical texts: "Not only the sections on the scenic Puja canon should be regarded as ritual texts but, at least, in the main, chapters on Gandharva music, dancing, dance poses, and gesticular symbols and techniques. Worship with postures, gestures, songs, music and dancing belongs to features shared by Agamic and scenic rites. At the same time, the Hindu ritual system allows to single out features common to all three worship practices under review—the Vedic sacrifice Yajna, *Natya-Sastra* rites and the Agamic Puja."[91]

Bharata (NS 28.1) had classified musical instruments into four categories based on the Gandharva instruments: 1) stringed instruments called Tata; 2) wind-blown instruments called Sushira; 3) percussion instruments called Avanaddha; and 4) cymbals called Ghana.[92] This fourfold classification of instruments has survived in the modern Sachs-Hornbostel system, created in 1914, and still used in ethnomusicology today. This classification consists of chordophones or stringed instruments, aerophones or air-driven instruments, membranophones or skin-covered instruments, and idiophones or self-sounding instruments.

Natya-Sastra chapter 31 is entitled "On the Instruments of Time-Measure." The measurement of rhythm was deemed extremely important in Gandharva music, as it paralleled the counting of syllables in Vedic mantra recitation. Out of all percussion instruments, the cymbals appear to have been given the most emphasis, as they provide the most distinct and accurate manifestation of time measure. Sarmadee explains with reference to the text itself: "The *Natya-Sastra* classifies these [percussion instruments] as Ghana, giving a representative status to the percussion instrument Tala [cymbal], assigning every significance to the art of its correct handling. This seems to put it straight that a cymbalist was the main Taladhari [counter of time measure] those days. Possibly the term Tala, meaning time measure itself, may have had something to do with this on the most intimate level. This renders the instrument rather basic."[93]

The awareness of the significance of cymbals in ancient forms of musical time measure makes a contribution toward a deeper understanding of the wide prevalence of cymbals in the devotional music (Bhakti Sangit) of the medieval and modern periods. This importance is reaffirmed by Sarmadee: "The implications are to be adequately appreciated that of all other instruments, the Ghana, and then a particular variety of it, namely Tala, acted as almost the sole guardians of rhythm, during the age represented by the *Natya-Sastra*. This is bound to mean much for any historical survey of facts concerning the evolution of art-music in India."[94] The fact that cymbals were associated with special songs in the vernacular called Dhruva in the *Natya-Sastra* also speaks to the search for an understanding of the prevalence of Dhrupad vernacular songs in Bhakti Sangit.

Bharata gives many details about the Dhruva songs used in the drama to propitiate the gods and facilitate the drama performance. The definition of Dhruva is given in NS 32.8: "The Dhruva is so-called, because in it words, *varnas* [syllables], *alankara* [ornaments], tempo, Jati [melody] and *panis* are regularly (*dhruvam*) connected with one another."[95] Dhruvas are thus rigidly constructed songs that required adherence to principles of melody, rhythm, and linguistic conventions of meter. NS 32.36 states: "Those (Padas) which are regularly composed in pursuance of the [rule of] syllables in a meter, are called the Dhruvas."[96]

Dhruvas were primarily rendered in Prakrit, not in Sanskrit. While Sanskrit refers to the refined and polished language, often artificial, of the gods and Brahmins, Prakrit refers to the natural, unrefined, ordinary language of the common people that had less rigid grammatical construction. An entire chapter of *Natya-Sastra* (chapter 32) is devoted to the Dhruva songs, indicating the great importance that they held in the traditions of Puja, drama, and early music. NS 32.440 states: "The language in the application of Dhruvas should be Suraseni [Prakrit]. Sometimes it may be Magadhi when [the Dhruvas of] the Natkuta [class] are to be made by the wise." The distinction between Sanskrit and Prakrit is clearly made with regard to dramatic presentation in NS 32.441, which states: "Sanskrit songs have been prescribed by the authorities in case of heavenly beings; and in case of human beings half-Sanskrit [songs] should be used."[97] The "half-Sanskrit" songs are called Ardha-Sanskrit, or a mixture of Sanskrit and Prakrit. In the section NS 32.56–354 more than 116 examples of songs in Prakrit in various meters are given, including many classes of Vedic meters which are applied to Prakrit songs, including Gayatri, Anustubh, Tristubh, Brihati, Jagati, Pankti, and others.

In order to appreciate the parallel worlds of Sanskrit and Prakrit, the recent work of Wendy Doniger is helpful. She describes the process of adopting local and regional dialects into brahmanical traditions as "Deshification." Deshification is the flipside of Sanskritization, the adoption of Sanskrit words and structural components into regional traditions. According to her, the exchange has always been a two-way street: "The opposite of Sanskritization, the process by which the Sanskritic tradition simultaneously absorbs and transforms those same popular traditions, is equally important, and that process might be called oralization, or popularization, or even, perhaps, Deshification (from the 'local' or Deshi traditions). . . . The two processes beget each other."[98]

The earliest inscriptions in India were in fact Prakrit (Pillar Edicts of Emperor Asoka, ca. 265 B.C.E.), and there has always been a vibrant Prakrit literary tradition alongside that of Sanskrit. As such, Prakrit did not "derive" from Sanskrit as is commonly held by many South Asianists, but most likely formed a substratum from which Sanskrit emerged fully formed. Doniger has explained that

> it must have been the case that the natural language, Prakrit, and the vernaculars came first, while Sanskrit, the refined, secondary revision, the artificial language, came later. But South Asianists often seem to assume that it is the other way around, that the dialects are "derived from Sanskrit" because it won the race to the archives and was the first to be written down and preserved, and we only encounter vernaculars much later. So we say that Sanskrit is older, and the vernaculars younger. But Sanskrit, the language of power, emerged in India from a minority, and at first its power came precisely from its non-intelligibility and unavailability, which made it the power of an elite group.

A point that has been rarely affirmed by scholars, yet with which common sense would agree, is that whoever spoke Sanskrit in the ancient world must have also spoken a regional language associated with his or her place of birth: "Many priests and scholars can speak Sanskrit, but no one ever spoke only pure Sanskrit. Sanskrit and oral traditions flow back and forth, producing a constant infusion of lower-class words and ideas into the Brahmin world, and vice versa."[99]

Like the Vedic chant, Dhruvas had to be metrical, as confirmed in NS 32.432: "The words of a song cannot be without meter. Hence after considering [the contents of] the Dhruva song, one should put it in a suitable meter."[100] NS 32.482 affirms the overall importance of Dhruva songs for the drama: "Without any song, the drama does not attain [the capacity of giving] joy."[101]

The prominent use of Prakrit songs in the early dramas gradually led to the dominance of vernacular dialects in Indian classical and devotional music. As such, the Dhruva was most probably the prototype of the medieval genre of Prabandha which was the basis of classical devotional forms sung in vernacular, called Dhrupad (Dhruvapada) in the North and Kriti in the South. The rapidly developing music of India also expanded to include materials from outside the original repertoire.

DATTILAM OF DATTILA

Beside the *Natya-Sastra*, the *Dattilam* is the most important ancient treatise on Gandharva Sangita. The *Dattilam* is a very short work of 243 verses composed by the sage Dattila. A single manuscript published in 1930 is believed to be authentic (see Sastri, K. Sambasiva, ed. 1930). Many scholars opine that *Dattilam* must have been a larger work, with material on dance and theater, but Mukund Lath rejects these claims, stating that "we think that there are sufficient grounds to believe that the *Dattilam*, as extant, is a work complete in itself and is found in its original form; that it is of a fairly early date and represents a tradition independent of the *Natya-Sastra* in many respects, though parallel to it."[102] But since the author Dattila is listed in the *Natya-Sastra* as a son of Bharata who was sent to conduct dramas on earth, we may safely assume that Gandharva Sangita was intimately connected with drama from the beginning and that *Dattilam* was originally a text on music and drama.

Dutch scholar E. Wiersma-Te Nijenhuis, in *Dattilam: A Compendium of Ancient Indian Music* (1970), pioneered the study of the *Dattilam* with a translation of the text and a full commentary citing many other Indian sources. Nijenhuis believes that the *Dattilam* is later than the *Natya-Sastra* yet is closely connected and even modeled upon it. The author Dattila, if not a son, was perhaps a disciple of Bharata. The very first verse of the *Dattilam* lays down the subject of Gandharva, the ancient term for classical music: "After having paid honor to the Great Lord [Siva], and to Brahma and other gods, and also to the teachers, I shall give a brief exposition of the theory of music (Gandharva-Sastra), which considers only the most essential things." The second verse indicates the process whereby Gandharva was transmitted to Narada and then to humans: "In the very beginning music (Gandharva) was given by the Self-Existing One (Svayambhu [Brahma]) to Narada and the other Gandharvas. Then, it was duly taken down to the earth by Narada."[103]

In the third verse of *Dattilam*, Gandharva Sangita is precisely defined: "A collection of notes (Svara), which is based on words (Pada), which is well-measured by time-measurement (Tala) and which is executed with attentiveness, is called music (Gandharva)."[104] This definition is basically the same as that which is found in NS 28.8.

APURVA AND ADRISHTA

The historical traditions of Gandharva Sangita, as outlined in both *Dattilam* and *Natya-Sastra* and despite being more practically associated with Puja and sacred drama, came to share an important technical ritual dimension with the Vedic sacrifice as interpreted by Mimamsa philosophy. In the Yajna sacrifices correct pronunciation and performance of the rites guaranteed success and even entrance into heaven. This goal was realized through the principle of merit accumulation within the mind or soul of the practitioner over a lifetime of ritual activity on earth. Though the rites would finish, the intangible result derived from its execution remained invisible to the performer, only to be reclaimed after death in the form of a heavenly reward. The original notion was evident in NS 31.370, where it is stated that "songs and instrumental music [performed in] the worship of gods, [bring] limitless merit [Punya]."[105]

This notion of merit or Punya was advanced and developed from within the context of Vedic sacrifice and transformed into the more sophisticated theory of Apurva or Adrishta by the philosophical school of Mimamsa. This school held that the unseen results of sacrifice were believed to be transferred to the soul of the performer only to be reclaimed after death. This theory permeated Mimamsa linguistics and especially the practice of mantra recitation, where there was believed to be a quantified accumulation of meaning/merit via chanted syllables. The monistic school of Advaita Vedanta had rejected all of these ideas in favor of the view of Bhartrihari and Sphota theory whereby meaning inhered in the entire sentence construction rather than individual syllables. The various linguistic schools and their differences have been discussed in chapter three of the present author's earlier work, *Sonic Theology: Hinduism and Sacred Sound.* What is most significant here is that the musical tradition of theistic worship, beginning with Gandharva Sangita and continuing to Bhakti Sangit, appears to be well aligned with the Mimamsa theory of Apurva or Adrishta. In the music traditions, however, the accumulation of invisible merit by both the musician and the listener was conveyed not through the ritual units of sacrifice but through the rhythmic units or beats (Matras) that were measured by the playing of cymbals or drums. The result was the same: Svarga (heaven) or Moksha. This invisible principle continued to underlie the sacredness of music governed by measured rhythm up to current times.

Indications of the early soteriological parallel between Gandharva music and Mimamsa interpretations of Vedic ritual have appeared in recent scholarship. Solveig McIntosh, in her study of ancient Indian music, *Hidden Faces of Ancient Indian Song* (2005), states that,

> in general, all formalized music was known as Gandharva and was even considered a secondary Veda. More specifically, it meant music that was intended for Adrishta Phala, for obtaining the unseen result, for religious merit or praising the gods. This was a highly grammatical music and in the *Natya-Sastra* [of Bharata] was used in a specific sense. The main components of Gandharva were Svara, Tala, and Pada (tone, time, and word or syllable) with specific rules for obtaining unseen spiritual results. Vocal music, Vina and the flute formed the triad of Gandharva music with the main emphasis on vocal music and with Vina and flute lending a special harmony.[106]

The direct correlation between the sacrificial Apurva or Adrishta and the accumulation of unseen merit in Gandharva music was first expounded in 1978 by Mukund Lath in his *A Study of Dattilam:* "A properly performed Vedic sacrifice was said to result in Adrishta (or Apurva, a concept synonymous with Adrishta). The same belief existed regarding Gandharva. Gandharva was in fact a Gana-Yajna ['musical sacrifice']—a sacrifice with musical movements, taking the place of the usual rites. As in a Yaga [Yajna], each specific musical movement (which was here analogous to a rite) was to be performed strictly according to injunctions; the true adherence to the enjoined rules led to Adrishta."[107]

Parallel to the Vedic theory of sacrifice, the performers of drama and music "earned" their way to heaven or to Moksha through correct performance: "Gandharva was not only immutable like the Vedic mantras, its performance was not unlike the performance of a Vedic sacrifice." Like Vedic sacrifices, "Gandharva was governed by strict commands regarding do's and don'ts. Every movement in it had to strictly follow the injunctions or vidhis laid down for it. These injunctions were preserved in the manuals on Gandharva (such as the *Dattilam*). . . . A properly performed Vedic sacrifice was said to result in Adrishta (or Apurva, a concept synonymous with Adrishta). The same belief existed regarding Gandharva." Since it adopted the principle of Adrishta, Gandharva music was prescriptive for the attainment of heaven: "Apurva or Adrishta is a concept elaborated by the Mimamsakas and is intrinsically connected with the liturgical spirit behind the performance of Vedic rites and sacrifices. The goal of Vedic sacrifices is the attainment of heaven, hence such ancient injunctions as . . . one desirous of heaven should perform sacrifices."[108]

In reply to reservations about the idea of a delayed reward of sacrifices, Lath explains how the energy, or Sakti, of the rite accrued to the performer of the rites: "Yagas generate a certain transcendental power or Sakti which remains even when the Yaga is over and has become non-existent. It is this Sakti, accruing to the performer of a Yaga, which at the appropriate time results in heaven. This Sakti was named Apurva (= Adrishta)."[109]

Gandharva Sangita as the primary form of ancient Indian music was essentially vocal. It employed as its main percussion instrument the Jhanjh, hand cymbals, to demarcate the Matras, or rhythmic units of Tala, as they unfolded. While there are classical forms today that have eliminated cymbals in their performance (for example, Hindustani Dhrupad, Khyal and Thumri), hand cymbals are still used in India for purely religious music or Bhakti Sangit and especially in Haveli Sangit and Samaj Gayan. But one may easily suspect that, even without cymbals, the marking of musical time with any percussion instrument (that is, Tabla or other drums) would generate Adrishta Phala (unseen merit). This may certainly be argued, but Lath stresses that the text bears witness to the singular importance of cymbals in the accumulation of merit: "A distinct feature of Gandharva Tala was the peculiar nature of the instrument used. Tala measures were demarcated chiefly by sounding bronze cymbals. To this day in India, the Jhanjh and Manjira (large and small bronze cymbals) are specifically connected with music in a religious or devotional setting."[110] While Lath has not elaborated on these types of music, we claim that similar notions of Apurva (earning merit toward salvation) hold for the temple music known as Haveli Sangit and Samaj Gayan performed from the medieval periods to the present. Dhruva songs are believed by Lath to have their modern parallel only in the Natya Sangit of Marathi theater and in Hindi films.

Some of the basic characteristics of Gandharva Sangita may thus be summarized:

1. Three fundamental ingredients: Svara (group of notes, melody; *meya* ["to be measured"]), Tala (well-measured rhythm, as "cloth is measured by a yard-stick"), and Pada (set to words).
2. Gandharva Music was primarily vocal, sacred, and unalterable, performed according to predetermined rules and regulations, as in the Vedic Sama-Gana: "Gandharva was, in its rigidity and timelessness, believed to be somewhat akin to the Vedas and it was, indeed, considered to be quite as immutable and sacred."[111]
3. Svara and Tala governed the arrangement of Pada, lyrics. In other words the literal meaning of the song was linked to melody and rhythm; literary meter followed the Tala patterns.
4. Seven Svaras (*arohi*-ascending); the scale in *Dattilam* was ascending: *sa re ga ma pa dha ni,* and only certain notes could be dropped according to rules regarding the singing of Tanas, patterns of notes in series.
5. Three Sthanas or octave ranges—*mandra* (lower), *madhya* (middle), *tara* (higher).
6. Tala measured Svara primarily by striking on metal, called Ghana. Cymbals (Jhanjh) were the main method of observing and punctuating rhythm: "The distinct instrumental basis of Tala in Gandharva was apparently the 'Ghana.'"[112] Moreover, "a singer could make sounded beats through clapping his hands, but this could not be so clearly audible as the sounds produced from cymbals. . . . Therefore cymbal playing with its neutral yet audible sounds was employed during Gandharva for a better attainment of Samya." As interpreted by Lath, "the effect of these pre-ordained Tala-measures with their set intricate patterns sounded on cymbals and ritually indicated through gestures, and accompanying the equally well-regulated Gandharva melody must have been a solemn and sublime experience."[113]
7. Rhythm consisted of sounded and unsounded beats or Matras: "The unsounded and sounded beats were of equal importance in Gandharva and were set to specific pre-ordained patterns."[114] The marking of Tala patterns with cymbals was a principal difference from Sama-Gana, for "Sama was always free of Tala accompaniment."[115]
8. Adrishta (unseen salvific Sakti or power to attain heaven) and Drishta (pleasing to gods and humans) effects: "Gandharva was Drishtadrishta Phala–both an immediately pleasing aesthetic effect as well as an Adrishta fruit."[116] Regarding Adrishta, it was tied with Vedic ritual hermeneutics and

ritual yet found its way into Gandharva Sangita: "Apurva or Adrishta is a concept elaborated by the Mimamsakas and is intrinsically connected with the liturgical spirit behind the performance of Vedic rites and sacrifices."[117] Gandharva-Sangita was not part of Vedic sacrifices but imbibed the same spirit.

9. *Samya* was the moment of precise coordination of Tala, Svara, and Pada, and which produced Adrishta. This was the primary function of melody and rhythm: "The only function of Ghana could be the attainment of Samya, a neutral balance or equipoise between Tala and Svara structures."[118] With attainment of heaven or Moksha as the ultimate goal, we can establish the following trajectory: playing of cymbals > Samya > Adrishta > heaven or Moksha. This continues today in the modern process of stressing the *Sam* (the first Matra of a Tala) in classical music, which resonates in many ways with the ancient features of Gandharva. Furthermore, regarding the use of cymbals, Lath has given the following explanation: "Keeping to the strict time-demarcation, tempos and yatis (tempic regulations) were a must in Gandharva; for only thus could Samya and the resulting siddhi (or, in other words, Adrishta) accrue. Care was being exercised for this purpose. A singer could, in principle, himself keep time through proper attentiveness (avadhana) and by marking Tala with his hands, yet in order to keep check on the singer (who was after all capable of human error) and also to allow him to sing at ease, it was necessary to appoint someone to keep time with a cymbal."[119]
10. Purvaranga was the ritual of deity propitiation before a drama or play. Gandharva music accompanied the dance (Tandava or Lasya created by Siva and Devi) and both achieved Adrishta.
11. Modifications of the Pada to conform to Svara and Tala were carried over from Vedic Sama-Gana. This flexibility with regard to the Pada meant that the communication of literary meaning was compromised in favor of the maintenance of strict rules of melody and rhythm. Abhinavagupta, a commentator on the *Natya-Sastra,* said that "in rendering words during Gandharva singing, the meaning of words could be overlooked; that is to say, it was not necessary for a Gandharva singer to render words in such a way as to make its literary meaning clear to the listeners."[120] As such, "in Gandharva, too, the hymns or psalms that were sung, had a metric base. But in singing them the metric arrangement of words or letters was not necessarily honored. An immediate communication of meaning was here unimportant and the words could be dragged or compressed as decreed. In Gandharva, formations of tempo, yati (regulation of tempo) and similar elements had to be made as prescribed, for Gandharva was used for a ritualistic propitiation of a Deity."[121] Specific examples of modifications of the Pada in Gandharva Sangita have

been listed in the *Dattilam:* distortion of a word, such as *agne* to *ognayi;* stretching or disjoining syllables, such as *vitaye* to *vo yi* to *ya yi;* stretching a syllable as in *ye* to *ayi;* repetition of words, as in *ya yi ya yi;* unwarranted break in the Pada, as in *gunano havyadataye* to *gunanoha vyadataye;* insertion of meaningless syllables (Stobha) foreign to the Pada, as in *au ho, va, ha u, eha u, ho yi, ho yi i, auho-i, oha-i.*[122]

12. Stobha, when specifically ordained and inserted to fill up the Tala patterns, was believed to lead to Adrishta. The process of interpolating Stobha syllables into Vedic Sama singing was carried over into Gandharva. A similar practice of syllable insertion may be observed in the addition of the syllables *eri ha, e ha, eri mai, aba han* in the verses of Haveli Sangit and Samaj Gayan, forms of medieval Bhakti Sangit.

Another theoretical connection of Gandharva Sangita with Vedic rituals is revealed in terms of the series of notes (Tanas) that are described in *Dattilam* 31: "They are called Agnistoma, etc. by Narada and the other experts, because they produce the religious merits of these sacrifices, if they are applied in propitiating the gods."[123] In other words when one sings the various patterns of notes in a Gandharva composition, one reaps the fruit of the specific types of Vedic sacrificial rituals.

Despite the theoretical contiguity between the Saman singing and Gandharva Sangita, reservations have arisen regarding their practical affiliation. Although there are strong claims of Vedic pedigree for Gandharva Sangita, there are some factors that suggest a rethinking of the history along the lines of the Yajna-Puja distinction discussed earlier. For one, the term *Gandharva* as either a class of musicians or as the name for music is absent from the Vedic texts. This has been noted by Nijenhuis: "As far as I know, most modern scholars agree with A. A. Macdonell, *Vedic Mythology* (Strassburg 1987, 137), that there is no distinct trace in the Rig-Veda of Gandharvas functioning as celestial singers. I wonder why nobody paid attention to the strange phenomenon that the well-known musical function of the Gandharvas, which is so clearly pointed out in the epics, should be completely absent in the RV."[124] And while in Vedic texts the term *Gandharva* as a form of music does not occur, in epic poetry the term *Gandharva* occurs many times, in *Mahabharata* and *Ramayana.* Nijenhuis states: "The author of the *Ramayana* uses the same musical terminology as Bharata, Dattila and the other ancient Indian musicologists, when he describes the musical skill of the minstrels Kusa and Lava."[125] It has also been noted that the playing of cymbals and the marking of Tala did not occur in Vedic rituals or Sama-Gana.

In addition, unlike Sama-Gana which was organized around particular sacrificial goals, Gandharva Sangita was, by application, directed to petitioning specific deities such as Siva and Vishnu. In harmony with the directives of the

Natya-Sastra and early drama, classical music became a special kind of Puja in honor of the gods. It was a "Yajna free of the immense expenses involved in Vedic sacrifices," in Lath's words, and was especially pleasing to Siva and the gods. Lath affirms this latter point: "There exists a strong Saiva influence in Gandharva: Siva is its chief deity, all the hymns in it are addressed to Siva and its complementary dance forms, the Tandava and the Lasya, were created by Siva and Devi."[126] All these facts suggest that the introduction of the Puja rituals into ancient drama necessitated the construction of a separate classical music with its own myth of origin that also drew upon features outside of the Indo-Aryan sphere.

Musicologist K. C. Brihaspati has articulated the lofty position of Gandharva Sangita with regard to the religious benefits associated with it: "Gandharva is highly propitiatory for the Devas. It is more effective in propitiating the Devas than Japa, Tapas, Yajna and Upasana. This is the Adrishta Phala (unseen benefit) of Gandharva which goes mainly to the Prayokta (performer) and secondarily to the Srota (listener). The Gandharva yields delight to the Gandharvas."[127]

Musicologist Prem Lata Sharma has indicated some structural differences between Sama-Gana and Gandharva Sangita, which have some broader implications as interpreted by the author: "Gandharva is to be distinguished from Sama-Gana. The tonal structure of Sama was in a descending order (Avarohatmaka) and there was no Grama-Vibhaga (classification of Gramas) in Sama, but Gandharva established the classification of Gramas with the evolution of the Arohavaroha (ascending and descending order)."[128]

This technical distinction based on different scales possibly suggests a profound reorientation in the shift from Yajna to Puja. Sama-Gana, in its utilization of the descending scale, was oriented toward calling the gods downward to earth for receipt of sacrificial favors. This process has been referred to as epiclesis in the field of liturgical studies and has many counterparts in other world religions. The world of sacrifice also involved forms of mutual exchange: propitiation (seeking favor or blessing in return for offerings) and expiation (seeking forgiveness of sin in return for offerings). Gandharva Sangita, in its use of the ascending scale along with the descending, was oriented upward toward the deities in the heavens in the mood of petition, supplication, or devotion (Bhakti). The human realm could approach the divine realm through the arts. Thus music in Puja, and later in Seva, by being utilized as a kind of *imitatio dei* (replication of divine archetypes), was directed toward pleasing and entertaining the gods rather than summoning them into a situation of exchange or negotiation as in the sacrificial rituals.

S. S. Janaki, upon consulting the commentator Abhinavagupta, had also observed that while there were fundamental differences between Sama-Gana and Gandharva Sangita, reconciliation was the ideal possibility: "There have been doubts about mentioning the closeness of Saman and Gandharva. Abhinavagupta clarifies here [in his commentary on *Natya-Sastra*] some doubts which arise in our mind regarding the similarity between Sama Giti, the source and the Gandharva developed from it. Truly the musical aspect of these two types is not the same. So, where is the necessity for mentioning the two together?" Yet differences are glossed over when the ultimate goal is recognized to be identical: "The answer to this is that although there is no structural similarity between Sama and Gandharva, the fruit of the rendering of both these musical types is the same, namely that they lead to Moksha by contributing to unique bliss. In fact such unique music is the proper sacrifice offered to gods without expending material wealth; truly, the Supreme Being is delighted more with this divine music rather than the Puranic reading or exposition and Yogic practices."[129] Before any reconciliation would occur, however, strict reservations were developing about Gandharva Sangita from a certain class of Brahmin priests who sought to ban it from the inner circles of Vedic orthodoxy.

RESTRICTIONS ON MUSIC

Although the theoretical connections between the ancient Gandharva Sangita and early Puja rituals may be established in the classical period on the basis of selected Sanskrit texts, that is, *Natya-Sastra* and *Dattilam*, there were practical issues that arose in response to the growing popularization of music, as in the trend toward non-Sanskrit lyrics and the adoption of new musical ideas. India had passed through a Buddhist period in which music was viewed with suspicion, such that Emperor Asoka (ca. 250 B.C.E.) banned Samajja performances (musical festivities). In our case the transition into the temple Hinduism of the early medieval period encompassed a confrontation with brahmanical orthodoxy that needed to be resolved in order for music to sustain its abiding connection with Hindu religious life.

The classical period in Hindu tradition is often cited as a period of consolidation of Hindu laws under the rubrics laid down in the Dharma-Sastras. The rules and regulations pertaining to Varna (caste duties), Ashram (life stages), and Samskara (life-cycle rituals) for the twice-born classes (the upper three castes of Brahmin, Kshatriya, and Vaisya) were articulated and enforced by strict Brahmin pundits. The principal Dharma-Sastra was the *Laws of Manu* or *Manu-Samhita*. There were also Dharma-Sutras and other literatures, all classed as Smriti. This period is thus sometimes called the Smriti Period, from the second century B.C.E. to the second century C.E. The principal focus of the prevailing religious authorities during the classical or Smriti Period was on the teaching and learning of the Veda in all its aspects. Yet there were some foreboding signs with regard to music and religion.

During the classical period Vedic orthodoxy had already begun to distance itself from Gandharva Sangita and to proclaim music and dance forbidden to devout or "twice-born" Hindus. This movement was led by a class of orthodox Brahmins, sometimes called Smartas. In principle Vedic chant, under the dominion of these Brahmins, was gradually withdrawn from association with musical art, dance, and instruments. Whereas Sama-Gana ("Vedic song") was respected and believed to lead to Moksha, Laukika-Gana ("worldly song") was frowned upon and believed to lead only to material enjoyment. Consequently Gandharva music was viewed more and more as Laukika-Gana, meant for frivolous entertainment and unsuitable for serious students of Vedic study. Sarmadee has explained this trend with reference to the Smriti texts: "According to Smriti, song and dance was forbidden for the twice-born (dvija). Those persisting in the art of Kusilava [artistic musicians] were dubbed as adharma (irreligious or shirkers of the duties assigned to them). Manu and Yajnavalkya both declare Silpa (craft) as forbidden for it is 'an occupation suited only to the low-born' (see *Manu-Samhita* 10, 100 and *Yajnavalkya-Smriti* 5, 120)."[130] According to the *Manu-Samhita*, "students residing in scholastic dormitories (Guru-Griha) for the purpose of attaining knowledge should keep away from Gita, Vadya and Nritya." He further states that, "according to some Sutras, the entire class of Brahmanas was to treat Gita [song], Vadya [instrument] and Nritya [dance] as totally tabooed."[131]

Initially a response to the growing popular appreciation of music, the Smarta orthodoxy nonetheless spawned a backlash with a new and stronger revivalism, leading to the rapid creation and absorption of regional music and vernacular dialects into the structures of classical Gandharva music. These new forms of music, often termed Bhakti Sangit, were later adopted by new sectarian schools that endorsed the growing trends of image worship and temple Hinduism found in the medieval period. In spite of the orthodox prohibitions, music seems to have flourished, as Sarmadee recounts: "The dominant social tendency of the time is thus to be viewed in its objectivity; that in spite of all taboos and prescriptions the Laukika did find itself capable of representing the art-music of the time. In fact, it is so on record that, as a result of the raging antagonism, this has been a period of immense and unique activity towards the development of song and dance and drama, both as a form of popular occupation and also as a means of expression through art."[132] In fact, the strong prohibitions were in most cases ignored by the populace: "The injunctions, so vehemently promulgated by the designers of the Smriti-Sutras, mostly appear to have been observed with indifference."[133]

The indigenous regional and vernacular influences on Hindu religious music and literature were thus not impugned or discouraged by any form of strict or artificial promulgation of orthodoxy. These traits, already present in the Vedic era, only continued to grow and be absorbed into the mainstream traditions. Even with the advent of Buddhism and Jainism, each with their vernacular expressions, the canon of Sanskrit culture could only respond with flexibility, being duly enriched by the ever-enlarging corpus of religious and artistic production. Sarmadee has made the following observation on this phenomenon: "The momentum thus gained by these arts during the Mauryan period was maintained till the age of the Guptas arrived. In between, the Sungas created conditions which revived Aryanism, and in the process Sanskrit regained its position as a Deva-vani [divine speech]. Thenceforth, it is seen that the ways of life—Aryan, Bauddha, and Jain—do thrive side by side. Sanskrit accommodates Pali and Prakrit, even Apabhramsha. So do the musical arts, the Vaidika and the Laukika. The aesthetic norms do likewise readjust themselves."[134]

3

Medieval India

Temple Hinduism and Bhakti Sangit

THE MEDIEVAL PERIOD OF INDIA (ca. fourth to seventeenth century C.E.) is characterized by the rise of Hindu temple worship and devotional music or Bhakti Sangit. The rapid spread of devotional Bhakti traditions, beginning in the south and extending to the north, stimulated many new forms of architectural, literary, and musical expression. In architecture there was the splendid rise of Hindu temple construction in honor of the great iconic deities, especially Siva and Vishnu. In terms of literature there was the emergence of Deshi Sahitya, literature in regional vernacular dialects of Prakrit or Apabhramsa, ranging from the time of Harshavardhana (seventh century C.E.) to Alauddin Khilji (thirteenth–fourteenth century C.E.). And as the Vedic system of fire sacrifice (Yajna) was gradually superseded by the worship of icons or images (Murti) in Puja rituals, religious music was separated from drama and became autonomous, subsequently integrating itself within Hindu temple liturgies that were established in service of the newer deities. This marks the next phase in the study of sonic liturgy in Hindu tradition.

Generally referred to as Bhakti Sangit, the devotional music in the Hindu temples of this period may be more specifically labeled as Kirtan or Bhajan. Bhakti Sangit generally paralleled the evolving classical music traditions that also derived much of their structure from Gandharva Sangita. We differentiate the spelling of *Sangita* from *Sangit* with regard to the language of the texts. Whereas *Sangita* refers to the ancient classical music based on Sanskrit texts and utilizing the formal modes known as Jatis, *Sangit*, pronounced as such in the vernacular, refers here to the devotional music in the vernacular languages that is based on Deshi (regional) tunes and Ragas. The classical musical texts of the *Brihaddesi* (ca. 900 C.E.) of Matanga and the *Sangita-Ratnakara* (thirteenth century) of Sarngadeva, as well as the plays of India's greatest literary figure Kalidasa, chronicle these modifications and developments.

In the immediate post-Vedic period, the classical music known as Gandharva Sangita was heavily dependent on the drama tradition. By the time of the Smriti literature (ca. 200 B.C.E.), the negative response of the Smarta Brahmins served to estrange the theater and its music from the centers of religious orthodoxy. But as the musical tradition began to build up a momentum by absorbing many regional and indigenous aspects, it gained in popularity among the masses and compelled recognition from the intelligentsia. After being co-equal with drama up until the time of Sarngadeva (thirteenth century), music as Sangita divorced itself from drama and took on a permanent life of its own. Shahab Sarmadee has explained this adaptive process: "By the opening centuries of the Christian era the art-music of India—whether in the wake of its own continuity or by evolving out a new dynamism—stood almost at par with Natya [drama]. It becomes as well evident that Gita and Vadya naturally combined to express in full the aesthesis of melody and rhythm—unaided even by Nritya [dance]. From now on to the time Sarngadeva testifies to the effect (early thirteenth century), and thence to the present-day, history establishes Gita as the Pradhana-anga [chief branch] of India's folk and art-music alike."[1]

TEMPLE HINDUISM

As religious trends moved beyond the sacrificial Yajna, Puja rites ascended to center stage as successive kings and rulers of provinces in India patronized the worship of their favored deities through temple construction and the consecration of shrines. As a sequential phase in the unfolding Hindu tradition, Richard H. Davis describes this phenomenon as "temple Hinduism" and underscores the central role of temples in Hindu worship by the end of the first millennium C.E.: Temple Hinduism became "the dominant religious and political order of South Asia in the seventh and eighth centuries, and which remained so for five hundred years. . . . Though it drew upon earlier Indian formations such as the Vedic sacrificial system, medieval temple Hinduism clearly distinguished itself from Vedism in several fundamental respects."[2]

One important difference was the consolidation and solidification of theistic worship around a lesser number of deities. The earlier Hindu tradition is often cited as hosting numerous divinities, sometimes figuratively calculated as 330 million gods and goddesses. While this phrase has become a cliché, it does indicate the enormous diversity within Hindu worship and mythology. Yet already in classical times there were trends that sought to consolidate deities into categories or "families." Accordingly, one prominent conception that was popularized in medieval Hindu theism was the idea of the Trimurti—Brahma, Vishnu, and Siva. According to P. V. Kane, this trinity of gods was based on function: "The Trimurti, i.e. the conception of the triune combination of Brahma, Vishnu and Siva into one Godhead is also an ancient one. The *Mahabharata* (Vanaparva) gives expression to the idea that Prajapati creates the world in the form of Brahma, sustains it in the form of the great Purusha and annihilates it in the form of Rudra."[3]

Temple Hinduism, while also including the worship of minor deities throughout its phases, centered around two major deities that rose to prominence after the Vedic period, Vishnu and Siva. According to Davis, "temple Hinduism directs itself primarily toward two gods, Vishnu and Siva. Each is viewed by his votaries as the highest overlord of the cosmos, the transcendent and encompassing divinity. The supreme character of the divinity is repeatedly expressed in appellations such as Purusha ('cosmic Person'), Paramesvara ('the highest Lord'), and Visvesvara ('Lord of everything')."[4] The importance of Siva was grounded upon a belief in the god's ancient roots: "Siva worship appears to be the most ancient worship that is still prevalent."[5] While the cults of Siva and Vishnu sometimes rivaled each other, they were believed to be inherently compatible, according to classical sources: "Though in later times the followers of Siva and Vishnu abused each other, the *Mahabharata* and some of the Puranas exhibit a most tolerant spirit and say there is no difference between the two."[6] The third member of the Trimurti, Brahma, found disfavor among the Hindu population and gradually declined in popularity.

AGAMA TRADITION

The developing Agama literatures reflected the broad base of temple worship and devotion that was galvanizing around the major gods Siva and Vishnu as well as the Great Goddess (Devi) during the early medieval period (500–900 C.E.). The Agamas are divided into three classes: the Agamas proper, denoting Siva as the supreme god; the Samhitas or Pancaratras, denoting Vishnu as the supreme god, and the Tantras, centered round the goddess Devi or Sakti.

The essential features of the Agamas with respect to Siva have been summarized by Davis: "The Agamas spell out in detail the organization of the temple cult, from the ritual procedures and architectural guidelines needed to construct and animate Siva temples, through the regular program of daily worship and subsidiary rites, to the much larger occasional festivals. . . . They set forth a sequence of transformative rituals—initiations and consecrations—that progressively incorporate the subject into the Saiva community, move him toward liberation, and empower him to act as a temple priest or adept. . . . They are the primary ritual texts of medieval Saivism."[7]

The special significance of the Pancaratra literature for understanding the rituals and practices of medieval Vaishnavism has been described by Hinduism scholar H. Daniel Smith: "The injunctions found in this Pancaratra literature . . . account for and give textual authority for the bulk of the activities undertaken in temples, in public and in the home by most Vishnu-worshippers today."[8]

In terms of actual sources the literatures unequivocally declare that Siva, Vishnu, or the Goddess revealed the texts of the Agamas, the Pancaratras, and the

Tanttras, respectively, directly to human beings. Unlike the Vedic literatures, which were viewed as authorless (*apaurusheya*) and not revelations from a particular god, the Saiva Agamas laid claim to divine origin and authorship from Siva: "All Agamas originate from a single source, namely from the highest god, Siva."[9] The Saiva Agamas were said to emanate from the five faces of Siva, referred to as Sadasiva. As the focus of Vedic literature was on ritual or liturgical activity, mostly in the form of Yajnas, the focus of the Agamas was also on ritual or liturgical concerns: "Most of the contents of the Agamas concern ritual activity. Siva sets forth, most often in the optative mood, those actions best calculated to lead his auditors to the highest states of attainment. Subsequent members of the Saiva community have carefully guarded and preserved these instructions, regularly copying over the manuscripts and passing them on to new priestly generations over many centuries."[10] Similar details are associated with Vishnu or the Goddess in the other branches of the Agama literary traditions.

Both the Saiva and Vaishnava medieval temple liturgies evolved out of the Agama traditions of Puja. While objects were offered into the fire in the Vedic rites, objects were offered to deities on altars in temple Puja. In the Puja system the items were meant for the enjoyment of the deity rather than as offerings tendered for a tangible (or intangible) benefit of the patron or community. As Davis recounts, "in Puja, a worshipper invokes or invites the deity into some material form, most often an image or icon visually and symbolically representing the deity, and presents to him both material offerings such as food and clothing and devoted services such as the recitation of his praises, music, dance, and songs. Agama texts classify all these material and performatory presentations to the deity as 'services' (Upacara). Vishnu and Siva, as gods simultaneously transcendent and immanent, enter into a variety of both anthropomorphic and aniconic objects so that their devotees may see them and make their offerings of homage."[11]

In Puja the divine service always takes place in reference to an altar upon which are placed statues or images (Murti) requiring regular worship. Puja in temples and shrines gradually developed into a complicated daily service that was enhanced during special monthly and seasonal observances. Puja is generally centered on pleasing the Lord in the temple with offerings of food, water, incense, flowers, fan, sweets, camphor, lamp wick, unguents, and conch. Music and devotional songs were key items in this arsenal of offerings. While many Pujas continued to include unaccompanied Stuti or Stotra (hymns of praise) to the deities in Sanskrit, they also contained more and more vernacular hymns and songs accompanied by musical instruments. And Bhakti devotion was the kernel of inspiration behind an entire culture of devotional expression. With its origin in the Tamil region of the South, the Bhakti movements gave birth to many sectarian movements throughout the subcontinent: "*Bhakti* cults sprang up all over India in the wake of the Tamil devotional movements."[12]

BHAKTI MOVEMENT

Temple Hinduism and the Agamas reflect a sea change in the human attitude toward the divine. In Vedic times the relation between the human realm and the divine was most often that of mutual exchange, quid pro quo. Deities responded to the Yajnas or sacrifices in kind, with incremental benefits to the human community acquired through the appropriate and calculated series of offerings and incantations. In medieval temple Hinduism and the Agamas, however, the relation became one of humility and subservience to a supreme power. According to Davis, in temple Hinduism "the relations between high gods and humans are, likewise and even more so, asymmetrical and hierarchical, not reciprocal as in the Vedas."[13]

This new approach to the divine, while not utterly absent in the Vedic cultus, is signified by the word *Bhakti,* which means devotion to God along with appropriate behavior and ritual action. The approach is explained with respect to the proper attitude and demeanor of the devotee: "The proper attitude for a person to take toward Vishnu or Siva is that of Bhakti: recognition of God's superiority, devoted attentiveness, and desire to participate in his exalted domain. The god is in no way compelled by human devotion, nor by any ritual action humans may undertake (as the Vedic exegetes claimed of sacrificial ritual), but he may freely choose to grant favor (prasada) or grace (anugraha) to those humans who have properly recognized and served him."[14] The attitude of Bhakti placed human beings in a position whereby they could approach the gods on their terms.

The widespread adoption of Bhakti actually began outside the formal parameters of either Vedic sacrifice or temple Hinduism. Arising in rural areas among nonpriests and common folk, it was subsequently formalized into temple liturgies and festivals. Bhakti is the concept of approaching God exclusively through love and devotion, as enunciated in classical Hindu literature, especially the epics, the Puranas, and the *Bhagavad-Gita.* Bhakti-Marga or Bhakti-Yoga is the path outlined for the pursuit of the divine through devotional service. With respect to its overwhelming success in the present, Hinduism scholar Klaus K. Klostermaier has observed that "the majority of Hindus are followers of the Bhakti-Marga, whose exterior manifestation in temples, images, processions, feasts, and popular gurus characterizes so much of present-day India." Bhaktas, persons following Bhakti as a lifetime commitment, are in fact organized into a large number of sampradayas, denominations or sects, with the Vaishnavas in the majority: "Numerically, the Vishnu-Bhaktas, with their many subdivisions, are the most important group. Siva-Bhaktas come second and Devi-Bhaktas or Saktas rank third, followed by the rest."[15] While Saivism includes Siva and the worship of his many manifestations as supreme deity, Saktism encompasses the goddess Devi as supreme feminine power such as Durga or Kali. Other important divisions are the Smarta Brahmins who venerate a sequence of five major deities, the Advaita non-dualist traditions including neo-Vedanta, lesser-known sects of minor divinities, modern synthetic movements, and local cultic forms.

By the fifth and sixth centuries C.E. regional Bhakti movements emerged in rural South India favoring a devotionally centered Hindu experience over one governed by priests and rituals. These new waves embraced songs and hymns in vernacular dialects. In fact, Bhakti became the primary motivational force for creating and performing religious music by many poet-saints from this period: "Bhakti has inspired thousands of Indian poets and singer-saints, whose hymns are still popular with large masses of Hindus."[16] In the South two main groups of poet singer-saints promulgated devotion to Siva and Vishnu in the Tamil language, respectively: the Saivite Nayanars and the Vaishnava Alvars. These collections of poetry in Tamil represent the first hymnals of devotional music in the vernacular. Later in the Southwest there were the vernacular Kirtanas or devotional songs and poems in Kannada language of the Haridasa Kuta saints such as Purandara Dasa. In the Southeast the later Telugu songs of Annamacarya and Tyagaraja formed a large part of the repertoire of Carnatic music. The Bhakti movements that took form after the ninth century C.E. in the North also comprised poet-saints who broke away from the Sanskrit canon by composing verses in vernacular languages, sometimes referred to as Prakrit or Apabhramsa. The northern saints wrote in Marathi, Gujarati, Braj Bhasha, and Bengali, the languages the common people. As noted by Wendy Doniger, "in North Indian towns and villages, people spoke Prakrits, the 'natural' or 'unrefined' languages, often regarded as dialects, in contrast with Sanskrit, the 'perfected' or 'artificial' language."[17]

Describing this overall process of vernacularization as "Deshification," whereby regional dialects began to overrun the Sanskrit heritage from the past, Doniger notes that this trend was augmented by royal patronage of vernacular expressions such that Deshi Bhashas, regional languages associated with Prakrits, in many cases usurped the primacy of Sanskrit:

> Once people departed from the royal road of Sanskrit literary texts, there were thousands of vernacular paths that they could take, often still keeping one foot on the high road of Sanskrit. The constant, gradual, unofficial mutual exchange between Sanskrit and the vernacular languages, the cross-fertilization, underwent a dramatic transformation toward the middle of the second millennium: Local languages were now promoted officially, politically, and artistically, replacing the

> previously fashionable cosmopolitan and translocal language, Sanskrit. Instead of nourishing and supplementing Sanskrit, the vernacular languages as literary languages began to compete with Sanskrit as the language of literary production. This process has been called, in imitation of Srinivas's Sanskritization, . . . vernacularization.[18]

Indeed as the Bhakti movements gained momentum in the North, the regional literary expressions coincided with the local spoken languages and thus created unstoppable waves of new literary production.

In the rapidly expanding Bhakti literary corpus, newer and lesser-known forms and images of the gods and goddesses were glorified in song and narrative poetry. For example, the childhood images of the god Krishna became very popular for the first time and even took precedence over the mature forms found in the Sanskrit literature. This included the forms of Makhan Chor (butter thief), Venu Gopala (flute player), and Govinda (cowherd boy), which came to more prominence than, for example, Krishna as charioteer on the battlefield or as king of Dvaraka. While Krishna's childhood was not neglected in the early canonical texts, the credit for the wider dissemination of specific childhood pastimes and images is given by historians to these new Bhakti poets and artisans who regaled the youthful Krishna. John S. Hawley has noted this point with regard to Krishna as butter thief, one of the most enduring aspects of Krishna's personality: "In the oldest sources, in fact—the *Harivamsa* and the Vishnu and Brahma Puranas—we hear nothing at all of the butter thief. . . . The legacy of the butter thief is ancient indeed. . . . But it was a popular legacy, so it came to expression primarily in vernacular and nonbrahminical texts and in the eloquent realm of art."[19]

In temple Hinduism the Bhakti attitude was combined with the ritual actions outlined in the Agamas and Puranas to establish liturgical structures and routines that would sustain themselves for hundreds of years. Puja, replacing the Vedic Yajna, became the ritual model for the liturgical expression of Bhakti toward consecrated images and icons. As Davis explains, "the internal attitude of Bhakti is most visibly externalized in temple Hinduism through ritual action, of which Puja is the model. In this sense, Puja replaces the Vedic sacrifice (Yajna) as the paradigmatic ritual act of Indian religiosity during this period."[20]

In the ancient Tamil region, the southernmost region of India, there was already a complex fusion between the Indo-Aryan religion and indigenous features: "In this region, such basic elements of brahmanical gods, and the veneration of Brahmins as specialists in the sacred, had already become part of Tamil religion and culture; at the same time, aspects of the earlier indigenous religion played an important part in the shaping of Tamil Saivism and Vaishnavism."[21] In fact, it was in this area that the two earliest vernacular anthologies of songs emerged and were adopted into medieval temple liturgies in the spirit of Bhakti. They were the *Tevaram* in Saivism and the *Divya Prabandham* in Vaishnavism. While the *Tevaram* is the compilation of the poems composed by the Nayanars, devotees of Siva, the *Divya Prabandham* comprises the poems of the Alvars or Vaishnava devotees of Vishnu or Krishna. Hinduism scholar Friedhelm Hardy notes the intertwining of these two traditions: "The Saiva Nayanars and the Vaishnava Alvars were contemporaries, fellows, and rivals in the great religious movement that swept over the Tamil region in the sixth, seventh, and eighth centuries A.D. The similarities of vision are reflected in a shared vocabulary and imagery."[22] The Nayanars and Alvars came from varied backgrounds, ranging from kings and soldiers to Sudras and untouchables, and together are sometimes accounted as South India's seventy-five apostles of Bhakti because of their importance in the rise of the Hindu Bhakti movement. Tamil scholar Indira Peterson assesses the great significance of the Tamil works of these two groups for the study of Hinduism and the Bhakti movement: "The hymns of the Nayanars and the Alvars, the early Tamil Saiva and Vaishnava saints, may be credited with many 'firsts': they are the first literary expression of emotional *Bhakti*; the first sizable corpus of full-fledged 'religious' poems in Tamil; and the first Hindu sectarian scripture in vernacular language."[23]

TAMIL SAIVISM

Tamil Saivism represents one of the most popular large-scale devotional movements within Hinduism. The Vedic prototype for the Puranic Siva is the god Rudra, who is mentioned in several places in the Veda. Rather than a simple benevolent deity, Rudra, as a god of the wind or storm, is often characterized in the *Rig-Veda* as a malevolent figure who is intent on disturbing the Vedic rites. By the time of the Upanishads, however, Rudra seems to have metamorphosized into the Supreme Person (Purusottama), as described in the *Svetasvatara Upanishad.* Moreover, in the Brahmana literature he enjoys a rise in popularity and is addressed affectionately by means of several Sanskrit prayers called Stotras. A famous set of verses called the *Satarudriya Stotra* as found in the *Yajur-Veda* was employed as a model for many of the important vernacular expressions that were forthcoming in the Tamil region. Peterson has explained that "within the Saiva tradition, one Sanskrit stotra stands out as the most influential model for the Tevaram hymns: this is the *Satarudriya* ('The Hundred Names of Rudra') hymn in the *Yajur Veda.* This ancient litany is addressed to Rudra-Siva, the Vedic prototype of the classical Siva Mahadeva." The *Satarudriya* hymn provides a kind of link between the Vedic and the Agamic worship of Siva and continued to appear in all or most Agamic worship: "This litany [*Satarudriya*] has had a very important role in Saiva ritual in both the Vedic and the Agamic traditions, whence the likelihood of the hymn being a direct influence on the Nayanars. The *Satarudriya* or 'Rudram' is the principal Vedic text used to accompany important Agamic temple rites and, in particular, the *abhiseka* (bathing/anointing) ritual for the image of the deity in the temple."[24] Even more significant is the fact that the most famous Siva mantra known all over the Hindu world has its origin in this hymn: "The *Satarudriya* is of particular significance to Tamil Saivas, since it is in this text that the five-syllable sacred formula (*pancaksara-mantra*) *namah sivaya* ('Hail Siva!'), the supreme sacred formula (mantra) in Tamil Saiva doctrine, appears for the first time."[25]

Beside the Vedic textual roots for Rudra-Siva, Tamil Saivism drew on many indigenous elements that were grounded in the ancient Tamil civilization. Most of these elements or features have been retained and blended together with the influx of the Vedic tradition to provide Saivism in the South with a unique status, as explained by Hardy: "Among the regional languages of India, Tamil alone had an early classical civilization, religion, and literature of its own, quite distinct from the Indo-Aryan heritage of Sanskrit and Brahmanism. Although the indigenous Dravidian civilization of the Tamils was progressively 'Sanskritized' by early contact with brahmanical civilization of the North, it retained its distinctive character even as late as the period of the Tamil Saiva saints. As the first literary expression of a popular and regional religious culture in Hinduism, the *Tevaram* hymns reflected many features of Tamil culture, and differed in many respects from the authoritarian sacred texts of the Great Tradition."[26]

Rather than resisting the insemination of Vedic culture and traditions into the land, the indigenous poets elevated their own language and culture to the same level: "With the religion of the Vedas and Puranas the Tamils accepted the ideas of Sanskrit as the sacred tongue and the Vedas as *sruti*, 'revealed' scripture. Appar and his fellow poets gave the Tamil language, and hymns in Tamil as well as Tamil music, equal status with the sacred 'northern' language and its scriptures."[27] The theological point with reference to Siva and his reception of Tamil devotion was argued, such that the new Tamil songs were viewed as equally pleasing to the Lord: "To the Tamil Saiva worshippers, . . . the part played by these hymns in ritual is a point of great doctrinal significance, legitimizing and confirming their belief that Siva loves the offering of Tamil song equally with the Sanskrit mantras."[28] This notion of divine acceptance has been played out over the centuries in the context of ritual, whereby the *Tirumurai* or songs of the Alvars are considered the equivalent of Vedic mantras: "The Tirumurai is sung simultaneously with the Veda, an act that affirms their sectarian view that the Tevaram hymns are equal to the Vedas as scripture and mantra."[29] In addition, an orthodox school of theistic Vedanta named Saiva Siddhanta arose within this new milieu of Saivism that provided Sanskrit or brahmanical sanction to the emerging vernacular expressions. This school, along with the Kashmiri Saiva school, was the most scholastic of the Saiva traditions.

Indira Viswanathan Peterson, in *Poems to Siva: The Hymns of the Tamil Saints* (1989), describes, for the first time in English, the ritual context of the *Tevaram* hymns, which serve as the primary vernacular scripture of Tamil Saivism. The name 'Tevaram' was given in the sixteenth century as a collective title to the works of the three principal Nayanars: Appar, Campantar, and Cuntarar. *Tevaram* (from *deva*, god, and *aram*—garland; collection of sweet songs to a god) is part of the larger corpus of Siva hymns called the *Tirumurai* composed by the entire 63 Nayanars (fifth–tenth century C.E.). The *Tevaram* hymns, set to about twenty-one different Pans (scale formulas from ancient Tamil tradition), are sung or performed in over 250 Siva temples throughout South India. In the eleventh century, volumes one through seven of the complete twelve-volume text (*Tirumurai*) were discovered by Nampi inside the Cidambaram Temple, the famous temple devoted to the Dancing Siva or Nataraja. Much of the remaining five volumes of the *Tirumurai* remain undiscovered. The bulk of the discovered '*Tevaram*' consists of the roughly eight hundred hymns composed by the three most prominent Nayanars, Campantar (Sambandar), Appar, and Cuntarar (Sundarar). Appar had earlier converted to Jainism and became a leading monk, but devotion to Siva healed his disease, and so he converted to Saivism. He was then tortured by Jains for deserting the religion, but survived unscathed.

The three Nayanars were itinerant devotees of Siva who, while visiting various Siva shrines, composed hundreds of hymns and songs of adoration and praise of Siva. According to Peterson, nearly every song of these Nayanars may be associated with a particular shrine or temple: "The *Tevaram* songs are distinguished by their pervasive orientation to shrines and sacred places. The poet-saints dedicated nearly every one of their hymns to a temple of Siva. Together, Appar, Campantar, and Cuntarar sang hymns to Siva as the god of shrines situated in 274 sacred places."[30] Subsequently many of the shrines visited by them received patronage and refurbishment by rulers: "The *Tevaram* saints and their hymns had a lasting impact on the temple, the center of Tamil Bhakti culture. The Cola kings enlarged and rebuilt extant Siva shrines and built great structural temples in stone, particularly in the places visited by the Nayanars."[31] The prefix *tiru-* (sacred, auspicious) was used before the names of the shrines visited by the Nayanars.

The bond that the Tamil people have with their landscape is reflected in the deep orientation toward sacred spaces that is found in the *Tevaram* hymns, which symbolize the quintessential Bhakti experience by uniting love of the land, love of the hymns, and love of Siva: "The power of the saints' songs has indeed moved generations of Tamil Saivas to treasure and to love them, to know and sing and listen to them. The sequence of identifications made by the poet-saints, that love of

Siva is the love of Tamil places, Tamil landscapes, the Tamil language and music, ends with the inclusion of the *Tevaram* hymns, the songs of the Nayanars, as the final element. The text becomes a symbol for the Bhakti experience in its entirety: Love of the *Tevaram* hymns is love of Siva."[32] This attitude underscores the prerequisite notion that "Tamil *Bhakti* requires that God be perceived—by poet and reader or listener—through the lens of passionate love, personal involvement."[33]

The image of God in Tamil Saivism can only be properly understood through the eye of love. The devotees, therefore, place the hymns of the Nayanars on the highest platform, equal if not surpassing the Veda in some respects. Since the poets were involved in intense love of Siva, the devotees relish their vision above all else: "None but those who love God can see him, and only through his grace can they obtain a vision of him. It follows, then, that only those who love Siva can, having seen him, describe him. In the Tamil Saiva view, an 'objective' description of Siva is meaningless; the only true image of God is that which is seen in the poet-devotee's loving eye."[34] Through the hymns, then, the devotees and Siva are inextricably bound by the true sentiments of Bhakti, which is not mere devotion or servitude but an enduring passion: "*Bhakti* connotes not only 'devotion,' in the sense of reverence, attachment, and loyalty, but 'love' . . . in all its dimensions. The Siva of the Tamil hymns is not just an awesome, transcendent, brahmanical deity and the manifestation of sacred power on the Tamil model; he and his devotees are bound to each other by a powerful mutual love."[35]

The adoption of the *Tevaram* hymns into Siva temple liturgies guaranteed their preservation and utilization as key factors in the sustenance of the Bhakti traditions. The close affinity between the Tamils and the Agama system of ritual worship helped to solidify many of the practices of deity worship and temple arts that so characterize Hindu India today. As explained by Peterson: "The importance given to the temple and ritual worship in the Tevaram hymns highlights the most striking feature of early Tamil Bhakti. Many later Bhakti sects protested against or detached themselves from image, temple, and ritual worship. By contrast, the Tamil cults were closely associated with the teaching and ethos of the large body of ritualistic literature called the Agamas and Tantras, which developed along with the spread of theism, image worship, and temple worship in Hinduism. From the age of the poet-saints to the present, the temple or shrine has occupied a central position in the literature and practice of Tamil Saivism and Vaishnavism."[36] In accordance with Agamic spirituality, "the poets saw their songs as formal 'offerings of song' or 'garlands of verse' . . . offered in place of 'garlands of flowers,' which formed part of the ritual milieu of the temple. In venerating the songs as sacred texts and officially incorporating the Tevaram into the temple ritual, Tamil Saiva tradition only affirms this view."[37] And in line with the earlier discussion of Puja, in Tamil Saivism, Puja fulfilled the role of communal worship by combining indigenous and Vedic elements: "The *puja* ritual combines many non-Vedic ideas with a similar emphasis on ritual purity and the power of ritual. In the South Indian temple, *puja* is performed by priests according to Agamic prescriptions. The devotees in the Nayanars' hymns support temple ritual and perform private and communal *puja* rites that are open to all."[38]

The experience of rendering and hearing the poems of the Nayanars in the Siva temples is described in terms that resonate with the developing notion of sonic liturgy as a total aesthetic experience including the arts: "In the religion of the Nayanars, ritual is also a personal and sensuous mode of experiencing the beauty and glory of God. . . . For Appar, Campantar, and Cuntarar, ritual is beautiful. It is an important component of *Bhakti* as aesthetic experience. Ritual is an essential means for expressing one's love for the Lord; it can be as emotionally charged as dancing and singing. Lastly it consists of acts of offering and service, the ideal way of life for the true devotee."[39]

The Tamil Siva temple personnel included a number of functionaries to carry out various duties associated with the Agamic rituals. During the Pallava and Cola dynastic periods, a new type of participant called the Otuvar gained ascendency with regard to the recitation or singing of the *Tirumurai:* "The institution, established in Pallava and Cola times, of employing specialists called *otuvar* ('one who chants or sings') to sing selections from the Tirumurai texts during the worship ritual and on other public occasions, continues in major Siva temples in the Tamil region."[40] Details of the duties of the Otuvar are given by Peterson with reference to the current context: "Today, the Otuvar in the Tamil Saiva temple stands just outside the *garbhagriha* (inner sanctum) of the temple during the two or three daily Puja rituals performed by the brahmin priests. . . At the end of the (sixteen) ceremonial honors (*sodasopacara*) extended to the deity during the Puja, the Otuvar, in accordance with the injunction of the Agamic ritual manuals, which states: 'Then, following the ceremony, there should be singing in the Dravida language,' sings two or more selections from the *Tirumurai* texts."[41] Unlike the later Vaishnava traditions in which a composition was linked by a Raga to specific time of day or season, it appears that the Otuvar had more liberty with regard to the practical application of the hymns: "The *Tevaram* singing of the Otuvar is. . . part of the temple ritual, but it is not tied to ritual contexts alone, nor is it prescribed that a specific song be sung on a specific day."[42] There are also instances when the Otuvars sing in unison as part of a choral group, sometimes in antiphonal style (two alternating groups), as part of festival processions.[43]

The musical details of the singing of the *Tevaram* hymns (Patikams) have passed through several phases reaching back to the ancient Tamil civilization when songs were rendered in archaic scales known as Pans. After an apparent break in tradition, current practitioners trace the performance style to a legend about the eleventh-century reconstruction of the music of the *Tevaram* hymns by Nampi: "The scholar [Nampi] finally managed to reconstruct the melodic and rhythmic aspects of the hymns with the help of a female descendent of the musician who accompanied Campantar on his travels. The story of the discovery of the *Tevaram* hymns in written form and the reconstruction of their ancient musical modes (pan) suggest that prior to the eleventh century there may have been a break in the oral tradition through which the *Tevaram* hymns were transmitted."[44]

According to Peterson, while the actual melodies of the ancient Pans as well as some of the instruments are now extinct, the tradition that survives since Nampi is secure in preserving the musical integrity of the poems as songs:

> The traditional arrangement of the hymns in manuscripts and printed editions is the *panmurai*, or arrangement according to the musical modes. The hymns were set to music in 23 of the 103 pan scale-types of ancient Tamil music, and were once sung to the accompaniment of the ancient Tamil stringed instrument, now extinct, known as the Yal. Though the ancient tunes have not survived, the musical dimension of the hymns plays an important role in the Tamil Saiva apprehension of them; it is also the key to a clear understanding of their metrical and rhythmic aspects. Since at least the eleventh century the oral tradition of the professional singers of the hymns in the temples has been the principal means for the preservation and transmission of the saints' poems as songs.[45]

The Nayanar hymns, called *patikams*, were indeed musical in their original form. Incorporating innovations in Tamil poetry, they were novel creations that were tailored to the new Bhakti movements: "The Nayanars combined the basic metrical patterns of Tamil verse with prosodic principles largely new to Tamil poetry, creating a large number of new 'musical' meters, as well as a new song form, the Patikam, with its ten stanzas and refrain, eminently suited to the spirit and themes of the new religion of Bhakti." In fact, several features of the *Tevaram* tradition draw attention to the musical nature of the *patikams*.

In terms of their subject matter and formal characteristics, and also by way of their function as sacred utterances in a ritual context, the *patikams* may be viewed as closely associated with early Sanskrit Stotra (praise poem) prayers that were derived from the Vedic hymns: "The primary function of the Vedic hymns, the earliest religious literature in Sanskrit, is praise of the gods in the context of the sacrificial ritual. Many features of the Vedic hymns are carried over into the early Sanskrit Stotras that are addressed to the gods of the classical pantheon and found in longer sacred texts such as the *Bhagavad-Gita* and other portions of the epic *Mahabharata*, as well as in 'secular' poems by court poets such as Kalidasa (A.D. fourth century) and Bhairavi (sixth century). In their simplest form these hymns are catalogues of the names, epithets, and attributes of the deity."[46]

Carnatic music is the name of the classical music tradition in South India since the thirteenth century, when it was separated from the northern Hindustani music. The Raga (melodic formula) emerged as the dominant form of pan-Indian melodic expression as described in such musicological texts as the *Brihaddesi* and the *Sangita-Ratnakara.* Since the correct *pan* settings were lost, the *Tevaram* hymns were eventually set to classical Ragas in order to endure as significant features of temple liturgy. Like the Raga, "the ancient Tamil scale-types (Pan) were associated with particular times of the day and particular moods; when the classical Pan modal system was strictly followed, the choice of hymns must have been guided by the need for singing in the appropriate pan."[47] Yet the *Tevaram* hymns held to a slightly different rhythmic pattern based on the meter of the text rather than rhythmic pulsations, and so the adoption of the Tala system of rhythmic cycles was a direct alteration of the original Nayanar hymns, as described by Peterson:

> The Raga tunes in which the Otuvars sing the hymns can be seen as contemporary "equivalents" of the ancient Pans, which were Tamil variants of the pan-Indian Raga concept, but the use of Tala, a fixed beat cycle on the model of Carnatic music, is a departure from the original conception of the rhythmic aspect of the hymns. . . . Whereas in the Carnatic song, a metrical or non-metrical text is "set" to a Raga tune and fit into one of a few standardized cyclical beat patterns, the metrical pattern of the *Tevaram* Patikam itself acted as the rhythmic framework of the hymn; equally important, this metrical pattern also indicated the tune, the melodic mold, in which the line of text would be sung.[48]

To this day Otuvars memorize about eight tunes and eight beat patterns for rendering the *Tevaram* songs. Reflecting on current practice, Peterson states that "in singing the *Tevaram,* the singer may select two or more verses from a hymn and render them in a set tune developed from a particular Raga scale and regulated by a cycle of beats called Tala, sometimes keeping time with hand cymbals (Talam). This rendering is done in a simple straight-forward manner. The Otuvar may attempt a few original grace notes, ornaments, and flourishes, but the basic melody is simple, and the melodic pattern itself has been fixed by tradition and learned by rote."[49] The playing of hand cymbals (Talam) is significant in that this practice was part of Gandharva Sangita and remains in use today.

The foregoing discussion of Tamil Saiva devotional songs is not a mere glance at history but a description of a musical practice that, like the Vaishnava hymns to be discussed in the next section, remains a significant element within the framework of sonic liturgy as a vibrant living tradition:

> In a continuous tradition going back at least to the time of the recovery of the hymns, the *Tevaram* has remained the fundamental instrument for Tamil Saivas

> in their personal, communal, and ritual worship of Siva. Devotees and professional hymn singers sing and recite the hymns, in informal as well as ceremonial settings. The Patikams can be heard in homes, temple courtyards, concert halls, and festival processions. Holy men sing them on city streets and country roads. The rise in popularity of other gods and cults, as well as the "secularization" of modern Tamil life, appears to have in no way diminished the affectionate regard in which Tamil Saivas hold the three Nayanars and their songs.[50]

TAMIL VAISHNAVISM

The broad category suggested by the term *Vaishnava* includes the veneration of Vishnu, Narayana, Lakshmi, Krishna, Radha, Rama, Sita, and the remaining avataras (incarnations) with their female consorts, saints, and sectarian leaders and followers.

The earliest literary sources of Vaishnava religion include the Vedas and several of the appended Brahmana texts. Vishnu appears in the *Rig-Veda* as an important solar deity within a pantheon of Vedic gods and goddesses. He gained wide significance when combined with the gods Narayana and Prajapati of the *Satapatha-Brahmana*. In further combination with the Rig-Vedic Purusha (Primal Man) and the Bhagavan of the Bhagavata sect, Vishnu as Krishna later became the principal hero and deity of the *Mahabharata*. Pious tradition places the historical Krishna at the beginning of the Kali Age about 3000 B.C.E., yet historical analysis uncovers a gradual process whereby Vishnu was assimilated with Narayana and Vasudeva-Krishna to bear the title of Bhagavan, as in the *Bhagavad-Gita* and the later *Bhagavata-Purana*. With his prominence in the *Mahabharata*, Krishna assumed the mantle of one of the most important deities in theistic Hinduism. The Sanskrit canon of Krishna comprises the texts and commentaries on the *Mahabharata* (including *Bhagavad-Gita*), *Harivamsa* (attached to the *Mahabharata*), *Vishnu-Purana*, *Brahma-Purana*, and the slightly later *Bhagavata-Purana*. Strong textual support in Sanskrit for Vishnu worship is also evident in the Pancaratra Samhitas, considered part of the Agama literatures.

Vishnu, an ancillary Vedic god who later emerged as central to temple Hinduism, was originally closely tied to the musical power of the Saman chant in Vedic sacrifice: "Music and Vishnu are connected in the sphere of sacrifice. . . . The music that is used in the sacrifice is henoistically mentioned to be ultimately connected to Vishnu."[51] In the *Mahabharata* and *Vishnu-Purana*, two central authorities for the developing theistic tradition of Vaishnavism, there are several references to the link between Vishnu and the *Sama-Veda* tradition. In *Mahabharata* VI 32.35: "Among the Samans, the Brihat-Saman is Vishnu-Krishna manifestation." In *Mahabharata* VI.32.22: "The Sama-Veda is considered as one of the manifestation of Vishnu-Krishna (vedanam samavedo 'smi; *Mahabharata* VI.32.22, [which is also a verse found in the *Bhagavad-Gita*]." In *Vishnu-Purana* I.9.21: "Vishnu is said to be identical with the Saman and the goddess Lakshmi with the Udgiti which forms a part of the Saman." Carrying forward the Vedic tradition of performing music to please the gods, G. U. Thite cites two other authoritative sources in reference to Vishnu: "In worshipping Vishnu, one should use vocal and instrumental music as well as dance (*Vishnudharmottara* III.341.19 ff)"; "Vishnu becomes pleased when music is performed in his honor (*Jaiminiyasvamedha* XII.22)."[52]

The first Vaishnavas were followers of Vishnu and Narayana, known as the Bhagavatas and Pancaratras, respectively. They both rejected the Vedic sacrificial cult and embraced the path of devotion or Bhakti through the system of Agama rituals. The former group accepted the Varna system (class or caste divisions) and brahmanical status, while the latter rejected it, originally flourishing among ascetics and those influenced by the Tantric tradition. Vishnu and Narayana were previously worshipped separately by the Bhagavatas and Pancaratras, yet a new amalgam, including the addition of Vasudeva-Krishna, contributed toward the rise of Krishnaism as a vital division of theistic worship.

In support of this devotional trend toward Vishnu or Narayana, sampradayas or orthodox schools were created during the middle medieval period (900–1300 C.E.) in South India by renowned Vaishnava saints (Acharyas). In formal opposition to the nondualist Advaita Vedanta school of Shankara (ca. 800 C.E.), these sampradayas espoused theistic Vedanta, believed to be more faithful to the original intention of Vedanta. They were the Srivaishnava Sampradaya founded by Ramanuja Acharya (ca. 1055–1137 C.E.), the Madhva Sampradaya founded by Madhvacharya (1199–1278 C.E.), the Nimbarka or Kumara Sampradaya founded by Nimbarka Acharya (ca. twelfth century), and the Rudra Sampradaya founded by Vishnuswami (ca. thirteenth century). Either dualist or modified nondualist in philosophical outlook, they built up a considerable literature in Sanskrit that included commentaries on the Upanishads, the *Vedanta-Sutra*, and the *Bhagavad-Gita*. Known as the Catuh-Vaishnava Sampradaya (Four Authorized Vaishnava Schools), they affirmed nonhereditary lineages that stretched all the way back to distinguished ancient Vedic sages and gods yet also advanced forward into formidable bureaucratic organizations with large temple compounds and thousands of followers. For most members of these Vaishnava lineages, the Sanskrit *Bhagavata-Purana* was a key text for giving brahmanical sanction to devotion with its direct exposition of the principles of Bhakti. In this text Bhakti was elevated as a distinct doctrine and mode of religious life superior to knowledge (Jnana) and works (karma). In fact, Bhakti was proclaimed as the quintessential means of achieving not only Moksha but communion with Vishnu (or Krishna) in the afterlife as well.

One of the most important directives of the Vaishnava sampradayas was the uplifting of the status of Bhakti vernacular writings within their respective liturgical traditions. Each of these groups conferred authentic, that is, Sanskritic, sanction to the emerging vernacular expressions of Bhakti. For example, in the Srivaishnava Sampradaya there were the Tamil poems of the Alvar saints such as Nammalvar, whose *Tiruvaymoli* is understood as the "Tamil Veda." In the Madhva Sampradaya there were the Kirtanas or devotional songs and poems in Kannada language of the Haridasa Kuta saints such as Vyasatirtha and Purandara Dasa. For the Kumara Sampradaya, there were the Braj Bhasha poems of Sri Bhatta and Sri Harivyasadevacharya. Little was known of the Rudra Sampradaya until its revival in the Vallabha Sampradaya in the sixteenth century. Nonetheless, in all four of these traditions there was significant vernacular infusion.

The earliest Vaishnava lineage to adopt a vernacular canon into temple liturgy was the Srivaishnava tradition, the largest and most powerful school of Vaishnavism in the South. Although Tamil Vaishnavism, or Srivaishnavism, is readily associated with Vedic orthodoxy and the Sanskrit literary tradition, it initially emerged under the aegis of indigenous and vernacular contributions. The first human founder of the lineage, two centuries before Ramanuja Acharya, was Nathamuni, who was so entranced by a Tamil devotional song that he changed his life and devoted himself to collecting and setting to music the entire corpus of the *Divya Prabandham*, the collection of Tamil songs of the Alvars, groups of lower caste musicians who inaugurated the Bhakti movement in the Tamil region. According to Hardy in "The Formation of Srivaisnavism" (2001), Nathamuni heard a beautiful song from some itinerant singers that described the physical qualities of Krishna in Tamil: "When Nathamuni witnessed this, he became fascinated by it and thought, 'To cultivate the enjoyment of His physical qualities by means of this Tamil song is so much sweeter than experiencing Krishna by means of yoga. He prostrated himself before them, and he received from them that song. . . . A single religious song in Tamil, accidentally brought to his attention by some pilgrims, opens up an entirely new religious universe for the yogi Nathamuni, and he is eager to explore it further." After receiving the entire one thousand stanzas of the song, "Nathamuni returns home to institute a tradition of singing the scriptures that have been revealed to him, called the 'Tamil Veda,' in a religious style (*deva-gana*)."[53] Nathamuni had been given the *Tiruvaymoli* composed by the Alvar named Nammalvar (Catakopan), which is often referred to as the Tamil Veda: "It is clear that Nathamuni received one large collection of religious songs, the *Tiruvaymoli* (Skt.: *Sahasragiti*), and three shorter works, all by Catakopan (Skt.: Sathakopa], and this is at least the core of the Tamil Veda."[54]

According to Tamil scholar Vasudha Narayanan, the Srivaishnava tradition of singing the Tamil Veda was first established by Nathamuni: "Nathamuni, it is said, instituted the chanting of verses from this anthology (alongside the Sanskrit Vedas, which alone had been traditionally recited) both in home and temple worship."[55] Furthermore, Nathamuni "is said to have set the entire *Divya Prabandham* to this form of divine music, choreographed the songs, and taught it to his two nephews." The sacred tradition passing through *guru-sisya-parampara*, teacher to disciple, has been maintained for nearly a thousand years through the hereditary descendents of Nathamuni who are known as Araiyars: "This art of singing and dancing the verses of the *Divya Prabandham*, apparently instituted by Nathamuni, has continued through the male descendents and disciples of the two nephews in what came to be known as the *araiyar* tradition."[56] The counterpart to the Saiva Otuvars, the Vaishnava Araiyars have been strictly preserving the sacred melodies and rhythms of the Alvar songs.

The Alvars are the most distinguished poets in the Srivaishnava Sampradaya and are considered the true founders. Hardy has outlined the line of transmission in Srivaishnavism, which appears to ignore the traditional Vedic pedigree by placing the Alvars as the earthly inaugurators of the tradition: "All versions of the Srivaishnava guru-parampara begin with the accounts of their lives. They are regarded as the human founders of the tradition. . . . In short, the line of transmission runs as follows: Vishnu (Laksmi), Visvaksena, Nammalvar, (Madhurakavi), Nathamuni, Yamuna, Ramanuja, and the later Acharyas. What is particularly striking here is the fact that all the Vedic Rishis are ignored, and even Vyasa is not mentioned."[57] Though history and local topography records their humanlike deeds and devotional contributions in the form of songs and hymns, their presence on earth is understood to be divine, such that they, along with the later Acharyas such as Nathamuni, Yamunacharya and Ramanuja, are viewed as avataras of Vishnu's associates and weapons in the heavenly realm of Vaikuntha. Hardy has summarized this outlook:

> Vishnu has decided to incarnate himself in the many temples as their *arcas*, temple statues, and that many of the eternally liberated beings (*nitya-suris*), such as his general Visvaksena, his weapons Sudarsana, Pancajanya, Kaumodaki, Nandaka, and also Bhumi, will be born on earth to sing his praise in a language comprehensible to all (which is Tamil!) and promulgate the saving truth. These incarnated heavenly beings are the Alvars and the subsequent Acharyas. Each Alvar is therefore the embodiment of a being who has never been in samsara and now is also free from the influence of karma. His or her life on earth is purely due to an order by Vishnu and is meant to be part of a grand and more effective new stratagem of salvation.[58]

The most famous of the Alvars, Nammalvar, is said according to the tradition to be the earthly manifestation of Visvaksena, Vishnu's assistant in heaven.

Narayanan affirms the divine origin of Nammalvar and even extends his presence in the community by likening him to the notion of the Vedic living word which is sustained through ritual recitation: "Nammalvar, whose origin is perceived as not human, stays with human beings, and his continued presence is requested and affirmed, year after year. Like the Vedas, which have no origin but which exist among human beings, Nammalvar continues to live among his devotees. The living word is enshrined in his presence, and the continued presence of the word and Nammalvar in the Srivaishnava community is affirmed through the festival and, in fact, every act of recitation."[59]

Vasudha Narayanan, in *The Vernacular Veda: Revelation, Recitation and Ritual* (1994), has described the revelation associated with the Alvar poet Nammalvar and how it was the first vernacular work to hold equal status with the Veda. Entitled the *Tiruvaymoli,* this collection of verses by Nammalvar, is the first revealed scripture in the vernacular. It holds immense importance within the entire fold of Bhakti literature for a variety of reasons, including its egalitarian application in ritual: "Canonized as scripture, the *Tiruvaymoli* has been of seminal importance in the piety and liturgy of the Srivaishnava community of south India and extraordinarily significant in the history of Hindu literature. It was the first 'vernacular' work within the Hindu consciousness to be considered as revealed; it was also the first work in a mother tongue to be introduced as part of domestic and temple liturgy. Unlike the Sanskrit Vedas, which could only be recited by male members of the upper castes, the *Tiruvaymoli* has been recited by men and women of all castes of Srivaishnava society."[60] The liberal approach to caste hierarchy, according to Narayanan, is found within the tradition since Nammalvar: "By incorporating the verses of Nammalvar, who was apparently born in a low caste, and by acknowledging him as the ideal devotee of Vishnu, the Srivaishnava tradition questions the hierarchy of the caste system, which denied salvific knowledge to the sudra. Class hierarchy, at least at certain moments of Srivaishnava history, is rejected in favor of devotee/faith hierarchy and the potential equality of all devotees."[61]

The cultural impact of the *Tiruvaymoli* must be assessed within the wider context of the rise and spread of Bhakti literature throughout India: "The devotion voiced in the *Tiruvaymoli* was transmitted through the Sanskrit text known as the *Bhagavata-Purana,* the teacher Ramananda (ca. 1360–1470), as well as through Sanskrit hymns and oral tradition and appeared in different forms in the teachings of Caitanya, Vallabha, Sur Das, Kabir, and Guru Nanak."[62] Moreover, the proper approach to the text must take into account its role in the larger cultural complex involving music and drama as well as literary interpretation: "A Study of the *Tiruvaymoli,* . . . involves a study of its revealed status, recitation schedules, musical gatherings, oral and written commentarial traditions, and dramatic performances in temples."[63]

While most of the great teachers and Acharyas of Srivaishnavism wrote in Sanskrit, their works and commentaries have absorbed the vernacular spirit of the poetry and theology of the Alvars, who were technically outside the Vedic fold, into a new "dual system of Vedic authority," termed Ubhaya Vedanta. As confirmed by Peterson, "through a number of powerful arguments, the Acharyas established the authority of the words and ideas in the *Tivviyap Pirapantam* [*Divya Prabandham*] hymns of the Alvars as being equal to that of the Vedic literature. The resultant philosophy, flowing out of the two streams of 'scriptural' tradition, the Tamil and the Sanskrit, was called the 'ubhayavedanta' or philosophy of the two Vedas or Vedic traditions."[64] Since the *Tiruvaymoli* is believed to be authored by God, it becomes the vernacular counterpart to the Sanskrit Veda. This dual revelation in two separate languages contributes toward the notion of a unique process of revelation to the Srivaishnavas, termed "dual theology" by Narayanan:

> The *Tiruvaymoli,* a poem that reverberates with rich imagery, symbolism, and passion has been learned by heart, recited, studied, enacted, sung, performed, enjoyed, revered, and commented upon orally, in writing, and through ritual, for over a thousand years. It is seen as being authored by Nammalvar, God, and, ultimately, like the Sanskrit Vedas, it has no author. It is the vernacular Veda, and, by reciting it, singing it, interpreting it for the Lord, who has made himself visible in a shrine, the Srivaishnava is hearing and seeing the sacred and participating in the ongoing process of revelation. Because it is considered to be the essence of the Sanskrit Veda, and revelation in both languages is important, the Srivaishnavas make a unique claim to the heritage of ubhaya vedanta, or a dual theology.[65]

Additional support for the equal status of the Sanskrit and Tamil Vedas is given with reference to content and authorship: "Both reveal Vishnu as the Supreme Being. The Sanskrit Vedas, however, are authorless, but the *Tiruvaymoli* is spoken both by the human being Nammalvar and at the same time considered by the poet and the community as the utterance of Vishnu. In time it, too, is considered to be authorless."[66] The exegetical work of combing the "two Vedas" by Srivaishnava theologians continued unabated: "Showing the equivalency of the vernacular Veda to the Sanskrit one preoccupied the discourse of the early Srivaishnava teachers. They demonstrated at great length and considerable ingenuity that the contents of the Vedas and the *Tiruvaymoli* were similar."[67] For example, the one thousand verses of the *Tiruvaymoli* were believed to be similar to the one thousand branches of *Sama-Veda.*

A central argument for the dual revelation was framed around challenging the notion of the exclusivity of Vedic knowledge and making it accessible to all people: "Unlike the Sanskrit Veda, whose meaning was not always understood, the

Tamil hymns were comprehended, and theology was made accessible in a vernacular language. By incorporating selections from the *Tiruvaymoli* into temple ritual, the Srivaishnava community highlighted and articulated certain concerns that collectively challenge the traditional norms of Hindu culture. . . The first notion challenged was the claim that Sanskrit is the exclusive vehicle for revelation and religious communication. The recitation of Tamil verses in the temple and home brought the concepts and themes embodied in the verses within the domain of comprehension for all the local devotees."[68]

The word for temple liturgy or divine service in Tamil is *cevai,* from Sanskrit *seva.* Recitation is always considered part of this service to God and thus called *seva kalam,* time of service. According to Srivaishnavism, "recitation is service to the Lord, and it is this attitude that one should take when articulating the words."[69] While portions of the *Divya Prabandham* are recited in the daily and monthly cycles, there are special annual festivals in temples where the entire *Divya Prabandham* or the entire *Tiruvaymoli* is recited: "These festivals are usually the Brahmotsavam (the main temple festival, which takes place at different times in different temples); the Festival of Purification *(pavitrotsavam);* the Festival of Recitation (15 Dec.–13 Jan.); and Nammalvar's birthday (15 May-14 June)."[70] The birthday of Ramanuja Acharya in April or May is also marked by long recitations. A smaller version of the *Tiruvaymoli* comprising roughly 143 verses is called the *Koyil,* or Temple *Tiruvaymoli,* recited daily at home or in temples. The entire *Tiruvaymoli* is also recited for domestic rituals of investiture with the sacred thread, sixtieth-birthday celebrations, funerals, and annual ancestral rituals. There are cycles for reciting the entire work over ten-day periods. Some temples and shrines have about twelve to thirteen cycles of recitations, and others may have only two. In addition to these cycles, some verses of the *Tiruvaymoli* are set to dance as well as enacted in Srivaishnava temples during the Festival of Recitation (described below).[71]

The recitation of the *Tiruvaymoli* is believed to occur in the presence of the Lord, who is visibly incarnate in the deity in the temple and audibly incarnate in the sacred words. Central to the experience of Srivaishnava liturgy, whether at home or in the temple, is the participation of the devotee in the passion of Nammalvar and in his submission through the aural reception of his words in the presence of the deity. As explained by Narayanan, "Nammalvar is the paradigmatic soul searching for the Lord; the *Tiruvaymoli* portrays his and the Srivaishnava community's quest for salvation. Recitation is always in front of the deity; there is an experience of the sacred through sound and visualizing the deity in the temple or at home."[72] Since the recitation and singing were always performed in front of the deity, the human audience both listened to the sacred word and simultaneously had a vision of the Lord. As explained by Narayanan, "as the audience participated in the process of bearing witness to the aural revelation, it also participated in seeing the Lord in the temple or shrine, which in Srivaishnava theology is like having a visual revelation."[73]

The composition of the Alvar poems, including the *Tiruvaymoli*, was for the express purpose of recitation and musical rendering by devotees in a liturgical context. Any other means of contact with the poems would fall short of the original intention of the authors: "The poems were meant to be recited, sung, and heard, more often than not in a liturgical milieu, and reading them in translation, without the trappings of contextual familiarity, will be an experience that is vastly different from the Srivaishnava community's enjoyment of the sacred word."[74] For the purpose of preservation, the lineage of musician-reciters called the Araiyars has been sustained as the hereditary descendents of Nathamuni, who was chief cantor at the Srirangam temple, and his two nephews who first sang and danced the *Divya Prabandham*. There are also groups of *adhyapakas*, reciters who are not Araiyars. Unfortunately, beside the recitations of the Araiyars the medieval style of Srivaishnava temple music has not survived: "The modes of singing which existed in those days are no longer in existence; except for the Araiyar tradition, which claims continuity, there is no other form of singing which is said to reach back over the centuries." The current method of Araiyar performance is recitation with cymbals rather than in the form of Carnatic music: "The Araiyar tradition is closer to recitation than to classical south Indian music today. The Araiyars use cymbals to beat time—and the recitation has traditionally been called 'singing.' For the better part of the last seven hundred years the *Divya Prabandham* has been recited rather than sung in the brahmanical temple context. It is, however, quite probable that the Alvar hymns have been rendered in song by the nonbrahmanical castes for several centuries."[75]

As in Vedic literature, the power of music in relation to Vishnu is attested in Srivaishnava writings: "According to biographical literature, even the Lord Vishnu is said to be entranced by music; in some instances he is reported as being so under the influence of the beauty of music that he accedes to the requests of the devotee."[76] But while the importance of music in the Srirangam Temple is documented up to the fourteenth century, for a number of reasons the temple music tradition has declined since that time. One reason is the tremendous rise in commentarial activity at the expense of attention on music and singing. Another is the development of music itself, which relied more and more on creativity and improvisation which are disparaged in the performance of anything considered "Vedic." Since the *Divya Prabandham* is viewed as the Tamil Veda, any alteration or rearrangement of phrases or words that would creatively occur in musical rendition would be inappropriate. As explained by Narayanan, "in certain forms of classical singing a phrase is sometimes repeated several times, or words are rearranged slightly to get the best possible musical effect. Rearrangement of words, even for aesthetic pleasure, would be unacceptable if the poem is considered to be a Veda; every syllable is supposed to be where it is supposed to be, and the order of the words is supposed to follow a cosmic order that outlives even the destruction of the universe. Thus, when the words are to be said in a definite order a musical rendering that would sacrifice this sequence would not be accepted."[77]

An historical reason for the decline may also be part of the equation, as it is orally remembered that hundreds of Araiyars were put to death by the Muslim invasions of Tippu Sultan (1790s): "Their cymbals were melted and recast into a large bell. The cymbals that the Araiyars carried symbolized their musical service to the Lord. This story seems to be a poignant account of the dying of certain forms of musical performances in the temple context."[78]

Yet from the fifteenth century there was a resurgence in classical music in the form of Bhakti Sangit, which involved the setting of devotional poems to classical Ragas and Talas. In the South the classical tradition is called Carnatic, whereas in the North it is labeled Hindustani. The early repertoire of Carnatic music focused on the songs of Purandara Dasa, a fifteenth-century saint in the Kannada-speaking region, which were sung in Ragas and Talas. While already present in the singing of the Saiva *Tevaram*, the Carnatic trend in this regard eventually touched the *Divya Prabandham*, with mixed responses: "Classical music in south India has undergone many changes, and in recent years there has been a tremendous revival in setting the *Divya Prabandham* to ragas. . . . Verses from the *Divya Prabandham* are set to classical modes of Carnatic music by many well-known singers and choreographed by dancers in the Bharata Natyam style."[79] Purists bemoaned the fact that the music would exit the temples and become part of an oral experience without the visual presence of the deity, thus effectively truncating the tradition. There was also some trepidation toward classical music such that, "rendering it [*Divya Prabandham*] in ragas diverts the attention from the words to the music, and it now becomes mere entertainment."[80]

Nonetheless, the significance of the temple experience of simultaneously seeing the deity and hearing the Lord's messages in Srivaishnava ritual context cannot be overestimated: "According to the Srivaishnava, just as the imperceptible God makes himself accessible (in sacred places) by manifesting himself in a visible manner to human eyes, he, out of his mercy, reveals the sacred word and makes it audible to human beings. For the Srivaishnava divine presence in visual form and in sound simultaneously creates the experience of salvation."[81] The concept of Seva thus entails both the visual and the aural in a total experience in resonance with our notion of sonic liturgy: "Reciting the sacred word while visualizing the Lord enshrined in a temple or home seems to be the principal way through which the Srivaishnava experiences revelation. . . . The intertwining of both vision and sound is seen in the word used for both activities in the Srivaishnava parlance: both seeing the Lord and reciting the holy word are called Seva, 'service.'"[82]

The poem known as the *Tiruvaymoli* is viewed as the audible counterpart to the visible manifestation of Vishnu in the temple image, each of which complements the other. In Narayanan's words the reciter of the poem enters a "paradigmatic circle of praise" that perennially binds him or her to God: "On one level the Srivaishnava community believes that the Lord composed the poem and the poet only 'voiced' the divine word (the poem itself makes this internal claim to revelation). The devotee who recites these words participates in a paradigmatic circle of praise: Vishnu uttered the *Tiruvaymoli* through the poet, who sang it in praise of Vishnu; every Srivaishnava reciter is this poet, communicating God's word back to him. According to Srivaishnavas, the revelation of the holy word in the *Tiruvaymoli* is homologous to the manifestation of the deity in the temple."[83]

Narayanan has captured the experience of Srivaishnava Puja in her description of a Festival of Recitation at the Srirangam Temple, combining sound and light, word and image:

> In Srirangam, as the camphor is lit in the "Hall of a Thousand Pillars" and the flame lights up the visible form of Vishnu, the Brahmin cantors at the other end of the hall begin the recitation of the poem known as the *Tiruvaymoli*, or "Sacred Utterance." Through light and sound, vision and recited words, with eyes and ears, the congregation is put in touch with the heavenly realm, which they believe descends to earth for those ten days that it takes to recite the poem. For the duration of ten days, when the poem is recited and acted, the "gates of heaven," large doors at the northern side of this temple, are flung open, and the pilgrims (over 400,000 in 1989–90) stream through them to see the divine form of the deity and to hear the recitation of the holy words of the *Tiruvaymoli*.[84]

Moreover, a personal sense of presence is brought to the reader: "One looked at the Araiyar's expressions and heard the tone and meaning of his words, the rhythm of his cymbals. Frequently one looked at the other side to see the camphor lamp being waved in front of the Lord and had a darshan of him while hearing the sacred word. The cymbals and words on one side, the lamp and the deity's form on the other: together, through sound and sight, word and form, by having the inaudible and the invisible be accessible to the ear and the eye, there seemed to be an apprehension and communication of reality and truth in those few hours by and within the Srivaishnava community congregating in the sacred arena, in the Hall with a Thousand Pillars."[85]

BHAKTI SANGIT

The earlier change in attitude from Yajna to Puja, from sacrifice to devotional worship, was paralleled by a transformation in music; from the rigid constraints of Gandharva Sangita into a more flexible medium that incorporated melodies and styles from various regions of India. As this new music was systematized in temple liturgies, it became standardized as an accompaniment to Puja. The general musical genre associated with the Bhakti movements and devotional practices is generally referred to by music historians and scholars as Bhakti Sangit ("devotional music"). Rather than employing this term, however, many later groups and practitioners of Bhakti Sangit preferred the terms *Kirtan* or *Bhajan* when referring to individual songs or musical forms. While compositions in Sanskrit exist, most songs in these genres are rendered in vernacular dialects.

Two important musicological texts of this period chronicle the transformation of the classical tradition along with its adoption of what has been called Deshi Sangit, music of the common people: Matanga's *Brihaddesi* ("Great Deshi") in the ninth century and Sarngadeva's *Sangita-Ratnakara* ("Treasure House of Music") in the thirteenth century. The *Brihaddesi* is the principal source for understanding the musical changes of the early medieval period: "It is the first of its kind to speak with exclusive authority on the art-music being the natural product of the ensuing middle ages in the country. Secondly its unmitigated accent on Prayoga (non-theoretical bias), even in matters wherein tradition is to be inevitably upheld, establishes its relevance as a unique record of art-facts of contemporary importance."[86]

The author of the *Brihaddesi*, Matanga, was an accomplished flute player and devotee of Siva. He introduced the term and concept of Raga and incorporated the Tantric notions of Nada-Sakti into the theory and practice of musical contemplation. Importantly he documented the rise and adoption of local and regional folk types of melodies and songs, known as Deshi Sangit, into the growing repertoire of classical Sangita. According to Sarmadee, the *Brihaddesi* "marks the supersession of the highly formalized Marga music [Gandharva Sangita] by the regional folk-music, termed as Deshi. It also elaborates upon the transition from Giti to Raga-Giti. It announces the advent of Raga, heralds a new era."[87]

As also evident in the *Brihaddesi*, Giti (song) had by now acquired its own status, separate from Natya-Giti, or drama song: "*Brihaddesi* happens to be the solitary document representing the period (seventh to ninth century). Above all, it testifies to the effect that Gita had become a Pradhana-anga [chief part] of the art music of the time. On this account the tribal, the aboriginal together with the regional types of tunes were in high demand."[88]

Matanga had done yeoman service to the history of Indian music by stressing the significance of the vernacular and regional dimensions and consolidating them into a single idea: "The art-facts found mentioned in the *Brihaddesi* do speak . . . of the changing times. The term Desha and its gaining wide recognition, significantly does itself indicate that every region was culturally conditioned to stress its own priorities. As a result the musical preferences of various regions could come up on the surface and be consolidated. Matanga has tried to link these up, as well. He has therefore adopted the word Deshi as a term commonly accepted to connote the art of music itself. He has also considered it as all-important and has, therefore, called it the Great Deshi (*Brihaddesi*)." Matanga has clearly defined *Deshi* at the opening of *Brihaddesi:* "the popularly practiced music possessing all the ingredients to suit every taste and to satisfy every urge of the kind; thereby it is pleasing even to and may be practiced, by a child (Bala), an Abala (a young maiden), a Gopala (cowherd), a Kshitipala (the ruler of a territory), and the rest, as per their desire."[89]

The *Brihaddesi* as a pivotal text also defines for the first time the idea of a Raga: "That which colors the consciousness (citta) of all people (jana) is the Raga."[90] The notion that a particular scale or mode "colors" the mind or is infused with a special type of emotion bespeaks the influence of the folk and popular dimensions and was revolutionary in its impact: "Raga evolving itself to become the body and soul of Indian music, thenceforth, may as well be considered as an event of great consequence."[91] Upon further inquiry it seems that the whole notion of a Raga is linked to vernacular expression: "The resurgence of Raga and its recognition as a hallmark of Deshi is, therefore, to be regarded as a natural corollary to the conditions which prevailed and did come to a point by the time *Brihaddesi* was put on the anvil. It ought to have been in this context that initially Raga could make itself form part of the term Raga-Gitis. Furthermore, that these Gitis, representing their own Bhasha (language of the region) could draw on the latter as a perennial source of upcoming popular tunes."[92]

The plays of Kalidasa, the famous sixth-century-C.E. playwright and poet of the Gupta Period, also provide us with clues as to the growing preference for vernacular expression and the absorption of regional music into the courts and religious domains of the time. The music that is described by Kalidasa had much more in common with the Laukika (ordinary people) as compared with the Vaidika (Vedic) traditions. In fact, according to Shahab Sarmadee, "the facts of life found portrayed in Kalidasa . . . go to show that the dividing line between Vaidika and the Laukika in Indian music did by that time become faint and feeble.

A uniform theory vitalized from the roots got enforced, and the art-form engendered by it became technically active and aesthetically alive."[93] Sarmadee expands on this aspect of Kalidasa, who proclaims the inherent beauty of folk and vernacular musical expressions and classifies them according to Sanskrit aesthetical norms, even associating, for the first time, the emotional and artistic term *Raga* ("color, attachment") with tonal beauty:

> The emphasis found in Kalidasa upon melodic improvisations . . . , and upon Gitis necessarily being in Prakrit and Apabhramsa languages, demonstrates the same. The term Dhun (once, Dhvani [musical sound]), denoting a melodic tune, makes understandable even now, the nature of tonal excellence an original folk-tune might have possessed in those days. Also, that the same out-of-the-ordinary Dhvani-property of a folk-tune, was believably conceived by Kalidasa and others as an "extra indefinable color"; therefore the word Raga adopted for it—whether as an adjective or as a noun. It could have been for the same reason, again, that Kalidasa is led on to imagine the words Gita, Rasa, and Raga (same as Ranga [color or pleasure]) as most congenial companions, and uses them in his plays accordingly.[94]

The second landmark musical text of the period was the *Sangita-Ratnakara* (SR) of Sarngadeva (1210–1247 C.E.), which, following the *Brihaddesi* of Matanga, testified to the rising favorable trend toward Deshi music: "The Gandharva type of music was on its way out and the classical Deshi tunes, as well as mixed and new tunes, were taking its place."[95] This also paralleled the gradual demotion of Natya (drama). It is thus possible to distinguish the two periods as pre-Sarngadeva, when Gandharva Sangita was connected to Natya (drama), and post-Sarngadeva, when Sangita was divorced from Natya. Sarngadeva is himself a witness to this trend: "The portents are clear, as Sarngadeva does find it necessary, or at least possible, to disregard Natya and omit it altogether in favor of the triad, called Sangita."[96]

The triad or trinity of Sangita as described by Sarngadeva consisted of song, instrumental music, and dance: "The epoch-making fact that the threesome—Gita (song), Vadya (instrumental accompaniment) and Nritta (dance)—did constitute the art-music of medieval days in India, seems to have been first registered by Sarngadeva [gitam vadyam tatha nrittam trayam samgitam ucyate, SR 1, 1. 21]. . . . Similarly his stress on the point that among the three, Gita was to remain Pradhana (paramount), has also been mostly his."[97] And Gita was linked to the emerging Tantric notion of Nada-Brahman, thus bringing us back to Hindu metaphysics and brahmanical tradition. In fact, Sarngadeva began his entire treatise "by paying homage to Gita, the embodiment of Nada, thus establishing that fact that during the time he lived and wrote, Gita was the best exponent of the philosophy of Nada-Brahma, therefore supreme [gitam nadatmakam—'nada constitutes the essence of Gita']."[98]

KIRTAN AND BHAJAN

The musical features of the ancient Yajnas, Sama-Gana, and of the early Pujas, Gandharva Sangita, were thus gradually fused together with local and regional musics, such that, within the context of medieval temple Hinduism, they evolved into devotional music or Bhakti Sangit. Rather than ritual accompaniments to a sacrificial exchange between the human and the divine, music (and dance) became "entertainment" or "service" (Seva) for a deity in the form of Kirtan and Bhajan, the most prominent musical expressions of Bhakti.

As central features of Hindu sonic liturgy, Kirtan and Bhajan are still the most important and most widely used terms for Hindu devotional music in India and in the Indian Diaspora. As two almost interchangeable terms, they were first used in a generic sense of praise or worship of a deity. At some uncertain time they were affixed to musical genres and performance, and for the past thousand years or more have been primarily associated with a musical event comprising songs of glorification and worship of God or the chanting of names of a deity. As devotional music, they fit under the umbrella term *Bhakti Sangit,* devotional music that became central to the Bhakti traditions of the medieval period. The summary statement of musicologist Stephen Slawek is instructive:

> Kirtan [as well as Bhajan] was of major importance to the maintenance and proliferation of the religious beliefs and practices of popular Hinduism. . . . Kirtan means glorifying someone or something by reciting or discoursing upon his or its fine attributes. This sense of meaning is still current; but, more commonly, Kirtan is associated with a musical setting of a text that glorifies a deity. While it is not possible to determine exactly when the term acquired a musical meaning, there is no doubt that the modern usage of Kirtan as a musical term is an extension of the practices of the medieval Bhakti saints who used Kirtan as a means of disseminating the emotional devotionalism that they espoused.[99]

Despite apparent uniformity in the use of the terms *Kirtan* and *Bhajan,* however, Bhakti religious traditions employ them in particular ways.

As forms of devotional music, Kirtan and Bhajan are similar in function to the Western hymn *(hymnus,* "song of praise or worship") or psalm (*psalmos,* "plucked song of praise") as found in classical and biblical traditions and Sufi Islamic songs of praise in South Asia. Bhajan shares with the words *Bhakti* and *Bhagavan* ("Lord") the common Sanskrit root *bhaj,* "to share, to partake of" (as in a rite). *Bhagavan* means the Lord who possesses *bhaga,* good fortune, opulence. *Kirtan* and *Bhajan*, as terms for religious or devotional music apart from Vedic chant and the evolving classical traditions, are thus directly linked to the growing Bhakti movements and are performed so that God, "Bhagavan," is praised, worshipped, or otherwise appeased in a mutual exchange of loving affection or Bhakti.

Authoritative Sanskrit references to Kirtan and Bhajan are found in the *Bhagavad-Gita* and the *Bhagavata-Purana*, two principal Vaishnava scriptures that endorse the practice of Bhakti. These two Sanskrit texts are so influential that sectaries of other deities and lineages utilize them as authorities for their own practices.

The *Bhagavad-Gita* (BG) provides two sequential verses that contain all three of these terms—*Kirtan, Bhajan, Bhakti*—with a shared objective. BG 9.13–14 states: "Great souled men . . . love-and-worship [bhajanty] Me. . . . Me do they ever glorify [kirtayanto], . . . to Me do they bow down, devoted-in-their-love [bhaktya], and integrated ever (in themselves) they pay me worship."[100] The terms *Kirtan* (kirtayanto) and *Bhajan* (bhajanty), however, appear here without a necessary musical connection.

The *Bhagavata-Purana* (BP), reaching its final form by the ninth centuriy C.E., contains copious references endorsing Kirtan and Bhajan as near-statutory practices within Bhakti worship, with some of the musical dimensions becoming explicit in certain passages. An important feature of the *Bhagavata-Purana* is that it is interpreted to promote vernacular expressions of Bhakti, thus inspiring entire movements of poetry and music.

In BP 7.5.23 Bhakti is described with reference to nine prescribed activities, of which Kirtan is the second: "Hearing and glorifying/chanting [*kirtanam*] about the sacred name, form, qualities, paraphernalia and pastimes of Lord Vishnu, remembering them, serving the feet of the Lord, offering worship to the image of Lord, offering prayers to the Lord, becoming His servant, considering the Lord one's friend, and surrendering everything unto Him; these nine processes are known as pure Bhakti service" (translation mine). Kirtan and Puja are inextricably linked in BP 11.19.20: "Eagerness to hear My deathless tale again and again and to expatiate on it; the hymning of My glories [*anukirtanam*] and solicitous assistance at My worship [*pujayam*]."[101]

In key sections of the *Bhagavata-Purana*, Kirtan and Bhajan are understood to be expressed musically in the form of song and even dance. The practices of Bhakti are closely associated here with the Sanskrit terms *Gayan* ("singing") and *Gita* ("song"). *Gita* had long been used as the standard term for a vocal song in Gandharva Sangita. The BP 11.11.23 indicates ways of worship that cause the mind to become fully immersed in the contemplation of God, including listening to divine stories, singing, and enacting divine deeds: "The man who hears with faith the auspicious tales of My exploits, which purify the worlds, sings [*gayann*] the glories of My life and work, dwelling in his mind on them with love, often imitating them in his own person, and devotes himself to Dharma, Artha, and Kama for My sake, putting his trust wholly in Me—that man gains a rock-like devotion to Me, the Eternal, O Uddhava."[102]

The relevance of music and singing as a pure expression of spontaneous Bhakti is confirmed in BP 11.14.24: "The man who is filled with love for Me [*bhakti*], whose voice falters with emotion, whose heart melts within him, who weeps often and sometimes laughs, who sings aloud [*udgayati*] and dances unabashed, purifies the world."[103]

Gita ("song") is prescribed as part of daily worship, according to BP 11.27.35: "Bathing the image after the ceremonial cleaning of the teeth, oiling and ceremonial massaging or anointing with 'panchamrita,' holding the mirror to the face, offering food and dainties, and entertainment with song [*gita*] and dance, should be features of the daily worship, if he can manage it, or should be done at least on special days such as the Parvas."[104]

In BP 11.11.36, song (*gita*), dance (*tandava*), and instrumental music (*vaditra*) are mentioned as equal components of the divine service in the temple: "Reciting the story of My births and exploits; celebrating important events connected with Me; conducting festivals in My temples with congregational singing [*gita*], dancing [*tandava*] and music [*vaditra*, 'instruments']."[105]

BP 11.27.45 states that hymns and songs must be in vernacular dialects or Prakrits: "Chanting in My praise the hymns of the ancients and the panegyrics of latter-day singers [*prakrtair*], he should throw himself down on the ground like a stick, making his prostrations to Me with the words 'Be Pleased, O Lord, to shower Thy grace on Me.'"[106] Here, the use of Prakrits and vernaculars as suitable for the praise of God is given scriptural authority by the *Bhagavata-Purana*, which prescribes Sanskrit hymns (Paurana Stotra) as well as verses composed in Prakrit ("local languages," that is, Hindi, Braj Bhasha, Bengali, Marathi, Tamil, Telugu, and so on). Backed by this pronouncement, the Vaishnava Bhakti traditions have produced an immense corpus of vernacular devotional poetry that makes up the bulk of Indian classical and devotional music performed in temples all over India.

According to the *Bhagavata-Purana*, the easiest method of evoking the divine presence in the Kali Yuga is Samkirtan, the congregational glorification and incessant repetition of God's name. BP 11.5.32 underscores the importance of Samkirtan as part of Bhakti worship in the present age of Kali in order to guarantee spiritual fulfillment. BP 11.5.32 states: "In Kali, too, they worship according to the modes prescribed in various Agamas; let me describe them. Men of enlightenment worship Him, Who is of a brilliant sapphire-blue in complexion [Krishna], along with different parts of His body, His ornaments, weapons and attendants, according to modes of worship in which the singing of His praises and the recital of His names [*samkirtana*] play a predominant part."[107]

The high significance of Samkirtan (Nam-Kirtan) for destroying all sins is reaffirmed in the final concluding verse in BP 12.13.23: "I offer my adoration to Hari, the Supreme, the recital of Whose names [*nama-sankirtanam*] destroys all sins, and humble submission to Whom brings surcease of sorrow."[108] Following the directions given in the *Bhagavad-Gita* and the *Bhagavata-Purana,* Bhakti practitioners acknowledged Kirtan and Bhajan as primary forms of Bhakti Sangit, musical access to the divine. Hence, rivalling Sanskrit invocations and prayers, vernacular songs in the form of Pada-Kirtan (lyrical praise songs) came to prominence in the liturgical and devotional contexts of the emerging Bhakti traditions throughout various regions, first in the South and then in the North. In addition to the largely liturgical Pada-Kirtan, there was a rapid growth of Nam-Kirtan in groups encouraging greater outreach among the masses. The huge popularity of certain forms of Nam-Kirtan in the towns and villages of India is due in large part to the belief in the need for, and the efficacy of, a simplified chant that was sufficient for liberation in the present age of declining morals (Kali Yuga).

Kirtan and Bhajan performance, like almost all types of Indian music, requires musical instruments. Percussion instruments, as well as a drone, are most essential. Membranophones and idiophones include pairs of hand cymbals called Kartal or Jhanjh, drums such as the Tabla, Pakhavaj, Dholak, or Khol, and occasionally bells, clappers, or tambourines. Bowed chordophones such as the Sarangi or Esraj may provide melodic support for the singing, but the harmonium has tended to replace these. A drone is provided by a Tanpura, if not by the harmonium or a Sruti box, a small pumped instrument used in Carnatic music.

The terms *Kirtan* and *Bhajan,* often used interchangeably in common parlance, differ when linguistic and contextual aspects are examined. For example, *Kirtan* (Sanskrit, *kirti,* "praise, glorify") refers strictly to a song that praises or glorifies God or a deity, and *Bhajan* (Sanskrit, *bhaj,* "share, partake," cognate with the term *Bhakti*) refers to a song that results in a personal communion or emotional exchange with the divine. Geographic factors also shape distinctive meanings. In the North *Kirtan* may refer to the act of devotional singing itself, with *Bhajan* meaning a specific song. In the South the reverse is found. Most recently *Bhajan* often signifies a solo devotional song performed at the conclusion of a concert of North Indian classical vocal music: "Bhajan has become commonly associated in North India with devotional songs sung in a semi-classical style by Hindustani vocalists."[109] In certain cases *Bhajan* refers to a specialized type of praise song associated with a religious movement or guru, some perhaps non-Hindu; for example, Sai Bhajans in honor of Satya Sai Baba, Jain Bhajans or "Stavans" in honor of Mahavira.

Two divisions of Kirtan and Bhajan frequently employed by scholars may or may not be used by the groups performing them. Kirtan that contains lyrics which describe the nature or activities of a deity is Pada-Kirtan (*pada*, "words, lyrics"), whereas Kirtan that merely contains a series of names of a deity is Nam-Kirtan (*nama*, "name," "epithet") or Samkirtan. There is a parallel distinction related to the term *Bhajan: Pada-Bhajan* (rarely used) and *Nam-Bhajan.* In actual use the terms *Kirtan* or *Bhajan* most often refer to Pada-Kirtan unless qualified as Nam-Kirtan, Nam-Bhajan, or Samkirtan, and so forth. Musically Nam-Kirtan (or Nam-Bhajan) compositions tend toward speedier tempos and simpler melodies, while Pada-Kirtan songs tend toward slower tempos and more complex musical structures based on Ragas and Talas. In addition, the performance of Pada-Kirtan normally requires formal training in Indian music, whereas Nam-Kirtan (or Nam-Bhajan), being of simple structure, does not.

Pada-Kirtan is most often performed in small groups, with participants seated on the floor in proximity to a lead singer. The term *congregational* may sometimes apply, but there are significant types of Pada-Kirtan, known in South India as Kriti and in the North as Haveli Sangit, Samaj Gayan, Shabad Kirtan (Sikh) and Padavali-Kirtan, that are performed by professional or well-trained musicians with less audience participation. A principal exception is the Arati song, which is most often a standing, congregational Pada-Kirtan. Nam-Kirtan, while occasionally performed on the floor, is primarily a standing event, even in temples. Otherwise Nam-Kirtan is often performed outdoors in public as walking Nam-Kirtan or Samkirtan (also called Nagar Kirtan). The most developed form of Pada-Kirtan in Bengal, called Padavali-Kirtan (or Pala-Kirtan), is frequently a standing event since the drum used (Khol) is more suitable for stand-up performance. Players of the Khol often combine drumming with elaborate dancing movements and gestures.

For Pada-Kirtan performance a separate space in the temple facing or adjacent to a deity or picture is frequently designated for singers and musicians. Reading lyrics from an anthology, the lead singer accompanies himself/herself on the harmonium, flanked by players of drum (Pakhavaj, Tabla, or Dholak) and hand cymbal (Kartal or Jhanjh). The harmonium is an Indian floor version of the upright portable reed organ used by nineteenth-century Christian missionaries, yet the metal reed used is of South Asian origin. Group members generally repeat the lines in unison after the leader in a call-and-response format, though the leader may also sing solo with occasional refrains sung by the group. To facilitate devotional music, varieties of printed hymnals are available.

Nam-Kirtan or Nam-Bhajan that is performed in solitude may be combined with Japa-Mala (bead counting and recitation), Om and mantra invocations, recitation of scripture, and private Puja worship. Japa-Mala, one of the most widespread individual devotional practices, may be carried out in declamatory fashion in one or two monotones or muttered in near silence.

PADA-KIRTAN IN BHAKTI TRADITIONS

While the Sanskrit sources cited above have endorsed Kirtan and Bhajan, musical and nonmusical, as authentic and legitimate courses of Bhakti practice, various styles or types of vernacular Kirtan and Bhajan flourished within specific lineages and traditions. And since Bhakti literature quickly became an expanding body of song-texts in regional vernacular languages, assorted forms of Pada-Kirtan emerged among various language and ethnic groups.

Many composers of vernacular Pada-Kirtan song-texts throughout India in the middle and late medieval periods were strongly influenced, directly or indirectly, by the *Gita-Govinda*, a Sanskrit work of twelfth century C.E. Bengal/Orissa by Jayadeva that became a landmark in devotional literature. Jayadeva was a court singer and musician to Raja Laksmana Sena (1179–1209 C.E.) in Navadvipa, West Bengal. The Sena kings were Vaishnavas and played a prominent role in the propagation of Vaishnavism in the region. The *Gita-Govinda* comprised twenty-four separate songs called Ashtapadis, each with eight verses distributed over twelve Sargas or chapters. The subject matter was the intimate love-sports of Radha and Krishna, which was already established and gaining in popularity: "The theme of the love-play of Krishna and Radha was known long before the emergence of Jayadeva. . . . Jayadeva skillfully reoriented his lyrics on the basis of earlier forms and conventions." Yet the influence of Jayadeva on Vaishnava devotional traditions is unparalleled: "Except Jayadeva no other poet has had so profound an influence on the Vaishnava cultural renaissance of the sixteenth, seventeenth and eighteenth centuries. Even today the Ashtapadis are recited throughout the country in musical concerts and dance performances."[110]

The *Gita-Govinda* became nearly synonymous with the proliferation of the arts and music associated with the Krishna cult: "The *Gita-Govinda* is still amongst the most popular works of Sanskrit. Its songs are still recited in the Jagannatha Temple at Puri, Guruvayur Temple in Kerala; also in some of the temples of Mathura. Its Padavali has been profusely used in Hindustani and Carnatic music. As a book of songs, it has also inspired poets like Vidyapati and Chandi Das, who are seen so faithfully following Jayadeva. Above all, it did make the arts of poetry, music and painting synchronize their efforts at glorifying almost all the aspects of Krishna-Lila."[111] Most of the original Ragas identified in the *Gita-Govinda* are no longer known, however, such as, "Patamanjari, Gauda, Gavasa, Aru, Gunjari, Deva-gri, Desakh, Bhairavi, Kamod, Dhanasi, Varadi, Valaddi, Malari, Malasi, Gavuda, Kahnu-Gunjari, Vangala, Sivari, and Savari."[112]

While the actual melodies or Raga formations are lost, it is known that the literary structure of the *Gita-Govinda* contained linguistic innovations in Sanskrit meter and poetics (that is, distributions of vowels and consonants, alternating refrain and stanzas) that would greatly inform new patterns of vernacular musical composition. In fact, the notion of a unifying structure or paradigm behind Kirtan, Bhajan and even classical music was finally set in motion by Jayadeva in his *Gita-Govinda*, whereby a closed form consisting of a refrain (Dhruva) and eight stanzas (Pada or Caranam) was presented. Musicologist Harold Powers summarizes the wide-ranging effects of Jayadeva's influence on Pada-Kirtan composition:

> After each stanza the refrain is sung, and the text is structured semantically and often grammatically so that the independent refrain is also a logical or even necessary completion of the stanza. In the performance of devotional Kirtan ("praise song") a leader and a group normally sing the stanzas and refrain alternately. There is a musical as well as textual contrast between the theme of the refrain and the theme of the verse, and there is usually a musical and a textual end-rhyme common to refrain and verse. These three textually determined features—leading back, contrast of refrain and verse, and musical rhyme—are fundamental to the performing practice not only of Kirtan singing (or, as devotional song is now often called, Bhajan) but also of Hindustani and Carnatic classical music.[113]

Following Jayadeva's innovations, the outpouring of similarly structured vernacular devotional poetry addressed almost every deity in the Hindu pantheon, although it was primarily directed toward Vishnu and his incarnations of Krishna and Rama. First in the South, the Haridasa saints such as Narahari Tirtha (who actually resided in Orissa, the place of Jayadeva), Sripadaraya, and Purandara Dasa wrote Kirtanas in Kannada language expressing devotion to Hari (Vishnu or Krishna), Annamacharya in Telugu to Sri Venkatesvara (Vishnu), Syama Sastri in Telugu devoted to the Goddess, and Tyagaraja in Telugu to Rama. In the North, Sur Das, Nanda Das, Paramanand Das, and Swami Haridas wrote in Braj Bhasha about Krishna; Hita Harivamsa wrote in Braj Bhasha about Sri Radha; Tulasi Das addressed Rama in Avadhi; Tukaram and Namdev in Marathi expressed devotion to Krishna; Mira Bai in Rajasthani addressed Krishna; Govinda Das wrote about Krishna in Brajaboli, and Chandi Das in Bengali expressed devotion to Radha and Krishna. Many of these poems were either composed directly for, or later incorporated into, Hindu temple liturgies that perpetuated specific Bhakti traditions or sectarian religious lineages.

Dhrupad represents the most important musical genre that was adopted for Pada-Kirtan in the North and is still associated with several Vaishnava traditions of Puja and Seva. Kritis as well as early Kirtanas were and are still the principal forms of vernacular vocal music in South Indian Pujas. While the lyrics of these forms include devotional praise and the depiction of pastimes of chosen deities, musically they are based upon Ragas and Talas in the Indian music tradition that are believed to be derived from divine inspiration and employed for the purpose of giving pleasure to the deities and the devotees.

DHRUPAD

Dhrupad, as the most important classical vocal form of music in northern India during the late medieval period (ca. 1400–1700 C.E.), is so named because its song-texts have a "fixed" (*dhru, dhruva*) relation between the syllable, note (Svara), and rhythmic unit or beat (Matra). The name, derivative of Dhruva-pada—an older variety of devotional music—means simply refrain and today means both a form of poetry and a style of music in which the poetry is sung. The term *Dhrupad* is thus nominally related to the ancient theater songs known as Dhruva, which were mostly rendered in the vernacular Prakrit dialects of the day. In the late medieval period, Dhrupad was composed of songs primarily in the Braj Bhasha dialect of Hindi. Dhrupad is thus the oldest surviving genre of classical singing in northern India.

A Dhrupad composition comprises four parts, usually represented by four lines of a complete poem, termed Sthayi, Antara, Sancari, and Abhog. Under the influence of the *Gita-Govinda* and its alternating structure of refrain and verse, Dhrupad songs developed into a four-part structure based on the refrain (Dhruva, or Sthayi) and additional three or more lines of text: Antara, Sancari, and Abhog. In theory these four parts each have a separate melody within the confines of a specific Raga that serve to unfold the pure characteristics of the Raga. Modern practice has tended to reduce these to the first two, as in the genre of Khyal, the Dhrupad's direct successor in form and popularity. Besides having the four parts, Dhrupad is rendered in the strict rhythms of Cautal (twelve beats) and Dhamar (fourteen beats), among others.

Like most Indian classical music, Dhrupad is modal or monophonic music, having a single melodic line and no harmony in the Western sense. The modal scales are known as Ragas, and each Raga has its own complicated framework of melodic rules. Apart from other genres of folk and popular music, Dhrupad is in slower tempo, mostly in Cautal (twelve beats) and Dhamar (fourteen beats). It has less melodic development and a limited set of ornaments. Based on available evidence, the current form of Dhrupad seems to have originated as a form of devotional singing in Hindu temples in the Braj area. But it is also believed to be traceable to the Vedic period, since there is mention of Dhruva as a kind of vernacular song in ancient texts such as the *Natya-Sastra*.

Because Dhrupad is highly regulated, it bears similarity in concept to the ancient Gandharva music discussed above. And like many of the Hebrew psalms in ancient Israel, most Dhrupad songs were composed with the intention of cultic performance as part of a sonic liturgy. Dhrupad spread wherever it was patronized in temples and courts and developed into a high art form. Dhrupad-style compositions in different Ragas were also composed and retained as part of temple liturgies in religious lineages. These were performed by trained singers and musicians at the appropriate times of the day and seasons of the year.

A nominal connection between Vaishnava temple music and Dhrupad singing is found in reference to the *Bhagavata-Purana:* "While classical musicians often refer to Sarngadeva's *Sangita-Ratnakara,* and more specifically to the description of Prabandha contained in it, as the theoretical fundament of classical Dhrupada, the scriptural confirmation of the superiority of the temple Dhrupad over other genres of Vaishnava devotional music is sought not in a musicological treatise, but rather in the text that forms the theological basis of Vaishnavism, namely the *Bhagavata Purana.*"[114] The Sanskrit verse in the *Bhagavata-Purana* that specifically refers to devotional music (that is, Dhruvam as "Dhrupad") is from chapter 33 of the tenth book (10.33.10), which offers an elaborate description of the Rasa-Lila, Krishna's famous round dance which he performed with the Gopis (cowherd women) of Vraja on the side of the Yamuna River during the full moon in autumn. The passage describes a musical exchange between the Gopis and Krishna. In Graham Schweig's translation: "One of them, together with Mukunda, sang out in pure embellished tones, freely improvising on a melody. Pleased by her performance, he honored her, saying, 'Well done! Well done!' Another one sang out that melody in a stylized rhythmic pattern, and he offered her much praise."[115]

In the second half of the stanza, the appearance of the term *dhruvam* is very significant and indeed refers to a type of song in the ancient music style of Gandharva Sangita. Importantly Dhruvam was a fixed metrical song that was mostly rendered in the vernacular or Prakrit dialect of the time and survives by name in the tradition of Dhruvapada or Dhrupad. In her studies of Vaishnava temple music, Selina Thielemann has commented on this passage: "The usage of the term Dhruva, which is nowadays interpreted as Dhruva Pada (that is, Dhrupad) and quoted as evidence for the superior position of Dhrupad among the song types of devotional music. In the present context, the term Dhruva refers clearly to a melody set to a fixed metric pattern, that is, to a composition as distinct from a freely improvised melody, but if we keep in mind that Dhruva Pada is most likely to have been the original and principal type of composition in Vaishnava devotional singing, the interpretation of Dhruva as Dhruva Pada gains indeed authority."[116]

Thielemann has cited a celebrated Vaishnava authority in connection with the interpretation of this passage: "Interpretations by contemporary Bhagavata scholars equate 'Dhruva' with 'Dhruva Pada' i.e. 'Dhrupad.' Thus, Shri Purushottam Goswami ji Maharaj of Vrindaban explained in a commentary on the present verse [sermon on April 26, 1995] that the Gopi referred to in the text was honored by the Lord as she proceeded to sing Dhrupad, and he continued by saying that Dhrupad derives its special spiritual significance from the power inherent in the twelve Matras of its metric cycle, i.e. Cautal."[117] He also attributed this same spiritual power to the fourteen beats of Dhamar Tala.

This statement about the power of the individual beats or Matras suggests a connection between Indian musical rhythm and Vedic chanting. We have discussed the Mimamsa notion of earning merit toward liberation in Vedic sacrifices and ancient Gandharva music through the principle of Apurva, whereby the result of a sacrifice may be delayed and stored up for the future. We have been arguing that this principle also holds for much of the temple music from the medieval period to the present day, including Dhrupad-influenced Bhakti Sangit. While the melody and rhythm types of Dhrupad songs are grouped according Raga and Tala nomenclature, the basic principle of Apurva functions independently of the particular Raga or Tala that may be employed. As the syllables of the text are vocally rendered in the strict manner of rhythmic units or Matras, the Sakti or power of the letters also unfolds within the mind of the performer or listener according to Varnavada linguistics (see Beck, 1993), accumulating unseen merit or Adrishta through the principle of Apurva. A distinct feature of Gandharva music was the peculiar nature of the instruments used, whereby Tala measures were demarcated by sounding bronze cymbals. While not present in classical Dhrupad today, the Gandharva practice of cymbal playing was carried over into Bhakti Sangit in the form of the Jhanjh and Manjira, large and small bronze cymbals. Prevalent in the singing of the medieval Saiva Otuvars and Vaishnava Araiyars of the Tamil region, cymbal playing remains a prominent feature of music in a religious or devotional setting to this day. There are also extensive references to musical instruments in medieval Bhakti poetry, especially the use of drums, cymbals, and other percussion instruments. These references are now more fully understandable in terms of the soteriological function of ritual music.

The inner dimension of rhythm or Tala emphasized in Gandharva music was hence retained in Bhakti Sangit, with special attention to the counting of beats in measured time. Tala refers to a specific number of Matras or beats in a time cycle (6, 8, 10, 12, 16, and so forth). For example, Cautal of twelve beats has twelve Matras, divided into *tali* (clap), *khali* (open hand), or simply as a counted beat or Matra. The name *Cautal,* the most prominent Tala in Dhrupad compositions, refers to its four *talis* or claps; it also has two *khalis* or open hand. It is our contention here, based upon examination of Vedic models of ritual chant and ancient Gandharva musical theory, that by virtue of the specific order, counting, and performance of these Matras, the hidden principle of Apurva allows for invisible "soteriological merit" in the form of Sakti deposited in the soul of the performer. This unseen merit is also called Adrishta and is believed to accumulate for the benefit of the singer, player, or listener. As such, there is a natural correlation between the notion of Matra as "syllable, long or short" and a rhythmic beat in music; thus in music a long vowel of a syllable would encompass two or more beats, while a short vowel is normally limited to one. When all factors are considered, including linguistics, there is an extraordinarily sophisticated salvific system that operates with or without the full knowledge of the participants.

Classical Dhrupad became popular in the Hindu and Muslim courts during the late medieval period. Abu Fazl, who was the courtier and chronicler at the court of the Emperor Akbar (1555–1605), wrote a work called the *Ain-e-Akbari* in which he defined Dhrupad as "four rhyming lines, each of indefinite prosodial length of words or syllables." The subject matter is mostly religious but also includes praise of royal figures, musical symbolism, and romantic themes. The most famous musical name associated with the court of Emperor Akbar was Tansen. Originally a Brahmin born in Gwalior and trained in music by Swami Haridas, Tansen later converted to Sufi Islam when he took up residence at Akbar's court in Fatehpur Sikri. Tansen was a renowned composer, poet, and singer of Dhrupad. His son Vilas Khan sang at Jahangir's court, and his daughter Sarasvati married Misri Singh, whose descendents included Niyamat Khan (Sadarang), singer and composer at the court of Mohammad Shah Rangile (1719–1748). While there was a line of Vina players that culminated in Ustad Dabir Khan, who died in the 1960s, there are very few today who can sing Dhrupad in the Tansen (Seniya) Gharana. The famous Dhrupad family of Dagar claims a separate lineage from Tansen.

By the eighteenth century Dhrupad singing began gradually to decline and was replaced by a more fluid improvisatory genre called Khyal, developed and popularized by Niyamat Khan (Sadarang). It allowed for more display of virtuosity and was configured as less religious and more like courtly entertainment. At this time new instruments were being developed such as the sitar and the sarod that mirrored the rendering of Khyal with regard to fast tempos and rapid passages in succession.

Despite the emergence of Khyal in the Muslim courts, the Dhrupad tradition of music in temple Hinduism has always been especially prominent in the areas associated with Krishna such as Mathura and Agra. According to musicologists Ritwik Sanyal and Richard Widdess,

> until recently, certain temples in the famous Hindu religious centers of Mathura and Vrindaban employed Brahman singers who performed the classical genres of

Alap and Dhrupad. There, temple towns have been centers of pilgrimage for many centuries, due to their association with the God Krishna, who was born in Mathura and spent his childhood in the groves of Vrindaban. Vaishnava devotional sects dating from the fifteenth and sixteenth centuries maintain important temples in the region; in many of these temples, devotional singing of the Padas of Vaishnava poet-saints—Sur Das, Swami Haridas, Hita Harivamsa and others—takes place daily before the image of the deity. Professional or non-professional singers may be employed to lead the singing. Today, these singers do not normally perform in classical styles, but the influence of Dhrupad is apparent in some cases. In the past, some temple singers were distinguished exponents of the classical styles.[118]

The Mathura tradition of Dhrupad singing has continued with some famous luminaries associated with this Bhakti tradition of singing. In the first part of the twentieth century, Candan Caube (1869–1944) was a highly regarded Dhrupad singer of the Mathura Gharana. Dhrupad festivals are still occasionally held in his memory. As noted by Sanyal and Widdess, "a few distinguished representatives of the tradition are known today, including Laksman Prasad Caube, Satyabhan Sharma and the late Balji Caube (son of Candan), all of whom have performed at recent Dhrupad festivals. In addition to vocalists, a number of virtuoso Pakhavaj players are to be found among the Mahants or temple priests of Mathura and Vrindaban."[119]

One of the most extraordinary examples of collaboration between musicians of different religions for the purpose of maintaining continuity of musical style over centuries occurs in the realm of Hindustani vocal music. Despite the gradual decline of the Mughal Empire under Akbar and his descendents, many Muslim musicians of the Dhrupad tradition held fast to their repertoires of compositions expressing devotion to Hindu deities, preserving and developing their unique musical styles. The nearby Muslim capital city of Agra became a nexus for this interchange, as explained by Sanyal and Widdess: "The Gharana [lineage] of Muslim hereditary singers associated with Agra, the former Mughal capital some 30 miles distance from Mathura, is also noted for its Dhrupad tradition."[120] In fact, the Agra Gharana musicians were originally performers of Dhrupad-Dhamar and claimed descent from Hindu Rajput singers. They took to singing Khyal as late as the nineteenth century, when Ghugghe Khuda Baksh took up Khyal from Gwalior. But Dhrupad-Dhamar has been a strong focus of the Agra Gharana, as evidenced in the music of Ustad Faiyyaz Husain Khan (1886–1950), the most famous name in this Gharana. He was initially trained in Dhrupad and Dhamar, and several recordings survive of his formidable Alap and Dhamar performances. Beside Ustad Faiyyaz Khan, there have been many great Muslim musicians in this tradition who were exemplary performers as well as composers: Ustad Khadim Husain Khan, Ustad Latafat Husain Khan, Ustad Ata Husain Khan, Ustad Sharafat Husain Khan, and Ustad Yunus Husain Khan. Waseem Ahmed Khan is a rising star among the current generation. Today, coming full circle, a number of Hindu musicians have been trained in the style of Agra Gharana and perform the Dhrupad-style Alap followed by a Dhrupad-Dhamar or a Khyal. Male singers who include Pandits Vijay Kichlu, Ravi Kichlu, Kumar Mukherjee, K. G. Ginde, M.R. Gautam, Dinkar Kaikini, and C.R. Vyas, as well as such female singers as Smt. Purnima Sen, Lalith Rao, Subhra Guha, Ruby Malik, and Tapasi Ghosh, have helped to preserve and disseminate the Agra Gharana style among their many students and disciples.

Sanyal and Widdess have noted the close affinity between the Mathura and Agra traditions of singing: "A close relationship existed at one time between the Mathura and Agra musical traditions, to the extent that singers from Mathura taught Dhrupad to, and learned Khyal from, singers from Agra: it is even said that Muslim singers from Agra sang in the Hindu temples of Mathura. Consequently it is not surprising to note certain similarities in the style of ornamentation in Alap between contemporary Mathura singers and recordings of Faiyyaz Husain Khan." Some of the details of this parallel compatibility have been explained:

> Performance of Dhrupad by Mathura singers laid considerable stress on the composition. The words are taken from the devotional poetry of Sur Das and other Vaishnava poets. Cautal compositions normally have the full complement of four lines, and the words are delivered in a deliberate and clear manner; the composition may be repeated, at the basic tempo or in diminution, but there is comparatively little improvisation (Layakari). This is as one would expect given the religious context of performance, in which the words are of at least as much importance as the music. Intricate Layakari may be performed, however, in Dhamar. In the Agra tradition, as befits a court setting, full-length Alaps were performed, as can be heard in a number of historical recordings of Faiyyaz Husain Khan.[121]

In the classical arena of today, Dhrupad is normally performed by a solo singer or a duo to the beat of a double-headed barrel drum, the Pakhavaj. Duos of singing brothers have been popular: Dagar Brothers, Kichlu Brothers, Gundecha Brothers, and others. The songs are mostly in praise of Hindu deities, but Islamic or simply regalist lyrics have been composed and added to the repertoire. In concert performance the text of the Sthayi is usually preceded by an introductory improvised section called the Alap, without instrumental accompaniment. Sung without words, it uses instead sets of syllables in a repetitive fixed pattern, such as *a re ne na, te re ne na, ri re re ne na, te ne toom ne.* This practice is often called Nom-Tom. According to the Dagar Brothers, these syllables were derived from sacred syllables of Vishnu mantras such as *Om Hari Ananta Narayana.* It has became the trend in modern concerts of Dhrupad that the Alap will comprise the greater part of the performance, lasting up to an hour, beginning in slow tempo with a gradual, controlled development of the Raga.

KRITI

In South India the vernacular songs of the sixth–ninth century Vaishnava Alvars and Saivite Nayanars provided the foundation for the later development of the Kirtana and the Kriti, the most refined Carnatic classical-devotional composition. The use of the term *Kirtan* (*kirtana*) as a purely musical form of Bhakti devotion was perhaps first adopted by the Haridasas in the 1300s, though there are precedents in the earlier worship songs of the Lingayat sect (Saivism). The Haridasas were itinerant Vaishnava followers of the Dvaita school of Madhvacharya (1238–1317 C.E.) who sang vernacular songs of devotion (Kirtanas) that also criticized social ills and worldliness. Patronized by the rulers of the Vijayanagara Empire (1336–1646) in Karnataka, the Haridasas almost singlehandedly elevated devotional Kirtan to a major phenomenon and forged the beginnings of Carnatic classical music. As innovators in vernacular songs they had also been influenced by the linguistic structure of the *Gita-Govinda:* "The refrain (Dhruva) and the stanzas (Caranam) of its [*Gita-Govinda*] eight-stanza form (Ashtapadi) set the pattern for the structure of Kirtana, also involving a refrain (Pallavi) and stanzas (Caranam)—a structure developed by the Haridasa singers of Karnataka in and after the 1300s."[122] As one of the most illustrious members of the Haridasa movement, Purandara Dasa (1480–1564), hailed as the "Father of Carnatic Music," composed thousands of Kirtanas. He was a major inspiration of Tyagaraja (1759–1847), whose devotional Kritis in Telugu to Rama comprise the major portion of the current repertoire of South Indian music. Tyagaraja is recognized as one of a trinity of great musician-poets from Tiruvarur that included Syama Sastri and Muttuswami Dikshitar, composers of songs to the goddesses Kamakshi and Minakshi.

The Kriti (from Sanskrit *kri*, "to create") is a South Indian form of classical Pada-Kirtan that evolved out of the earlier, two-section Kannada Kirtanas of Purandara Dasa. The two-section Samkirtanams of the Telugu composer Annamacharya (1424–1503), who was based at the Tirupati Temple, were also important precursors. The new Kriti thus had three distinct sections: Pallavi (refrain), Anupallavi (second-verse elaboration of refrain), and Caranam (stanzas). The creative development in the Anupallavi was the addition that made the Kriti a distinct genre of Carnatic classical music. Kritis are essentially devotional but have increased their versatility as pieces performed in a wide variety of contexts. Regarding the relation between Kriti and Bhajan, "there are areas of overlap between Kriti and Bhajan; some Kritis are performed congregationally by Bhajan groups, and a Bhajan or another 'light' piece may be performed at the end of a Carnatic concert [as in Hindustani concerts in the North]."[123]

PADAVALI-KIRTAN

Padavali-Kirtan is a distinctive genre of vernacular Pada-Kirtan found in Bengal and Orissa. Developing primarily out of the late medieval songs of poets Vidyapati and Chandi Das, but also drawing upon Baul music, Panchali recitation, Buddhist Charya Giti, and folk idioms, Padavali-Kirtan became the most sophisticated form of devotional music in eastern India. To reach its present structural form it was adapted and modified from the slower Dhrupad style of Braj music by Sri Narottam Das (1531–1587 C.E.), a follower of Sri Caitanya who organized a large Kirtan festival in Kheturi in 1572. His originating style of Padavali-Kirtan is sometimes called Garanhati Kirtan, named after the region in present-day Bangladesh. Later styles incorporated influences of Hindustani vocal forms such as Khyal, Thumri and Tappa.[124]

Padavali-Kirtan combines the recitation of religious narratives (*katha*) with songs in various tempos and rhythms composed by Bhakti saints in Bengali and Brajaboli languages. This genre did not become inextricably linked with temple liturgies and as such has remained a form of devotional art-song that survives as a singular performative tradition. A Padavali-Kirtan session nonetheless revolves around a theme from Radha-Krishna pastimes, with names such as Mana, Purva-Raga, Rasa-Lila, Dan-Lila, and Mathura-Gamana. The songs also include short improvisatory phrases called *akhar* inserted into the lyrics of the original songs by the singers themselves for the purpose of interpreting or reiterating the meaning of the poem using colloquial expressions for the benefit of local audiences. The normally "standing" performers include one or more vocalists, a Khol (double-headed clay drum) player, a hand-cymbal player, and sometimes a violinist or flautist.

While the tradition is dwindling today, there are still singers of Padavali-Kirtan, both male and female, who have the ability to improvise Akhars on the spot. Nanda Kishor Das, Rathin Ghosh, Mriganka Chakravarti, Vinapani, Radharani, and Chabi Bandyopadhay are names of important twentieth-century performers and recording artists.

The two principal traditions of Bhakti Sangit fall under the rubric of Pada-Kirtan (or Pada-Bhajan). During the late medieval period (1400–1700 C.E.) they arose within the worship of four new Krishna sampradayas as genres of liturgical music yet are better known as Haveli Sangit and Samaj Gayan. The tradition of Haveli Sangit is predominant within the Seva worship of the Vallabha Sampradaya or Pushti Marg tradition, and Samaj Gayan is a unique form of interactive singing that comprises the Seva worship of the Radhavallabha, Nimbarka, and Haridasi sampradayas.

4

Seva and Haveli Sangit

AS THE PRACTICES OF TEMPLE HINDUISM evolved and became standardized in the medieval period, the Bhakti movements spread throughout India, and by the fourteenth century the deity of Krishna had become the most popular object of Bhakti devotional music. While there are numerous examples of devotional music directed at other deities such as Siva, Ganesha, and the goddesses Durga and Sarasvati, the prevalence of Krishna-centered devotional music by this time is evidenced by the enormous literary output in the form of song-texts and poetry. The *Bhagavata-Purana*, with its account of the life of Krishna and consistent endorsement of devotional music, reached unprecedented authority. Selina Thielemann has noted the strong bond between Vaishnava devotion and music: "Since Bhakti is the main content of Vaishnavism, music has always been an important part of Vaishnava traditions, and singing became the primary mode of worship. At all times, and to the present-day, Bhakti saints wrote hymns and eulogies and sang them in praise of their deities."[1] She has also affirmed the superiority of music over other forms of worship in Vaishnava devotion with regard to its dialectic principle: "Music and singing have been of central importance in the Vaishnava Bhakti movement since its very beginnings. . . . A person endowed with devotion makes the musical offering out of love for God, and it is his devotion that enables man to partake of divine blessing in the form of music. . . . It is important to note that the dialectic principle can work only in devotional religion, because it presupposes an active and two-sided relationship between man and the divinity."[2]

Most devotees of Krishna strive to invoke and recall his presence in ritual worship by hearing and singing his names and praising his activities, specifically through the medium of vernacular song-texts or hymns. While the Sanskrit Puranas and epic texts describing the life and pastimes of Krishna have proliferated throughout the elite and literary sectors of Indian society, the production of vernacular versions and descriptions of his pastimes in the form of devotional songs is now being recognized as equally significant for the study of Hinduism. Hindi scholar Heidi R. M. Pauwels has placed these vernacular compositions on a par with the Sanskrit prayers as equally important for the academic study of

Hindu traditions: "One of the favorite vehicles of the [Bhakti] movement is the genre of devotional songs in the vernacular of the Braj area, the region closely associated with Krishna. Studying these apparently simple Braj Bhasha devotional songs reveals the complicated processes underlying them. Roughly speaking, the songs are the result of a merging of the Brahmanic Puranic tradition (itself complex), Sanskrit poetics usually associated with the court tradition, and popular devotional and even secular folk traditions. In other words, these songs are excellent materials for the study of Hinduism."[3]

SRI KRISHNA

While Vishnu worship had been firmly established among the aristocracy in the early medieval period, it was Krishna who found the widest representation in literature, music, and popular culture. Through a kind of coalition with the gods Vishnu, Narayana, and Vasudeva, Krishna gained even greater strength and attraction through the ability of his cult to absorb many indigenous and regional elements. This trend has been observed by Sarmadee in terms of cultural syncretism: "It had been a period [medieval] when new Gods developed, better suited to the rustic mentality . . . ; the most successful of these was Vishnu-Narayana-Krishna, who dominates the final redaction of the *Mahabharata*. . . . It was easy to absorb all prominent ancient or local cults as incarnations or numina of the god. This syncretism gave a cultural unity to the land." These syncretistic tendencies of Krishna, along with the Siva, brought about drastic changes throughout India: "Besides Vasudeva-Krishna and Vishnu-Narayana-Krishna, the other prominent god is Siva, who has features reminiscent of the three-faced Indus figure surrounded by totem animals. With his Gana companions, and a family headed by the mother goddess Parvati, Siva has been the other inspiring source for the popularization of a syncretic religion in the whole of this subcontinent."[4]

As we have seen, there was strong patronage of Siva and Vishnu in southern India during the middle medieval period. In the North the deity of Krishna, primarily as an incarnation of Vishnu, found favor among the Gupta Dynasty of rulers that held power for several centuries. This is attested by varieties of concrete evidence offered by scholars: "By the Gupta period, the worship of Krishna was widespread across the subcontinent. Epigraphic and numismatic evidence indicates that most of the Gupta sovereigns, while patronizing a number of Hindu sects, were devout Vaishnavas; and a number of the Guptas referred to themselves as *paramabhagavatas*, 'topmost devotees of Bhagavan,' another title used to refer to Krishna. It is during this period that the Puranic literary genre attained the final stages of its compilation, and it is in these texts that the story of Krishna reaches its fullest expression."[5]

The *Harivamsa,* attached to the epic *Mahabharata,* is the first description of Krishna's life and pastimes. Yet it is in works called the Puranas that the mythological incarnations of Vishnu are described with great detail. Produced later than the *Vishnu-Purana,* the *Bhagavata-Purana* remains the principal literary source for the childhood pastimes of Krishna and most probably reached its final form in the ninth century C.E. According to the accounts in these Sanskrit sources, as well as depictions in sculpture and other visual art, Krishna ruled his own kingdom and was the descendent of an illustrious dynasty carefully chronicled and preserved by scribes and Puranic authors. In fact, Krishna is the only deity in the Hindu pantheon whose entire earthly life, from birth to death, has been presented in Sanskrit literature. His life spanned more than one hundred years according to the *Vishnu-Purana.* Krishna had many wives (16,108), children (180,000 sons, according to *Vishnu-Purana* 5.32), and grandchildren. Krishna's earthly career covered the entire region of northern India. There are also hundreds of material pilgrimage sites and shrines commemorating specific events in Krishna's life. In addition there are thousands of references to Krishna's life in literature, both classical and vernacular. The classical Sanskrit sources, including especially the *Bhagavata-Purana* but also the epics and other Puranas, offer the following biographical portrait of Krishna.

Krishna is generally accepted within the Hindu tradition as the eighth of ten incarnations of Vishnu, descending on earth at the beginning of the present age of Kali and at the end of the previous Dvapara age, in about 3000 B.C.E. Whenever there is a general rise in unrighteousness, Vishnu is believed to descend as an avatara in order to punish the evildoers and deliver the righteous devotees from the cycle of rebirth. At this particular juncture there was a preponderance of demons from former times who had taken birth as evil kings and were threatening the stability of Hindu dharma. Planning his strategy of descent, Vishnu is said to have pulled two hairs from his head, one black (Krishna) and the other white (Balarama).

Many centuries before descendants of the Yadava family had settled around the town of Mathura in North India. Overthrowing his pious father Ugrasena, the evil King Kamsa was the principal villain and reason for the descent of Vishnu. With the support of his father-in-law, King Jarasandha of Magadha, he precipitated a reign of terror in the region. Krishna, while understood to have taken a divine birth, was born to Devaki, the sister of Kamsa, and her husband Vasudeva of the same illustrious Yadava family, a lunar dynasty descended from the Moon. In a situation filled with intrigue similar to that in the Jesus narrative, Krishna's parents had to face a horrible ordeal. Kamsa had heard in a vision that the eighth son of Devaki would kill him, and so he had her and Vasudeva imprisoned in a Mathura jail, where he murdered six of her sons out of fear. Kamsa was told that the seventh child had aborted. However, this child, known as Balarama, who was another avatara of Vishnu sent to help Krishna, had actually been miraculously transferred to the womb of Vasudeva's second wife, Rohini. When Krishna finally took birth, divine intervention allowed for the blackish-colored child to be carried out of jail and switched with a female child in the nearby village of Gokula, where his new "foster parents," Yasoda and her husband Nanda, lived as wealthy dairy farmers. Thus when Kamsa tried to kill the eighth child of Devaki, the child was a girl and had to be spared.

Krishna's early life was spent growing up with his elder brother Balarama in an idyllic rural setting. However, Krishna and his family were besieged by demons sent by Kamsa who heard about a miraculous child in the Braj area. Krishna, as a beautifully divine child, was naturally adorable to everyone in the village, but he could also wield frightening consequences for those evil beings who entered his turf. This series of demons included a witch, whirlwind, cow, serpent, bird, sea dragon, ox, horse, and goat, all of which were destroyed by the child prodigy and his brother. Further exploits included lifting Govardhan Hill to protect the villagers from the rainfall of the jealous Lord Indra and stealing the clothes of the cowherd girls of the village of Vrindavana, where his family had subsequently settled. As Krishna approached teen age, he gained a reputation for dallying with the local cowherd maidens and wives by enchanting them with his flute, leading ultimately to a midnight Rasa Dance in which he multiplied himself in order to satisfy their amorous desires. All of these childhood pastimes created an unprecedented outpouring of affection for and deep attachment to Krishna by the villagers that became a paradigm for religious devotion in Vaishnava tradition.

One day Kamsa invited Krishna and Balarama to Mathura to witness a fourteen-day sacrifice, using this as a ruse to destroy them. Akrura, a devotee of Krishna himself, was sent by Kamsa to collect the brothers in Vrindavana, but he also warned them of Kamsa's evil designs. The residents of Vrindavana experienced deep emotional trauma upon their departure yet were assured of their return after helping the Yadava clan. In Mathura, Krishna and Balarama performed a few healing miracles, killed an evil elephant, defeated two wrestlers, and ultimately killed Kamsa along with his eight evil bothers. After this, Vasudeva and Devaki, released from prison, proceeded to arrange for their sons' education in the sixty-four arts and archery at the hermitage of the sage Sandipani Muni. After their return, it became difficult for the brothers to remain in Mathura. The evil Jarasandha, king of Magadha and father of two of Kamsa's wives, led a large coalition of kings with their armies into revenge on the Yadavas, who were temporarily impoverished and thus forced to retreat. Krishna quickly built a new capital city of Dvaraka on an island off the northwest coast of India, where his parents Vasudeva and Devaki were kept safely. Through a series of events, Krishna and fellow Yadavas accumulated wealth and built up a large kingdom and army. Krishna then married Rukmini as his chief queen but continued to marry many other women (for example, Jambavati, Satyabhama, Kalindi, Satya, Kaikeyi) who either fell in love with him or were given by grateful kings or princes in return for his valor and good deeds. In one unprecedented event in all world religious history, Krishna married the 16,000 daughters of Narakasura who were released by him from captivity and built each of them a palace in Dvaraka, where he multiplied himself in order to satisfy all simultaneously! In terms of progeny, it is mentioned that Krishna had ten sons from each of eight wives.

The rest of Krishna's earthly sojourn is bound up with the fate of the five Pandava brothers and their common wife Draupadi. The Pandavas, including Arjuna, Yudhisthira, Nakula, Sahadeva, and Bhima, were also Yadavas, being the sons of Pandu and Kunti, Krishna's paternal aunt. Krishna took pity on their miserable plight of being cheated by the Kauravas out of their wealth and kingdom in a loaded dice game. Despite the efforts of Krishna to negotiate peace between the rival families—the Pandavas and their allies versus the Kauravas, including the hundred sons of Dhritarastra and Gandhari—steps were taken toward an all-out war on the battlefield of Kurukshetra in northern India. Krishna lent his skill as a charioteer to Arjuna, and the stage was set for the epic eighteen-day war chronicled in the *Mahabharata*. After speaking the famous *Bhagavad-Gita* discourse to Arjuna, who had suddenly been overcome with grief and panic about performing his duty in battle, Krishna and the Pandavas fought relentlessly and scored a victory in that war. The Yadava clan returned to Dvaraka to celebrate, yet evil omens lay ahead. Gandhari, angered at her loss of sons and kin, cursed Krishna to die in the forest and the entire Yadava Dynasty to be destroyed within thirty-six years. Such dire events did come to pass, as the Yadavas killed one another in drunken quarrels, and Krishna was struck with an arrow in the foot by the hunter Jara, who mistook him for a deer. Arjuna then cremated Krishna, after which he rose up as Vishnu to return to the heavenly Vaikuntha and receive worship there as Narayana. Krishna's brother Balarama, who had stayed with him throughout most of his life except for the war, died just before him at the same location and rejoined Vishnu. The lengthy and variegated life of Krishna, spanning nearly one hundred and twenty years, thus drew to a close. The evil King Kamsa and many of his cohorts were certainly vanquished, yet it is believed that with the withdrawal of Krishna and Balarama from the world, the evil and decadent fourth age of Kali Yuga commenced in which we are presently embroiled.[6]

The geographic location in northern India where Krishna was born and displayed his childhood pastimes is recognized by the name of Braj (Vraja in the Sanskrit texts). Yet *Braj* does not refer to an area with clearly defined boundaries and "has never been used as the official name of a political territory or administrative division."[7] The term comes from the Sanskrit *vraja,* meaning a place where cattle roam, where Krishna tended his cows many years ago. Nonetheless, Braj is often defined as the religious and cultural sphere occupying about eighty-four square miles in western Uttar Pradesh and eastern Rajasthan where the spoken language Braj Bhasha predominates. The area includes the entire districts of Mathura and Bharatpur, as well as adjacent parts of other districts, such as the towns of Aligarh, Hathras, Agra, and Alwar. The single most important town in the Braj area in terms of the intensity of Krishna devotion and worship is Vrindaban, the place where the adolescent Krishna is believed to have exhibited his childish pranks, heroic feats, and amorous pastimes roughly five thousand years ago.

The people of Braj, or Brajbasis as they are usually called, "have taken the image of the romantic and pastoral Krishna to their hearts and have made him the central character in their folklore. They are proud to be associated with the land in which Krishna spent his youth and delight in telling visitors stories about the deeds he performed in their neighborhood. In keeping with their pastoral background, they are lovers of all dairy products and, if they indulge in a feast, prefer to gorge themselves on butter, ghee, and sweets made from milk, rather than any other kind of delicacy. They are also proud of their dialect, usually referred to as 'Braj Bhasha.' It is universally admired for its sweetness and is popularly assumed to be the language that Krishna spoke while he lived and played among the rustic people of Braj. Because it was thought to be the dialect most appropriate for describing Krishna's pastoral adventures, it became the most widely used form of literary Hindi from the sixteenth to the nineteenth century. Throughout this period Braj was a centre of inspiration for anyone concerned with the adventures of Krishna and Radha."[8] While the geographic Braj remains an important locus today for the study of Krishna, it the "spiritual" Braj that has taken on a life of its own within human consciousness: "Even though there is hardly a trace of his mythological environment, the presence of Krishna remains alive in the hearts and minds of the people."[9]

Krishna worship in India generally centered upon his humanlike form. The deity forms of Krishna are venerated according to the events in his earthly life, including birth, childhood miracles, adolescent dalliances with cowherd girls, romantic trysts with his favorite milkmaid Radha, marriages with various queens, slaying of adversaries, ruling of dynasties, and speaking holy teachings (*Bhagavad-Gita*).

The popularization of Krishna worship went hand in hand with the dramatic rise in the use of vernacular lyrics embedded in musical forms: "Music proved itself to be the natural choice to act as a vehicle of desired expression. The rise of the Krishna cult made this more imperative. It could develop, therefore, a popular halo around it. The widely spoken non-Sanskrit languages of regional origin had by then managed to become one of the chosen media for the purpose. Therefore, the more Krishna-worship proselytized itself, the better sustenance could these Deshi (regional) dialects procure for themselves. . . . And as the creed of Bhakti took over, using poetry and music as its sole media, a fresh impetus was provided to both."[10] As the love of Krishna became embedded in the hearts of the populace, a cultural renaissance resounded through the countryside that validated the intimate connection between religious worship and musical experience: "With Prema [deep love] as one of its principles, and Shringara its own mood, the Krishna-theme provided to poets, writers, artists, musicians and dancers an inspiration of vast magnitude. For all of them Krishna was now a god who made music."[11]

The earliest Sanskrit source for Krishna, the *Harivamsa* (second century B.C.E., attached to the *Mahabharata*), reveals the close connection between music and dance within his cultic expression. Sarmadee recounts: "In the *Harivamsa*, the music-inspiring personality of Sri Krishna is for the first time fully introduced. . . . In it we come to know the youthful Krishna of the Gopis, the Krishna of Hori, Dhamar, the Krishna of the Krishna-Gopika Rasa-Krida. This Krishna is to be found nowhere else but in *Harivamsa*. . . .The subsequent Vaishnava literature mainly draws on *Harivamsa*." Already by the time of the *Harivamsa* (HV) there is a strong presence of Laukika music as mentioned in the Smriti texts: "HV [20.3] tells of Laukika and Vaidika Ganas having equal sway during the period. Laukika was the common art of song and dance practiced by the common people as Gandharva; but Vaidika, on the other hand, concerned itself exclusively with Sama-Gana, for example, in connection with Yajna-Yaga."[12]

In chapter 89 of *Harivamsa*, Gandharva music is elaborately discussed in terms of regional representation: "In song and dance compositions, various Deshi-Bhashas of vast popularity were employed. Costumes and other paraphernalia meant for these dance-dramas were also of all designs and colors. They boldly spoke of the regions they came from, and of the people who patronized them."[13] In terms of musical theory, however, the text displays the same terminology as such older music texts as the *Dattilam*: "*Harivamsa* gives credit to a system based on seven Svaras and twenty-two Srutis as also on Sthanas, Murchanas and Gramas."[14] This statement indicates that, while the technical terminology of Indian music remained relatively constant over the centuries, the substance of the songs and melodies began to vary from region to region as new ideas were absorbed and refined.

Described first in the *Harivamsa*, the famous Rasa Dance or Rasa-Lila was an early song and dance tradition in which both men and women participated. This tradition is related to something called the Mandalakara Rasa-Nritya (circle-dance in a Mandala), in which the female performers whirled around clapping each other's palms: "The same dance-type, with its emphasis differing from region to region, has been a presentation par excellence of all times." The Rasa-Lila is said to have been inaugurated by Krishna from the Hallisaka dance, along with Chalikya Gana, mentioned as Chalikya Gandharva (Gandharva chorus-singing):

> In *Harivamsa,* Chalikya-Gandharva has been mentioned in relation to Chalikya-Krida, which makes it possible to believe that it was a sort of Nritya-Gita performed by Gopa tribesmen on the occasion of their community festivals. Both men and women sang this Gita (Chalikya) and danced together. Similarly there is mention of Hallisaka-Gana. It has been said that Sri Krishna started Hallisaka along with Chalikya-Gana; hallisakam tu svayam eva Krishnah savamsa-ghosham naradeva parthah; Sri Krishna performed Hallisaka to the tune of his flute. It was presumably a kind of Rasa-Nritya. The commentator, Sankara of *Harsacarita,* thinks that Hallisaka was a form of a Mandali-Nritya [circle-dance] in which the dance number was done by female dancers, led by a male-dancer in the middle.[15]

This information constitutes further evidence that the Gandharva tradition remained alive despite absorbing many indigenous elements that furthered the cause of Bhakti and temple Hindu traditions.

The highest spiritual aspiration of the advanced Krishna devotee is direct participation in or observation of the eternal pastime of the Rasa Dance, wherein Krishna attracts all the ladies of Braj with his flute in a round dance that is performed on a full-moon night of autumn. In the Rasa Dance, according to both the Sanskrit *Bhagavata-Purana* and *Ananda-Vrindavana-Campu,* and greatly expanded upon in the Hindi and Bengali versions and descriptions, there is a dynamic plethora of pulsating music and rhythm. After the *Bhagavata-Purana,* which describes the Rasa Dance in twenty-two chapters in book 10, the *Ananda-Vrindavana-Campu* by Kavi Karnapur (sixteenth century C.E.) is the best contemporary Sanskrit source that represents the complete fusion of Krishna devotion with Indian music or Bhakti Sangit. Kavi Karnapur was born in 1524 and wrote several works in Sanskrit on themes of Vaishnava tradition. His father was Sivananda Sen, a close associate and follower of Sri Caitanya, making him an important authority in the field of Gaudiya Vaishnavism. One of his later works, *Gaura-Ganoddesa-Dipika,* was composed in 1576. It is said that he wrote *Ananda-Vrindavana-Campu* in his later years in Vrindaban, so it probably appeared shortly after the latter text.

Two chapters (17, 18) of *Ananda-Vrindavana-Campu* describe the Rasa Dance episode with the extensive addition of classical musical terminology and references to Gandharva music. Corresponding to BP 10. 33.10, the

Ananda-Vrindavana-Campu states: "One Gopi, joining Krishna in His singing, sang pure melodious tones with full feeling in the Gandharva scale made pleasant by suitable jati [parent modes], sruti [microtones] and gamakas [tremolo effects]. Pleased, Krishna showed great appreciation for her performance, saying 'Excellent! Excellent!' She pleased Krishna by singing the seven notes of the scale embellished with twenty-two srutis [microtones] presented with the principal ornaments in the introductory passages (alapa)."[16] Many other passages in the *Ananda-Vrindavana-Campu* highlight the centrality of classical music within the context of Rasa dancing and love-play, all centering on the eternal couple of Radha and Krishna. Endless Gandharvas, demigods, and demigoddesses accompany the dance with songs and instrument playing: "Impelled by the festive sight and desiring to dance like the blissful Gopis, the goddesses of dancing, singing, and playing instruments appeared personally at the Rasa dance."[17] More than two dozen classical Ragas (male melodies) and Raginis (female melodies) are mentioned with regard to their presiding deities. All four classes of instruments, including wind, string, drumming, and percussion (including especially cymbals) are well represented in concert with the dancing Gopis. Legions of technical terms are also present, such as *svara* (note), *sruti* (microtones), *jati* (parent scale), *murcchana* (scale variation), *vadi* (principal note), *samvadi* (secondary note), *anuvadi* (penultimate note), *tana* (rapid improvisatory passages), and so on, all in connection with the Rasa Dance event. With regard to the singing of Dhrupad, the text states that "the Gopis sang a type of song called *suddha prabandha* [a type of early Dhrupad]."[18] In addition, many rhythmic *bols* (syllables) expressing the dance beats of the drum (for example, *tat thei tat thei*) occur throughout the text and were repeated verbatim in Hindi and Braj Bhasha poetry of the time period. There is little question that the Gopis and Krishna were believed here to be well skilled in classical Indian music and most probably sang in the vernacular. The entire Rasa Dance event was surrounded with music, as skilled players of instruments accompanied the dance: "The instrumentalists, situated outside the circle, assisted the pastime of the Lord by playing according to the dancing of the Gopis."[19]

KRISHNA SAMPRADAYAS

By the sixteenth century, several new Krishna sampradayas were founded in the Braj region, or modified from previous Vaishnava sampradayas, during the late medieval or Mughal Period (ca. 1500–1750 C.E.). These new movements favored Krishna as the Supreme Being, over and above Vishnu. As noted by Hinduism scholar Edwin F. Bryant: "Moving forward to the sixteenth century and the theologies of what are sometimes referred to as the Krishnaite schools, we find the emergence of organized Krishna lineages that reversed the commonly held relationship between Vishnu and Krishna, positing Krishna as the source of Vishnu rather than a derivative incarnation of Vishnu."[20]

The Krishna sampradayas founded in Braj drew almost exclusively on the Braj Bhasha vernacular poetry produced from within their own respective traditions. And rather than selecting an important site associated with Vishnu mythology or the adult life of Krishna as their base, they established headquarters in the rural vicinity of Braj in northern India, the specific geographical region of Krishna's birth, infancy, and childhood pastimes. These new sampradayas included the Pushti Marg or Vallabha Sampradaya founded by Vallabhacharya in the early sixteenth century (linked with the earlier Rudra Sampradaya, thirteenth century), the Radhavallabha Sampradaya founded by Sri Hita Harivamsa (not linked with any former sampradaya) in the mid-fifteenth century, the Nimbarka Sampradaya founded by Nimbarka (twelfth century, revived in the sixteenth century; not linked with any former sampradaya), the Haridasi Sampradaya founded by Swami Haridas (sometimes linked with the Nimbarka Sampradaya) in the mid-fifteenth century, and the Gaudiya Sampradaya of Bengal founded by Caitanya in the early sixteenth century (linked with the Madhva Sampradaya, thirteenth century).

Instead of focusing attention on the heroic and pedagogical images of Krishna found in the *Mahabharata* and the *Bhagavad-Gita,* the new Krishna sampradayas cultivated devotion to the childhood and adolescent Krishna and explored the emotional feelings experienced between Krishna and the Braj family members, friends, and associates with whom he had reportedly lived. More than simple piety or petition expressed in Puja, however, this intense form of Bhakti was a total spiritual exercise (Seva) directed toward attaining various emotional states (Rasa) that reflected the intimate love of Krishna believed to have been relished by the founders—emotional states said to have been savored originally by the living residents of the Braj area during the actual advent of Krishna roughly five thousand years ago. The young cowherd women (Gopis), both married and unmarried, of the rustic region of Braj became special icons of devotion, as they were purported to have ascended to the highest stages of intimacy and love of Krishna, the supreme goal of Bhakti.

The new communities further distinguished themselves by highlighting Krishna's favorite female consort, Radha, said to be the ultimate object of his enduring love and affection in Braj. Essentially unknown in Vaishnava traditions before the seventh century C.E., Radha became an important goddess or divine Sakti after being equated with Lakshmi, Vishnu's wife, and other Vaishnava consorts in the developing vernacular literature as well as in Tantric circles. Radha was originally described as simply one of the Gopis, but then, as she conquered Krishna with her beauty and love, she ascended to the level of the quintessential devotee of Krishna.

The emphasis on the Sakti or female energy of a male deity was linked to an upsurge of Tantric writings during the middle medieval period. In the Tantric tradition every god, Deva, has a relation with a female deity, a Devi or Sakti, usually as his wife or consort. At a certain point Krishna was paired with Radha, often described as an incarnation of Lakshmi. In their adoration and veneration of Radha alongside Krishna as a dual divinity superior to Vishnu, most of these new groups nonetheless preferred to distance themselves from the Tantric traditions that were receiving social disapproval for unsavory and unorthodox practices. They preferred instead to follow in the wake of the Vaishnava innovations presented in the twelfth-century Sanskrit text *Gita-Govinda* by Jayadeva in Bengal. In this work the youthful Krishna is consistently coupled with his lover and consort Radha. The verses of the *Gita-Govinda* showcased the pure relationship between Krishna and Radha. In the *Gita-Govinda* the former avatara of Vishnu known as Krishna, along with his consort Radha, had fully usurped the primacy of Vishnu as the Supreme Being (*Jagadisa*), becoming the avatarin or source of the avataras. The rise of Radha and Krishna into theological prominence in the Bhakti traditions of Vaishnavism was underscored by her presence in this work, which was enormously influential.

SEVA AND MUSIC

The system of temple Hinduism of the new sectarian movements differed from the typical Puja structure and context that had developed by the middle medieval period. Instead of the term *Puja*, meaning the ordinary pious worship available to the public, they preferred *Seva*, meaning a fully concentrated and exemplary devotional service available to the initiated members of the sect. This new form of sonic liturgy entailed a more all-encompassing ritual process that bound communities of believers together in a joint effort to achieve not simply Moksha but the highest aesthetic and ecstatic experiences in association with Krishna and his companions in the spiritual Vrindaban. Bhakti was cultivated for its own sake.

The emotional experience of Seva produced by the music in the minds of the singer and the listeners is known as Bhava, and it varied according to the type of Raga employed, the meaning of the Pada or literary composition, and the atmosphere provided by the decorations in the temple. As explained by Braj scholar A. W. Entwistle: “As with other devotional activities, the aim of the singing is to evoke Bhava. The lyrics usually describe a particular incident in the life of Krishna. . . . Most sects have special anthologies containing lyrics by a number of poets that are arranged into sequences appropriate for a particular moment in the daily ritual or for a festive celebration.” The devotional songs “serve to enhance and complement the mood evoked by the decoration of the deity.” These songs also bring about a sense of unity in the congregation: "Besides having an emotionally cathartic effect on the participants, this form of worship has always played an important role in creating a feeling of solidarity among the devotees."[21] It is perhaps this solidarity of feeling between the human and divine realms, sometimes known as *koinonia* in the West, that constitutes the most important reason behind the longevity of these traditions. Because of this, great attention has been given to the protection and preservation of the musical traditions in the new sampradayas.

As part of the Seva experience the new Krishna sampradayas cultivated unique forms of Bhakti Sangit that were related in kind to the Dhrupad music in the contemporary ruling courts, both Hindu and Muslim. While there are some folk-like elements in these genres, the presence of Dhrupad structures and features suggests the borrowing of classical styles from the surrounding regions. As explained by Selina Thielemann: "As for North India, there is no written support for the use of the term Dhrupad to denote the devotional songs of the Vaishnavas before the time when Dhrupad had actually been introduced to the courts, that is, before the late fifteenth and early sixteenth centuries. The earliest references to Dhrupad in the context of the Vaishnava temple music tradition specifically that of Braj, are the Haveli Dhrupad ('temple Dhrupad [Haveli Sangit]' of the Vallabha Sampradaya and the Dhrupads of Swami Haridas (ca. 1480–1575). Both Swami Haridas and Vallabha, the founder of the Vallabha Sampradaya, are contemporaries of Raja Mana Simha."[22]

Musicologist Sharma disagrees with Thielemann, however, having contended that Dhrupad was born in Braj and not "imported" from surrounding courts: "In the realm of Indian music, Braj and Dhrupad-Dhamar are nearly synonymous. Dhrupad-Dhamar sprouted in Braj, flourished in Braj, and spread to regions beyond Braj with the passage of time. That is the reason why an inquiry into any Dhrupad musician about . . . his lineage's education and upbringing ultimately reveals his Braj connection."[23] Sharma follows this up with his affirmation that Dhrupad originated in Hindu temples in pre-Mughal times and was the "Mother of all Hindustani classical music":

> All the Padas are related to Krishna Lila; there is a natural relation between the Dhrupad and Krishna Lila, not an artificial one. In the courts at Gwalior, the singers, in order to satisfy the needs of the court itself, molded the music. Whatever the courtiers wanted, the musicians did. But in the temples, that was not the case. In the temples, the style was reproduced in its original form. The musicians owned it. The singers controlled the style, and there was no question of distortion, as there was a religious faith behind it. Therefore the form we hear today is very much to be taken as the original form. It survives today, and reflects the old

temple Dhrupads of pre-Mughal times. The old traditional form of Dhrupad-Dhamar is found even today in these temples. We call it Kirtan, not Haveli Dhrupad. It is the Mother of all Hindustani classical music. Even the language of Braj, Braj Bhasha, comprises 95% of Hindustani classical vocal music.[24]

Dhrupad historian Induram Srivastava had also suggested that wandering Vaishnava religious, rather than stationary temple musicians, had inaugurated the Dhrupad-style devotional songs of the period, stating that, contemporary with Raja Mana Simha, "it was usual for Vaishnava mendicants to roam around with their Vina and sing Dhrupads in the form of devotional songs. This was the genesis of Haveli Dhrupad (the temple Dhrupad)."[25]

Judging from an assessment of the earliest available manuscripts of the Pada-Sangrahas (song anthologies), it is nonetheless undeniable that the oldest form of Haveli Sangit was very close to the tradition of classical music based on the Sanskrit treatises on music written as early as the fourteenth century C.E. This is especially evident in the usage of traditional Ragas and Talas (rhythms) as mentioned in the individual songs themselves. These include Ragas which had been assigned a gender, a time of day, or a season in texts such as the *Sangita-Makaranda* by Narada (ca. fourteenth or fourteenth century) and especially the *Rasa-Kaumudi* of Srikantha (ca. 1575). The somewhat sophisticated use of Raga classifications in the Haveli Sangit tradition thus indicates a familiarity with the courtly tradition of classical music found in Central and South India during early medieval times, a tradition rich in theoretical and aesthetical formulations. The most likely scenario may be that the formal classical style of Dhrupad was conceived in the Hindu courts, and the devotional or temple Dhrupad (Haveli Dhrupad) was fashioned in Braj from the classical ingredients already prevalent since the early medieval period.

Sharma has offered us a useful insight, nonetheless, in revealing that one of the most important common denominators among all the new Braj Vaishnava sects, as well as many other religious groups, was the adoption and modification of Dhrupad-style music for their Seva traditions of worship. He explains that, "being the birthplace of Lord Krishna, the repository of all aesthetic happiness (Rasa), and the place of his pastimes, this land of Braj has been adopted by many heads of religious sects for establishing their devotional worship and service. Thus many sampradayas like Vallabha, Radhavallabha, Haridasi, etc., were originally headquartered there. Apart from the many temples representing various forms of worship of Radha-Krishna, temples of various other deities and religious concerns such as Ramanandi, Ramanuji, Nirvani, Niranjini, Advaitavadi, Sahajiya, Sakti, Siva, also exist there." Despite differences in theology or philosophy, a common factor in all these disparate groups is devotional music, since "all religious leaders considered music as essential for propagation of their faiths in order to make them more attractive. Though there may be differences in the content of their Padas (stanzas), there is no difference in principle in their style of singing. Thus, all of the temples of Braj, barring Sri Rangaji Mandir of Vrindaban where South Indian Karnatak music prevails, are engaged in adorning and furthering the Braj Gayaki of Dhrupad-Dhamar. For these reasons, it could prosper to such an extent."[26] We note here that Samaj Gayan, the other important form of Bhakti Sangit or Pada-Kirtan discussed earlier, was also indebted to the Dhrupad style compositions current during this time.

The commonality of Dhrupad-style singing noted above among the Vaishnava and other sects of this period resonates with this author's earlier work on sonic theology, where it was concluded that, despite theological and cultic differences among many Hindu religious groups, they all shared similar notions of sacred sound in the form of Nada-Brahman and Nada-Sakti in their metaphysical doctrines and theories of language.

Under the name of Kirtan, Haveli Sangit became established within the Pushti Marg Seva sometime during the lifetime of Vallabhacharya, according to the medieval sources. Unfortunately there is little evidence from written sources about the precise nature of Haveli Sangit. In the Varta literature, sectarian discussions in Braj Bhasha prose concerning the biographies of great devotees in the tradition, there are accounts of at least eight original poet-musicians attached to the worship of the original deity of Sri Nathji at Govardhan in Braj. There is also mention of certain favorite compositions of these poets, but there is no description of the manner in which they were sung or performed. The eight poet-musicians are collectively known as Ashtachap, or "Eight Seals," since they each ended their poems with their signature or "chap." Their music is sometimes referred to as Ashtachap Sangit and is believed to have been close to the Dhrupad and Dhamar music prevalent in Braj at that time.

Yet there are subtle differences between Haveli Sangit and the classical Dhrupad songs. Musicologist Anne-Marie Gaston has emphasized the literary content of the songs in Haveli Sangit as opposed to modern concert Dhrupad: "Both Dhrupad and Haveli songs are generally in Braj Bhasha, a dialect of Hindi which, through its association with the mythology of Braj as Krishna's birthplace, became an important literary dialect from the fifteenth to the nineteenth centuries. . . . The name Dhrupad is indicative of the importance of its literary content. Present-day Haveli Sangit gives even greater importance to the text. As it is, concert presentations of Dhrupad tend to emphasize the musical content with a greater elaboration of the Raga."[27]

Moreover, the authenticity of Haveli Sangit as a unique though classically based form of devotional music is supported by the information gathered by Gaston in her study of Nathadvara: "The Nathadvara musicians stated that Haveli

Sangit was closely related to the art music form, Dhrupad-Dhamar. It is generally accepted that both Haveli and Dhrupad-Dhamar evolved from an earlier musical form, Prabandha, and both share many musical characteristics. Nevertheless, Haveli Sangit is a religiously inspired genre in which enthusiasm and devotion are more important than musical intricacy. As a result, Haveli Sangit, as performed in the temples of Nathadvara, is simpler and more straightforward than Dhrupad-Dhamar."[28]

Regarding comparative scholarship of the music of the new Krishna sampradayas, including Haveli Sangit and Samaj Gayan in comparison with classical Dhrupad, mention must be made here of Thielemann's work. Selina Thielemann, in *Musical Traditions of Vaisnava Temples in Vraja. A Comparative Study of Samaja and the Dhrupad Tradition of North Indian Classical Music* (2001), presents and analyzes many examples of Braj Bhasha compositions in both Indian and Western notation. In the first volume of this two-volume work, she examines the five major musical traditions of Braj, beginning with the Caitanya Sampradaya, followed by Radhavallabha Sampradaya, Nimbarka Sampradaya, Haridasi Sampradaya, and Vallabha Sampradaya, and in the second volume she compares these traditions with the classical Dhrupad. Our discussion here will take note of some of her conclusions.

VALLABHA SAMPRADAYA

The largest and most important of the Krishna sampradayas, for our purposes, is the Vallabha Sampradaya or Pushti Marg tradition, founded by Sri Vallabhacharya (1479–1531 C.E.) in Gokula, just outside of Mathura, in roughly 1495 C.E. Vallabhacharya was a Vaishnava scholar-saint who, though originally hailing from southern Andhra Pradesh, focused his preaching efforts mostly in northern Uttar Pradesh, with subsequent sectarian fruition mainly in the states of Rajasthan and Gujarat. He propagated a philosophy of Suddha Advaita Vedanta, a theistic version of Vedanta aimed at establishing the "purified" Brahman as Krishna. For this sect Krishna was not only an avatara of Vishnu; he was also Brahman himself, the ultimate reality.

Vallabha tradition holds that Vallabhacharya received the principal initiatory mantra of the sect, the Brahma Sambandha Mantra (the mantra that binds—*sambandha*—one to Brahman who is Krishna), directly from Krishna himself in Gokula near Mathura in the year 1494 C.E. He then initiated Damodar Das as the first member of the sampradaya with the mantra: *sri krishnah saranam mama*—Sri Krishna is my Refuge. Vallabhacharya was then given the epithet Mukhavatara, having heard the sacred sound from Krishna's mouth. During his lifetime the only person authorized to initiate disciples (that is, to impart the holy sound of the mantra given by Krishna) was Vallabhacharya himself. After his demise this privilege was handed to his two sons by divine decree and then on to his seven grandsons. A hereditary lineage of initiation has been strictly maintained.

The devotional doctrine of Vallabhacharya is known as Pushti Marg, "the Way of God's Grace," derived from a phrase in the *Bhagavata-Purana* 2.10.4 (*poshanam tad-anugrahah*). The path of Pushti Marg is a lifetime plan for complete surrender to Krishna and is believed to be superior to all other Vaishnava paths. For example, instead of progressing through gradual stages through several lifetimes according to the teachings of Ramanuja, Nimbarka, or Madhva, Pushti Marg offers immediate Moksha to its followers after death. When death occurs the souls of its followers first merge into Brahman and are then placed in divine bodies and allowed to participate in the eternal love dance (Rasa-Lila) of Krishna and the Gopis. This eternal state of Moksha is facilitated and sustained by constant repetition of the Brahma Sambandha Mantra and the singing and listening to Kirtan or Haveli Sangit, songs offered as part of the devotional liturgy in Vallabha temples.

The Pushti Marg tradition was host to a legion of exemplary poets who have described the transcendental pastimes of Krishna with the firm intensity of Bhakti coupled with literary genius. These poems form part of the permanent devotional experience in that they are constantly sung and heard within the context of a sonic liturgy. From the literary perspective, religious studies scholar A. Whitney Sanford, in *Singing Krishna: Sound Becomes Sight in Paramanand's Poetry* (2009), stresses the role of both sight and sound in Hindu worship through an analysis of the poetry of the Pushti Marg poet Paramanand: "It is important to know that sight and sound are privileged modes in the divine encounter in the Hindu tradition. . . . Paramanand induces the devotee to 'see' through what he or she 'hears.'"[29] Poems in Pushti Marg are not mere poetry for literary consumption or appreciation, but effective tools as well, with which the aspiring devotees catch a glimpse of the divine world of Krishna Lila: "The poet takes the listener by the hand and walks them through the daily life of Krishna and, in turn, through an annual cycle of predictable repetitive events. . . . It is through the repetition of these cycles [both Nitya (daily) and Utsava (festival)] that devotees gradually transform their vision from Laukika, this mundane world, to Alaukika, Krishna's supramundane world."[30]

When Vallabhacharya came to Govardhan in the late-fifteenth century to see the self-manifested deity of Sri Nathji, the form of Sri Krishna lifting Govardhan Hill, he had a temple constructed on the hilltop and formally installed the deity for worship in roughly 1519 C.E. Although the worship of Sri Nathji began as soon as Vallabhacharya started performing Seva in a small erected hut over the newly found deity, the routine of Ashtayam Seva (service during eight periods of the day) took several years to reach the standardized form. As explained by Entwistle: "Two of Vallabha's own disciples, the poets Krishna Das and Kumbhan Das, were appointed as manager (adhikari) and singer (kirtaniya), and Saddu Pande was given responsibility for organizing the supply of raw materials needed for the offerings."[31] The view that Kumbhan Das was the first of the Ashtachap poets to sing before the deity of Sri Nathji, making him the first Haveli Sangit singer, is generally accepted by scholars. The four elder Ashtachap poets, Kumbhan Das (1469–1584), Sur Das (1478–1580), Paramanand Das (1494–1585), and Krishna Das (1497–1580), are believed to have been initiated directly by Sri Vallabhacharya himself, while the younger four, Govind Swami (1506–1586), Chitaswami (1517–1586), Chaturbhuj Das (1531–1586), and Nanda Das (1534–1584) were initiated by Vallabha's second son, Vitthalnath (1516–1586).

Vitthalnath is said to have inaugurated the elaborate liturgical system, Ashtayam Seva, in which the worship of Sri Nathji was divided into eight periods of the day with variations in the seasonal worship, including special songs and decoration for different festivals. Prior to this time the most famous of the Ashtachap musicians, Sur Das, sometimes said to be the first full-time singer, used to sing for the deity in addition to Kumbhan Das: "When Sur Das was initiated by Vallabhacharya into the sampradaya, he was given the duty of singing Kirtan—hymns of praise—before the svarupa of Sri Govardhan Nathji. Later, when the sampradaya was under the guidance of Vallabhacharya's younger son Vitthalnath, Sur Das' Kirtan singing was formally integrated into the daily periods of worship in the temple of Sri Govardhan Nathji."[32] At the same time Vitthalnath incorporated various musical instruments into the Kirtan Seva. Further details about the Ashtayam ("eight periods") service are outlined below.

PUSHTI MARG SEVA

The liturgical Seva of Sri Nathji in Pushti Marg included special daily Kirtan songs and decorations and others for seasonal festivals. The daily cycle, called Ashtayam or Nitya-Krama, from morning to evening, was divided into eight periods, with Kirtans sung in appropriate Ragas for the times of the day. The annual cycle, called Varshotsava, consisted of different festivals (Utsava) celebrated throughout the year, such as Holi, Ratha Yatra, Sravan, Krishna Janmastami, Radhastami, Rasa-Lila, Annakut, Dipavali (Diwali), and Vasant Panchami. In Pushti Marg one follows a rigid calendar of worship that restricts the music and the Ragas employed according to time of day and season, hot or cold: "In the Vallabhite temples . . . a strict calendar is followed for the Ragas, and there are specific melody types for the cold and hot seasons respectively."[33]

The two types of Seva, the daily and the seasonal, form the foundation of the liturgical life of Pushti Marg. The daily rituals, Nitya-Krama, are impossible to understand without familiarity with the daily life of the deity of Krishna. As such, the daily cycle depicts a typical day in the life of Krishna as Gopal, a cowherd boy who lives at home with his parents Mother Yasoda and Nanda Baba. His day is punctuated by eight Darshan periods (Jhanki) in which he (the deity) is visibly adored by the Hindu public and during which three items must be offered—Sringara (dress and decoration), Bhog (food and drinks), and Raga (music, that is, Haveli Sangit)—as established by Vitthalnath. Since music was obligatory at each of the eight Darshan periods, lasting roughly ten to fifteen minutes each, it became an important component of the Vallabhite tradition. From Mangala, in which Sri Nathji is awakened in the morning by 6:00 A.M., to Sayan, or bedtime in the evening at 7:30 P.M., music must be performed as an offering throughout the day. Accordingly all of the Ashtachap poet-musicians mentioned above were assigned to a specific Darshan period so that they would compose and perform their own compositions as offerings to the deity at their respective times. For example, Sur Das, the most renowned of the eight Ashtachap members, sang at the time of Utthapan (4:00 to 4:30 P.M.) when the deity is awakened from his afternoon nap. Paramanand Das sang at the time of Mangala and was followed by Nanda Das who sang at Sringara, the time when Krishna is dressed for the day between 7:00 and 8:00 A.M. After this, Gopal goes out to tend to the cows in the morning with his cowherd friends. This is called Go-carana or Gwala (8:00–9:00 A.M.), the time when Govind Swami used to sing.

There is evidence that Govind Swami was especially expert in the art of music and was a sort of mentor to the other members of the Ashtachap. In the Varta literature it is even mentioned that the famous singer of Emperor Akbar's court, Mian Tansen, studied music under Govind Swami. Tansen is assumed here to be an initiated member of Pushti Marg, since "it is mentioned in 252 *Vaishnavas*, where he meets Govind Swami, an expert singer who teaches Tansen later in his life."[34] Though perhaps apocryphal, the account of this occurrence gives additional credence to the view that Ashtachap music was a form of Dhrupad, since the music of Tansen was rendered in classical Dhrupad style, as attested by several reliable sources.

The main meal of the day is offered to Krishna between 10:00 and 11:00 A.M. This period is known as Raj Bhog and included the music of Kumbhan Das. Following his "lunch," Sri Nathji would take his afternoon nap until 4:00 P.M., when he was awakened by the music of Sur Das. After an hour or so, the evening meal was served at Sandhya Bhog (5:00–5:30 P.M.), accompanied by the music of Chaturbhuj Das. This was followed by a worship service between 6:00 and 6:30 P.M. known as Sandhya Arati and sung by Chitaswami. The last event in the daily worship routine of Sri Nathji was the Sayan or bedtime service. At this service Krishna Das used to serenade the deity to sleep at between 7:00 and 7:30 P.M. We must remember that Sri Nathji is in the form of a young boy, with a daily schedule resembling that of a princely child. Throughout Pushti Marg Seva a courtly ambience surrounds the deity and his ministrations.

The Ashtachap poets were also identified with different characters in the pastimes of Sri Nathji. For instance, they are known as Ashta Sakha, or the eight cowherd friends of Krishna during the daytime, and as the Ashta Sakhi, or the eight female friends of Krishna during the night. These correspondences are given below, alongside the eight divisions, with times and appropriate Ragas for the daily cycle under the times:[35]

Mangala 6:00–7:00 A.M.	Paramanand Das	Tosa Sakha
	Lalit, Bhairav, Vibhas	Chandrabhaga Sakhi
Sringara 7:00–8:00 A.M.	Nanda Das	Bhoja Sakha
	Vilaval, Ramkali, Gunakali	Chandralekha Sakhi
Gwala 8:00–9:00 A.M.	Govind Swami	Sridama Sakha
	Asavari, Todi, Devgandhar	Bhama Sakhi
Raj Bhog 10:00–11:00 A.M.	Kumbhan Das	Arjun Sakha
	Sarang, Deshi, Asavari	Visakha Sakhi
Utthapan 4:00–4:30 P.M.	Sur Das	Krishna Sakha
	Bhimpalasi, Dhanasi	Campakalata Sakhi
Sandhya Bhog 5:00–5:30 P.M.	Chaturbhuj Das	Visal Sakha
	Gauri, Purvi, Puriya	Vimala Sakhi
Sandhya Arati 6:00–6:30 P.M.	Chitswami	Subal Sakha
	Sri, Jaitasri	Padma Sakhi
Sayan 7:00–7:30 P.M.	Krishna Das	Rsabha Sakha
	Bihag, Yaman, Kamod, Kedara	Lalita Sakhi

The times of the eight Darshan periods differ slightly among the various regions. For this reason time periods of one-half to one hour are given to suggest an approximate time slot in which the roughly fifteen-minute musical Darshan period would be included. Each of the Ashtachap poets would prepare his own musical compositions to sing before Sri Nathji during his assigned period.

The Ragas mentioned alongside the times of the day are classified in the Vallabha tradition as either warm or cool. According to Sharma, "the morning cool ragas include Bhairav, Ramkali, DevGandhar, Vilaval, Vibhas, Maru, Sarang, Dhanasri, Suha, and Malhar, while the evening cool ragas are Purvi, Gauri Nat, Kalyan, Iman, Sorath, Kanhara, Adana, Jaijayavanti, and Malhar. The morning warm Ragas include Lalit, Malkauns, Pancham, Khat, Todi, Asavari, Malar,

Vasant, etc., while the evening warm ragas are Nayaki, Kedar, Bihag, Bihayari, Raisi, Jaitsri, Kafi, and Vasant. Ragas Bhairav and Purvi may be sung all through the year in the morning and evening respectively."[36] These distinctions are also recognized and carried out in the seasonal calendar of the annual festivals.

The seasonal cycle of Kirtan is called the Varshotsava (Varsha - year + Utsava - festival). Different festivals or Utsavas are celebrated throughout the year, in which various aspects of Seva, including Raga (music), Bhog (food), and Sringara (dress), are arranged. The format for the calendar year includes the following important festivals, with lunar date specifications, where the appropriate Ragas, whether warm or cool, are listed:[37]

Ratha Yatra (Asarh Shukla 2): Raga Malhar is performed in all Jhankis.
Sravan (Sravan Krishna 1): Hindol and cool Ragas other than Malhar are sung.
Sri Krishna Janmastami: all Ragas except for Lalit are sung on this day.
Asvin Shukla 1–7: 9 days of Padas (stanzas) of Nau Vilas are sung in Raga Malhar at Sayan (deity bedtime).
Kartik Shukla 11 (Prabodhini): warm Ragas are sung but only Raga Lalit for the entire day.
Makar Sankranti (approx. Paush Krishna 30 until Shukla 15): Ragas Lalit and Malkauns are performed.
Margashirsha (Krishna 1): Padas of Vratacharya begin, and warm Ragas are sung at all Jhankis everywhere. All Sarang Ragas are stopped.
Vasant Panchami (Magh Shukla 5 until Phalgun Krishna 30): Raga Vasant is sung in all Jhankis.
Phalgun Shukla 1: cool Ragas begin again.
Aksaya Tritiya (Vaisakh Shukla 3): Raga Sarang is sung in Raj Bhog Arati and Raga Hamir in Sandhya Arati.
Snana-Yatra (Jyestha Shukla 15 until Ratha Yatra): In the morning, during the Padas of Khandita, Ragas Suha and Sugharai are sung, while at the evening Bhog and Arati, Raga Sorath is sung.

There are many hymnals and liturgical manuals for Pushti Marg Seva, but most of them are divided according to the categories listed above. Although there are thousands of songs that are distributed throughout the many temples and shrines of this tradition, many songs are shared among temples because their description of temple decorations appropriate for the time of day or season are of exceptional quality. Ethnomusicologist Meilu Ho has explained this phenomenon in more detail:

> Temple Kirtan almanac-systems (Kirtan Pranali) are the guidebooks for a temple singer. Handwritten copies are found in temples. Many use printed copies that

> they have published themselves. . . . These almanacs outline the songs to be used for 365 days of the year. In practice, they vary from temple to temple in terms of actual song sung, but temples will share the same songs with regard to which best express the primary emotional intent of the day. The color, type, style, and fabric of Krishna's clothes, his headdress, and special food offering (if any) are included in the daily prescriptions for songs, as these are the business of the kirtaniya.[38]

Thielemann confirms this observation, as well as the fact that the Pushti Marg is unique in its position as the most longstanding tradition of meticulous Seva with regard to time of day and season: "The Vallabha Sampradaya owns by far the most extensive amount of printed textbooks for liturgical use. The verse collections are structured according to the requirements of daily and seasonal ritual service, with exact indications as to the Raga and the proper day and time of singing. The Vallabha Sampradaya is the only community that has maintained, on a large scale, the continuous practice of music throughout the day to accompany every single ritual act in the temple."[39]

Gaston, in *Krishna's Musicians: Musicians and Music Making in the Temples of Nathadvara, Rajasthan* (1997), discusses the complicated nature of Seva in the most important and largest Pushti Marg center in Nathadvara:

> In common with many other Krishna temples, worship in the Shri Nathji Haveli has two essential ingredients: Bhakti or devotion to God, and Seva or service [to God]. All work in the Haveli is regarded as Seva to Shri Nathji. Music, which has always been one of the most important components of the religious rituals of the Shri Nathji Haveli, is one form of Seva. It is presented up to seventeen times a day. Seva of Shri Nathji must be performed with Bhakti, and complete selflessness and humility, with obsessive attention to ensuring his comfort and maintaining his status as a manifestation of god on earth. Seva and Bhakti are inextricably interwoven, neither can exist without the other. Bhakti gives the raison d'etre for the various activities associated with the worship of Sri Nathji.[40]

All in all, the entire system of Pushti Marg Seva comprises one of the most sophisticated forms of sonic liturgy in Hindu tradition.

The manner in which the creative arts have been integrated into Pushti Marg Seva is only beginning to be apprehended by outsiders. From altar backdrops to temple architecture, from delicate miniature paintings to decorative floral designs, from gourmet cooking to exemplary needlework, from classical Vina playing to choral singing, the Indian arts have all been channeled into the Pushti Marg Seva in ways that require many years of study to capture their full significance. The Pushti Marg philosophy of Suddha Advaita Vedanta has informed the Pushti Marg approach to the divine and affirmed that there is a fundamental unity between the worshipped and the worshipper. This understanding played a definitive role in their traditions of Seva, whereby all of the various "material" dimensions of worship, including sight, taste, smell, sound, and touch, are conflated in a kind of liturgical mysticism.

Despite language and cultural difference, scholars such as Meilu Ho have attempted to grasp the concept and articulate the notion of holistic blend of the arts and liturgical experiences in the Vallabha Seva: "The emphasis on the utilization of the arts in liturgical service (Seva) is a part of the philosophy of Brahmavad (Theory of Brahman), where the material world is seen but as sparks of the cosmic source of fire; a variegate external forms of the same essence. Embracing the most refined of material culture is to offer the best possible to the lord, who is no different from the substances being offered. The visual, culinary, customary, and musical arts are all components of the completed notion of Seva, that is, tan-man-vitaja Seva, or service using one's body-mind-material possessions."[41] Furthermore, she states that "performing Seva, in that it conflates—materially, temporally, spatially—one's existence in this and that world, may be understood as a form of non-dualistic experience. In this way, performance of service is not merely a ritual, but is also a philosophy practiced. The seemingly symbolic gestures of a ritualistic act take on a larger-than-life meaning, bringing the doer into participation and experience of the divine world."[42]

Focusing on the musical and culinary dimensions, we may catch a glimpse of the intimate yet everlasting encounter with the divine as experienced in the Pushti Marg sonic liturgy, as interpreted by Ho: "When singing songs during the food offering, the song text empowers one to partake of the food together with the Lord. Capping off the Seva with song singing pulls one into the life of the cosmic world, and the food one earlier purchased is now being eaten by Krishna and by one (and other compatriots), who play the part of the divine friends in the cosmic world of the song text." Ultimately, the devotee is transfixed by the Lord and savors the communion in perpetuity: "I suggest that the experience of music—self-performance primarily and listening secondarily—in the particular context of doing Seva, approximates the overwhelming, melting sensation of Rasa-relishing, or God-relishing—only that it is not a transient feeling, a momentary mystical state, but a continual and extended one."[43]

HAVELI SANGIT

Haveli Sangit is not the original name of the music of Pushti Marg. While often described as "music performed in the Havelis or palaces of Krishna worship," the term *Haveli Sangit* is actually of recent vintage. In the early hymnals and literature of this sect, the Dhrupad-style songs of the Vallabha tradition are called

Kirtan. While Vallabhacharya was not a performing musician, Kirtan is mentioned several times in his Sanskrit works as a highly beneficial means of service to the deity. This music acquired the distinctive name of Haveli Sangit as recently as 1955, when executives at All India Radio in New Delhi introduced this name to propagate Vallabha music to the public. *Haveli Sangit* literally refers to music in the Havelis ("houses," or "mansions" in Persian) that are prevalent in Rajasthan, where the center of the Vallabha sect shifted in 1672 C.E. to avoid Mughal persecution. Since some Mughal rulers in the seventeenth century were known to demolish any structure that looked like a Hindu temple, the Haveli or house was adopted as the preferred place of worship for Vallabhite *svarupas* (deities, the chief of whom is Sri Govardhan Nathji, known simply as Sri Nathji) in exile from Braj. The town of Nathadvara, north of Udaipur, in Rajasthan, was virtually created around the deity of Sri Nathji in order to become the center of the Vallabha Sampradaya. The most orthodox tradition of Haveli Sangit continues there in an unbroken lineage of musicians to the present day. For convenience, we use the term *Haveli Sangit* to refer to Vallabhite music at any stage in its historical development, since it is presumed by devotees of the tradition to be nearly identical with the original Kirtan. However, musicological analysis reveals some specific modifications in the music over the centuries. Nonetheless, the music of the Vallabha Sampradaya is highly significant and influential within the history of the Hindustani classical tradition.

Gopi Rasik Tailang, one of the Acharyas of the Vallabha Sampradaya stationed at Jatipur Temple in the area of Govardhan, explained the nature of Haveli Sangit in an interview, with reference to its continuity and meaning for the devotees over the centuries: "Haveli Sangit started developing with Sur Das, Nanda Das, Chaturbhuj Das, etc. When these poets of Ashtachap realized the usefulness of this system they gave a proper place for Kirtan in the daily worship. These Ashtachap sang about Lord Krishna in the way in which they beheld his Darshan, and since then innumerable devotees sing their Padas in the same manner even today. The public hears this music and enjoys it, and it has been a path of emancipation and God-realization for many of them."[44]

Sur Das, whose Hindi poetry is widely known throughout India from his main work the *Sur-Sagar*, exemplified the attitude shared by nearly all the Bhakti poets toward music and singing. For Sur Das, principal among the Ashtachap, singing was a viable means of salvation, as explained by John Stratton Hawley in his study of Sur Das: "If anything in the *Sur-Sagar* spells release and salvation, it is the act of singing itself. . . . Song, for Sur—singing to the Lord—is as close as one can come to salvation." Song is the means of fastening unto Krishna: "The act of singing the poem creates a bond between the singer and the Lord that suggests another valency altogether."[45]

The religio-aesthetical considerations of Haveli Sangit are fairly straightforward. The Upanishadic dictum *raso vai sah* maintains that the Absolute Truth is full of Rasa or emotional taste, pleasure. As Brahman, Krishna is believed to be the fountainhead and source of all Rasa, as well as the original musician (flute player). Krishna, being a transcendent personality, is extremely fond of Ragas (male) and Raginis (female) and relishes them so much that he requires their presence in his services. As the music is offered to Krishna out of Bhakti or love of God, the musician or devotee gains association with Bhagavan (Krishna) and reaches the Lord's abode known as Goloka. In the words of Mathura Haveli Sangit singer Pandit Lav Caturvedi, "through svara (musical notes), one reaches Isvara (Krishna)."[46] Though there is no etymological connection between these two terms, the pun is revealing with regard to the relation between music and the divine in Pushti Marg.

Accordingly, Gaston has described the soteriological dimension of Haveli Sangit, whereby the sonic liturgy containing the songs acts as a kind of catalyst for transporting the devotees to the spiritual world: "It is a fundamental belief of the Vallabha Sampradaya that all beings have the potential for a unique experience with Krishna. . . . The poetry in the songs awakens this potential by helping devotees to visualize themselves as actually participating in the life of Krishna. Language and music create the scene and the listeners are transported to the sacred land of Braj."[47]

The singular combination of poetic beauty and musical elation in Haveli Sangit thus comprises the devotional package that envelopes the devotee and links him or her to the higher realms of Krishna meditation. And it is specifically within the context of the sonic liturgy or Seva that this takes place. Ho has further discussed and analyzed the process of Seva with reference to music in the Pushti Marg tradition:

> In the Pushti Marg liturgy, music takes on the potency of an aid that is used daily, within a particular ritual environment, Seva, with the ultimate aim of achieving religious realization (Nirodh), in this lifetime. An experience is not the fleeting, evanescent kind achieved at the momentary heights of ecstasy primarily through the immediate socio-musical context. Rather, it is an ontological state that comes about through a lifelong cultivation of an emotional-aesthetic commonsense (Bhava) which possibility arises only with the assiduous service of the Lord over a lifetime. The power of the music lies in the manner in which it activates the imagination of the devotee during the execution of simultaneous embodied acts. With the aid of song, the mind and body takes on the life of one in the cosmic world, the Lila self, daily, persistently. And it is only through such continual engagement in the total Seva spanning one's life that one may aspire toward the ultimate goal.[48]

From the performance perspective, Haveli Sangit is a group endeavor. Normally one leader or lead singer sits with other members in close proximity on the temple floor or platform adjacent to the deity. Singing from an anthology of verses composed in the Braj Bhasha language, he or she often plays simultaneously on the harmonium (small portable reed organ) while the others sometimes repeat after him in call-and-response fashion. All singing is done in unison, since there is no harmony in the Western sense. Other instruments are employed, including a long drum known as a Pakhavaj, hand cymbals known as Jhanjh, a plucked drone lute known as a Tanpura, and sometimes a bowed lute or Sarangi. As indicated above, the Padas are sung in different Ragas or melodic configurations that express the mood or Bhava appropriate to the time and the Lila being described in the Pada itself. Thielemann concurs but notes a point of contrast with the other prominent form of Pada-Kirtan, Samaj Gayan: "Unlike Samaj Gayan, performances of Haveli Sangit are often held in soloistic setting by a singer and a number of accompanying instruments, without a chorus of responsorial singers. The Samaj setting, however, is not uncommon, and at certain temples, the rules require a certain number of supporting singers to assist the main vocalist. Pakhavaj, harmonium and cymbals are indispensable as accompanying instruments, but the ensemble is normally enriched by a Sarangi and other supporting melody instruments."[49]

Regarding rhythm in Haveli Sangit, the primary beats (Talas) are as follows: Cautal (12 beats), Dhamar (14 beats), Ada Cautal (14 beats), Adi Tal or Tintal (16 beats or in fast speed 8 beats), Jhaptal (10 beats), Sultal (10 beats), Rupak (7 beats), Dipchandi (14 beats) and Jhumra (14 beats). Dhamar is a form of Dhrupad-style Pada-Kirtan that refers to a slow/fast composition of fourteen beats that is sung primarily during the Holi season but also during other festivals such as Krishna Janmastami, Radhastami, Ekadasi, Dipavali (Diwali), and Annakut.

The Talas of Haveli Sangit have been traced to many of the original rhythms of Gandharva Sangita as delineated in the *Natya-Sastra* of Bharata. Sharma has explained this as follows: "Seven chief rhythms are described in Bharata's classic work on the dramatic arts, *Natya-Sastra*. According to percussionist expert Sri Govind Devraoji of Burhanpur, the present forms of those principal seven Talas are given: 1–Dhruva (Ada Cautal), 2–Math (Sul), 3–Rupak (Rupak), 4–Jhampa (Jhaptal), 5–Tripata (Tintal), 6–Ada (Cautal), 7–Ek Tal (Ektal). In Pushti Marg Sangit, with some variation, these seven beats are as follows: Cautal (12 beats), Dhamar (14 beats), Ada Cautal (14 beats), Adi Tal or Tintal (16 beat or in fast speed 8 beats), Jhaptal (10 beats), Sul Tal (10 beats), and Jhumra (14 beats)."[50] These correlations reveal the extraordinary continuity in Indian music over many centuries.

Despite the apparent freedom given to the performer of Haveli Sangit in improvisation and variations, Thielemann has carefully noted the restrictions on performance that are prevalent in most forms of Bhakti Sangit: "Improvisation must not be carried out in a manner as to obstruct the clear pronunciation of the words and to obscure their comprehensibility, but it serves solely to highlight the devotional message and the relevance of the text. It is this emphasis on the words rather than the notes that marks the fundamental difference between devotional and classical music."[51]

From the point of view of musical style, there are two prominent centers of Haveli Sangit today; (1) Braj, and (2) Nathadvara (Rajasthan). Although Pushti Marg temples are scattered all over India, the Kirtankars (performers of Kirtan) in each are found to be attached to either Braj or Nathadvara in their musical allegiance, such that their style of singing reveals at once the tradition from which they learned Kirtan. Haveli Sangit is still widely practiced and is found primarily in Rajasthan, Gujarat, and Maharashtra.

Just as initiatory succession in the Vallabha Sampradaya was kept strictly within the system of paternal family lineage beginning with Vallabhacharya himself, so the musical tradition of Haveli Sangit is believed, for the most part, to have been handed down from father to son, beginning with the Ashtachap poets who first trained their sons or close disciples in the art of Dhrupad-Dhamar singing. This singing tradition has remained hidden for centuries in that its dissemination or performance in public has been guarded, that is, until the 1950s. In 1991 the main temple or Haveli in Nathadvara was finally opened to non-Hindu visitors, paving the way for Western research and documentation.

Ho has produced the most complete study of Pushti Marg music in the English language, "The Liturgical Music of Pushti Marg of India: An Embryonic Form of the Classical Tradition" (2006). In this work, a Ph.D. dissertation, she never loses site of the liturgical context of Haveli Sangit within the Seva of Pushti Marg tradition, yet she also demonstrates its foundational influence on the Hindustani vocal tradition. The mandatory inclusion of Haveli Sangit in religious worship necessitated its preservation as part of a larger cultural experience, both visual and aural: "Because the service of song is required in liturgy, this temple tradition has maintained a vibrant musical practice that is difficult to match elsewhere. Whereas the visual, the fusing of secular and religious values permeated what eventually became a major painting style, in the same way, the values of Vaishnava culture have become embedded in the vocal repertoire of Hindustani classical music."[52]

A growing interest in Haveli Sangit among modern exponents and admirers of Hindustani classical music suggests that Haveli Sangit, or Ashtachap Sangit as an important precursor, will be preserved. Thielemann has described their close affinity: "The Ragas and Talas sung in Haveli Sangit are identical with those of North Indian classical music. In addition, ancient and uncommon melody types and metric cycles are practiced in Haveli Sangit."[53] But as the music was taken out of the temples and into the courts of the Mughal emperors, singing styles reflected certain changes characteristic of the transition from religious devotion to courtroom entertainment. Yet the basic structure, that is, the Ragas, Talas, and their execution, has remained intact over the centuries. Heading this revival, classical vocalist Pandit Jasraj has recorded CDs of Haveli Sangit with titles such as *Bhajan: Sur Padavali-Nitya Kram* (1983) and *The Inimitable Pandit Jasraj: Echoes of Temple Music* (1989) and performed packed concerts billed as "Haveli Sangit" in London's Royal Albert Hall and other venues. Classical singers Sanjiv Abhyankar and Rattan Mohan Sharma are continuing this tradition through concerts and recordings.

Sharma, who earlier testified to the seminal influence of Haveli Sangit on Hindustani classical traditions, further elaborates on this point in a 1996 work: "The tradition of Pushtimargiya music has been a matter of attraction for modern musicians. Its impact is clearly discernible in the *Kramik Pustak Malika* (6 vol., 1932), the largest anthology of classical music compositions, Dhrupad and Khyal, compiled by Pandit V. N. Bhatkhande. While some of the compositions in this collection are true copies of Pushtimargiya songs, or else used with slight modification, many of them are either incorrect or incomplete. As such, an important source of present-day Khyal and even Thumri can be found in the Gayaki of Haveli Sangit, making it, in a sense, 'the mother of North Indian classical music.'"[54]

Haveli Sangit is intrinsically tied to a unique form of spirituality, according to Sharma:

> Through the music of this tradition we can get many leads into the nature of Indian spirituality. The archaic form of many Ragas is still available to us. Moreover, we can hear the old Gayaki of traditional Dhrupad-Dhamar in the temples with the same deep devotion and faith, in every season and from morning to evening. Spirituality is the unique adornment not only of Indian music, but of the soul of India as a whole. Nowhere do we find this spiritual aspect as much as in the temples themselves. The present musical tradition continues to be deeply imbued with spirituality, such that it would be no exaggeration to say that the true spirituality of music has taken birth in this tradition. Deep faith and respect towards this tradition projects us back to the glorious past of Indian music.[55]

The Seva of Pushti Marg, including Haveli Sangit, thus forms a quintessential example of Hindu sonic liturgy in which the human and divine realms converge via ritual and music. It can also be observed that the Haveli Sangit tradition of Pushti Marg is one of the most venerable traditions of Indian music.

5

Seva and Samaj Gayan

BESIDE THE VALLABHA TRADITION OF Pushti Marg, there are three additional Krishna sampradayas flourishing in Braj that have adopted Bhakti Sangit as their central form of devotional expression. Instead of Haveli Sangit, they have cultivated the other most important form of Bhakti Sangit, Samaj Gayan. A form of northern Pada-Kirtan, it is found in at least three distinct traditions of Seva or liturgical worship. Samaj Gayan is the most vocally interactive style among the Pada-Kirtan genres, yet it is much less well known than Haveli Sangit or other forms. Possessing its own unique set of melodies, Samaj Gayan is a highly complex form of responsorial singing that requires serious training and diligence to perform properly. Despite being mostly obscured from the general public, Samaj Gayan is regularly performed and cultivated within the Seva or worship practices of the Radhavallabha Sampradaya founded by Sri Hita Harivamsa (1502–1552), the Nimbarka Sampradaya founded by Sri Nimbarka (ca. 1200), and the Haridasi Sampradaya founded by Swami Haridas (ca. 1475–1580), all centered in Vrindaban. Although Samaj Gayan conforms to the definitional parameters of Pada-Kirtan, the specific terms *Kirtan* and *Bhajan* are not employed in these three traditions.

SAMAJ GAYAN

The ordinary meaning of the word *Samaj* is "group" or "assembly," and *Gayan* means "singing." Samaj Gayan is the collective singing of devotional verses in a particular style. As a form of Pada-Kirtan that is related to the classical Dhrupad style, Samaj Gayan is based on similar notions of Raga and Tala and, like Dhrupad, incorporates a formal structure with strict rules of development requiring a basic knowledge of Indian musical tradition. Classical Dhrupad and Samaj Gayan are only sung in non-Sanskritic dialects such as Braj Bhasha and not in Sanskrit, which was believed to be the language of the gods, Narada Rishi, and the Puranic authors. But while Sanskrit is called Devanagari and is believed to be spoken by the gods, the Bhakti authors of North India claimed that Krishna and his associates, who are on a higher plane of power and intimacy than the other gods, speak and sing in Braj Bhasha, a dialect related to Apabhramsa Prakrit and medieval Hindi. Moreover, Braj Bhasha is less formal with regard to grammar and pronunciation, has more allowance for vowel sounds, and is thus sweeter to the ear and more suitable for singing.

Several differences, however, exist between classical Dhrupad and Samaj Gayan. Whereas the subject matter of Samaj Gayan is solely the glorification of Radha and Krishna, classical Dhrupad has enlarged its repertoire to include adoration of kings and heroes, descriptions of nature, and occasionally human passions and exploits. And while Dhrupad more strictly adheres to the form of classical Ragas as found in the treatises, Samaj Gayan compositions, though often resembling basic Raga structures, essentially comprise a repertoire of special melodies that are handed down orally in *guru-sisya parampara*, master-disciple succession. Hand cymbals or Jhanjh must always be used in Samaj Gayan but are virtually absent in Dhrupad concerts. And while concert Dhrupad must have unaccompanied Alap, there is no Alap in Samaj Gayan. Whereas classical Dhrupad is frequently sung solo, Samaj Gayan is never a solo singing event. The harmonium is almost always used in Samaj Gayan but is rarely found in Dhrupad presentations. Perhaps the principal difference lies in the fact that Samaj Gayan is always purely religious in intention and context, whereas Dhrupad had developed as courtly entertainment as early as the sixteenth century. The texts of Samaj Gayan are also much longer and comprise a significantly larger number of verses than Dhrupad. Selina Thielemann notes the complexity of Samaj Gayan in contrast to the simple fourfold structure of classical Dhrupad: "The most complex structure is found in Samaj Gayan, where the verses may comprise any number of lines from four onwards; very often the texts are extremely extended, and they have to be rendered in full during the performance owing to the sanctity of their devotional content. The sequence of Sthayi and Antara is repeated for each couplet; Sancari and Abhog (i.e. the final couplet) are melodically identical with Sthayi and Antara respectively."[1] Many of the minor differences, however, are circumstantial and do not obscure the basic similarity in design and structure.

The most conspicuous feature of Samaj Gayan is its completely interactive nature; at least two responsorial singers (Jhelas) are required to respond to each line, half-line, phrase, word, and exclamation of the main singer (Mukhiya) in a systematic fashion, including hand gestures. Samaj Gayan is the only genre of Indian music that has adopted this intricate process of intercommunication or articulation. As such, there is no solo Samaj Gayan, for it is said that without the Jhelas there can be no Samaj Gayan. The true essence of the singing tradition is constituted by the interactive "play" of the participants who temporarily assume the roles of the associates of Krishna and the Gopis. For example, the frequent response patterns of the Jhelas in Samaj Gayan include long exclamations of the short phrase *eri ha* or *iha* that are signs of affirmation believed to have been used by the Gopis in association with Krishna.

While the melodies of Samaj Gayan in themselves may contain similarities to classical Ragas and Talas, the interactive nature of the actual rendition differs considerably from classical performance. For example, the verse lines are systematically broken up into fragments with many seemingly unnecessary repetitions and exclamations. First the Mukhiya sings an entire line in a slow Tala such as Dhamar, with response from the Jhelas. Then the Mukhiya begins breaking up the line into phrases and adding appropriate words of exclamation (*eri ha, eri mai,* and so on), with the Jhelas repeating each fragment verbatim. The Pakhavaj player maintains the prescribed rhythm throughout each section but with variations. Then the Mukhiya and the Jhelas, after singing and repeating the first half and second half of each line in this way, repeat the entire line in a faster tempo such as Dipchandi (fourteen beats) or Keherva (eight beats). Once this is finished, the next line begins slowly again and proceeds in the same way. After all the lines have been rendered in this manner, the refrain is repeated several times in unison in a faster tempo such as Dipchandi or Keherva. The entire performance of a song following this process may last an hour or more depending on the number of lines of text. It is obvious that the Jhelas are experienced musicians who understand the dynamics of this style of singing. In most cases there is also an eager audience in the temple that follows closely every word and nuance for the duration of the song.

The instruments preferred for Samaj Gayan are the same as those for Haveli Sangit: the drum (Pakhavaj or Tabla), the hand cymbals (Kartal or Jhanjh), and the harmonium, a small portable reed organ, to accompany the lead singer. Occasionally a drone instrument such as a Tanpura or a bowed lute such as a Sarangi or Esraj is added for melodic effect. Since the text of the song is the main focus of the singing, there is little solo playing of instruments or any virtuosity for its own sake. The players are there to accompany the singers and enhance the overall effect of the lyrics as rendered in song as part of the Seva.

More specifics of the Samaj Gayan style are here described from firsthand observation by the author. The musicians are generally seated along two rows adjacent to the deity or altar platform. In most cases the percussionist faces the deity toward the end of the rows and the Jhelas face each other and the Mukhiya, who may be on either side. After an invocatory prayer honoring the founder and other Acharyas, the leader begins the Samaj session with a slow composition in either Dhamar Tala or Cautal, which speeds up intermittently according to the dynamics of the call-and-response format. Within the time frame (one to three hours), several songs are selected by the leader, and the session is usually closed with a few songs in lighter Talas (Dadra, six beats, or Dipchandi) that most everyone knows from memory. The songs are generally followed in the hymnal by both the musicians and the congregation. Unlike other genres of Indian music, Samaj

Gayan displays a much more intimate interaction between the lead singer and the responders. There is also a close adherence to the text, with little or no attention to individual creativity or improvisation as is found in courtly classical traditions.

Despite the absence of musical notation in the hymnals of these traditions, congregations of singers follow a familiar and established pattern of melody and rhythm learned through oral transmission. Many songbooks contain, above each song-text, the names of many of the familiar Ragas of current Hindustani classical tradition, such as Kanhara, Dhanasri, Kafi, Sarang, and Malhar. Yet the live performative tradition differs significantly from the indications in the songbooks, exhibiting different, more specialized, or even unknown forms of these otherwise general categories of Hindustani Ragas in their standard seasonal repertoires. And while some of the songs used throughout the liturgical year of these sects can be readily identified with standard forms of classical Ragas, there are several key songs which, though based on the Raga format, have their own individual character and are generally not to be heard outside the tradition. That is, although carrying a certain Raga's name above their place in the hymnal, the actual melody-lines defy particular classification. While they often similarly exhibit extremely elevated aesthetic moods or Rasas, they unfortunately cannot be systematized according to the Rasas experienced in the standard Raga rubric. Instead of strict prescriptions, as in the Haveli Sangit of the Vallabha Sampradaya, the Ragas listed above the poems in Samaj Gayan appear to be approximations, general guidelines, manuscript conventions, or simply cues for the singers added later by the editors of the anthologies. Yet the songs of these sampradayas should not be seen as deviations or imperfect renderings of earlier standardized scales or Ragas but more as archaic forms of the now classicized Raga or even survivals of extinct Ragas. This conclusion is based on observations regarding the extent to which the purity of their singing tradition is maintained and the efforts made to achieve this state and to further protect the tradition from deviation.

The first Krishna sampradaya to adopt Samaj Gayan as part of its Seva is the Radhavallabha Sampradaya, believed to have inaugurated it at the time of its own founding.

RADHAVALLABHA SAMPRADAYA

The Radhavallabha Sampradaya was founded in the sixteenth century (1535 C.E.) by Sri Hita Harivamsa (1502–1552 C.E.) in the town of Vrindaban in North India. Vrindaban (Sanskrit, Vrindavana) is believed to be the most important geographical location of the childhood activities of the incarnation of Krishna who was born, according to pious tradition, in roughly 3000 B.C.E. in the nearby town of Mathura. Hita Harivamsa is an important name in the early history of the medieval revival of the township of Vrindaban as a major pilgrimage center for

Hindus, along with Sri Caitanya and the Six Goswamis of the Gaudiya tradition, Vallabha and the Ashtachap poets, Sri Bhatta and Harivyasadevacharya from the Nimbarka Sampradaya, and Swami Haridas of the Haridasi Sampradaya. All of these saints are recognized by historians as pioneers in reestablishing Vrindaban as the center of the Bhakti tradition in northern India.

The standard account of the life of Hita Harivamsa, citing original sources, has been presented and commented upon by Hindi scholar Rupert Snell. The following is from the account of Uttamadasa, an eighteenth-century disciple of the Radhavallabha tradition. Hita Harivamsa's family was from the town of Deoband in Uttar Pradesh. His father, Vyas Misra, was a wealthy Brahmin astrologer who served at the royal court and was at first unable to conceive a child. Vyas, however, rejoiced at his brother's dream of a son who would soon be born to Vyas's family as a joint incarnation of Hari (Krishna) and Vamsa (Krishna's flute). Since the Misra family was often in transit, Sri Harivamsa took birth in the small village of Bada near Mathura, Krishna's own birthplace. From an early age the child was obsessed with the name and form of the goddess Radha, often receiving communication from her in dreams. Radha had told him to make known to the world a special mantra of her name and to rescue a Krishna deity from a well in his father's garden. Sri Harivamsa took these commands seriously by establishing this deity in a temple in his hometown. After marrying and raising three children, Sri Harivamsa was further ordered by Radha to leave his family behind and proceed to Vrindaban, but only after going to another village and accepting two daughters in marriage from a Brahmin, as well as another image of Krishna to be installed there. This deity was known as Radhavallabha (Dearest of Radha) and was installed in a new temple in Vrindaban in the year 1535.[2]

Hita Harivamsa's principal work in Braj Bhasha is the *Caurasi-Pad,* eighty-four verses covering the topics of Nikunja-Vihara (the intimate love pastimes of Radha and Krishna taking place in eternal time), the Rasa-Lila, Radha's Mana or pride, and descriptions of the spring and autumn scenery of Vrindaban. There are few direct theological assertions in the *Caurasi-Pad,* since the work is meant to be a poetical description of love situations between Radha and Krishna. In addition to the *Caurasi-Pad,* plus a Sanskrit work on Radha, there is only a short text in Braj Bhasha called *Sphut-Vani* as well as a prayer in Sanskrit to the goddess Yamuna.

Along with his significance as a pioneer in establishing Vrindaban as a religious center, Hita Harivamsa is important for his pivotal role in elevating Radha to supreme status and establishing the musical practice of Samaj Gayan as the core of the temple Seva. The theological move of elevating Radha above Krishna has been referred to as an "alternative Krishnology" and discussed further by this author elsewhere (see Beck, 2005). Most of the new Krishna sampradayas venerated Radha in some fashion, yet it was the Radhavallabha Sampradaya that became exclusively associated with Radha. Their emphasis on Radha was so influential that several of the movements that had originally revered primarily Krishna or the divine couple of Radha-Krishna began to focus more on Radha.

The name Radhavallabha refers to Krishna as "the dearest of Radha," as she is the principal figure in the theological hierarchy, with Krishna always at her side. Since its founding the Radhavallabha Sampradaya has venerated Radha above Krishna in its worship and doctrine. Radhavallabhites depicted Krishna not as the ultimate Supreme Being in the ordinary sense but as the most intimate servant of God, in this case the goddess Radha. In the words of Charles S. J. White, "Hari Vams is closely allied to the Vaishnava schools that have Krishna as the chief deity—the difference being that Hari Vams extols Radha above Krishna."[3] Snell has shown in his research that, while there are verses describing Krishna alone, "the protracted thematic sequence CP [*Caurasi-Pad* verses] 37–42 introduces themes in which Krishna is dependent on Radha and suffering in her absence."[4] This observation simply reaffirms the prior testimony recorded by one of the earliest Westerners to interview a member of this sect, J. N. Farquhar, in 1917: "Krishna is the servant of Radha. He may do the coolie-work of building the world, but Radha sits as Queen. He is at best but her Secretary of State. We win the favor of Krishna by worshipping Radha."[5]

The unique theology of the Radhavallabha Sampradaya has been summarized by historian of religions Charles S. J. White. Regarding the centrality of Radha, he says that

> Radha is the very ground of being. She is eternal power and the giver of bliss in the universe. Being absolute she is without form and qualities, and yet her devotees are her companions (*sakhi* or *sahacari*) who adore her while she is amorously sporting with Krishna. It is through Radha's physical manifestations and the grasp of her psychological character that a devotee at length finds the route to her eternal aspect. The love-play and the granting of all wishes and desires for the devotees are merely aids to that discovery. Radha is without equal in the universe for beauty, and her power constantly defeats the god of love, Kamadeva [cf. Cupid]. There are no negative emotions appropriate to her; hence she is without the characteristics of Devi or Sakti. Simply put, she is the goddess of love to Krishna.[6]

There are nonetheless precedents for the subordination of Krishna to Radha. Jayadeva in the *Gita-Govinda* (twelfth century C.E.) portrayed Krishna as subordinate to Radha in a particular verse in which he submits to Radha by having her place her feet on his head. *Gita-Govinda* 10.9 states, "Now like a diadem, crown this my head with the tender petals of your feet, a pleasurable balm for the venom of desire. And let it cure my suffering from the burning fire of desire."[7]

The Radhavallabha Sampradaya built upon this notion and solidified it into a permanent union in which Radha was placed as the Supreme Being.

The Radhavallabha Sampradaya flourished and sustained its singular religious perspective from its base at Vrindaban for more than five hundred years. While it was generally compatible with the post-Jayadeva Bhakti movements established during the Mughal Period, the Radhavallabha Sampradaya resisted affiliation with the previous orthodox Vaishnava sampradayas such as Ramanuja, Madhva, Nimbarka, and Rudra. As explained by Snell, "the Radhavallabha Sampradaya does not claim affiliation to the 'classical' Vaishnava Catuh-Sampradaya [Four Sampradayas], nor does it specifically profess any one of the major philosophical positions of classical Hinduism. Its claim to autonomy as a sampradaya in its own right rests on its following a particular mode or style of Bhakti, and in the maintaining of distinct lines of authority descending from Hita Harivamsa himself."[8] The Radhavallabha scriptural canon was devoted solely to the effect of creating a new theological understanding of Radha and Krishna, such that the tradition did not build upon previous Vedanta, Mimamsa, or Yoga philosophies as did other Vaishnava sects. Moreover, the Radhavallabha Sampradaya ignored the practice of traditional Hindu and Vaishnava rituals. According to Snell, "the use of Vedic ritual and the observance of certain generally accepted Vaishnava practices, such as the Ekadasi Vrata, are spurned as irrelevancies."[9] The Radhavallabha Sampradaya also venerated the householder stage of life as ideal and did not endorse renunciation of world and family in any form, as did some of the other Vaishnava groups.

The Radhavallabha experience of Shringara Rasa (conjugal love) in the form of the eternal Nitya-Vihara pastimes of Radha and Krishna was believed to transcend all other known experiences of Bhakti. The true experience of Bhakti in the form of Shringara Rasa was said for the Radhavallabhites to exist in the constant and simultaneous presence of both meeting and separation. And this could only be sustained in the married state of conjugal union. The Radhavallabha Sampradaya thus stressed almost exclusively the Nikunja-Vihara, or private love-play, dimension of the Krishna story, adopting conjugal love as its preferred devotional approach. This element was thus singled out from the extraordinarily diverse types of images and pastimes associated with Krishna. Radha and Krishna are eternally married yet continue to engage in conjugal activities wherever they find intimate pleasure, preferring the Nikunja or sacred grove. Snell explains the distinction that was maintained between "Nikunja Lila [private intimate relations in a secluded bower], in which the sublimated passion of Radha and Krishna provided the focus of the devotee's attention, and Braj Lila, the generality of Puranic Krishna mythology, regarded as inferior as a source of Rasa since its diversity is detrimental to the experiencing of single-minded absorption (*ananya bhava*) in the sport of the joint deity." Of course the full experience of the divine union of Radha and Krishna could not be experienced by the devotee through imitation or other participation but was only approximated by a kind of spiritual voyeurism that satiated the devotee in the form of a spectating Sakhi or handmaiden to the couple: "The role of the *Sakhi* in promoting (but not participating in) the Nikunja-Vihara is emulated by the devotee, whose highest aim is to achieve the vicarious delight of being an onlooker in the Nikunja. An Alaukika Vrindavana [otherworldly Vrindaban] is the setting for this divine activity, and takes the place of other Vaishnava conceptions of paradise such as Vaikuntha and Goloka [the abodes of Vishnu and the Puranic Krishna]."[10]

Accordingly, Radhavallabha eschatology centered upon the eternal love shared between Radha and Krishna in the form of divine conjugal union, which for the human devotees is the most sought after spiritual bliss. And while the poetic descriptions often appear erotic, the approach of the devout is nonliteral and meant to reflect a lofty realization of eternal Prema, or intense spiritual love. Salvation for the Radhavallabha devotees consists of permanent mystical participation in that divine romantic love. This is attained not through solitary renunciation or private devotions but by joining in the temple Seva and participating in the Pada-Kirtan sessions of Samaj Gayan, which are believed to reenact the divine pastimes as if they were happening at that particular moment.

For Radhavallabha devotees, the uniting of Radha and Krishna takes place both in the terrestrial Vrindaban, a location the devotee can aspire to visit, and at the highest levels of the cosmos in the eternal Vrindavana. Members of the Radhavallabha Sampradaya claim to utilize music and singing in the earthly Vrindaban during Seva to gain direct perception of the eternal pastimes of Krishna. Ramnath Prasad, a musician in this tradition, has remarked: "Since music and dance are the most thrilling aspects in the world, we are taking these songs and mixing them with music. And after singing them, the whole sound vibrates in our mind night and day . . . ; these songs bring some deep and very unspeakable joy in the mind. . . . That is why we go on and on singing these songs. Our only work is to watch their love affairs through the singing of these songs. Then the divine beauty manifests in different colors, aspects, and forms."[11]

Sri Rajendra Prasad Sharma, lead singer at the Satsanga Bhumi, Hitashram, and the Choti Sarkar Temple, is considered a Mukhiya,having studied the musical style and repertoire from the former principal singer of the sampradaya, Sri Damodar Dvivedi. The latter led the Samaj for more than thirty years, until 1996, and is recognized as a person who has entered the Nitya-Vihara, the eternal pastimes. Sharma has provided insights into the unique manner of mystical meditation on the deity during Seva through the musical construction of a verbal icon:

> When a Raga is being sung and Svaras are being used, then the words of the poem create an image of the Raga and personify it, making it a Murti [icon]. For example, when a devotee takes the role of a Sakhi and requests Radha to join in the Rasa-Lila where Sri Krishna has made all arrangements, a verbal icon or image is created that arouses the devotional consciousness. The emotion of this event, expressed by the Raga, becomes personified and serves as an object of meditation. The importance is not so much of the Raga as the Bhava or pathos surrounding the image. There may be any Raga, but the main idea is the expression of feeling; then only will the Bhajan be successful.[12]

From a religious viewpoint, by intensely participating in Samaj Gayan it is believed that the participants are not merely observing the pastimes of Radha and Krishna but actually participating vicariously as well. The manner and degree of spiritual elation obtained by the singers suggest their ability to experience aspects of the divine pastimes that are unavailable to persons who may simply read the song-texts. To what extent the current singers in this tradition are on this higher level is difficult to assess from the outside but has been attested by informants. It took many weeks to gain the confidence of the singers so that recordings could be made. In addition, the combination of many years of accumulation of merit through performance plus the grace of Krishna (and particularly Radha) enables the Samaj Gayan performers to make valid claims of their spiritual states.

The Radhavallabha repertoire of songs is distributed over an annual liturgical calendar. Most of the songs are strictly linked to the Seva in the temple, as well as to the specific pastimes of Radha and Krishna, such that outside of these occasions or holidays, the songs are not heard. Nearly all of their music is structured around a solar/lunar calendar of festivals, with dates that vary from year to year based on lunar calculations. These observations are confirmed by Sri Lalitacaran Goswami, former Acharya for the tradition: "Most of the devotional lyrics, except for some prayer Padas of Bhakti-kavya and some didactic stanzas, are linked to various festivals and jubilees. Worship of the deity and other routine functions . . . are carried out with the help of these Padas."[13]

The Radhavallabha Seva and Samaj Gayan have remained largely in secluded enclaves, relished only by the Rasikas, accomplished devotees who understand and appreciate the aesthetic feelings and devotional nuances of the literature and music. Yet the main temple is overcrowded on special festival days such as Holi, when giant syringes of colored water are squirted on pilgrims by priests from the altar, and Annakut, when the entire altar area is covered with sumptuous food offerings to Radha and Krishna. A select group of trained musicians is regularly employed by the Radhavallabha temple trusts. The basic instrumentalists and singers are paid a small stipend to maintain the daily regimen of Samaj Gayan throughout the liturgical year.

The daily schedule of Radhavallabha Seva revolves around the waking, bathing, feeding, dressing, and retiring of the deity of Radhavallabha, a statue of Krishna playing the flute. Radha is present but only as a leaf on a seat, signifying her presence as totally divine and otherworldly. Although Radha is the principal figure in this sect, the Radhavallabha temples in Vrindaban do not contain representations or statues of her. Radha, high above physical representation, is worshipped in the form of a small tablet inscribed with her name and placed, suitably adorned and garlanded with flowers, on Krishna's left side. According to White,

> the *gaddi* [throne cushion], placed alongside the *murti* [statue] of Radhavallabha, has a golden leaf suspended over it upon which is written the name of Sri Radha. Several reasons are given for service to Radha as the throne (*gaddi-seva*). First, Radha's beauty is indescribable (she is the Absolute and beyond all forms). Thus no icon would be suitable to represent her. Second, Radha is a teacher; because the symbol of the teacher is the *gaddi*, the mind of the devotee should be fixed upon it. Third, because Radha and Krishna are engaged in eternal bower sport, if they are depicted together, this would have to be the main subject of the icon. It would be improper to depict them so, and it has been avoided; the devotee is enjoined to fix his attention mentally upon Radha through contemplating the *gaddi*. Devotion to Radha is further shown through writing her name on creepers, stones, and pieces of wood . . . in various sacred places.[14]

The Radhavallabha temple priests maintain a strict regimen of daily worship, ensuring that all worship activities are preceded with the utmost cleanliness of all utensils as well as of their own person and dress. There are seven daily services before the deities during eight periods of the day (Ashtayam) in the Radhavallabha temple. According to the record, "He [Harivamsa] established the service of the deity with seven food offerings (*Bhog*) through the eight periods of the day (*yama*), according to the season."[15] The present system is outlined as follows:

> Mangala 6:00 A.M. The awakening of the deity and the offering of sweets, including butter and a lump of sugar. Stanzas 3 (Raga Vilaval, Tala Dhamar) and 13 of the *Caurasi-Pad* are sung. The Arati, or waving of lights in front of an image, is a feature of all hours of worship.
>
> Shringara 10:00 A.M. The icon is bathed and adorned; various costumes are prescribed according to the day and season. Incense, curds, and sweets are offered. Stanzas 9 (Raga Asavari, Tala Tintal) and 25 (Raga Khammaj, Tala Jhaptal) of the *Caurasi-Pad* are sung at this time.
>
> Raj Bhog 12:00 Noon. The main meal is offered to the deities, and it consists of rice, curry, dal, vegetables, curd, and sweets. Games such as caupada are played.

From this time onward the songs sung at the hourly services are from works other than the *Caurasi-Pad.*

Utthapan 4:00 P.M. The deities are awakened from their afternoon siesta with music and bathing. The deities go for a stroll.

Sandhya 6:00 P.M. Various sweets are offered and there is singing, together with the Arati. The Rasa-Lila sport begins at this time.

Sayan 8:00 P.M. The evening meal of fried foods, puri, halva, rahani, and other dishes is offered.

Saiya 10:00 P.M. The time of retiring the deity for the evening. Special songs for laying the deity to rest are sung before the curtains close.[16]

The Radhavallabha liturgical hymnal is the *Sri Radhavallabhji ka Varshotsava* (1978–1980) in three volumes, originally published in four volumes as *Shringara-Rasa-Sagara* (1956–1962). A second edition of two volumes of the new version was published in 1994 (volume 2) and 1996 (volume 3). Most of the *Caurasi-Pad* (84 songs) of Hita Harivamsa, as well as the complete *Sri Bayalis Lila* (42 Lilas, 22 Ragas) of Dhruva Das, are contained in this collection, perhaps the largest anthology of Braj Bhasha poems. Portions of the 482–verse, 32–Raga *Vyas Vani* of Hariram Vyas are also included. Caca Vrindaban Das (eighteenth century), the most prolific poet of the Radhavallabha Sampradaya with works numbering in the hundreds, is strongly represented.

All of the songs in the three volumes of the hymnal are organized according to the seasons and holidays that are celebrated in the main temple. The liturgical year begins at the start of volume one with the season of Vasant in the spring, and ends in volume three with *Sri Bayalis Lila* in the winter months.

Volume 1. Vasant (spring), Holi, Rasiya, Dol, Caitra, and Hit Badhai (appearance day of Sri Harivamsa)

Volume 2. Phul Racana (flower arrangements), Van Vihar (forest pastimes), Grisma Ritu-Jal Vihar and Nauka (summer water and boat pastimes), Ratha Yatra (chariot), Pavas Ritu (rainy season), Jhulan (swing ceremony), Rakhi, Sevak Badhai (appearance day of Sevakji Maharaj), Krishna Badhai (birthday of Krishna, Janmastami), Radha Badhai (birthday of Radha, Radhastami), and Samjhi

Volume 3. Rasa-Lila, Dasahara (Diwali), Caupar (game pastimes), Annakut (feast at Govardhan Hill), Vyahulau Utsav (wedding of Radha and Krishna), Patotsava, Khicari Utsav, Mohan Bhog, Phutkar (assorted songs), Sain ke Pad (evening songs and lullabies), and *Sri Bayalis Lila* (sung during the winter months)

Several of the festivals on the Radhavallabha calendar are actually extended over a fixed number of days. Thus the musicians may perform a selection of Padas over the seasonal time period, as there are many Padas in the songbooks appropriate to the occasion. According to Sri Rajendra Sharma, the spring season of

Vasant lasts for ten days, during which time any song from the chapter labeled "Vasant" may be sung, normally in Raga Vasant which may be sung any time during Vasant season. This is followed by the Holi season during which songs from the Holi section may be sung for thirty days until the full moon in March. Many of these songs, sung in a variety of Ragas but especially in Raga Kafi, are called Dhamar, often in Dhamar Tala of fourteen beats but not necessarily. After that, miscellaneous verses may be sung until the celebrations of Sri Hita Harivamsa's appearance begin. This period of Badhai songs lasts for twenty-five days, from Vaishakh Purnima (April) to Ekadasi of the second fortnight of the next month. Then the Phul Padas start, with beautiful flower decorations in the temples (called Phulbanglas) for a month. Following this, the rainy season (Savan, or Pavas Ritu) begins with many songs in special Ragas such as Megh Malhar and Gaur Malhar. Then the Jhulan season starts around mid-July, with many unique songs to accompany the deities of Radha and Krishna on their swings. When this is finished, there is preparation for the major festivals of late summer and fall, such as Krishna Janmastami (Krishna's birthday), Radhastami (Radha's birthday for one month, usually in September), and Samjhi (special songs along with beautiful sand paintings of Radha and Krishna). During Karttika season (October–November), there is the Rasa-Lila for one and a half months, then Diwali and Annakut, followed by the wedding of Radha and Krishna with very special songs. After the new moon of Diwali, the winter season begins, and for two-and-one-half months the *Sri Bayalis Lila* by Dhruva Das is sung in special tunes. Then we come full circle back to Vasant again.[17]

Samaj Gayan is the central musical and devotional expression of the Radhavallabha Sampradaya. Snell has observed that "special importance is attached to the singing of appropriate texts in Samaj, and a large body of sectarian literature, mostly in Braj Bhasha, exists for this purpose."[18] Members of the Radhavallabha Sampradaya even utilize music and singing in Braj Bhasha as a vehicle with which to gain direct access to ecstasy and pure religious experiences. In the introduction preceding his translation of the *Caurasi-Pad*, Sri Hita Harivamsa's main work in Braj Bhasha, Charles S. J. White comments on the musical dimension of this group: "Where the tradition of the sect provides for the composition of hymns or *bhajans* for group singing, such music becomes, through participation and understanding, a vehicle for the devotee to move beyond the external forms of the cult to an inner experience of ecstasy based on the intensity of his faith."[19]

In his works the celebrated spiritual leader and Acharya (guru) in the Radhavallabha tradition, Sri Goswami Lalitacaranji Maharaj, has outlined the importance of Samaj Gayan: "In the Pushti Marg and Radhavallabha temples, Kirtankars (performers of Kirtan) are appointed to sing Padas in front of the deity of Krishna at specific hours. The Kirtankars of the Radhavallabha Sampradaya are known as Samajis. The number of Samajis is at least four, one of whom is the Mukhiya (leader), one the Pakhavaji (player of the Pakhavaj drum), and two Jhelas (responsorial singers). The Mukhiya first sings one line of a Pada which is then repeated by the Jhelas. One of the Jhelas usually plays Jhanjh, and the other plays Tanpura or something else."[20]

While several groups in Vrindaban practice Samaj Gayan and hold music and singing as central to their worship, the Radhavallabha Sampradaya prides itself as the originator of Samaj Gayan. Whether or not this tradition was created by Radhavallabha followers, it is most likely native to the Braj area and must be considered a unique form of devotional singing that nonetheless has ties with the Dhrupad classical tradition. The Radhavallabha Sampradaya claims that it has maintained this musical tradition continually on a daily basis since its origination in the sixteenth century. The main temple of Sri Radhavallabha established by Hita Harivamsa houses the longest continuing tradition of Samaj Gayan, with performances twice daily. Several other branch temples have also maintained a daily regimen of Samaj Gayan. Modern scholarship has reaffirmed the longevity and continuity of this tradition with reference to a painting of Hita Harivamsa, Swami Haridas and Hariram Vyas sitting together in Samaj Gayan:

> The musicians of the Radhavallabha Sampradaya claim that their practice of congregational singing reaches back to the 16th century when it was initiated by the founder of the sampradaya, the poet Hita Harivamsa. This opinion is supported by a miniature painting dating from 1538, which shows Hita Harivamsa and his followers performing Samaj Gayan to the accompaniment of cymbals, barrel-drum and Tanpura. Beginning with Hita Harivamsa, the Radhavallabha tradition has developed a rich poetic heritage, and music has always played a predominant role in this community. The Radhavallabhite Samaj is perhaps the oldest tradition of Samaj Gayan to have been maintained on a continuous basis to the present. The principal religious center of the sampradaya, the temple of Radhavallabha in Vrindaban, arranges Samaj performances twice daily.[21]

Sri Rajendra Sharma, principal singer of this tradition, has reaffirmed that Samaj Gayan began within the Radhavallabha Sampradaya: "The origin of Samaj Gayan is only in Vrindaban and particularly in the Radhavallabha Temple. And if held elsewhere outside of Vrindaban, it is only in the Radhavallabha Sampradaya. There is no worship of Radhavallabha without Samaj."[22] This claim has been contested by members of the Nimbarka Sampradaya who state that Sri Bhatta, an early Braj Bhasha poet in their tradition, sang Samaj Gayan. But while some of the literature of the Nimbarka Sampradaya even claims that the legendary Narada Rishi of antiquity learned Dhrupad from the gods, there is no reference to Samaj Gayan, which differs from classical Dhrupad.

Sri Kisori Saran Ali of the Radhavallabha Sampradaya disputes all other claims to seniority by saying that Samaj is a relatively recent practice in other sampradayas: "Samaj Gayan has been recently adopted by the followers of Swami Haridas, while the Nimbarka Sampradaya and others are now also using Samaj Gayan in their communities. The Radhavallabha Sampradaya is most certainly the originator of this music, as it is attested in older manuscripts of this tradition and lacking in others."[23] Indeed, references to Samaj Gayan in early literature of the Radhavallabhites make their credentials appear stronger than those of others who lack such references and most probably adopted the style of singing from the Radhavallabha Sampradaya.

The song repertoire of Radhavallabha Sampradaya is unique and represents a valuable corpus that must be examined for its own melodic worth. In fact, many Ragas in Hindustani classical music today are less than one hundred years old, and many Ragas have been modified over time to become more refined with regard to their grammar and rules of performance. The Radhavallabha song collection is thus a glimpse into the remote past of devotional music, and the Radhavallabha Sampradaya has kept and protected its musical tradition from encroachment from outside so that it may be preserved in its pristine form. The tradition has its own rules and guidelines that are separate from Hindustani musical expectations.

The singing style of Samaj Gayan in the Radhavallabha Sampradaya relies on plain execution devoid of fast melodic embellishments, with much emphasis given to the clear pronunciation of the words. Regarding improvisation, Thielemann explains that "there is limited space for improvisation, which consists mostly of repetitions of parts of the text, modification of the basis melody, and phrases sung on the basis of extraneous syllables. Internal repetitions and phrases sung on extra syllables are standardized, but some freedom is permitted regarding additional repetitions of sections or part of them. The execution of *layakari* improvisation is not permitted."[24] With regard to Alap and the insertion of syllables, Thielemann has emphasized that

> the non-metricized Alap introductions are dispensed with, because they are merely musical entities and of no significance for the rendition of the devotional verse. Improvisation, too, is prohibited. The only type of variation which is not only legitimate, but whose execution is compulsory in Samaj Gayan, is the insertion of melodic phrases sung on the syllables eri ha. The musicians of the Radhavallabha Sampradaya claim to be the originators of the practice of inserting extra syllables, which is followed in Samaj singing of all Vaishnava communities of Braj. Further additional syllables such as ri mai may occur at the end of verses or verse-lines: these serve as verse-fillers in order to adjust the poetic line to the cycle of the musical meter.[25]

In the edition of the *Caurasi-Pad* published by the Radhavallabha Sampradaya headquarters in Vrindaban, there are various Ragas mentioned alongside the songs as follows, according to the number of occurrences: Sarang 16, Gauri 9, Kanharau 9, Vilaval 7, Dev Gandhar 7, Dhanasri 7, Kalyan 6, Vibhas 6, Malhar 5, Kedar 4, Todi 4, Asavari 2, and Vasant 2. This listing indicates some of the preferences for melodies in the rendering of these hymns. The present performance tradition is mostly faithful to these indications, yet many of the melodies are not strictly in Ragas. Thielemann offers additional explanations for the differences between the Ragas in Radhavallabha Sampradaya and the Hindustani tradition:

> The requirement of textual clarity is regarded to be the main reason for changes made to the conventional North Indian Raga structures in the musical practice of the Radhavallabha Sampradaya. Raga melodies that include difficult or uncommon melodic progressions, or scales in which certain notes have to be rendered with specific embellishments, have been simplified or mixed with other Ragas in order to create a melodic structure that is easily sung without disturbing the pronunciation of the words. The new Ragas thus created were not re-named, but retained their original denominations; hence the Ragas of Radhavallabhite Samaj Gayan do not necessarily have the same musical features as their nominal counterparts in North Indian classical music.[26]

With regard to the Tala cycles, there are very few discrepancies between the Radhavallabhite temple music practice and the classical tradition.

Tanas are patterns of notes sung with *a*, *i*, *u*, or *o*, and so forth that do not have linguistic meaning, resembling in some ways the Stobhas of Sama-Gana. These are mentioned in *Natya-Sastra* and *Dattilam* as constitutive parts of Gandharva Sangita. However, in Samaj Gayan, because of the strict focus on the words of the Pada, Tanas are discouraged, believed to be out of sync with the Vaishnava tradition of solemn and reverent worship. According to Sri Rajendra Sharma, "there is no scope for Tanas, as they will spoil the Sabda, the meaning of the words. There are some *murkis* [short melismatic phrases] but not Tanas. There is no scope for artistic display in the form of Tanas, etc. Such deviations affect the devotion, and are a distraction."[27] According to Sri Goswami Lalitacaranji Maharaj, "the Radhavallabhiya Samajis have their own distinctive style. To ensure and protect the clear pronunciation of Sabda (words), Alaps have been regulated in this style, and only prescribed Alaps are sung with Sthayi and Antara. There is no scope for elaborate Tanas in this style, and only very brief Murkis (ornaments) are tolerated."[28] The unanimous opinion of the informants regarding Samaj Gayan is thus that this music is primarily meant for devotion and worship and not for virtuosic display of musical skills or for pleasing human audiences. Sharma has commented that "Samaj Gayan is basically a Bhakti Sangit, meant for worship and not for *lok ranjan*, human entertainment."[29]

The musicians of the Radhavallabha Sampradaya do not employ specific terminology when referring to their music compositions. The only expression used by them is *Samaj* or *Samaj Gayan*, which denotes this method of singing in general. Thus the term *Dhrupad* is not used in the Radhavallabha Sampradaya. There are indeed Dhrupad-like compositions, but they are not referred to as Dhrupad, simply as Samaj Gayan. As clarified by Thielemann: "In the opinion of the Radhavallabhite musicians, Dhrupad is firstly a singing style (Gayaki) rather than a Tala, and secondly it belongs to the tradition of North Indian classical music which has to be strictly separated from the Samaj Gayan practice of the Vaishnava temples. . . . The Radhavallabhite musicians themselves do not employ the term 'Dhrupad' (or any other specific term denoting song types for that matter) with reference to Samaj Gayan."[30] The term *Dhamar* refers to the poetic repertoire sung during the Holi season, rather than to a composition in Dhamar Tala. Hori Dhamar compositions are not necessarily set to Dhamar Tala.

NIMBARKA SAMPRADAYA

Compared to other sampradayas, much less is known about the Nimbarka Sampradaya or its founder Nimbarka (ca. 1120–1200 C.E.). Nimbarka was born in the southern region of Andhra Pradesh, yet he appears to have spent most of his life around the town of Mathura in Braj. Nimbarka's philosophical works, including a commentary on the *Vedanta-Sutra*, propound a version of Vedanta known as Dvaitadvaita, in which God and the souls are the same yet different. Instead of promoting the worship of Vishnu and his consort Lakshmi, as in the Srivaishnava Sampradaya of Ramanuja, Nimbarka advocated personal devotion to the forms of Krishna or Gopala and his consort Radha.

The Nimbarka Sampradaya is the earliest of the new Krishna sampradayas. But since it dates back to the time of the Srivaishnava Sampradaya (ca. 1200 C.E.), it may be seen as a kind of bridge between the earlier Vishnu sampradayas and the new Braj sects. With regard to Samaj Gayan, there is a slight controversy over the age of this sampradaya's practice of it. Several of the leaders have claimed that Samaj Gayan originated with Nimbarka and explain that Dhrupad was originally taught to Narada Rishi in the heavens by Krishna himself and then passed down along the chain of disciplic succession to Nimbarka. For example, Sri Brajvallabh Saran, Vedantacharya of Nimbarka Sampradaya and director of Sriji Mandir and Sarasvati Press, Vrindaban, had stated that, "just as Devarshi Narada sang Dhrupad songs and lost himself in musical ecstasy, members of the Nimbarka sect continue performing Samaj Gayan in the Dhrupad tradition."[31] Despite this assertion, the Nimbarka Sampradaya seems only to have adopted Samaj Gayan formally in the mid–seventeenth century, after the Radhavallabha Sampradaya. Moreover, Nimbarka wrote only in Sanskrit, and there is no evidence of his having participated in the singing of Samaj Gayan, which was customarily conducted only in the regional Braj Bhasha language. Furthermore, the Nimbarka manuscript anthologies of songs in Braj Bhasha date back about 360 years, a fact mentioned by Sri Saran: "Manuscripts of old Pada collections show that since 1643 C.E. (Vikrama 1700), the Samaj Gayan tradition is continuous in this sect." However, Sri Saran cites the singing of Samaj Gayan in Sanskrit as a precursor to the Braj Bhasha practice: "Prior to the composition of poems in Braj Bhasha language, Samaj Gayan was performed in Sanskrit using the eight-stanza poems of *Gita-Govinda* by Jayadeva."[32] This assertion is probably inaccurate, since, while these verses may have been sung in Dhrupad style, the interactive practice of Samaj Gayan singing is believed to be unique to Braj.

The first Nimbarka poets in Braj Bhasha were nonetheless highly influential in the rising Vaishnava culture in the Braj region during the early sixteenth century. The poetry of Sri Bhatta is considered "Adivani," or the first Braj Bhasha poem in the region of Braj. According to Sri Saran, "Sri Bhatta is regarded as the first poet in the Nimbarka sect to write in Braj Bhasha for the purpose of singing Samaj Gayan. Several of his renowned disciples—Harivyasadevacharya, Parasuramadevacharya, Ruparasikadevacharya—have also composed poems in Braj Bhasha. A number of poets and musicians have become famous in the tradition of a disciple named Sri Brajabhusanadevacharya. Today in the Nimbarka sect, Samaj Gayan is performed using the Padas of these celebrated Acharyas."[33]

Sri Bhatta (ca. 1470–1570 C.E.) was the first Braj Bhasha poet in the Nimbarka Sampradaya, having composed the one-hundred-verse classic *Yugala-Sataka*. The *Yugala-Sataka,* recognized as the first devotional work in Braj Bhasha among the new Vaishnava sampradayas, became an exemplary model for the composition of devotional verses in the language. The number of times specific Ragas are mentioned alongside individual verses in manuscripts of this text indicate early preferences: Kedarau, Bihagarau 18, Sarang 17, Vilaval 11, Malhar 6, Gauri 5, Vasant 3, Vibhas, Kanhara, Rayaso, Maru 2, and Sorath, Pancam, Ramkali, Kafi, Cancari, and Hori 1. Unlike other anthologies, this volume also mentions specified Talas such as Campak, Ektal, Tintal, and Cautal. However, few or none of these indications are followed in current performance, as suggested by this comment of Thielemann: "The *Yugala-Sataka,* which indicates names of both Ragas and Talas, mentions a number of old melody types and Talas nowadays no more known or performed in the tradition of Vaishnava devotional music."[34]

Sri Bhatta's disciple and student Sri Harivyasdevacharya (ca. 1540–1630 C.E.) composed the principal liturgical hymnal used in Nimbarka Samaj Gayan singing, the *Mahavani*. Both Sri Bhatta and Harivyasdevacharya were spiritual disciples of the great Nimbarka scholar Pandit Kesava Kashmiri Bhatt (fifteenth century C.E., thirty-third Acharya of the sect) who was originally from Andhra Pradesh, as was Nimbarka, but later settled near Mathura in Braj. Twelve disciples of Sri Harivyasdevacharya founded the twelve branches of the Nimbarka Sampradaya, each of which included its own line of Acharyas, sometimes collectively referred to as Harivyasis. The leading Acharya of the first generation, Parashuram, was a prolific poet in Braj Bhasha who also established a center at Salemabad, near Kishangarh, in Rajasthan where Acharya Sriji Maharaj resided.

The text of *Mahavani* ("Great Hymns") has five divisions. The second section, Utsaha-Sukha, offers songs for festival celebrations and is used in all Samaj Gayan sittings today. The twenty festivals mentioned from Vasant to Diwali are those that are generally observed by the Nimbarka sect: Vasant, Holi, Dol, Candan Sringara, Jal Vihar, Ratha Yatra, Varsartu Vihar, Pahilil Tij, Hindora (Jhulan), Luhan, Pavitra, Rakhi, Pachali Tij, Lalaju ki Badhai (Krishna Janmastami), Priyaju ki Badhai (Radhastami), Samjhi, Vijaya Dasami, Rasotsava, Supathauni, Divari (Diwali).[35] The other sections of the work, many songs of which are meant for daily performance, are believed to be too "confidential" for the general public and are thus not performed. By *confidential* it is meant that the descriptions of the love-play of Radha and Krishna in these songs are so intimate that they risk being misinterpreted as erotic poetry rather than spiritual hymnology. Copies of the printed *Mahavani*, as well as other sacred texts, are especially revered by followers, and they are wrapped in colored or decorated cloth and kept above ground at all times.

Unlike the *Samaj-Srinkhala* of the Haridasi Sampradaya or the *Sri Radhavallabhaji ka Varshotsava* of the Radhavallabha Sampradaya, the *Mahavani* does not refer to Ragas or Talas above the poems or stanzas. While no tradition in Braj follows literally the Raga indications in hymnals, the Ragas that are sung by the Nimbarka sect can only be identified by listening to the singers' renditions of Samaj Gayan.

As there is no daily routine of Samaj Gayan in the Nimbarka Sampradaya, the normal practice consists of multiple-day sittings commemorating a special season such as Holi or the death of one of the Acharyas. These sittings last from one to four hours and continue from five to fifteen days in a fixed location. Since the Samaj Gayan of Nimbarka Sampradaya is only occasionally performed, it might be inferred that it is independent of liturgical practices. In truth, the arrangements of Samaj Gayan mostly center on the temple Seva and the priestly functions during the festival times. And because Samaj Gayan sessions consist of a complex ordering of prayers, songs, rhythmic cycles, texts, and gestures, the events themselves may be considered a sonic liturgy.

The Nimbarka Samaj occasions are known about far in advance, drawing a special crowd of people for the multiple-day event. There are therefore many more singers than one may find in daily Samaj Gayan. According to Thielemann's observations, "the setting for Samaj Gayan of the Nimbarka Sampradaya often involves one or two lead singers, and a chorus of five to ten Samajis. In general, it is the senior lead singer who conducts the performance, while the junior Mukhiya may take over parts of extended verses, in order to allow the senior Mukhiya to take rest. Indispensable accompanying instruments are the harmonium (played by the senior Mukhiya), cymbals (played by the junior Mukhiya) and Pakhavaj." Most compositions in the Nimbarka Sampradaya begin with a short unaccompanied Doha, several verses led by the lead singer, and then follow a slow elongated Dhrupad or Dhamar structure ending up in speedier tempos: "Most Padas, or compositions, are preceded by a Doha sung to free rhythm by the lead singer alone. Extended Dhrupad and Dhamar songs begin in slow tempo (Vilambit), and end in fast tempo (Drut). Dhamar compositions are characterized by a change of the musical meter to Tintal of sixteen beats towards the end of the verse." Furthermore, the execution is strictly "by the book" and without variation or improvisation: "Short musical compositions based on quatrains are presented in their basic shape only, with a number of repetitions, but without variations. The performance of extended compositions includes melodic variations, phrases sung on the basis of verse-filling syllables and portions sung in faster tempo than the basic composition. All modifications, however, are standardized and repeated literally for each verse-line respectively stanza. There is no improvisation of any type."[36]

Sri Saran concurs with this and emphasizes that, like the Samaj Gayan of the Radhavallabha Sampradaya, the Nimbarka tradition avoids the ornamentation of Tanas characteristic of Hindustani classical music: "In the introductory phrases known as Alapchari, except for a fine musical variance (Meed), Tanas have been avoided in Samaj Gayan, and even Khyal, Tappa, and Thumri styles have not been adopted. As in the days of old, the Dhrupad and Dhamar Talas follow a Vilambit, or very slow pace, rendition, with the performance being completed in a Drut, or fast-pace, one."[37]

In recent times the most prominent singer of the Nimbarka Samaj has been Sri Rup Kishor Maharaj of Cain Bihari Kunj, Vrindaban. Sri Vrindaban Bihari Goswami, Sri Navalkishore Das, and Sri Rasik Das are also prominent singers.

HARIDASI SAMPRADAYA

Swami Haridas (ca. 1500–1595 C.E.), often lauded as the "Father of North Indian Music," is generally considered the saintly teacher of Mian Tansen who sang at the court of Emperor Akbar (mid-sixteenth century) and whose disciples were almost solely responsible for the transmission of classical Dhrupad and Khyal throughout the courts of the Mughal Dynasty and thereafter. Believed to have been an expert singer and musician, Swami Haridas nonetheless refused appointment at the royal courts and preferred to spend his entire life absorbed in singing the praises and pastimes of Syama (Radha) and Kunjbihari (Krishna) while settled in the Vrindaban forest grove of Nidhuvan. Recognized by believers as an incarnation of Lalita (one of the eight principal cowherdesses of Krishna), Swami Haridas lived out his own path of devotion to Kunjbihari, the famous deity of Krishna who appeared miraculously before him and was installed within the forest of Nidhuvan. This deity was renamed Sri Banke Bihari and was later moved to another part of Vrindaban where a large temple was permanently established.

Drawing on the words of Swami Haridas himself (that is, *Ashta-Siddhanta* 17: "So long as you live, my heart, praise Hari"), Richard D. Haynes has summarized the salvific counsel of Swami Haridas that has influenced the activities of the entire Haridasi Sampradaya: "In general, his advice is to leave worldly pursuits and retire to Vrindavana, there to sing, meditate and contemplate the spot where God came once to earth."[38]

Swami Haridas's main poetical work in Braj Bhasha is the *Kelimala*. His only other work is a short philosophical tract called *Ashta-Siddhanta*. The *Kelimala* has direct references (verses 94 and 107) to singing and music in the context of the pastimes of Krishna and his consort Radha: "Haridas' lords, Syama and Kunjbihari, are companions in song [sangit sangi]"; and "In the midst of (their) secret love, according to the rules of emotion [Rasa], the numbers of Raga (melodies) and Ragini (more melodies) increase; Haridas' lords, Radha and Kunjbihari, are dyed in the colors of song."[39] Manuscripts of this work place the name of a Raga above each verse. The frequency of classical Ragas found in the *Kelimala* is Kanharau 30, Kedar 22, Kalyan 12, Sarang 11, Vibhas 11, Malhar 8, Gauri 6, Vasant 5, Vilaval 2, Gauda Malhar 2, and Nata 1.

The succeeding literary tradition of the Haridasi Sampradaya is entirely in the Braj Bhasha language and focuses almost exclusively on the depictions of the intimate love-play between Radha and Krishna in Vrindaban. Being highly specialized like the Radhavallabha Sampradaya, the Haridasi sect disassociates itself from traditional Sanskrit texts and scholarship having to do with other aspects of Vaishnavism such as avataras, vyuhas, yoga, siddhanta, penances, and calendrical observations.

Although Swami Haridas is said to have had connections with either the Nimbarka or Vallabha Sampradaya, he followed his own unique path of Sakhi-Bhava (the devotional mood associated with Krishna's Sakhis or maidservants) in isolation from other teachers and sects. However, there is evidence of an early bifurcation among his disciples involving two groups claiming legitimacy from Swami Haridas. The first group comprised the hereditary descendants of Jagannath, a priest of Sri Banke Bihari who was believed to have been Swami Haridas's younger brother. These descendents are known as Goswamis and govern the famous Sri Banke Bihari Temple. The other group comprised ascetics who claimed that Swami Haridas never had offspring or family connections and who continue to live and worship in a monastic compound known as Tatti Sthan on the banks of the Yamuna River. The ascetic followers have established a nonhereditary succession of eight Acharyas beginning with Swami Haridas: Vitthalvipuldev (1550–1635), Biharinidev (seventeenth century), Nagaridev (seventeenth century), Sarasdev (seventeenth century), Naraharidev (1640–1741), Rasikdev (1692–1758), Lalitkisoridev (1733–1823), and Lalitmohinidev (1750–1858). Among the Acharyas, Biharinidev was the most prolific, having written many Braj Bhasha devotional and doctrinal poems.

Haridasi Samaj Gayan is sung with the use of a standardized hymnal, *Samaj-Srinkhala* ("chain of Samaj songs"), published by the group's own trust and incorporating poems from the *Kelimala* written by Swami Haridas as well as poems of the succeeding Acharyas. In Thielemann's words, this text "lists its repertoires according to the birth anniversary celebrations of the community's main poet-saints. Seasonal repertoires are integrated within this order. Only verses of the Sampradaya's own poets are included into the collection."[40]

Unlike other hymnals, *Samaj-Srinkhala* mentions the names of particular Talas as well as Ragas above the stanzas. The Talas are primarily Dhrupad—12 beats, Dhamar—14 beats, and Tintal—16 beats. The names of the particular Ragas mentioned do not refer to the strict classical configuration of the Ragas. They denote instead specialized "tunes" constructed from the notes of the classical Ragas that have become familiar to both the musicians and the audiences. Thielemann has described the relation between the Ragas and Talas mentioned in the text and the Hindustani Ragas: "Whereas the Talas sung in the Haridasi Sampradaya correspond to those of North Indian classical music, the Ragas have been formalized during the 18th century, and Raga names refer to standardized melodic models rather than actual Raga scales." She then explains the rigid format of the musical execution: "The musical compositions are presented in their basic shape with a number of standardized repetitions and variations. Variations may include the repetition of phrases on the basis of verse-filling syllables. The entire presentation is governed by strict rules regarding progression and tempo. Improvisation as such does not exist, and there is no space to give into spontaneous musical inspiration."[41] One may conclude that, in comparison with the other Braj sects, the Haridasi Sampradaya has the strictest set of rules and regulations for singing Samaj Gayan.

Members of the sect attest that Swami Haridas did not practice Samaj Gayan as it is known today but rather sang a form of solo Dhrupad heard only by his most intimate followers. In addition, recent scholarship has suggested that Samaj Gayan was adopted by the Haridasis as late as the eighteenth century: "The tradition of congregational singing in the Haridasi Sampradaya is a relatively recent one that originated only during the 18th century."[42] Local informants outside of the tradition also recognize that the late adoption was used as a means to solidify the group of ascetics living in Tatti Sthan. According to Sri Vrindaban Bihari Goswami (Nimbarka Sampradaya) of the Vrindaban Research Institute, "the Harivyasis, members of the Nimbarka Sampradaya, and the Haridasis used to sing Samaj Gayan together for many years until a separation occurred. Followers of Lalitmohinidev of the Haridasi Sampradaya [eighteenth century], being a separate monastic group, began sitting separately and conducting their own regular Samaj Gayan."[43] If the Haridasi Samaj Gayan has been performed for only two hundred years, it represents the youngest continuous tradition of Samaj Gayan among the three studied here. There are, however, other voices on this issue.

Until his demise in 1993, Sri Govinda Saran Sastri was the director of the Swami Haridas Seva Samsthan and a renowned scholar of both Sanskrit and Braj Bhasha literature. His account of the development of Haridasi Samaj Gayan is perhaps the most authoritative on record, though he remains elusive about the precise transition from solo Dhrupad to Samaj Gayan style. He first describes the musical expertise of Swami Haridas: "A musician of a very high order, he had a mastery over all the Ragas and Raginis. The uniqueness of the music of Swami Haridas was such that, whichever Lilas of Krishna were rendered by him through music, Krishna was said to take pleasure in performing those Lilas. Swami Haridas sang about such Lilas in the Dhrupad style."[44]

Sri Sastri then describes the music of Swami Haridas in the company of his successor disciple: "Like Swami Haridas, Sri Vitthalvipuldev (ca. 1550–1650), his successor and disciple, was a proficient musician and Rasika poet, always absorbed in the Rasa worship of Sri Radha and Krishna through the medium of music. Occasionally Swami Haridas used to sing with Tanpura, or Sri Vitthalvipuldev would accompany him, and both would be absorbed in the emotions of the Lila according to the Rasa of the song. From time to time, saints and other Rasika followers of Swami Haridas would join them in their Samaj Gayan, describing the wonderful Lilas of Krishna and his divine consort. Whenever Swami Haridas used to sing, a sort of river of Rasa would start flowing."[45]

Sri Sastri seems to suggest that there was a gradual adoption of Samaj style by the early saints of the Haridasi tradition: "In approximately 1563 C.E. (1620 Vikrama Samvat), Sri Biharinidev came to Vrindaban and accepted the discipleship of Sri Vitthalvipuldev under the orders of Swami Haridas. He joined this

Rasika Samaj, and as a result the tradition of Samaj Gayan flourished all the more. Sri Biharinidev made the sea of music of the palaces of the Lord enjoyable and worth taking a dip in by all, and therefore he was known by the name of Gurudev. After Sri Biharinidev, all of the Acharyas, namely Sri Nagaridev, Sri Sarasdev, Sri Naraharidev, and Sri Rasikdev, were expert and innovative musicians, yet the impact of the original musical style of Swami Haridas could be discerned."[46]

Following in the tradition of their predecessors, the singers of Samaj Gayan continued it in the same form from then on with no major changes until the time of Sri Lalitkisoridev (1733–1823), who became the preceptor of the Haridasi Sampradaya. Sri Sastri notes here that "during this period many problems arose in preserving the principles of the sect and the form of worship. While oppression by fanatic Muslim rulers was on the rise, there was also tension between the various Hindu groups." Considering the possible deterioration of the Samaj Gayan tradition and lineage in these adverse conditions, "Sri Lalitkisoridev considered it necessary to crystallize the form and system of this wealth of music in order to preserve it. . . . The music was supposed to be devotion-based, with the predominant focus on the words and their repetition in order to rouse the sentiments. If this ideal of Samaj Gayan was not maintained, then the future of the pure tradition would be in jeopardy." Like the other new Krishna sampradayas, the Haridasi Sampradaya was based exclusively on the Nitya-Vihara Lilas of Krishna. For reasons regarding the preservation of the purity of tradition, Sri Lalitkisoridev "formalized the Ragas and Raginis according to the Padas to be sung at the various festivals of Sri Radha-Krishna, such as Sarad, Vasant, and Holi, and on other special occasions such as the birth celebrations of the Acharyas. Even today the same form is continuing without interruption in the Samaj Gayan of this sampradaya. Because of this far-sightedness, Sri Lalitkisoridev is regarded in the sampradaya as the second incarnation of Swami Haridas."[47]

The Samaj Gayan of the Haridasi Sampradaya, unlike that of the others, is performed only by initiated monks, that is, celibate male members. Like the others, however, those who participate have the full intention of entering Sakhi-Bhava, or the eternal love-play of Radha and Krishna, through their performance activities. They are sometimes referred to as the Sakhi Sampradaya. Throughout the year Swami Haridas's songs, as well as poems written by the other Acharyas of the sampradaya, are regularly performed in Samaj Gayan style by monks in Tatti Sthan, accompanied by Pakhavaj (drum) and responsorial singing by Jhelas—disciples and devotees. Of all the sampradayas, the Haridasi sect follows the most rigid calendar, according to which a particular Pada is sung on a particular day of the lunar year. Avoiding many of the popular Vaishnava festivals in favor of the birth anniversaries of their own Acharyas, this sect honors each Acharya birthday with a four-five day Samaj, except for that of Swami Haridas, which receives a seven-day celebration. Besides Tatti Sthan, where a grandiose Samaj Gayan is held on specified occasions, daily Samaj Gayan is also held at Haridas Nagar, led by Sri Chabilisaran Maharaj and his group of musicians.

The logistical organization of Haridasi Samaj Gayan centers on the image of Swami Haridas and the deity or framed picture of Sri Banke Bihari. There is an antiphonal style of singing in which all persons are divided into two groups, the Mukhiyas (leaders) and the Jhelas (responders), who are seated in front of the image or deity. The description by Sri Sastri confirms this division into two sides: "On the right side of the image sits the Mukhiya group, and on the left side the Jhela group, each in rows if necessary. In the space between are placed the musical instruments as well as old hand-written Vanis (manuscripts). As Samaj Gayan is dependent upon the written text for its execution, a standard edition has been published known as *Samaj-Srinkhala* ('chain of Samaj songs'). Samajis open these Vanis or books and place them with great respect in front upon a bookstand or platform."[48]

Regarding instruments, the harmonium is played mostly by the Mukhiya. It is said that

> previously the Mukhiya used to sit and play the Tanpura, just like Swami Haridas, but nowadays it is not so. If the Tanpura is played at all, it is played by other learners of the community. The Jhanjh (hand cymbals) is a compulsory instrument of Samaj Gayan, with specific rhythms that are highly regulated. Any person other than the Mukhiya may play them, but the Jhanjh player generally sits near the Pakhavajiya (drummer), whose place is just in front of the deity or picture, in between the two rows of Mukhiya group and Jhela group, at the other end. Generally the task of playing the Pakhavaj is performed by a Sadhak musician, one who is an initiated disciple. But if none is available the service can be entrusted to any other knowledgeable person. In the absence of a Pakhavaj or Pakhavaj player, sometimes the Tabla is played in Pakhavaj style, open-handed. At one time, the Sarangi (bowed lute) was a prominent musical instrument of the Samaj, but nowadays it is no longer compulsory.[49]

A special type of Samaj Gayan is performed on festival days and on the birthdays of the Acharyas and gurus. A description of the various Padas used during the festivals is provided by Sri Sastri:

> For the festivals and special celebrations, different Padas of the Acharyas are earmarked for each day, all sung in their own predetermined Raga and Tala. After the initial Pada, the Padas connected with the festival are sung. Out of these, the Padas of Guru Purnima, Jagara (wake), Sarad, Vasant, and Holi are generally short, while the Padas of other festivals are longer. Among these, the Padas known as Saheli and Samvari Saheli are so long that their singing takes more than three

hours each. When such lengthy Padas are sung, Bada Guru Mangala is omitted, and between stanzas there may be a break of five or ten minutes. Bana and Calsakhi Padas are Padas which are not very lengthy in themselves, but the tradition of singing them is such that it takes a comparatively longer time. Bada Guru Mangala is once again omitted when these Padas are sung.[50]

The Haridasi Samaj tradition is known for some very lengthy Padas commemorating the marriage celebrations of Radha and Krishna. As described by Sri Sastri: "Some lengthy Padas sung in the Samaj have particular names such as Bana, Jhumka, Suhelera, Saheli, etc. According to the subject matter of Bana, the Sakhis entice Radha (Priya) and Krishna (Priyalal) in the role of bride and bridegroom. In Saheli, Radha expresses her deepest feelings to her girlfriend. Suhelera is a love song sung during the coming together of the bride and bridegroom. In Jhumka, scenes of the beauty of Vrindaban are depicted in the fullness of Rasa. Today, Bana is sung by the ladies of Braj with great enthusiasm at the time of marriage." By the time a lengthy Pada is finished being rendered, Bhog (foodstuff) is offered to the deity. However, "Bhog Padas are not sung separately in the evening Samaj. Afterwards, the Mangala Badhai (birthday songs) of the gurus are sung. On festivals like Akshaya Tirtha and Guru Purnima the Padas of Mangala Badhai are not sung. But on the festival of the Appearance of Sri Banke Bihari (Krishna), the Mangala Badhai is sung. In the end, two Padas of 'Rupa Madhuri' are sung, the first of which was composed by Lalitmohinidev and the second by Lalitkisoridev. With the distribution of Prasad to everyone, the occasion of Samaj Gayan comes to an end."[51]

As an inside member of the Haridasi sect, Sri Sastri has disclosed the precise order of events in a typical Haridasi session of Samaj Gayan. Coupled with priestly activities of Seva, this description fits the notion of sonic liturgy at its best:

> When the whole Samaj is gathered together, the Mukhiya begins by singing Akara (Alap) and, by way of introduction (Mangalacarana), presents two stanzas of Guru Vandana (obeisance to Swami Haridas and the previous Acharyas). Along with the Mukhiya, the disciples as well as the audience of both groups sing these in unison. After this, the Bada Guru Mangala composed by Swami Krishnadas is sung. There are eleven stanzas of six lines each in this Guru Mangala, describing Sri Vrindaban Dham and the beautiful form of Krishna. By singing these Padas, the atmosphere becomes charged very quickly with the atmosphere of worship. The Chota Guru Mangala is sung after Bada Guru Mangala. It has only three Padas with four lines each, composed by Swami Pitambar, Sri Lalitkisoridev, and Sri Lalitmohinidev. Meanwhile a priest or other person connected with the community worships the Vanis (texts) with sandalwood paste, flowers, and so on, sprinkles perfume, and then offers Misri-Bhog with black pepper and elaichi (cardamum).

> Thereafter, first the Mukhiya, next other Samajis, then all the invited and respected guests, are honored with sandalwood paste, garlands, Misri-Prasad, and such, to the extent possible. Apart from black pepper, cardamom, and Misri-Prasad, betel leaves are offered to the Samajis so that their throats may be melodious. By the time this welcoming ceremony is performed, the musical rendering of Chota Guru Mangala is over. Thereafter, a Pada of Swami Haridas is sung.[52]

The style of singing the Padas is quite different from other traditions of Indian music. Though the Ragas and Talas are already specified, the verses are broken up into different parts or fragments. The accent or emphasis in some lines varies from the beginning to the middle without altering the Raga or Tala. Knowledge of these various accents is known only by oral transmission. Sri Sastri explains the process:

> First of all, the Mukhiya sings the entire line, and then the Jhela, after adding appropriate words of exclamation (eri ha, eri mai, eri ma, ha, etc.), repeats it verbatim. In this manner, after singing each line in the Sthayi and Antara style, and dividing it into several parts with the appropriate interjections and gestures, the process goes on and on. Both the Mukhiya and the Jhelas, after singing the first half and second half of a Caran (line), repeat the whole Caran once more. The entire Caran or line sung in this manner is called a "Tuk." But this rule may not apply to every Pada. In some Padas, two or more Tuks are drawn out of one Caran, or, according to the convenience and the speed of the Tala, two or three Tuks are made from one word only."

The idea is that every Pada has its own style of singing, and some of the Padas are repeated as a whole before proceeding further: "While repeating each line, the words '*eri ha*,' etc., are injected, with the same process followed in the repetitions of the second and third Carans. Suhelera is sung in this style. The last pair of lines in these Padas is sung in Drut Laya (faster pace) of Mul Tal (eight beats, similar to Keherva). Some middle pairs of Bana are also sung in Mul Tal. When Tuks are sung in Drut Laya after the Vilambit Laya (slower pace), the hearts of the Rasikas are enchanted with the sounds of the Pakhavaj in ways that cannot be described."[53]

In Vrindaban the most famous place of Samaj Gayan of the Haridasi Sampradaya is Tatti Sthan. All the functions and festivals are performed here in the traditional style. According to Sri Sastri, "under the guidance and leadership of Baba Sri Visvesvara Das, Samaj Gayan has been organized in the groves of Bihariji, for the last several years. And now that Swami Haridas Sampradaya Kuti has been constructed, Utsavas and festivals are being performed there under the patronage of respected Babaji Maharaj. With the assistance of Sri Govindadasji Mukhiya and Baba Radhasaran, daily Samaj Gayan is also being performed."[54]

In various venues in Vrindaban, Haridas's songs as well as poems written by other members of the Sampradaya are regularly performed in Samaj Gayan style, accompanied by Pakhavaj and responsorial singing by disciples and devotees. But since the beginning of the Mukhiya-Jhela system in the Haridasi Sampradaya, there has been a paucity of record keeping regarding the personnel of the lineage. According to information received from Tatti Sthan, the lineage of Mukhiyas is as follows: "Paramanandadas, Devadas, Gangadas, Ladilidas, Nevalidas, Ramanadas, Puranadas, Madanmohandas, Govindadas, Syamadas, Navaladas." However, historical details about the performances and longevity of each singer are a matter for further research. Another subject for further inquiry is the extent to which the original music of Swami Haridas is part of the present Samaj Gayan tradition. According to Sastri, "so far as the particular Bandish (composition or rendering) of Svaras is concerned, no attention was paid to this in Samaj Gayan because the system was simply passed down through oral transmission."[55] Recently, however, musicologists have begun studying the Bandish of Haridasi Samaj Gayan. The Haridasi sect also sponsors a series of regular festivals (Sammelans) of classical music in Vrindaban, especially Dhrupad.

Samaj Gayan represents one of the most important yet lesser-known branches of devotional music or Pada-Kirtan in India today. Its ritualized performance may be characterized as a unique form of sonic liturgy, with multiple levels and patterns of melody, text, and rhythm interspersed with gesture and liturgical activity. While the music of Samaj Gayan may be studied, with some caution in the context of Hindustani classical music, particularly Dhrupad, it should also be viewed as an important predecessor of modern classical music as well as an influence upon several other important forms of devotional music that were sweeping the northern regions and extending east and west. For example, the tradition of Padavali-Kirtan in Bengal can only be properly understood in relation to the temple music traditions of Vrindaban in the sixteenth century. Many other varieties of devotional music found in parts of North India can be stylistically traced back to the Bhakti musicians of the Braj area that especially include the Radhavallabhites, the Ashtachap poets, and Swami Haridas. But as there is still a sizeable amount of manuscript material that remains to be edited and analyzed critically, the bulk of scholarly determinations have yet to be formulated with regard to the direct and indirect influences of Samaj Gayan on the entire network of devotional music in India.

Conclusion

THIS BOOK BEGAN WITH A CALL TO WIDEN the concept of liturgy and liturgical studies beyond Christian parameters. Certainly the case has been made for the importance of studying ritual and liturgy in different religions. Yet because of a lack of attention to the implicit connections between ritual and music, we have adopted the category of sonic liturgy as a method of approaching the immense variety of sound events and musical expressions in the context of ritual and liturgy. In the ancient Mediterranean world music was viewed as a gift from the gods to humans. In ancient Greece sacrifices required the playing of flutes, cymbals, lyre, and tambourine. Music had a magical influence over the pagan gods and controlled the forces of nature.

In this work we have observed a wealth of these same features in India, where music is a gift of the god Brahma and the goddess Sarasvati in some texts and a benefaction of Siva in others. While the ancient Sama-Gana pleased the gods and brought control over the forces in charge of the natural world, musical instruments were actually played in heaven and transferred to the human realm to assist in the accumulation of salvational merit or Apurva. The Western concept of epiclesis, the calling down of the divine to the earthly plane for purposes of supplication, has found its perfect Eastern corollary in the Vedic Yajna, where priests called down the gods to the sacrifice in order to placate them and make offerings; Sama-Gana invited the Vedic gods to the Yajna in descending scales. Apotropaia, the notion of removing evil forces from sacred spaces, finds Eastern counterparts in both Vedic chant and the performance of drama and Gandharva Sangita. In all cases it is the liturgical context that provides the theater or arena for the conduct of sacred sonic procedures. In the case of Gandharva Sangita, musicians used ascending and descending scales to petition and commune with the gods in Puja rituals. In fact, we have noted that the introduction of the Puja rituals into ancient drama necessitated the construction of a new "classical music" with its own myth of origin that also drew upon features outside of the Indo-Aryan sphere.

Just as in Celtic culture where music was a connector to the Otherworld, in ancient Indian Vedic Sama-Gana, as well as in Gandharva Sangita, music was the principal vehicle that transported the musician and the listener to heavenly states in the afterlife. Performing music was even placed on a higher soteriological platform than sacrifices and the chanting of the rosary of divine names (Japa).

The pioneer phenomenologists of religion Rudolf Otto and Gerardus Van der Leeuw both affirmed that the experience of music was equivalent to the experience of the holy, that musical feeling was "wholly other." The ancient Indian philosophers of music such as Bharata and Dattila contended that, since music was pleasing to the gods, it brought about moral uplift and the permanent experience of divine bliss. The application of these modalities of thought vis-à-vis the notion of sonic liturgy highlights the importance of the Hindu phenomena associated with ritual and music.

We have also introduced liturgical studies and ritual studies as effective disciplines for the study of music and religion in non-Western cultures. Christian theologians, most specifically Louis Boyer and Edward Foley, have given us their foundational views on liturgy—as a universal autonomous agent that generates religious consciousness. With liturgy so broadly denoted, there was an urgent need for Christian thinkers to situate the concept within the general sacrality of the universe. Consequently the disciplines of phenomenology of religion and history of religions were enlisted to provide facts and theoretical formulations. All religious rituals were now part of this general sacred universe that was instituted by "the gods" in the beginning. As such, Bouyer argued that all rites reflect the prototypical and original human action, Richard Viladesau affirmed the theological foundation for all culture, including music, and Anthony Monti demonstrated that all works of art convey the presence of God, even when not labeled as such. Alongside these pronouncements, we have the ritual-studies axiom that culture cannot be defined apart from cult. With these premises on the table it behooved researchers in religious studies like me to begin applying the methods and structures of analysis of liturgical studies and ritual studies to Hindu traditions of worship.

Once all rituals and liturgies were seen to partake of the sacred world, all relevant music became appropriate as the "language of the rite," as integral, necessary. Music was observed to function in various ways: to engage the assembly, reveal the divine, enable communion between the divine and the human. Edward Foley discussed the acoustical properties of music, as well as the qualities of ritual music as being time-bound, as indicators of a personal presence, as dynamic, and as intangible. Though these qualities may have been designed to fit the biblical examples of liturgical music, they apply equally well to the Hindu traditions of temple music in the contexts of Puja and Seva.

Mary E. McGann further supported the primary role of music in liturgy by stating, with examples, that music and song were not mere decoration but expressed as well key features in the community. This holistic approach whereby music is inseparable from the totality of liturgical action is tailor-made for approaching the Hindu practice of Seva, where music is inextricably tied to art, poetry, and liturgical action. The examples of Haveli Sangit and Samaj Gayan have been discussed with the intention of showcasing this principle. McGann's own prescriptive research methods were interdisciplinary, as ours have been, including liturgical studies, ritual studies, and ethnomusicology. In addition she stressed developing empathy by learning the tradition from the inside and called for more cross-cultural studies in music and liturgy.

Taking another cue from Bouyer's premise that all rituals and myths are bound together in liturgical action, we have advanced the more comprehensive thesis that music is an important and vital balancing factor between word and action in all religious rituals, public and private, preventing their decline into the extremes of verbal pedagogy and mindless ritualistic action. The Hindu sonic liturgies examined here all fit into this paradigm, with the survival and sustenance of cultic belief and practice depending upon the continuance of liturgical patterns and formats as established by ruling kings, patrons, or sectarian religious founders. The notion of sacred music has also been given a more precise definition in these pages. The question of context is all-important; Stephen A. Marini has reminded us that the element of ritual context makes a song sacred and that music may indeed be the single most powerful medium of the ritual process.

Accordingly, historical data surrounding various Hindu liturgies—whether in the form of Yajna, Puja, or Seva—have been examined in light of the insights and premises noted above. We have seen how the simple process of mutual exchange between the human realm and the divine comprised the early Vedic system of Yajna, which utilized chant formulas and Sama-Gana hymns as part of the sacrificial action. Then, as non-Aryan dimensions and regional practices were absorbed, the concept of Puja gradually replaced Yajna as the primary vehicle of worship, incorporating early classical music called Gandharva Sangita. In time Puja was fueled by the new surge of Bhakti devotion and narrowed down primarily to the worship of Vishnu and Siva, yet it was greatly enhanced within the venue of Hindu temples and was later even replaced in many cases by Seva, a more all-encompassing form of devotional experience involving a lifetime commitment to a specific deity or teaching. In all of these forms of sonic liturgy, sacred music played a foundational role and gradually reached its apogee, in terms of classical sophistication, in the Seva traditions of the new Krishna sampradayas established in Braj by the sixteenth century. The remainder of this book focused primarily on the two principal forms of classical Pada-Kirtan in northern India: Haveli Sangit and Samaj Gayan.

We have advanced the concept of sonic liturgy here in order to highlight the very prevalent sonic dimensions of Hindu liturgies, that is, music and chant, when, in fact, most religious liturgies contain some form of music and chant. It has also been chosen because there is no single Sanskrit or Indian word for *sonic liturgy*. Each word employed in Hindu tradition—Yajna, Puja, Seva, and also Arcana, Arati, and so on—has culturally specific connotations yet would seem to fit possible metacategories from a wider perspective. By taking assistance from liturgical studies and other Western academic disciplines we have been able to create an elastic or "floating" concept like sonic liturgy which is "portable" and can be tentatively applied across a broad chronological and geographical spectrum of phenomena.

In the process of delineating and refining our concept of sonic liturgy, we have assembled and surveyed some of the best scholarship in the field of Indian religion and Indian music. Not one of these works by itself could have sufficiently presented our case; only after combining the insights of all of them are we able to connect the dots on the ground, so to speak, and draw the conclusions to this study. Hindu sacred music, referring to Indian music in the context of ritual and liturgy, that is, sonic liturgy, thus has the following characteristics.

Theory: Sacred music is rooted in the theoretical principle of Nada-Brahman, as outlined in the Tantras and other musicological literature.

Theory: Sacred music is a gift from the gods through Narada and Bharata, as presented in such Sanskrit musicological texts as *Natya-Sastra* and *Dattilam.*

Theory: Sacred music serves to rebuild and reinforce the cosmos, indicated by the linguistic prefix of the word for music, *Sangita, Sam-gita* (*sam-* , to bring together, perfect, refashion, combine; *-gita,* song, music).

Theory: Sacred music earns salvational merit through the Mimamsa principle of Apurva or Adrishta by marking and measuring musical time, a concept unique to India.

Theory: There is the natural intention to invoke praise of the divine through Bhakti devotion, endorsed in the form of Kirtan by the *Bhagavata-Purana.*

Composition: Verses contain Prakrit/vernacular as well as Sanskrit lyrics, as sanctioned by musicological texts and *Bhagavata-Purana.*

Composition: Melodies are based upon established Ragas, many of which are from Deshi regional sources.

Composition: Rhythms are based upon established Talas, in slow, medium, and fast tempos.

Composition: Melodies are set to Ragas that are frequently linked with times of the day or seasons of the year.

Practice: Rooted in Indo-Aryan features, such as the chanting of Sama-Gana, verses of the *Sama-Veda* are sung in descending scales of five to seven notes.

Practice: Ritual and music are also influenced by non-Indo-Aryan or indigenous features.

Practice: Gandharva Sangita, associated with sacred drama and early Pujas, was vocal music sung in ascending and descending scales of seven notes.

Practice: Almost all Hindu sacred music, including Gandharva Sangita and Bhakti-Sangit, involves the playing of cymbals or other percussive instruments

Practice: Bhakti Sangit strives toward a balance of Raga, Tala, and Pada (words), as exemplified in the Dhrupad songs of the North and the Kriti songs of the South.

Practice: The performance of Bhakti Sangit involves full attention of the participants; sacred music is not a soundtrack for altered states of consciousness but part of an all-encompassing experience, as idealized in the notion of Seva.

Practice: Performance may contain varying degrees of improvisation or not, depending upon the specific tradition.

Practice: Performance normally follows a formal structure and execution.

Practice: Bhakti Sangit usually involves a leader and a group of responders, with occasional antiphony.

Practice: In Bhakti Sangit musical instruments normally include drums, cymbals, harmonium, with optional strings, flutes and other idiophones.

Practice: In sonic liturgy sacred music is part of an order or sequence of ritual events involving epiclesis, propitiation, expiation, *koinonia,* or petition directed toward a deity or deities.

In the Hindu traditions covered, there is also a special emphasis on forms of music that are often highly sophisticated and involve degrees of musical skill. And while there are other traditions of religious worship in the world that have incorporated skilled musicians and conservative or restrained approaches to music, whether in terms of lyric, melody, or rhythm, the Hindu traditions demonstrate an unprecedented fusion and balance among these three factors, such that sacred music, in the form of intricate and often exhaustive combinations of Pada (word), Raga (melody), and Tala (rhythm), becomes not only a central feature of liturgical action, but also, in the case of Samaj Gayan, the liturgy itself.

Accordingly, the centrality of religion within the production of the arts, while present in Western history, is something that reaches a pinnacle in India. Anne-Marie Gaston has reminded us of this fact when she states that, "unlike contemporary artistic traditions in the West, many of the Indian arts continue to be heavily influenced by religion. Until recently, the situation was reminiscent of Europe before the Renaissance. Even today, the content of India's classical arts is taken largely from Hindu religious texts, and many current performance genres evolved from religious rituals." The temple worship traditions are therefore particularly fruitful in disclosing the fusion of the aesthetic and the religious in ways that are incomprehensible to outsiders: "It is therefore of particular interest to examine an artistic tradition which exists in a temple context still largely unmodified by outside influences." Many of the arts, especially music, were conceived and groomed within the confines of liturgical activity, as we have seen: "Although virtually all Indian performing arts trace their origins to religion, or have close ties with it, some are specifically devoted to presentation in religious contexts."[1]

Despite differences in theology or philosophy, a common factor among a myriad of Hindu traditions is the sonic liturgy that serves to generate religious consciousness. Within the sphere of liturgical action, although there may be differences in the content of the song-texts or in the order of execution, there is little difference in principle in the styles of singing or performance. For example, the wide commonality of Dhrupad-style singing has been noted among the many Vaishnava sects of the late medieval period. Moreover, many Siva and Sakta lineages utilize Dhrupad-style songs in their particular Pujas and liturgical activities, but that is a subject for future research. Nonetheless, all of this resonates with the author's earlier book on sonic theology, where it was concluded that, despite theological and cultic differences among many Hindu religious groups, they all share similar theoretical notions of sacred sound in the form of Nada-Brahman and Nada-Sakti in their metaphysical doctrines and theories of language.

In conclusion, the concept of sonic liturgy provides a useful and flexible template for the study of ritual and music in Hindu tradition, and the field of liturgical studies has contributed a meaningful language with which to begin describing and analyzing the gamut of Hindu approaches to ritual and music. But while there has been less attention given to the oral/aural dimension of religion in the field of religious studies, when scholars in liturgical studies talk in terms of a "multileveled auditory environment" or "soundscape" in worship, the Hindu traditions naturally comply in the sense that Seva, as a system of total service to the divine, is meant to incorporate all of normal sensate experiences. The Hindu sonic liturgy, then, as a human experience of the divine, is constituted as an interlocking and interactive network of musical and liturgical meaning.

We close with a few reflections by musicologist Marius Schneider on the nature of the voice, singing, and the ritual song of praise. In "The Nature of Praise Song," Schneider proclaims that "song, according to the ancient concept, did not accompany the sacrifice but in fact formed the core of the sacrificial process. . . . What resounds at the beginning of all things is a praise song. This song represents the first sacrifice. . . . Sound is the basic matter of the primordial world. Praise is the dynamics of this sound."[2]

According to Greek mythology, the creation of music itself is linked with its function of praise: "When Zeus created the world he summoned the gods to show them his work. The gods came and admired the creation in silence. Since none of them said anything about his work, Zeus asked whether anything was still missing. Then the gods answered: 'Your work is great and glorious, but the voice that would praise the great work is missing.' Thereupon Zeus created the Muse, for the existence of things is not complete as long as there is no voice to express it."[3]

Studies in Indo-European linguistics that have linked *vac* (Sanskrit) and *vox* (Latin) with the English *voice* have enabled religious studies scholars to focus on ancient India and the Vedic tradition as the oldest tradition relating praise song to sacrifice: "Sacrifice is the crimson thread that runs through the whole of human life. If this sacrifice is a sound sacrifice, a praise song, then man taps into the primordial acoustic energy of creation, which in the final analysis is the holy syllable AUM that 'fastens' everything together: the past, the present, and the future." Citing ancient Vedic literature (*Satapatha Brahmana* VIII 4. 3. 2) stating that "all that the gods do, they do through song," Schneider concludes that "the praise song is the body of the invisible and the primordial matter of all that has come into being."[4]

Through ritual action the singers of praise song thus evoke the primordial world of pure sound in both spiritual and bodily experience: "Through bone resonance, the singer experiences the reality of pure sound and its intimate link with the physical world, that is, the concrete reality of the spiritual. The spiritual then becomes physically perceptible and the physical is experienced spiritually. The bodily locations of the different sounds vary from school to school, but ritual singing always strives to arouse the sounds of the primordial world."[5]

In Hindu tradition the ritual singing of praise song goes beyond its mere doxological function to bring about self-transformation and self-realization: "Praise singing does not only mean the act of lavishing praise or bestowing power and magnificence on another being, but bringing one's own innermost nature into harmony with the word of creation from which all creatures have sprung. In the religions of the Brahmins, both of these duties of the praise song were one and the same because Atman, the highest God, resides in the innermost part of every person, and his redemptive power and truth must be revealed through song alone."[6]

NOTES

INTRODUCTION

1. Terry Muck, "Psalm, Bhajan, and Kīrtan," 14.
2. Rudolf Otto, *The Idea of the Holy*, 49.
3. Gerardus Van der Leeuw, *Religion in Essence and Manifestation*, 2: 453.
4. Gerardus Van der Leeuw, *Sacred and Profane Beauty: The Holy in Art*, 225, 227.
5. S. G. F. Brandon, *A Dictionary of Comparative Religion*, 457.
6. Catherine Bell, "Performance," 205.
7. Johannes Quasten, *Music & Worship in Pagan & Christian Antiquity*, 1.
8. Ibid., 16.
9. Ibid., 18.
10. Karen Ralls-MacLeod, *Music and the Celtic Otherworld*, 1.
11. Ibid., 5.
12. Ibid., 15.
13. Bruno Nettl, *Excursions in World Music*, 9.
14. Robin Sylvan, *Traces of the Spirit*, 6.
15. Mary Douglas, *Purity and Danger*, 78.
16. Victor Turner, *Image and Pilgrimage in Christian Culture*, 244.
17. Nathan D. Mitchell, *Liturgy and the Social Sciences*, 15.
18. Ronald L. Grimes, "Performance," 379.
19. Ibid.
20. Roy A. Rappaport, *Ritual and Religion in the Making of Humanity*, 31.
21. Nathan D. Mitchell, *Liturgy and the Social Sciences*, 33.
22. Roy A. Rappaport, "The Obvious Aspects of Ritual," 174.
23. Jan Snoek, "Defining Rituals," 13.
24. Alex Michaels, "Sanskrit," 86.
25. Ibid., 87.
26. Ibid., 89–90.
27. Ibid., 90.
28. Joseph Gelineau, "Music and Singing in the Liturgy," 441.
29. Joseph Gelineau, "The Path of Music," 137.
30. *Vatican Council II: The Conciliar and Post Conciliar Documents*, 82, 84.
31. Aidan Kavanagh, *Elements of Rite*, 103–14.
32. Ibid., 104.

33. Louis Bouyer, *Rite and Man*, 31.
34. Ibid., 57.
35. Ibid., 66.
36. J. D. Crichton, "A Theology of Worship," 5.
37. Richard Viladesau, *Theology and the Arts*, 41.
38. Ibid., 47.
39. Aidan Kavanagh, "The Role of Ritual in Personal Development," 148–49.
40. Louis Bouyer *Rite and Man*, 53.
41. Edward Foley, *Ritual Music*, 107.
42. Ibid., 115.
43. Ibid., 116.
44. Ibid., 109–10.
45. Ibid., 112.
46. Ibid.
47. Edward Foley, "Music, Liturgical," 869.
48. Ibid., 868–69
49. Edward Foley, *Ritual Music*, 116.
50. Ibid., 120
51. Edward Foley, "Music, Liturgical," 868.
52. Ibid.
53. Ibid., 869
54. Ibid.
55. Edward Foley, *Ritual Music*, 113–15.
56. Ibid., 108.
57. Mary E. McGann, *Exploring Music as Worship and Theology*, 20.
58. Ibid., 35.
59. Stephen A. Marini, *Sacred Song in America*, 7.
60. Mary E. McGann, *Exploring Music as Worship and Theology*, 11.
61. Ibid.
62. Ibid.
63. Terry Muck, "Psalm, Bhajan, and Kīrtan," 15.
64. Ibid., 16.
65. Ibid., 19.
66. Ibid., quoting Guy L. Beck, *Sonic Theology*.
67. Hilary Rodrigues, *Ritual Worship of the Great Goddess*, 149.
68. Vasudha Narayanan, "Diglossic Hinduism: Liberation and Lentils," 776.
69. Susan L. Schwartz, *Rasa*, 3.
70. Selina Thielemann, *The Music of South Asia*, 339.

CHAPTER ONE—ANCIENT INDIA: YAJNA AND SAMA-GANA

1. Rajesh Kochhar, *The Vedic People*, 37.
2. Ibid., 35.
3. Michael Witzel, "Indocentrism: Autochthonous Visions of Ancient India," 353.

4. Rajesh Kochhar, *The Vedic People*, 99.
5. C. Kunhan Raja, *The Vedas*, 29.
6. Ibid., 16.
7. Frits Staal, *Ritual and Mantras*, 65.
8. C. Kunhan Raja, *The Vedas*, 15.
9. Ibid., 21.
10. Brian K. Smith, *Reflections on Resemblance, Ritual, and Religion*, 13.
11. Ibid., 28.
12. Frits Staal, *Ritual and Mantras*, 65.
13. C. Kunhan Raja, *The Vedas*, 11.
14. Ibid., 41.
15. Frits Staal, *Ritual and Mantras*, 69.
16. Ibid., 67.
17. Ibid.
18. Musashi Tachikawa, Shrikant Bahulkar, and Madhavi Kolhatkar, *Indian Fire Rituals*, 2.
19. Frits Staal, *Ritual and Mantras*, 67–68.
20. Ibid., 67.
21. Ibid., 69.
22. Ibid., 137.
23. Alex Michaels, "Sanskrit," 252.
24. Ibid., 255.
25. Ibid., 258–59.
26. Ibid., 260.
27. Ibid., 261.
28. C. Kunhan Raja, *The Vedas*, 53–54.
29. Ibid., 69. In *Rig-Veda* 10.135.7, the abode of Yama is described as full of song and flute playing
30. Wayne Howard, "Vedic Chant," 242.
31. Solveig McIntosh, *Hidden Faces of Ancient Indian Song*, 44.
32. G. U. Thite, *Music in the Vedas*, 8.
33. G. H. Tarlekar, *Sāman Chants*, 6–7.
34. Ibid., 19–20.
35. Chitrabhanu Sen, *A Dictionary of Vedic Rituals*, 123.
36. A. H. Fox-Strangeways, *The Music of Hindustan*, 246.
37. Thakur Jaidev Singh, *Indian Music*, 1–2.
38. Shahab Sarmadee, *Nūr-Ratnākara*, 4.
39. Solveig McIntosh, *Hidden Faces of Ancient Indian Song*, 45.
40. *Kātyāyana Śrauta-Sūtra: Rules for the Vedic Sacrifices*, 27.
41. Chitrabhanu Sen, *A Dictionary of Vedic Rituals*, 58.
42. Ibid., 70.
43. G. H. Tarlekar, *Sāman Chants*, 20, 31–32. See also Thakur Jaideva Singh, *Indian Music*, 6.
44. Ibid., 21.

45. S. S. Janaki, "The Role of Sanskrit in the Development of Indian Music," 67.
46. V. Raghavan, "Music in Sanskrit Literature," 18.
47. Chitrabhanu Sen, *A Dictionary of Vedic Rituals,* 10.
48. Hermann Oldenberg, *The Religion of the Veda,* 217.
49. Thakur Jaidev Singh, *Indian Music,* 5.
50. Chitrabhanu Sen, *A Dictionary of Vedic Rituals,* 118.
51. Thakur Jaidev Singh, *Indian Music,* 11–12.
52. G. U. Thite, *Music in the Vedas,* 116–17.
53. Ibid., 68.
54. Ibid., 71.
55. Ibid., 94.
56. Ibid., 51–52.
57. Ibid., 61–62.
58. Ibid., 90.
59. Ibid., 11.
60. Brian K. Smith, *Reflections on Resemblance, Ritual, and Religion,* 50.
61. Ibid.
62. Ibid., 51.
63. Ibid., 63.
64. Ibid., 62.
65. Ibid., 63.
66. Rajagopala Aiyar, "Saṁskṛta and Saṅgīta," 64.
67. Brian K. Smith *Reflections on Resemblance, Ritual, and Religion,* 101–12.
68. Ibid., 82.
69. Ibid., 116.
70. Ibid., 101.
71. Ibid., 86.
72. Ibid., 100.
73. Ibid., 102–13.
74. Ibid., 117.
75. Ibid., 105.
76. Ibid., 109.
77. Ibid., 112.
78. Ibid., 68.
79. Francis X. Clooney, S.J., *Thinking Ritually,* 222.
80. Ibid., 241.
81. Ibid., 223.
82. Ibid., 225, citing *Mīmāṁsā–Sūtra* 2.1.5 and Śabara's commentary.
83. Ibid., 226.

CHAPTER TWO—CLASSICAL INDIA: PUJA AND GANDHARVA SANGITA

1. P. V. Kane, *History of Dharmaśāstra (Ancient and Medieval Religious and Civil Law),* vol. 2, 706–8.

2. Natalia Lidova, *Drama and Ritual of Early Hinduism*, 39.
3. Richard H. Davis, *Worshipping Śiva in Medieval India*, 8.
4. Ibid.
5. Ibid., 7.
6. P. V. Kane, *History of Dharmaśāstra (Ancient and Medieval Religious and Civil Law)*, vol. 2, 714.
7. Ibid., 708.
8. Ibid., 706.
9. Natalia Lidova, *Drama and Ritual of Early Hinduism*, 109.
10. P. V. Kane, *History of Dharmaśāstra (Ancient and Medieval Religious and Civil Law)*, vol. 2, 706.
11. Ibid., 707.
12. Shahab Sarmadee, *Nūr-Ratnākara*, 3.
13. Natalia Lidova, *Drama and Ritual of Early Hinduism*, 98.
14. Ibid., 96.
15. Ibid., 40.
16. Ibid., 96.
17. Ibid., 104.
18. Wendy Doniger, *The Hindus*, 259.
19. Natalia Lidova, *Drama and Ritual of Early Hinduism*, 6.
20. Ibid., 46.
21. Ibid., 39.
22. Ibid., 40.
23. Ibid., 107.
24. Ibid., 98.
25. Ibid., 118.
26. Ibid., 44.
27. Ibid., 42.
28. Ibid., 108.
29. Ibid., 109.
30. Ibid., 98–99.
31. Ibid., 43.
32. Ibid., 44.
33. Ibid., 47.
34. Ibid., 43.
35. Ibid., 44.
36. Ibid., 43.
37. Ibid., 40.
38. Ibid., 46.
39. G. H. Tarlekar, *Studies in the Nāṭya–Śāstra*, 16.
40. Susan L. Schwartz, *Rasa*, 13.
41. G. H. Tarlekar, *Studies in the Nāṭya–Śāstra*, 15–16.
42. Adya Rangacharya, trans., *Nāṭya–Śāstra*, 342.

43. Manomohan Ghosh, trans., *Nāṭya–Śāstra Ascribed to Bharata-Muni,* vol. 1, 102.

44. G. H. Tarlekar, *Studies in the Nāṭya–Śāstra,* 1.

45. Ibid., 3.

46. Manomohan Ghosh, ed. and trans., *Nāṭya–Śāstra Ascribed to Bharata-Muni,* vol. 2, 233–37.

47. G. H. Tarlekar, *Studies in the Nāṭya–Śāstra,* 4. Citing Max Muller on *Rig-Veda* I. 165.

48. Ibid., 5.

49. Ibid., 6.

50. Ibid., 10.

51. Ibid., 12–13.

52. Natalia Lidova, *Drama and Ritual of Early Hinduism,* 33.

53. Ibid., 37.

54. Ibid., 8.

55. Ibid., 8–9.

56. Ibid., 22.

57. Manomohan Ghosh, ed. and trans., *Nāṭya–Śāstra Ascribed to Bharata-Muni,* vol. 2, 65.

58. Natalia Lidova, *Drama and Ritual of Early Hinduism,* 13–14.

59. Ibid., 14.

60. Ibid.

61. Ibid., 12.

62. Ibid., 23.

63. Ibid., 100–101.

64. Ibid., 34.

65. Ibid., 34–36.

66. Manomohan Ghosh, ed. and trans., *Nāṭya–Śāstra Ascribed to Bharata-Muni,* vol. 1, 36–37.

67. Natalia Lidova, *Drama and Ritual of Early Hinduism,* 103.

68. Ibid., 104.

69. Ibid., 41.

70. Ibid., 51.

71. Ibid., 115–16.

72. Ibid., 106.

73. Ibid., 105.

74. Ibid., 107.

75. Ibid.

76. Ibid.

77. Ibid.

78. Shahab Sarmadee, *Nūr-Ratnākara,* 7.

79. Alain Danielou, *Introduction to the Study of Musical Scales,* 99.

80. E. Wiersma-te Nijenhuis, *Dattilam,* 62.

81. Ibid., 56–57.

82. Mukund Lath, *A Study of Dattilam,* xii.

83. E. Wiersma-te Nijenhuis, *Dattilam,* 17.

84. Mukund Lath, *A Study of Dattilam,* x, xiii.

85. Ibid., 109.

86. Manomohan Ghosh, ed. and trans., *Nāṭya–Śāstra Ascribed to Bharata-Muni,* vol. 2, 232.

87. Adya Rangacharya, trans., *Nāṭya–Śāstra,* 340.

88. Manomohan Ghosh, ed. and trans., *Nāṭya–Śāstra Ascribed to Bharata-Muni,* vol. 2, 232.

89. E. Wiersma-te Nijenhuis, *Dattilam,* 18–19.

90. Lewis Rowell, *Music and Musical Thought in Early India,* 75–85.

91. Natalia Lidova, *Drama and Ritual of Early Hinduism,* 50–51.

92. Manomohan Ghosh, ed. and trans., *Nāṭya–Śāstra Ascribed to Bharata-Muni,* vol. 2, 37.

93. Shahab Sarmadee, *Nūr-Ratnākara,* 67.

94. Ibid., 90.

95. Manomohan Ghosh, ed. and trans., *Nāṭya–Śāstra Ascribed to Bharata-Muni,* vol. 2, 106.

96. Ibid., 109.

97. Ibid., 151.

98. Wendy Doniger, *The Hindus,* 6.

99. Ibid., 5.

100. Manomohan Ghosh, ed. and trans., *Nāṭya–Śāstra Ascribed to Bharata-Muni,* vol. 2, 150.

101. Ibid., 155.

102. Mukund Lath, *A Study of Dattilam,* 3.

103. E. Wiersma-te Nijenhuis, *Dattilam,* 17.

104. Ibid.

105. Manomohan Ghosh, ed. and trans., *Nāṭya–Śāstra Ascribed to Bharata-Muni,* vol. 2, 92.

106. Solveig McIntosh, *Hidden Faces of Ancient Indian Song,* 79.

107. Mukund Lath, *A Study of Dattilam,* 82–84.

108. Ibid., 82.

109. Ibid., 83.

110. Ibid., 110.

111. Ibid., 81.

112. Ibid., 103.

113. Ibid., 105–16.

114. Ibid., 107.

115. Ibid., 110.

116. Ibid., 127.

117. Ibid., 82.

118. Ibid., 104.

119. Ibid., 105.

120. Ibid., 113.

121. Ibid., 108.

122. E. Wiersma-te Nijenhuis, *Dattilam,* 20–21.

123. Ibid., 21.

124. Ibid., 64.

125. Ibid., 62.

126. Mukund Lath, *A Study of Dattilam*, 91.

127. 1Prem Lata Sharma, "Colloquium on Gandharva," 169.

128. Ibid., 168.

129. S. S. Janaki, "The Role of Sanskrit in the Development of Indian Music," 73.

130. Shahab Sarmadee, *Nūr-Ratnākara*, 15.

131. Ibid., 16.

132. Ibid., 17.

133. Ibid., 19.

134. Ibid., 56–57.

CHAPTER THREE—MEDIEVAL INDIA: TEMPLE HINDUISM AND BHAKTI SANGIT

1. Shahab Sarmadee, *Nūr-Ratnākara*, 40.

2. Richard H. Davis, *Worshipping Śiva in Medieval India*, 6.

3. P. V. Kane, *History of Dharmaśāstra (Ancient and Medieval Religious and Civil Law)*, 724.

4. Richard. H. Davis, *Worshipping Śiva in Medieval India*, 6.

5. P. V. Kane, *History of Dharmaśāstra (Ancient and Medieval Religious and Civil Law)*, 724.

6. Ibid., 725. Jan Gonda, in *Viṣṇuism and Śaivism* (13), stated the differences simply: "In short Vishnu is, generally speaking, a friend nearer to man, Śiva a lord and master, ambivalent and many-sided."

7. Richard H. Davis, *Worshipping Śiva in Medieval India*, 10.

8. H. Daniel Smith, "The 'Three Gems' of the Pāñcarātrāgama Canon—An Appraisal," 45.

9. Richard H. Davis, *Worshipping Śiva in Medieval India*, 11.

10. Ibid., 12.

11. Ibid., 7–8.

12. Indira Viswanathan Peterson, *Poems to Śiva*, 52.

13. Richard H. Davis, *Worshipping Śiva in Medieval India*, 7.

14. Ibid.

15. Klaus K. Klostermaier, *Survey of Hinduism*, 210.

16. Ibid.

17. Wendy Doniger, *The Hindus*, 167.

18. Ibid., 6.

19. John Stratton Hawley, *Krishna, The Butter Thief*, 6.

20. Richard H. Davis, *Worshipping Śiva in Medieval India*, 7.

21. Indira Viswanathan Peterson, *Poems to Śiva*, 8.

22. Friedhelm Hardy, "The Formation of Śrīvaiṣṇavism," 6, n. 11.

23. Indira Viswanathan Peterson, *Poems to Śiva*, 4.

24. Ibid., 26–27.

25. Ibid., 27.

26. Friedhelm Hardy, "The Formation of Śrīvaiṣṇavism," 5.

27. Indira Viswanathan Peterson, *Poems to Śiva,* 40.

28. Ibid., 55.

29. Ibid., 56–57.

30. Ibid., 12. The link between song and shrine becomes more pronounced in the later Vaishnava traditions of linking Krishna's pastimes with specific landmarks or natural features in the Braj region.

31. Ibid., 14.

32. Ibid., 50.

33. Ibid., 29.

34. Ibid., 32.

35. Ibid., 36.

36. Ibid., 11.

37. Ibid., 24.

38. Ibid., 43.

39. Ibid., 43–44. This notion of sonic liturgy as a "total experience" is prominent in the Krishna sampradayas of the sixteenth century, as described below in chapter four and chapter five.

40. Ibid., 51.

41. Ibid., 60.

42. Ibid., 61. By way of comparison, the songs of Jain devotion, stavans, accompany Jain rituals, according to Mary Whitney Kelting (*Singing to the Jinas,* 25): "All Jain rituals are accompanied by stavan singing. . . . Although stavan often accompany some other ritual, stavan singing itself should be seen as Jain ritual both independent of, and in conjunction with, other activities. Stavan singing is not just present in but central to several rituals."

43. Ibid., 66.

44. Ibid., 15–16.

45. Ibid., 23.

46. Ibid., 25.

47. Ibid., 62.

48. Ibid.

49. Ibid., 51. The use of hand cymbals by the Otuvars ties in with the older Gandharva Sangita and prefigures the prominence of cymbals in the later Krishna sampradayas.

50. Ibid.

51. G. U. Thite, *Music in the Vedas,* 10.

52. Ibid, 9.

53. Friedhelm Hardy, "The Formation of Śrīvaiṣṇavism," 43.

54. Ibid., 44.

55. Vasudha Narayanan, *The Vernacular Veda,* 36.

56. Ibid., 80.

57. Friedhelm Hardy, "The Formation of Śrīvaiṣṇavism," 44.

58. Ibid., 46.

59. Vasudha Narayanan, *The Vernacular Veda,* 145. Hinduism scholars H. Daniel Smith and M. Narsimhachary, in *Handbook of Hindu Gods, Goddesses and Saints Popular in Contemporary*

South India, 132, discuss the difficulty in separating history from legend when it comes to the Alvars. While they were historical figures, the question may be raised as to their status as either saints or divine incarnations. Smith and Narsimhachary suggest that they were saints, including the most revered Nammalvar: "So highly revered have these saintly Alvars figures been among Srivaishnavas for many centuries, and so extravagant has been the praise heaped on them through the many generations, that it is now almost impossible to reconstruct with any confidence the historical circumstances surrounding the lives and deeds of any of them. What is beyond doubt, however, is that among the Srivaishnavas today, as has also been the case for several centuries up to now, the one among the twelve Alvars who receives highest acclaim for his saintliness is Nammalvar—a name that is really an epithet meaning 'Our Saint.'" In honor of Nammalvar, Srivaishnavas arrange for annual ten-day celebrations on his birth and departure times.

60. Ibid., 2. Smith and Narsimhachary (in *Handbook of Hindu Gods, Goddesses and Saints Popular in Contemporary South India*, 136–137) also stress the uniqueness of Nammalvar and his work the *Tiruvaymoli* in its original Tamil: "The function of Nammalvar in the spiritual life of Srivaishnavas is to serve as a mediator between man and God. His own human devotion was considered so exemplary that it is a perfection toward which every pious Srivaishnava should himself strive. The words in which he himself articulated his religious vision are so revered that it is considered sacrilege to treat them lightly in any way. Although the *Tiruvaymoli* has been translated into other languages, for purposes of utilizing it to help one move closer to God it must be recited aloud only in Tamil original."

61. Ibid., 140. Regarding gender egalitarianism and music, Kelting (*Singing to the Jinas*, 28) has compared the repertoires of men and women in Jain singing: "Men and women used similar melodies and vocal styles; men and women adhered to similar, though not identical, uses of stavan texts and melodies. The differing performances reflected their differing aesthetics and performance priorities."

62. Ibid., 2–3.

63. Ibid., 5.

64. Indira Viswanathan Peterson, *Poems to Śiva*, 53.

65. Vasudha Narayanan, *The Vernacular Veda*, 136.

66. Ibid., 38.

67. Ibid., 136–37.

68. Ibid., 138.

69. Ibid., 40. The notion of Tamil songs as a vernacular challenge to Sanskrit is paralleled in the later Braj Bhasha songs of the Krishna sampradayas that eclipse the role of Sanskrit in musical worship.

70. Ibid., 64.

71. Ibid., 4.

72. Ibid.

73. Ibid., 89.

74. Ibid., 11.

75. Ibid., 81. The use of hand cymbals by the Araiyars ties in with the older Gandharva Sangita and prefigures the prominence of cymbals in the later Krishna sampradayas.

76. Ibid.

77. Ibid., 83.

78. Ibid., 84.

78. Ibid., 88.

80. Ibid., 98.

81. Ibid., 144.

82. Ibid., 141–42.

83. Ibid., 143.

84. Ibid., 1.

85. Ibid., 144–45. The concept of sonic liturgy is exemplified here as a total spiritual and aesthetical experience that only increases by the time of the sixteenth-century Krishna sampradayas of Braj.

86. Shahab Sarmadee, *Nūr-Ratnākara*, 146.

87. Ibid., xxiv.

88. Ibid., 142.

89. Ibid., 143.

90. Ibid., 144.

91. Ibid., 145.

92. Ibid., 143–44.

93. Ibid., 59.

94. Ibid., 60.

95. Ibid., 276.

96. Ibid., 313.

97. Ibid., 260–62.

98. Ibid., 260.

99. Stephen Slawek, "The Definition of Kīrtan," 57–58.

100. R. C. Zaehner, *The Bhagavad-Gītā*, 279.

101. N. Raghunathan, trans., *Śrīmad Bhāgavatam*, vol. 2, 595. Additional prescriptive references to Kirtan in the *Bhāgavata-Purāṇa* are as follows: 2.1.11, 2.4.15, 4.31.25, 6.1.30, 7.11.8–12, 10.38.4.

102. Ibid., 561.

103. Ibid., 573.

104. Ibid., 630–31.

105. Ibid., 563.

106. Ibid., 632.

107. Ibid., 534. See also 535.

108. Ibid., v. 2, 698.

109. Stephen Slawek, "The Definition of Kīrtan," 61.

110. Shahab Sarmadee, *Nūr-Ratnākara*, 240.

111. Ibid., 241.

112. Ibid., 242.

113. Harold Powers, "India, Subcontinent of, I-II," 75.

114. Selina Thielemann, *Divine Service and the Performing Arts in India*, 27.

115. Graham Schweig, *Dance of Divine Love*, 68.

116. Selina Thielemann, *The Music of South Asia*, 357.

117. Selina Thielemann, *Divine Service and the Performing Arts in India*, 28.

118. Ritwik Sanyal and Richard Widdess, *Dhrupad*, 28.

119. Ibid., 28–29.

120. Ibid., 29.

121. Ibid., 29–30.

122. William Jackson, "Religious and Devotional Music." 262.

123. T. Viswanathan and Matthew Harp Allen, *Music in South India*, 17.

124. See Guy L. Beck, "An Introduction to the Poetry of Narottam Dās."

CHAPTER FOUR—SEVA AND HAVELI SANGIT

1. Selina Thielemann, *Musical Traditions of Vaiṣṇava Temples in Vraja*, vol. 1, 10.

2. Selina Thielemann, *The Music of South Asia*, 333–34.

3. Heidi R. M. Pauwels, *Kṛṣṇa's Round Dance Reconsidered*, 13.

4. Shahab Sarmadee, *Nūr-Ratnākara*, 18–19.

5. Edwin F. Bryant, ed., *Krishna*, 6.

6. This summary of the life of Krishna was assembled from entries found in Vettam Mani, *Puranic Encyclopedia: A Comprehensive Dictionary with Specific Reference to the Epic and Puranic Literature* (New Delhi: Motilal Banarsidass, 1975), 420–29.

7. A. W. Entwistle, *Braj*, 8.

8. Ibid., 10.

9. Ibid., 11.

10. Shahab Sarmadee, *Nūr-Ratnākara*, 41.

11. Ibid., 13.

12. Ibid., 9–10.

13. Ibid., 11.

14. Ibid., 13.

15. Ibid., 11.

16. *Ānanda-Vrindāvana-Campū*, 328–29.

17. Ibid., 325.

18. Ibid., 327.

19. Ibid., 328.

20. Edwin F. Bryant, ed., *Krishna*, 13.

21. A. W. Entwistle, *Braj*, 85.

22. Selina Thielemann, *Musical Traditions of Vaiṣṇava Temples in Vraja*, vol. 1, 21.

23. Satyabhan Sharma, "The Dhrupad–Dhamar Tradition of Braj," 126.

24. Interview with Dr. Satyabhan Sharma (October 20, 1992), Agra, U.P.

25. Induram Srivastava, *Dhrupada*, 22.

26. Satyabhan Sharma, "The Dhrupad—Dhamar Tradition of Braj," 128–29.

27. Anne-Marie Gaston, *Krishna's Musicians*, 122. According to John Stratton Hawley (*The Memory of Love*, 6), "Almost by definition, he [Krishna] must have spoken Brajbhasa in one of its earlier forms."

28. Ibid., 121.

29. A. Whitney Sanford, *Singing Krishna*, 10.

30. Ibid., 12.

31. A. W. Entwistle, *Braj*, 142.

32. Richard Barz, *The Bhakti Sect of Vallabhācārya*, 9.

33. Selina Thielemann, *Musical Traditions of Vaiṣṇava Temples in Vraja*, vol. 1, 492.

34. Meilu Ho, "The Liturgical Music of Pushti Mārg of India," 102.

35. Satyabhan Sharma, "The Dhrupad—Dhamar Tradition of Braj," 129.

36. Ibid., 130.

37. Ibid.

38. Meilu Ho, "The Liturgical Music of Pushti Mārg of India," 32.

39. Selina Thielemann, *Musical Traditions of Vaiṣṇava Temples in Vraja*, vol. 1, 492.

40. Anne-Marie Gaston, *Krishna's Musicians*, 27.

41. Meilu Ho, "The Liturgical Music of Pushti Mārg of India," 97.

42. Ibid., 20.

43. Ibid.

44. Interview with Sri Gopi Rasik Tailang (October 25, 1992), Jatipur, U.P.

45. John Stratton Hawley, *Sūr Dās*, 163, 170.

46. Interview with Pandit Lav Caturvedi (October 12, 1992), Mathura, U.P.

47. Anne-Marie Gaston, *Krishna's Musicians*, 122–23.

48. Meilu Ho, "The Liturgical Music of Pushti Mārg of India," 25.

49. Selina Thielemann, *Musical Traditions of Vaiṣṇava Temples in Vraja*, vol. 1, 492.

50. Satyabhan Sharma, "The Dhrupad—Dhamar Tradition of Braj," 131.

51. Selina Thielemann, *Musical Traditions of Vaiṣṇava Temples in Vraja*, vol. 1, 493.

52. Meilu Ho, "The Liturgical Music of Pushti Mārg of India," 97.

53. Selina Thielemann, *Musical Traditions of Vaiṣṇava Temples in Vraja*, vol. 1, 492.

54. Satyabhan Sharma, "The Dhrupad—Dhamar Tradition of Braj," 132.

55. Ibid.

CHAPTER FIVE—SEVA AND SAMAJ GAYAN

1. Selina Thielemann, *Musical Traditions of Vaiṣṇava Temples in Vraja*, vol. 1, 23.

2. Rupert Snell, *The Eighty-Four Hymns of Hita Harivaṁśa*, 20.

3. Charles S. J. White, *The Caurāsī Pad of Śrī Hit Harivaṁś*, 35.

4. Rupert Snell, *The Eighty-Four Hymns of Hita Harivaṁśa*, 329.

5. J. N. Farquhar, *An Outline of the Religious Literature of India*, 318.

6. Charles S. J. White, *The Caurāsī Pad of Śrī Hit Harivaṁś*, 28–29.

7. Durgadas Mukhopadhyay, ed. and trans., *In Praise of Krishna*, 89.

8. Rupert Snell, *The Eighty-Four Hymns of Hita Harivaṁśa*, 3.

9. Ibid., 5.

10. Ibid., 3.

11. Interview with Sri Ramnath Prasad at the Radhavallabha Temple in Vrindaban, U.P. (July 20, 1988). The content was transcribed and edited from an audiotape. Sri Prasad was the Esraj player during the Samaj Gayan at the main Radhavallabha temple in Vrindaban for many years.

12. Interview with Sri Rajendra Prasad Sharma in Vrindaban (March 23, 1993). The content was transcribed from an audio tape and translated from Hindi to English by Sri Hari Shankar Mathur, former director of the Sri Rangaji Temple in Vrindaban.

13. Sri Goswami Lalitacaranji Maharaj, "The Musical Style of the Rādhāvallabha Samāj Gāyan," 136–37.

14. Charles S. J. White, *The Caurāsī Pad of Śrī Hit Harivaṁś*, 32.

15. Ibid., 31.

16. Ibid., 32.

17. Interview with Sri Rajendra Prasad Sharma (March 23, 1993), Vrindaban, U.P.

18. Rupert Snell, "Metrical Forms in Braj Bhāṣā Verse," 361.

19. Charles S. J. White, *The Caurāsī Pad of Śrī Hit Harivaṁś*, 31.

20. Sri Goswami Lalitacaranji Maharaj, "The Musical Style of the Rādhāvallabha Samāj Gāyan," 136.

21. Selina Thielemann, *The Music of South Asia*, 305.

22. Interview with Sri Rajendra Prasad Sharma (March 23, 1993), Vrindaban, U.P.

23. Interview with Sri Kisori Saran Ali (July 22, 1992) in Vrindaban; transcribed from an audio tape and translated from Hindi to English by Sri Hari Shankar Mathur. Sri Kisori Saran Ali is a recognized authority on the Radhavallabha tradition and has published many works in Hindi.

24. Selina Thielemann, *Musical Traditions of Vaiṣṇava Temples in Vraja*, vol.1, 213–14.

25. Selina Thielemann, *The Music of South Asia*, 306.

26. Ibid., 305–6.

27. Interview with Sri Rajendra Prasad Sharma in Vrindaban (March 28, 1993). The content was transcribed from an audio tape and translated from Hindi to English by Sri Hari Shankar Mathur.

28. Sri Goswami Lalitacaranji Maharaj, "The Musical Style of the Rādhāvallabha Samāj Gāyan," 136–37.

29. Interview with Sri Rajendra Prasad Sharma (March 28, 1993) in Vrindaban, U.P.

30. Selina Thielemann, *Divine Service and the Performing Arts in India*, 29.

31. Sri Brajvallabh Saran, "Samāj Gāyan in the Nimbārka Sampradāya," 135.

32. Ibid., 132–33.

33. Ibid., 133.

34. Selina Thielemann, *Musical Traditions of Vaiṣṇava Temples in Vraja*, vol. 1, 282.

35. *Śrī Mahāvāṇī*, edited by Sri Govinda Saran, 51–196.

36. Selina Thielemann, *Musical Traditions of Vaiṣṇava Temples in Vraja*, vol. 1, 282.

37. Sri Brajvallabh Saran, "Samāj Gāyan in the Nimbārka Sampradāya," 135.

38. Richard Haynes, "Svāmī Haridās and the Haridāsī Sampradāy," 250.

39. Ibid., 324, 330.

40. Selina Thielemann, *Musical Traditions of Vaiṣṇava Temples in Vraja*, vol. 1, 357.

41. Ibid.

42. Ibid.

43. Interview of Sri Vrindaban Bihari Goswami (March 28, 1993), Vrindaban, U.P. A prominent lead singer in Samaj Gayan, Sri Goswami is also a research scholar attached to the Vrindaban Sodh Samsthan (Vrindaban Research Institute).

44. Sri Govinda Saran Sastri, "Samāj Gāyan in the Haridāsī Sampradāya," 138. Sri Sastri, while originally belonging to the Nimbarka Sampradaya and editing many of their scriptures, was residing with the Haridasi Sampradaya in 1993.

45. Ibid.

46. Ibid., 138–39.

47. Ibid., 139.

48. Ibid., 140.

49. Ibid., 140–41.

50. Ibid., 141.

51. Ibid., 141–42.

52. Ibid., 141.

53. Ibid., 142.

54. Ibid., 143.

55. Ibid., 144.

CONCLUSION

1. Anne-Marie Gaston, *Krishna's Musicians,* 21.

2. Marius Schneider, "The Nature of Praise Song," 37–39.

3. Ibid., 50.

4. Ibid., 41.

5. Ibid., 48.

6. Ibid., 49.

GLOSSARY

Abhinavagupta—ca. 950–1020 C.E.; one of the greatest philosophers and mystics of India who wrote a commentary on the *Nāṭya-Śāstra.*

Acharya (Ācārya)—great spiritual teacher or founder of a lineage.

Adhvāryu—Vedic priest associated with the *Yajur-Veda.*

Adrishta (adṛṣṭa)—"unseen," referring to the unseen merit that accrues to the sacrificer or musician through the principle of *Apūrva.*

Āgama—medieval collection of revealed texts in Sanskrit that comprises instructions for rituals, temple construction, and religious practices for the followers of Śiva, Vishnu, or other deities. This category includes the Śaiva Āgamas, the Vaishnava Pāñcarātras, and Śākta Tantras.

Agni—the god of the sacred fire in the Vedic religion.

Agra Gharana—the oldest and richest tradition of Hindustani classical vocal music, with direct ties to the Dhrupad and Dhamar music of the temples in Mathura and Vrindaban.

Ālāp—introductory presentation of a *Rāga* in Indian music without percussion accompaniment.

Āḻvār—group of twelve Tamil poet-saints from ca. fifth century to ninth century C.E. who produced roughly four thousand songs and poems that had been collected by the tenth century and comprise the early hymnal for the Śrīvaishnava Sampradāya. The complete work is known as the *Divya-Prabandham.*

Apabhraṁśa—an early class of Prākrit language that developed into Braj Bhāṣā and Hindi.

Apsarās—dancers in the heavenly court of Indra.

Apūrva—the principle outlined in Mīmāṁsā philosophy whereby the result or merit of a sacrifice, quantified through ritual time units and the syllables of mantra chanting, is delayed or stored within the soul of the sacrificer to be reclaimed at a future time, usually in heaven or in the form of immortality. This principle also operates within the domain of music and the counting of rhythm.

Ārati—the ceremony of making a series of offerings, including flowers, incense, water, food, and the like, as part of the *Pūjā* ritual service.

Aryan (Ārya)—a term meaning "noble" or "cultured," normally associated with a language group. The ancient Indians and Iranians are the only groups to have employed the term to themselves.

Ashtachap (aṣṭachāp)—a group of eight poet-saints associated with the Pushti Mārg or Vallabha Sampradāya, the most famous being Sur Das. They were among the forerunners of northern Hindustani classical music as they wrote and sung compositions in the genre of Dhrupad and

Dhamar. Their poems comprise the bulk of the Pushti Mārg hymnals in use, of which there are many.

Ātman (Daiva Ātman)—the spiritual soul of the living entity, believed according to Vedanta philosophy to be equivalent or part of Brahman.

Balarāma—the elder brother of Krishna who was also an incarnation of Vishnu.

Bhagavad-Gītā—Sanskrit text; famous discourse by Krishna in eighteen chapters that forms part of the epic *Mahābhārata.* Many pious Hindus consider this work to be the best summation of Hindu teachings, especially with regard to Bhakti.

Bhāgavata-Purāṇa—Sanskrit text; the most famous of the Vaishnava Purāṇas, describing in detail the various *avatāras* (incarnations) of Vishnu and presenting the entire life of Krishna in the tenth book.

Bhakti Sangīt—Devotional musics, especially those that have incorporated the classical traditions. Music as part of temple worship from medieval times to the present, including the sub-categories of *Kīrtan* and *Bhajan.* Bhajan is a sub-category of Bhakti Sangīt, referring to worship music or music as an offering to God.

Bharata Muni—the legendary author of the musical treatise *Nāṭya-Śāstra* (ca. 400 B.C.E.) outlining the theory and practice of Gandharva Sangīta.

Bhāva—emotional state or experience derived from witnessing drama or music.

Brahmā—the Creator God of Hindu tradition, part of the Trimūrti, the group of three great gods that also includes Vishnu and Śiva.

Braj Bhasha (Braj Bhāṣā)—dialect of medieval Hindi prominent in the northern region of Braj and beyond and one of the favorite vernacular languages for devotional poetry describing Krishna.

Brihaddeśī—Sanskrit text; musical treatise of the eighth or ninth century C.E., the first musical work to identify the concept of a *Rāga and to incorporate Tantric discussions of Nāda-Brahman.*

Caurāsī Pad—Braj Bhasha text; eighty-four verses composed by Hita Harivaṁśa, founder of the Rādhāvallabha Sampradāya.

Cautal—the most prevalent rhythm in Dhrupad music, consisting of twelve beats.

Cēvai—the Tamil term for *Sēva,* or divine service.

Darshan (darśana)—seeing the deity; school of Indian philosophy.

Dattilam—Sanskrit text; ancient musical work by the sage Dattila describing Gandharva Sangīta.

Devakī—the birth mother of Krishna.

Devī—Sanskrit term for female divinity or goddess.

Dhamar—a rhythm used in Dhrupad music, consisting of fourteen beats.

Dhrupad—the oldest surviving form of classical music in northern India, originally Dhruvapada ("fixed verse").

Dhruva—the reference in *Nāṭya-Śāstra* to a type of vernacular song used in the early dramas and in worship of the gods.

Divya Prabandham—Tamil text; the collection of Tamil hymns composed by the Āḻvārs, used as a hymnal by the Śrīvaishnava tradition.

Durgā—a great goddess or Śakti in Hinduism, wife of Śiva.

Ekaśruti—one note or sound; refers to the monotone chanting of the *Rig-Veda.*

Esrāj—musical instrument; a bowed chordophone.

Gandharvas—class of heavenly musicians who sing in the court of Indra.

Gandharva Sangīta—the ancient classical music of India as described in the *Nāṭya-Śāstra* and the *Dattilam.*

Gītī/Gītā—song or musical composition in Indian tradition.

Gīta-Govinda—Sanskrit text; well-known devotional work of the twelfth century by Jayadeva.

Gopāla—name for Krishna as a cowherd boy.

Gopī—name for the wife of a cowherd friend of Krishna

Grihya—domestic rituals in the Vedic religion.

Haridāsī Sampradāya—one of the Krishna *sampradāyas* founded in Braj by Swami Haridas in the sixteenth century C.E.

Harivamśa—Sanskrit text; early work attached to the *Mahābharata* that presents descriptions of Krishna's life and pastimes.

Haveli Sangīt—the Dhrupad-influenced Bhakti Sangīt of the Vallabha Sampradāya.

Hita Harivaṁśa—the founder of the Rādhāvallabha Sampradāya in the sixteenth century.

Holi (Horī)—Hindu Spring Festival of Colors.

Homa (also *havan*)—a small fire sacrifice; refers to fire worship in the Tantric tradition.

Hotri—Vedic priest associated with the *Rig-Veda.*

Īśvara—"Controller" or "Lord" in Hindu tradition, the personification of Brahman; may refer to Śiva, Vishnu, or simply "God."

Janmāṣṭamī—annual birthday celebrations of Krishna in August and September.

Japa—the low-volume solitary muttering or chanting of divine names or mantras, often with the counting of beads.

Jarjara—the heavenly pole of Indra, one of the first objects of image worship in the *Nāṭya-Śāstra.*

Jhāñjh—hand cymbals used in Bhakti Sangīt, especially Haveli Sangīt and Samāj Gāyan.

Jhaptal—rhythm in Indian classical music consisting of ten beats.

Jhelā—singers who accompany Samāj Gāyan performance.

Kalidāsa—the most famous poet and playwright of medieval India.

Khyāl—the most prevalent form of Hindustani vocal music, derived partially from Dhrupad.

Kinnāras—the heavenly musicians who play on instruments in the court of Indra.

Kīrtan—"praise song"; devotional music, a genre of Bhakti Sangīt.

Kōyil—short version of the *Tiruvāymoli.*

Kriti—classical song of Carnatic music in southern India.

Laukika—worldly or secular status, referring to the entertainment value of music or drama.

Laya—tempo in Indian music.

Mahābhārata—Sanskrit text; the famous epic of India describing the feud between the Pāṇḍavas and the Kauravas culminating in an eighteen-day battle. The *Bhagavad-Gītā* is the sermon of Krishna to his friend and disciple Arjuna that was delivered just before the battle commenced.

Mahāvāṇī—Braj Bhasha text; the hymnal of the Nimbārka Sampradāya compiled by Śrī Harivyāsdevācārya.

Maṇḍala—a circle or square diagram used in Hindu and Buddhist ritual.

Mantra—Sanskrit word or phrase used in Vedic ritual or Hindu piety.

Manu—one of the first two human beings, along with his brother Yama; the composer of the Laws of Manu, *Manu-Samhitā.*

Mārga—path or discipline.

Mathurā—the town in Braj, in northern India, where Krishna was born.

Mātrā—a single beat in Indian music. The term is cognate with the English words *meter* and *measure.*

Mīmāṁsā—branch of Indian philosophy that interprets the Vedic rituals and their injunctions. Famous philosophers of this school are Jaimini, Śabara, Kumārila Bhaṭṭa, and Prabhākara Miśra.

Moksha (mokṣa)—liberation from *Samsāra* or the cycle of rebirth.

Nāda-Brahman—the concept of sacred sound in Hindu tradition, encompassing both linguistic and nonlinguistic sound (music).

Nāda-Śakti—the feminine potencies of sacred sound attached to the letters of the Sanskrit alphabet which are released when chanted or sung.

Nām-Kīrtan—chanting the names of God in a musical setting.

Nammāḻvār—the most famous of the twelve Āḻvārs of Tamil Vaishnavism.

Nārada Rishi—the son of Brahmā who brought music to earth and taught it to the human race.

Nārāyaṇa—a name for Vishnu as the object of ritual devotion in the Pāñcarātra tradition.

Naṭarāja—the image of the dancing Śiva.

Nāṭya-Śāstra—Sanskrit text; ancient musical work by the sage Bharata describing Gandharva Sangīta.

Nāthamuni—First Acharya of the Śrīvaishnava tradition, who set the hymns of the *Divya Prabandham* to music.

Nāyañārs—sixty-three Śaiva poet-saints whose collected works appear in the Tamil hymnal known as the *Tēvāram.*

Nikuñja-Vihāra—The eternal pastimes of Rādhā and Krishna taking place in the forest grove of the spiritual abode of Vrindāvana.

Nimbārka—the twelfth-century founder and Acharya of the Nimbārka Sampradāya.

Nrittya—dance

Oṁ/AUṀ—the cosmic sound of creation, reiterated at the beginning of Vedic rituals, mantras, and most Hindu Pujas and recitations of scripture. As a potent symbol of Brahman, it is believed to encapsulate all the letters and sounds of the Sanskrit alphabet and contains spiritual properties.

Øtuvār—singer-musicians in the Tamil Śaiva tradition of temple Hinduism.

Pada-Kīrtan—a devotional music composition involving sung poetry and verse.

Pakhāvāj—long barrel drum used in northern Hindustani music and Bhakti Sangīt.

Pāñcarātra—the corpus of Sanskrit ritual texts of medieval Vaishnavism belonging to the Āgama tradition.

Pāṇini—the best-known Sanskrit grammarian, ca. fifth century B.C.E.

Prākrit—the vernacular counterpart of Sanskrit, believed to encompass the many indigenous languages and vocabularies that influenced the birth and development of Sanskrit through its many stages.

Prasād—“mercy”; sacraments or offered remnants of food and so on.

Pūjā—ritual worship of images that replaced the Vedic fire sacrifice (*Yajña*) as the central rite of Hinduism.

Punya—merit or spiritual credit accumulated through ritual or pious deeds.

Purāṇa—Sanskrit texts; a class of lengthy historical and mythological narratives compiled in medieval India.

Pūrvara ga—the preliminary *Pūjā* to the gods as outlined in the *Nāṭya- Śāstra*.

Purusha-Sūkta—"The Hymn of the Cosmic Man" in the *Rig-Veda* (RV 10.90).

Pushti Mārg—"the path of grace"; another term used for the Vallabha Sampradāya.

Rādhāṣṭamī—annual birthday celebrations of the appearance of the goddess Rādhā in September and October.

Rādhāvallabha Sampradāya—the Vaishnava tradition or Krishna sampradāya founded by Hita Harivaṁśa in the sixteenth century in Braj.

Rāga—a special set of notes from a musical scale; a "mood" in Indian music; term first described in the *Brihaddeśī*.

Rāmānuja—the best-known *Acharya* and theologian of the Śrīvaishnava tradition.

Rasa—emotional state or mood, as in the eight Rasas described in the *Nāṭya-Śāstra*.

Rāmāyaṇa—the second great epic of Hindu tradition, describing the descent of Vishnu as Rāma, his heroic recovery of his wife, and the destruction of evil in the world.

Rig-Veda—the original Veda, comprising ten books of metrical hymns and other materials.

Rishi—"seers," Vedic poet-sages who received the revelation of the *Rig-Veda*.

Rupak—rhythmic cycle of seven beats in Indian music.

Śabda-Brahman—concept of sacred sound or sonic Absolute as presented in the Upanishads. While Śabda-Brahman is associated with linguistic meaning, Nāda-Brahman as outlined in the Āgamas also includes nonlinguistic sound and music.

Śakti—feminine principle or goddess.

Śaktism—the traditions of goddess worship or veneration.

Sāma-Gāna—the performance of *Sāman*, the hymns of the *Sāma-Veda*.

Samāj Gāyan—the unique style of collective singing as found in Braj, especially in the Rādhāvallabha, Haridāsī, and Nimbārka *sampradāyas*.

Samāj-Śriṅkhalā—Braj Bhasha text; hymnal used by the Haridāsī-Sampradāya.

Sāman—a hymn of the *Sāma-Veda* rendered in musical notes.

Sāma-Veda—one of the four Vedas that include the hymns set to music and sung by Udgātri priests.

Sampradāya—tradition or scholastic lineage in Hindu tradition.

Samsāra—the cycle of rebirth in Indian religions.

Samskāra—life-cycle rituals in the Hindu tradition.

Samya (sam)—the confluence of note, beat, and word in Gandharva and classical music, especially on the first beat of the *Tāla* or time cycle; believed to bring about enhanced *Adrishta* or spiritual merit.

Sangīt—in this work, the designation of music normally sung in the vernacular; that is, Bhakti Sangīt.

Sangīta—in this work, the designation of music as delineated in the Sanskrit texts; Gandharva Sangīta.

Sangīta-Ratnākara—Sanskrit text; musical work by Śārṅgadeva in the thirteenth century C.E.

Sanskrit—the classical and liturgical language of India used by priests and scholars; the language of the Vedas and successive literature; the priestly counterpart to the vernacular Prākrit.

Sārangī—bowed chordophone musical instrument.

Sarasvati—goddess of learning and music in Hindu tradition.

Śārṅgadeva—author of the well-known musical treatise *Sangīta-Ratnākara.*

Sevā—"divine service"; an expanded system of *Pūjā* that involves a total experience and commitment to a deity or guru.

Shringāra (śṛṅgāra)—the first of the eight *Rasas* outlined by Bharata; passionate love.

Śiva—one of the great gods of the Trimūrti; the destroyer of the cosmos.

Śloka—a verse in Sanskrit, arranged in one of a variety of meters.

Smārta—a post-Vedic conservative tradition of worshipping five deities established by Brahmins.

Smriti—"that which is remembered"; texts and traditions that follow the Śruti or Vedic revelation.

Somā—an intoxicating plant used in Vedic rituals, unknown today but prevalent in ancient India and Iran.

Śrauta—public rituals in the Vedic religion.

Śrīvaishnava Sampradāya—Tamil Vaishnava tradition established by Nāthamuni in the tenth century c.e. and carried forward by Yāmuna and Rāmānuja.

Śruti—Vedic revelation; also the finest microtone in Indian music.

Stobhā—meaningless syllables inserted into the prose of the *Sāma-Veda* to fill out the melody or metrical requirements for singing.

Stotra—a group of Sanskrit verses focused on a theme or addressed to a specific deity.

Stuti—Sanskrit hymn of praise.

Sūkta—Sanskrit hymn from the Vedic literature.

Sūtra—short form of Sanskrit verse style used in authoritative texts or treatises such as *Yoga-Sūtra* and *Dharma-Sūtra.*

Sūtradhara—the head priest of the *Pūjā* in the ancient dramas as described by Bharata.

Tablas—pair of small drums used in Hindustani music.

Tāla—rhythm or rhythmic cycle used in Indian classical music, comprised of *tali* (claps) and *khali* (waves).

Tāna—series of musical notes arranged in phrases of ascending and descending passages. The term may also refer to "fixed-tone" in Vedic chant.

Tēvāram—Tamil text; collection of the hymns of the Nāyañārs, Śaiva poet-saints.

Tiruvāymoḷi—Tamil text; the hymns of the best-known Vaishnava Āḻār, Alvar.

Trimūrti—the three great gods of Hindu tradition: Brahma the Creator, Vishnu the Preserver, and Śiva the Destroyer.

Udgātri—Vedic singer-priest associated with the *Sāma-Veda.*

Upacara—referring to the sixteen activities of *Pūjā.*

Upanāyana—the ceremony of initiation of young boys into the Hindu tradition; one of the principal *Samskāras* or life-cycle rituals.

Vāc—the goddess of speech in the Vedas, precursor to the goddess Sarasvati.

Vādya—a musical instrument.

Varṇa—the four social divisions of society sometimes referred to as caste.

Vāsudeva—name of Krishna as the son of Vasudeva.

Vallabha—the founder and *Acharya* of the Pushti Mārg tradition, also known as the Vallabha Sampradāya.

Veda—"knowledge" received as revelation in the form of four collections of Sanskrit verses; the four Vedas handed down orally by Brahmins for more than three thousand years.

Vedānta—branch of Indian philosophy based upon the Upanishads, interpreted in various ways, carrying forth ontologies of monism, qualified nondualism, dualism, and so forth, according to the scholastic lineage or *sampradāya*.

Vrindāvana—the spiritual residence of Krishna.

Vrindaban—the earthly hometown of Krishna in India.

Yādava—the lunar dynasty associated with Krishna and the Pāṇḍava heroes of the *Mahābhārata*.

Yajamāna—the sacrificer or patron of the sacrifice in the Vedic ritual.

Yajña—fire sacrifice in Vedic religion.

Yama—the first human being, along with his brother Manu. Yama was the first human to reach the netherworld through sacrifice by following the rituals outlined by Manu.

Yāmuna—the *Acharya* before Rāmānuja in the line of Śrīvaishnavism.

BIBLIOGRAPHY

Ānanda-Vrindāvana-Campū, by Kavi Karṇapur. Translated by Bhanu Swami and Subhag Swami and edited by Mahanidhi Swami. Vrindavana, U.P.: Mahanidhi Swami, 1999.

Barz, Richard. *The Bhakti Sect of Vallabhācārya*. Faridabad: Thomson Press, 1976.

Beck, Guy L. "An Introduction to the Poetry of Narottam Dās." *Journal of Vaiṣṇava Studies* 4.4 (Fall 1996): 17–52.

———. "Religious and Devotional Music: Northern Area." In *Garland Encyclopedia of World Music*. Vol. 5: *Indian Subcontinent*, edited by Alison Arnold, 246–58. New York and London: Garland, 2000.

———. *Sonic Theology: Hinduism and Sacred Sound*. Columbia: University of South Carolina Press, 1993.

———. *Vaishnava Temple Music in Vrindaban: The Rādhāvallabha Songbook*. With 18 CDs. Kirksville, Mo.: Blazing Sapphire Press, 2011.

———. "Vaiṣṇava Music in the Braj Region of North India." *Journal of Vaiṣṇava Studies* 4.2 (Spring 1996): 115–47.

———, ed. *Alternative Krishnas: Regional and Vernacular Variations on a Hindu Deity*. Albany: State University of New York Press, 2005.

———, ed. *Sacred Sound: Experiencing Music in World Religions*. With CD. Waterloo, Ont.: Wilfrid Laurier University Press, 2006.

Bell, Catherine. "Performance." In *Critical Terms for Religious Studies*, edited by Mark C. Taylor. 205–24. Chicago: University of Chicago Press, 1998.

Bouyer, Louis. *Rite and Man: Natural Sacredness and Christian Liturgy*. Notre Dame, Ind.: Notre Dame University Press, 1963.

Bradshaw, Paul, ed. *The New Westminster Dictionary of Liturgy & Worship*. Louisville, Ky.: Westminster John Knox Press, 2002.

Brandon, S. G. F. *A Dictionary of Comparative Religion*. New York: Charles Scribner's Sons, 1970. Entry entitled "Music," 457.

Bryant, Edwin. *The Quest for the Origins of Vedic Culture*. New York: Oxford University Press, 2001.

———, ed. *Krishna: A Sourcebook*. New York: Oxford University Press, 2007.

Buhnemann, Gudrun. *Pūjā: A Study in Smārta Ritual*. Vienna: Publications of the De Nobili Research Library, 1988.

Chakrabarty, Ramakanta. "Vaiṣṇava Kīrtan in Bengal." *Journal of Vaiṣṇava Studies* 4.2 (Spring 1996): 179–99.

Clooney, S. J., Francis X. *Thinking Ritually: Rediscovering the Pūrva Mīmāṁsā of Jaimini.* Vienna: Publications of the De Nobili Research Library, 1990.

Crichton, J. D. "A Theology of Worship." In *The Study of Liturgy*, edited by Cheslyn Jones, Geoffrey Wainwright, and Edward Yarnold, S.J., 1–29. New York: Oxford University Press, 1978.

Danielou, Alain. "The Modal Music of the Hindus." Part 5 of *Introduction to the Study of Musical Scales.* London: India Society, 1943.

Davis, Richard H. *Worshipping Śiva in Medieval India: Ritual in an Oscillating Universe.* Delhi: Motilal Banarsidass, 2000.

Denny, Frederick M., and Rodney L. Taylor, eds. *The Holy Book in Comparative Perspective.* Columbia: University of South Carolina Press, 1985.

Doniger, Wendy. *The Hindus: An Alternative History.* New York: Penguin, 2009.

Douglas, Mary. *Purity and Danger: An Analysis of Concepts of Pollution and Taboo.* Baltimore: Penguin, 1970 (1966).

Driver, Tom F. *Liberating Rites: Understanding the Transformative Power of Ritual.* New York: Booksurge Publishing, 2006.

Entwistle, A. W. *Braj: Centre of Krishna Pilgrimage.* Groningen: Egbert Forsten, 1987.

Farquhar, J. N. *An Outline of the Religious Literature of India.* Oxford: Oxford University Press, 1920.

Feld, Steven, and Keith H. Basso, eds. *Senses of Place.* New York: School of American Research Press, 1996.

Fink, S.J., Peter E., ed. *The New Dictionary of Sacramental Worship.* Collegeville, Minn.: Liturgical Press, 1990.

Foley, Edward. "Music, Liturgical." In *The New Dictionary of Sacramental Worship*, edited by Peter E. Fink, S.J., 854–70. Collegeville, Minn.: Liturgical Press, 1990.

——. *Ritual Music: Studies in Liturgical Musicology.* Beltsville, Md.: Pastoral Press, 1995.

——, ed. *Worship Music: A Concise Dictionary.* Collegeville, Minn.: Liturgical Press, 2000.

Fox-Strangeways, A. H. *The Music of Hindustan.* 1914. Reprint, Delhi: Oriental Books Reprint Corporation, 1975.

Gaston, Anne-Marie. "The Hereditary Drummers of Śrī Nāthjī Temple: The Family History of Pakhavājī Guru Puruṣottam Dās." *Dhrupad Annual* 4 (1989): 16–57.

——. *Krishna's Musicians: Musicians and Music Making in the Temples of Nathdvara, Rajasthan.* New Delhi: Manohar Publishers, 1997.

Gelineau, Joseph. "Music and Singing in the Liturgy." In *The Study of Liturgy*, edited by Cheslyn Jones, Geoffrey Wainwright, and Edward Yarnold, S.J., 440–54. New York: Oxford University Press, 1978.

——. "The Path of Music." In *Music and the Experience of God*, edited by Mary Collins, David Power, and Mellonee Burnim, 135–47. Edinburgh: T & T Clark, 1989.

Ghosh, Manomohan, ed. and trans. *Nāṭya-Śāstra Ascribed to Bharata-Muni.* Complete Sanskrit Text and English Translation in 4 vols. Varanasi: Chowkhamba Sanskrit Series Office, 2007 (1967).

Gonda, Jan. *Viṣṇuism and Śivaism: A Comparison.* London: School of Oriental and African Studies, 1970.

Grimes, Ronald L. *Beginnings in Ritual Studies.* 1982. Rev. ed. Columbia: University of South Carolina Press, 1994.

———. "Performance." In *Theorizing Rituals: Issues, Topics, Approaches, Concepts,* edited by Jens Kreinath, Jan Snoek, and Michael Stausberg, 379–94. Leiden & Boston: Brill, 2008.

———. *Rite Out of Place: Ritual, Media, and the Arts.* New York and Oxford: Oxford University Press, 2006.

———. *Ritual Criticism: Case Studies in Its Practice and Essays on Its Theory.* Columbia: University of South Carolina Press, 1990.

Gupt, Bharat. "Origin of Dhruvapada and Krishna Bhakti in Brijabhasha." *Sangeet Natak* 64–65 (April–September 1982): 55–63.

Hardy, Friedhelm. "The Formation of Śrīvaiṣṇavism." In *Charisma and Canon: Essays on the Religious History of the Indian Subcontinent,* edited by Vasudha Dalmia, Angelika Malinar, and Martin Christof, 41–61. Oxford: Oxford University Press, 2001.

———. *Virahā-Bhakti: The Early History of Kṛṣṇa Devotion in South India.* Delhi: Oxford University Press, 1983.

Hawley, John Stratton. *Krishna, The Butter Thief.* Princeton: Princeton University Press, 1983.

———. *The Memory of Love: Sūrdās Sings to Krishna.* New York and Oxford: Oxford University Press, 2009.

———. *Sūr Dās: Poet, Singer, Saint.* Seattle: University of Washington Press, 1984.

Haynes, Richard D. "Svāmī Haridās and the Haridāsī Sampradāy." Ph.D. diss., University of Pennsylvania, 1974.

Heesterman, J. C. "Veda and Dharma." In *The Concept of Duty in South Asia,* edited by Wendy Doniger O'Flaherty and J. D. M. Derrett, 80–95. Columbia, Mo.: South Asia Books, 1978.

Heine, Steven, and Dale S. Wright, eds. *Zen Ritual: Studies in Zen Buddhist Theory in Practice.* New York: Oxford University Press, 2007.

Henry, Edward O. *Chant the Names of God: Music and Culture in Bhojpuri-Speaking India.* San Diego: San Diego State University Press, 1988.

———. "The Vitality of the Nirgun Bhajan: Sampling the Contemporary Tradition." In *Bhakti Religion in North India: Community Identity and Political Action,* edited by David Lorenzen, 231–50. Albany: State University of New York Press, 1995.

Hirschkind, Charles. *The Ethical Soundscape: Cassette Sermons and Islamic Counterpublics.* New York: Columbia University Press, 2006.

Ho, Meilu. "The Liturgical Music of Pushti Mārg of India: An Embryonic Form of the Classical Tradition." Ph.D. diss., University of California, Los Angeles, 2006.

Houseman, M., and C. Severi. *Naven, or the Other Self: A Relational Approach to Ritual Action.* Leiden: Brill, 1998.

Howard, Wayne. *Sāmavedic Chant.* New Haven and London: Yale University Press, 1977.

———. "Vedic Chant." In *Garland Encyclopedia of World Music.* Vol. 5: *Indian Subcontinent,* edited by Alison Arnold, 238–45. New York and London: Garland, 2000.

———. *Veda Recitation in Vārānasī.* Columbia, Mo.; South Asia Books, 1986.

Hume, Robert E. trans. *The Thirteen Principal Upanishads.* 1921. Reprint, Oxford: Oxford University Press, 1977.

Humphrey, Caroline, and James Laidlaw. *The Archetypal Actions of Ritual: A Theory of Ritual Illustrated by the Jain Rite of Worship* New York: Oxford University Press, 1994.

Jackson, William. "Religious and Devotional Music: Southern Area." In *Garland Encyclopedia of World Music.* Vol. 5: *Indian Subcontinent,* edited by Alison Arnold, 259–71. New York and London: Garland, 2000.

Jamison, Stephanie W. *Sacrificied Wife / Sacrificer's Wife: Women, Ritual, and Hospitality in Ancient India.* New York: Oxford University Press, 1995.

Janaki, S. S. "The Role of Sanskrit in the Development of Indian Music." *Journal of the Music Academy, Madras* 56 (1985): 66–98.

Jha, Ganganatha, trans. *Ślokavārttika of Kumārila Bhaṭṭa.* 1908. Reprint, Calcutta: The Asiatic Society, 1985.

Jones, Cheslyn, Geoffrey Wainwright, and Edward Yarnold, S.J., eds. *The Study of Liturgy.* New York: Oxford University Press, 1978.

Kane, P. V. *History of Dharmaśāstra (Ancient and Medieval Religious and Civil Law).* Vol. 2. Poona: Bhandarkar Oriental Research Institute, 1941.

Kavanagh, Aidan. *Elements of Rite: A Handbook of Liturgical Style.* Collegeville, Minn.: Liturgical Press, 1990.

———. "The Role of Ritual in Personal Development." In *The Roots of Ritual,* edited by James Shaughnessy, 145–160. Grand Rapids, Mich.: Eerdmans, 1973.

Kelting, Mary Whitney. *Singing to the Jinas: Jain Laywomen, Mandal Singing, and the Negotiations of Jain Devotion.* New York: Oxford University Press, 2001.

Klostermaier, Klaus K. *Survey of Hinduism.* Albany: State University of New York Press, 1989.

Kochhar, Rajesh. *The Vedic People: Their History and Geography.* New Delhi: Orient Longman, 2000.

Kreinath, Jens, Jan Snoek, and Michael Stausberg, eds. *Theorizing Rituals: Issues, Topics, Approaches, Concepts.* Leiden & Boston: Brill, 2008.

Kunhan Raja, C. *The Vedas: A Cultural Study.* Waltair, A.P.: Andhra University, 1957.

Lath, Mukund. *A Study of Dattilam: A Treatise on the Sacred Music of Ancient India.* New Delhi: Impex India, 1978.

Leaver, Robin A., and Joyce Ann Zimmerman, eds. *Liturgy and Music: Lifetime Learning.* Collegeville, Minn.: Liturgical Press, 1998.

Leeuw, Gerardus Van der. "Music and Religion." Part 6 of *Sacred and Profane Beauty: The Holy in Art.* New York: Holt, Rinehart and Winston, 1963.

———. *Religion in Essence and Manifestation.* 2 vols. 1938. Reprint, Gloucester: Peter Smith, 1967.

Lidova, Natalia. *Drama and Ritual of Early Hinduism.* Delhi: Motilal Banarsidass, 1994.

Lorenzen, David N., ed. *Bhakti Religion in North India: Community Identity and Political Action.* Albany: State University of New York Press, 1995.

Maharaj, Sri Goswami Lalitcaran.ji. "The Musical Style of the Rādhāvallabha Samāj Gāyan." *Journal of Vaiṣṇava Studies* 4.2 (Spring 1996): 136–37.

———. *Śī Hit Harivaṃś Gosvāmī: Sampradāya aur Sāhitya.* Vrindaban: Venu Prakasan, 1957.

Marini, Stephen A. *Sacred Song in America: Religion, Music, and Public Culture.* Urbana and Chicago: University of Illinois Press, 2003.

McGann, Mary E. *Exploring Music as Worship and Theology: Research in Liturgical Practice.* Collegeville, Minn.: Liturgical Press, 2002.

McIntosh, Solveig. *Hidden Faces of Ancient Indian Song.* Burlington, Vt.: Ashgate Publishing Company, 2005.

Michaels, Alex. "Ritual and Meaning." In *Theorizing Rituals: Issues, Topics, Approaches, Concepts,* edited by Jens Kreinath, Jan Snoek, and Michael Stausberg, 247–61. Leiden & Boston: Brill, 2008.

——. "Sanskrit." Section of "Ritual: A Lexicographic Survey of Some Related Terms from an Emic Perspective," edited by Michael Stausberg. In *Theorizing Rituals: Issues, Topics, Approaches, Concepts,* edited by Jens Kreinath, Jan Snoek, and Michael Stausberg, 86. Leiden & Boston: Brill, 2008.

Mitchell, Nathan D. *Liturgy and the Social Sciences.* Collegeville, Minn.: Liturgical Press, 1999.

Monier-Williams, Monier. A *Sanskrit-English Dictionary.* 1899. Reprint, Oxford: Oxford University Press, 1920.

Monti, Anthony. A *Natural Theology of the Arts: Imprint of the Spirit.* Burlington, Vt.: Ashgate Publishing, 2003.

Muck, Terry. "Psalm, Bhajan, and Kīrtan: Songs of the Soul in Comparative Perspective." In *Psalms and Practice: Worship, Virtue, and Authority,* edited by Stephen Breck Reid, 7–27. Collegeville, Minn.: Liturgical Press, 2001.

Mukhopadhyay, Durgadas, ed. and trans. *In Praise of Krishna: Translation of Gīta- Govinda of Jayadeva.* Delhi: B. R. Publishing Corporation, 1990.

Müller, Friedrich Max. *Biographies of Words and the Home of the Aryas.* London: Longmans Green, 1888.

Mutatkar, Sumati, ed. *Aspects of Indian Music: A Collection of Essays.* Delhi: Sangeet Natak Akademi, 1987.

Narayanan, Vasudha. "Diglossic Hinduism: Liberation and Lentils." *Journal of the American Academy of Religion* 68.4 (December 2000): 761–79.

——. *The Vernacular Veda: Revelation, Recitation, and Ritual.* Columbia: University of South Carolina Press, 1994.

Nettl, Bruno. *Excursions in World Music.* 3rd ed. Upper Saddle River, N.J.: Prentice-Hall, 2001.

Neuman, Daniel M. *The Life of Music in North India.* Detroit: Wayne State University Press, 1980.

Nijenhuis, E. Wiersma-te. *Dattilam: A Compendium of Ancient Indian Music.* Leiden: Brill, 1970.

Nitya Kīrtana: Rasa Ratnākara. Foreword by Kesavram Sastri. Bikaner: Mundhra Foundation, [1990].

Oldenberg, Hermann. *The Religion of the Veda.* Translated by Shridhar B. Shrotri. Delhi: Motilal Banarsidass, 1988.

Ong, Walter J. *The Presence of the Word.* New Haven: Yale University Press, 1967.

Otto, Rudolf. *The Idea of the Holy.* 2d ed. Translated by John W. Harvey. New York: Oxford, 1958.

Paden, William E. *Religious Worlds: The Comparative Study of Religion.* Boston: Beacon Press, 1988.

Pauwels, Heidi R. M. *Kṛṣṇa's Round Dance Reconsidered: Harirām Vyās's Hindi Rās–pañcādhyāyī.* Surrey, U.K.: Curzon Press, 1996.

Penner, Hans H. "Language, Ritual, and Meaning." *Numen* 32 (July 1985): 1–16.

Peterson, Indira Viswanathan. *Poems to Śiva: The Hymns of the Tamil Saints.* Princeton: Princeton University Press, 1989.

Powers, Harold. "India, Subcontinent of, I-II." In *The New Grove Dictionary of Music and Musicians.* Vol. 9, edited by Stanley Sadie, 69–141. London: Macmillan, 1980.

Quasten, Johannes. *Music & Worship in Pagan & Christian Antiquity.* Washington, D.C.: National Association of Pastoral Musicians, 1983.

Raghavan, V. "Music in Sanskrit Literature." *National Centre for the Performing Arts Quarterly Journal.* 7 (December 1978): 17–38.

——. "Sāmaveda and Music." *Journal of the Music Academy, Madras* 33 (1962): 127–33.

Raghunathan, N., trans. *Śrīmad Bhāgavatam.* 2 vols. Madras and Bangalore: Vighneswara Publishing House, 1976.

Rajagopala Aiyar, P. K. "Sāma Veda and Saṅgīta." *Journal of the Music Academy, Madras* 52 (1981): 62–71.

——. "Saṁskṛta and Saṅgīta." *Journal of the Music Academy, Madras* 53 (1982): 57–78.

Ralls-MacLeod, Karen. *Music and the Celtic Otherworld: From Ireland to Iona.* Edinburgh: Polygon, 2000.

Ranade, H. G., ed. and trans. *Kātyāyana-Śrauta-Sūtra: Rules for the Vedic Sacrifices.* Poona: Ranade Publications, 1978.

Rangacharya, Adya, trans. *Nāṭya Śāstra.* 1996. Revised edition, New Delhi: Munshiram Manoharlal, 2003.

Rappaport, Roy A. "The Obvious Aspects of Ritual." In *Ecology, Meaning and Religion.* Richmond, Calif.: North Atlantic Books, 1979.

——. *Ritual and Religion in the Making of Humanity.* Cambridge: Cambridge University Press, 1999.

Ray, Sukumar. *Music of Eastern India: Vocal Music in Bengali, Oriya, Assamese and Manipuri with Special Emphasis on Bengali.* Calcutta: Firma KLM, 1985.

Reid, Stephen Breck, ed. *Psalms and Practice: Worship, Virtue, and Authority.* Collegeville, Minn.: Liturgical Press, 2001.

Rodrigues, Hillary Peter. *Ritual Worship of the Great Goddess: The Liturgy of the Durgā Pūjā with Interpretations.* Albany: State University of New York Press, 2003.

Rosenstein, Lucy L. *The Devotional Poetry of Svāmī Haridās: A Study of Early Braj Bhāṣā Verse.* Groningen: Egbert Forsten, 1997.

Rowell, Lewis. *Music and Musical Thought in Early India.* Chicago: University of Chicago Press, 1992.

Samā–Śriṅkhalā. Edited by Sri Govinda Saran Sastri. Vrindaban: Sri Swami Haridas Seva Samsthan, 1988.

Sanford, A. Whitney. *Singing Krishna: Sound Becomes Sight in Paramānand's Poetry.* Albany: State University of New York Press, 2009.

Sanyal, Ritwik, and Richard Widdess. *Dhrupad: Tradition and Performance in Indian Music.* SOAS Musicology Series. London: Ashgate Publishing, 2004.

Saran, Sri Brajvallabh. "Samāj Gāyan in the Nimbārka Sampradāya." In Guy L. Beck (Spring 1996), 132–35.

Sarmadee, Shahab. *Nūr-Ratnākara: A Bio-bibliographical Survey and Techno-historical Study of all Available Important Writings in Arabic, Persian, Sanskrit and other Allied Languages on the Subject of Song, Dance and Drama*. Volume 1. Kolkata: ITC Sangeet Research Academy, 2003.

Sastri, K. Sambasiva, ed. *Dattilam*. Trivandrum Sanskrit Series no. 102. Trivandrum: Government Press, 1930.

Sastri, Sri Govinda Saran. "Samāj Gāyan in the Haridāsī Sampradāya." In Guy L. Beck (Spring 1996), 137–44.

Sax, William, Johannes Quack, and Jan Weinhold, eds. *The Problem of Ritual Efficacy*. New York and Oxford: Oxford University Press, 2009.

Schafer, R. Murray. *The Soundscape: Our Sonic Environment and the Tuning of the World*. Rochester, Vt.: Destiny Books, 1993.

Schneider, Marius. "The Nature of Praise Song." In *Cosmic Music: Musical Keys to the Interpretation of Reality*. Edited by Joscelyn Godwin, 35–52. Rochester, Vt.: Inner Traditions, 1989.

Schwartz, Susan L. *Rasa: Performing the Divine in India*. New York: Columbia University Press, 2004.

Schweig, Graham. *Dance of Divine Love: The Rāsa Līlā of Krishna from the Bhāgavata Purāṇa, India's Classic Sacred Love Story*. Princeton: Princeton University Press, 2005.

Seligman, Adam B., Robert P. Weller, Michael J. Pruett, and Bennett Simon. *Ritual and Its Consequences: An Essay on the Limits of Sincerity*. New York and Oxford: Oxford University Press, 2008.

Sen, Chitrabhanu. A *Dictionary of Vedic Rituals: Based on the Śrauta and Grihya Sūtras*. New Delhi: Concept Publishing, 1978.

Sharma, Prem Lata. "Colloquium on Gandharva with Prem Lata Sharma, Sadagopan, and K. C. Brihaspati." In Prem Lata Sharma, *Indian Aesthetics and Musicology: The Art and Science of Indian Music)*, 164–70.Varanasi: Amnaya-Prakasana Bharata-Nidhi Trust, 2000.

——. *Indian Aesthetics and Musicology (The Art and Science of Indian Music)*. Varanasi: Amnaya-Prakasana Bharata-Nidhi Trust, 2000.

——. "The Indian Musicological Perspective on Text and Music." In *Text, Tone, and Tune: Parameters of Music in Multicultural Perspective*, edited by Bonnie C. Wade, 177–83. New Delhi: A.I.I.S. and Oxford University Press, 1993.

Sharma, Satyabhan. "The Dhrupad—Dhamar Tradition of Braj (Haveli Sangīt of the Vallabha Sampradāya)." In Guy L. Beck (Spring 1996), 126–32.

Singh, Thakur Jaideva. *Indian Music*. Edited by Prem Lata- Sharma. Calcutta: Sangeet Research Academy, 1995.

Slawek, Stephen. "The Definition of Kīrtan: An Historical and Geographical Perspective." *Journal of Vaiṣṇava Studies* 4.2 (Spring 1996): 57–113.

Smith, Brian K. *Reflections on Resemblance, Ritual, and Religion*. Delhi: Motilal Banarsidass, 1998.

Smith, H. Daniel. A *Descriptive Bibliography of the Printed Texts of the Pāñcarātrāgama*. 2 vols. Gaekwad Oriental Series158, 168. Baroda: Oriental Institute, 1975, 1980.

——. "The 'Three Gems' of the Pāñcarātrāgama Canon—An Appraisal." *Vimarśa* 1.1 (1972): 45–51.

Smith, H. Daniel, and M. Narsimhachary. *Handbook of Hindu Gods, Goddesses and Saints Popular in Contemporary South India.* New Delhi: Sundeep Prakashan, 1997.

Snell, Rupert. *The Eighty-Four Hymns of Hita Harivaṁśa: An Edition of the Caurāsī Pada.* Delhi: Motilal Banarsidass / London: School of Oriental and African Studies, 1991.

——. "Metrical Forms in Braj Bhāṣā Verse: The Caurāsī Pada in Performance." In *Bhakti in Current Research 1979–1982*, edited by Monika Theil-Horstmann, 353–83. Berlin: Dietrich Reimar Verlag, 1983.

Snoek, Jan. "Defining Rituals." In *Theorizing Rituals: Issues, Topics, Approaches, Concepts*, edited by Jens Kreinath, Jan Snoek, and Michael Stausberg, 3–14. Leiden & Boston: Brill, 2008.

Śrī Mahāvāṇī. Edited by Sri Govinda Saran Sastri. Vrindaban: Sri Nimbark Prakashan Trust, 1975.

Śrī Rādhāvallabhajī kā Varṣotsava. 3 vols. Compiled by Sri Goswami Lalitacaranji Maharaj. Vrindaban: Sri Radhavallabha Mandira Vaishnava Committee, 1978, 1979, 1980.

Srivastava, Induram. *Dhrupada: A Study of its Origin, Historical Development, Structure, and Present State.* New Delhi: Motilal Banarsidass, 1980.

Staal, Frits. *Ritual and Mantras: Rules without Meaning.* Delhi: Motilal Banarsidass, 1996 (New York: Peter Lang, 1989, 1993).

——, ed. *Agni: The Vedic Ritual of the Fire Altar.* 2 vols. Delhi: Motilal Banarsidass, 2001 (Berkeley, Calif.: Asian Humanities Press, 1983).

Stausberg, Michael, ed. "Ritual: A Lexicographic Survey of Some Related Terms from an Emic Perspective." In *Theorizing Rituals: Issues, Topics, Approaches, Concepts*, edited by Jens Kreinath, Jan Snoek, and Michael Stausberg, 51–98. Leiden & Boston: Brill, 2008.

Sylvan, Robin. *Traces of the Spirit: The Religious Dimensions of Popular Music.* New York: New York University Press, 2002.

Tachikawa, Musashi, Shoun Hino, and Lalita Deodhar. *Pūjā & Saṁskāra.* Delhi: Motilal Banarsidass, 2001.

Tachikawa, Musashi, Shrikant Bahulkar, and Madhavi Kolhatkar. *Indian Fire Rituals.* Delhi: Motilal Banarsidass, 2001.

Tarlekar, G. H. *Sāman Chants: In Theory and Present Practice.* With audiotape. Delhi: Sri Satguru Publications, 1995.

——. *Studies in the Nāṭya–Śāstra: With Special Reference to the Sanskrit Drama in Performance.* Delhi: Motilal Banarsidass, 1975.

Thielemann, Selina. *Divine Service and the Performing Arts in India.* New Delhi: APH Publishing Group, 2002.

——. *The Music of South Asia.* New Delhi: APH Publishing Group, 1999.

——. *Musical Traditions of Vaiṣṇava Temples in Vraja: A Comparative Study of Samāja and the Dhrupad Tradition of North Indian Classical Music.* 2 vols. New Delhi: Sagar Publishers, 2001.

——. "Samāja, Havelī Saṁgīta and Dhrupada: The Musical Manifestation of Bhakti." *Journal of Vaiṣṇava Studies* 4.2 (Spring 1996): 157–77.

——. *Singing the Praises Divine: Music in the Hindu Tradition*. New Delhi: APH Publishing Group, 2000.

——. *Sounds of the Sacred: Religious Music in India*. New Delhi: APH Publishing Group, 1998.

Thite, G. U. *Music in the Vedas: Its Magico-Religious Significance*. Delhi: Sharada Publishing House, 1997.

Trautman, Thomas R., ed. *The Aryan Debate*. New Delhi: Oxford University Press, 2005.

Tripathi, Gaya Charan. *Communication with God: The Daily Pūjā Ceremony in the Jagannātha Temple*. New Delhi: Indira Gandhi National Centre for the Arts, 2004.

Turner, Victor. *Image and Pilgrimage in Christian Culture*. New York: Columbia University Press, 1978.

——. *The Ritual Process: Structure and Anti-Structure*. Chicago: Aldine Publishing Company, 1969.

Vatican Council II: The Conciliar and Post Conciliar Documents. Edited by Austin Flannery, O.P. Northport, N.Y.: Costello Publishing Company, 1975.

Vesci, Uma Marina. *Heat and Sacrifice in the Vedas*. 2d ed. rev. Delhi: Motilal Banarsidass, 1992.

Viladesau, Richard. *Theology and the Arts: Encountering God through Music, Art, and Rhetoric*. Mahwah, N.J.: Paulist Press, 2000.

Viswanathan, T., and Matthew Harp Allen. *Music in South India: The Karnatak Concert Tradition and Beyond*. New York.: Oxford University Press, 2004.

Wade, Bonnie C. *Music in India: The Classical Tradition*. Englewood Cliffs, N.J.: Prentice-Hall, 1979.

White, Charles, S.J. *The Caurāsī Pad of Śrī Hit Harivaṁś*. Honolulu: University Press of Hawaii, 1977.

Widdess, Richard. *The Rāgas of Early Indian Music; Modes, Melodies and Musical Notations from the Gupta Period to c. 1250*. Oxford: Clarendon Press, 1995.

Williams, Ron G., and James W. Boyd. *Ritual Art and Knowledge: Aesthetic Theory and Zoroastrian Ritual*. Columbia: University of South Carolina Press, 1993.

Witzel, Michael. "Indocentrism: Autochthonous Visions of Ancient India." In *The Indo-Aryan Controversy: Evidence and Inference in Indian History*, edited by Edwin F. Bryant and Laurie L. Patton, 341–404. New York: Routledge, 2005.

Yugala-Śaṭaka of Śrī Bhaṭṭa. Edited by Sri Brajvallabh Saran. Vrindaban: Sriji Mandir, 1992.

Zaehner, R. C. *The Bhagavad–Gītā*. Oxford: Clarendon Press, 1969.8

INDEX